Between the Material and the Possible

BETWEEN THE MATERIAL AND THE POSSIBLE

Infrastructural Re-examination and Speculation in Art

Edited by
Bassam El Baroni

Sternberg Press, London
Edith-Russ-Haus, Oldenburg
2022

PRELUDE

SECTION I: Infrastructural Critique

SECTION II: Infrastructural Speculation

SECTION III: Infrahauntologies: On Invasive Legacies and Futures

END MATTER

PRELUDE

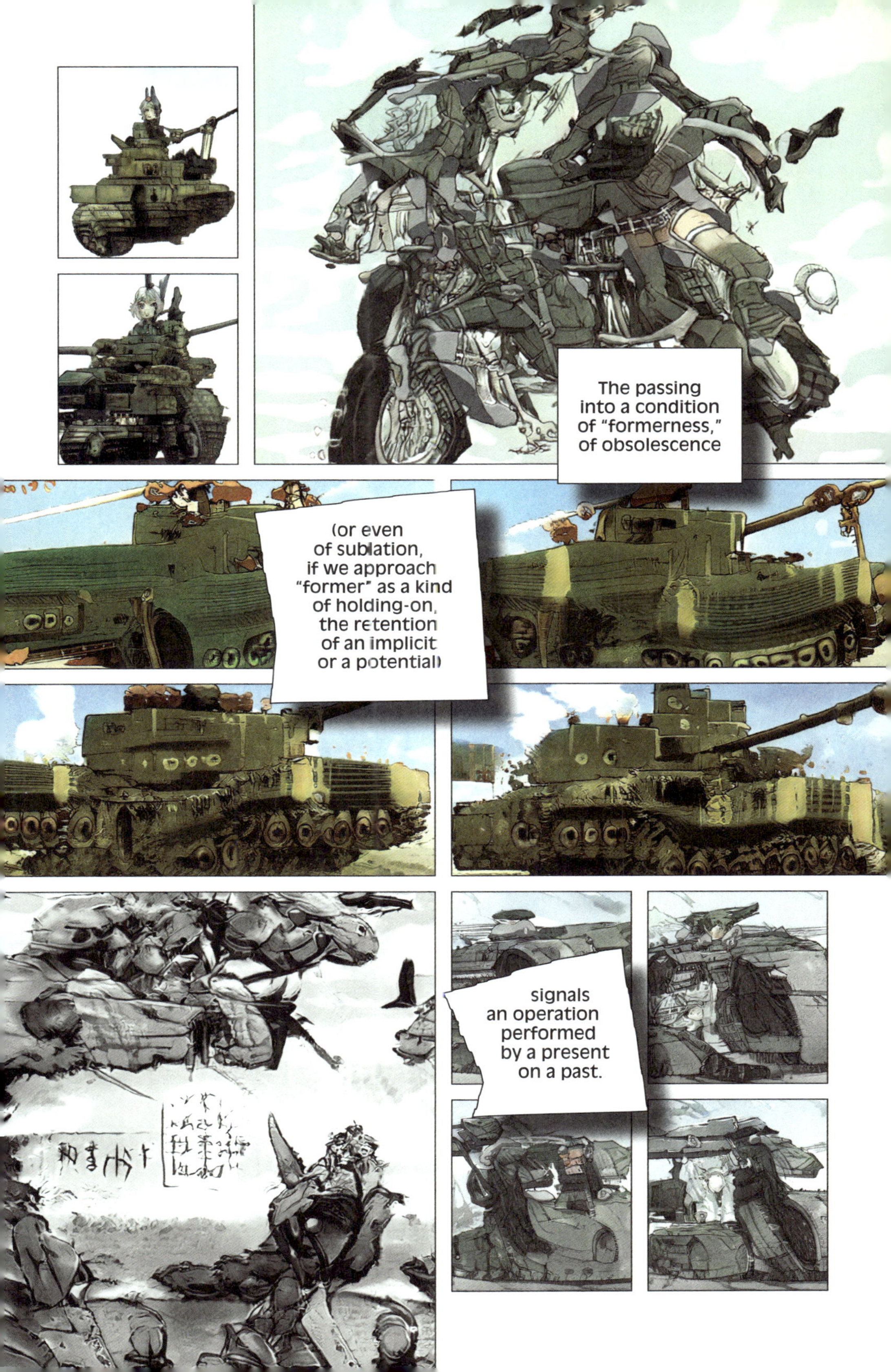
The passing into a condition of "formerness," of obsolescence
(or even of sublation, if we approach "former" as a kind of holding-on, the retention of an implicit or a potential)
signals an operation performed by a present on a past.

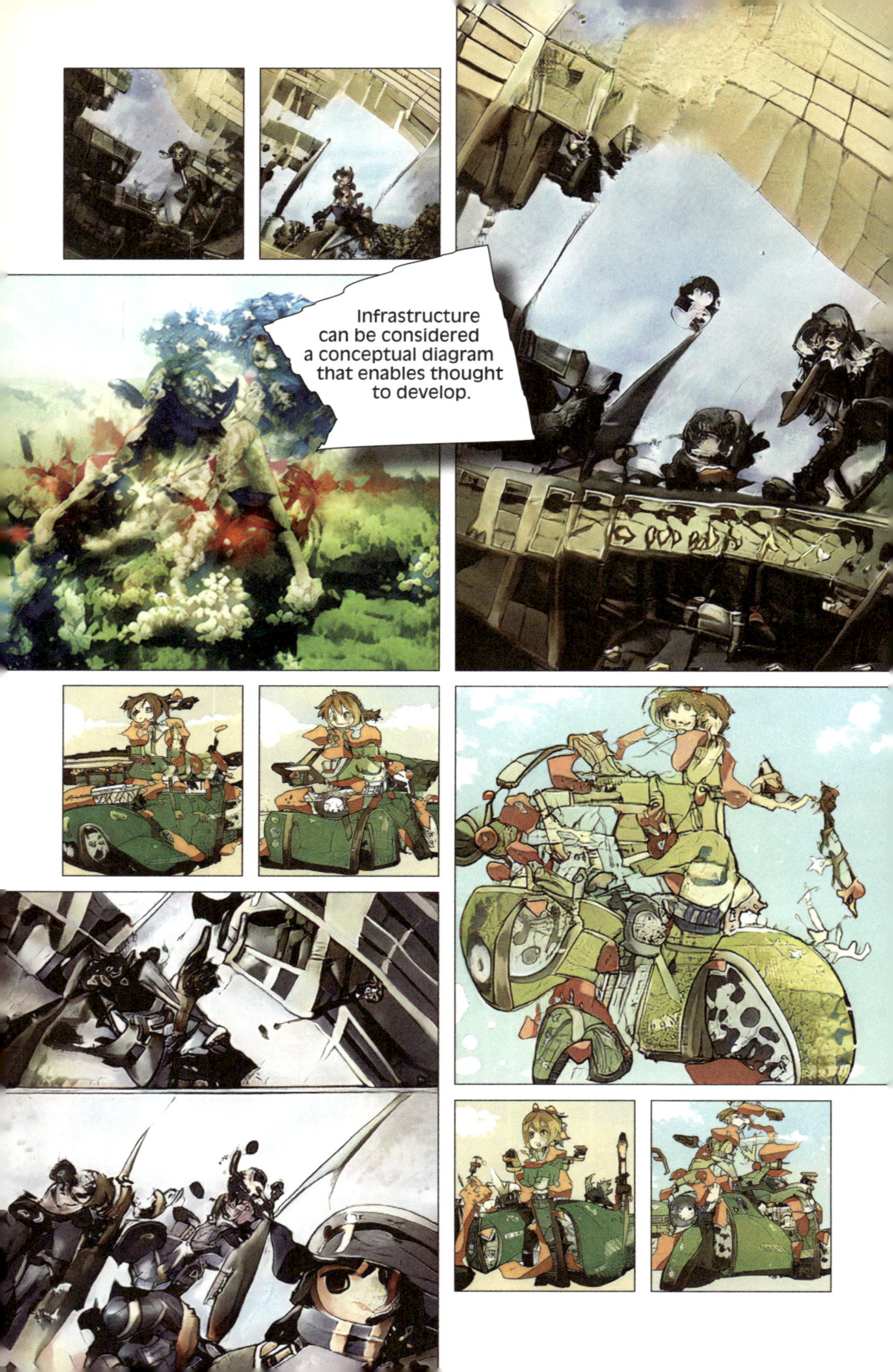
Infrastructure can be considered a conceptual diagram that enables thought to develop.

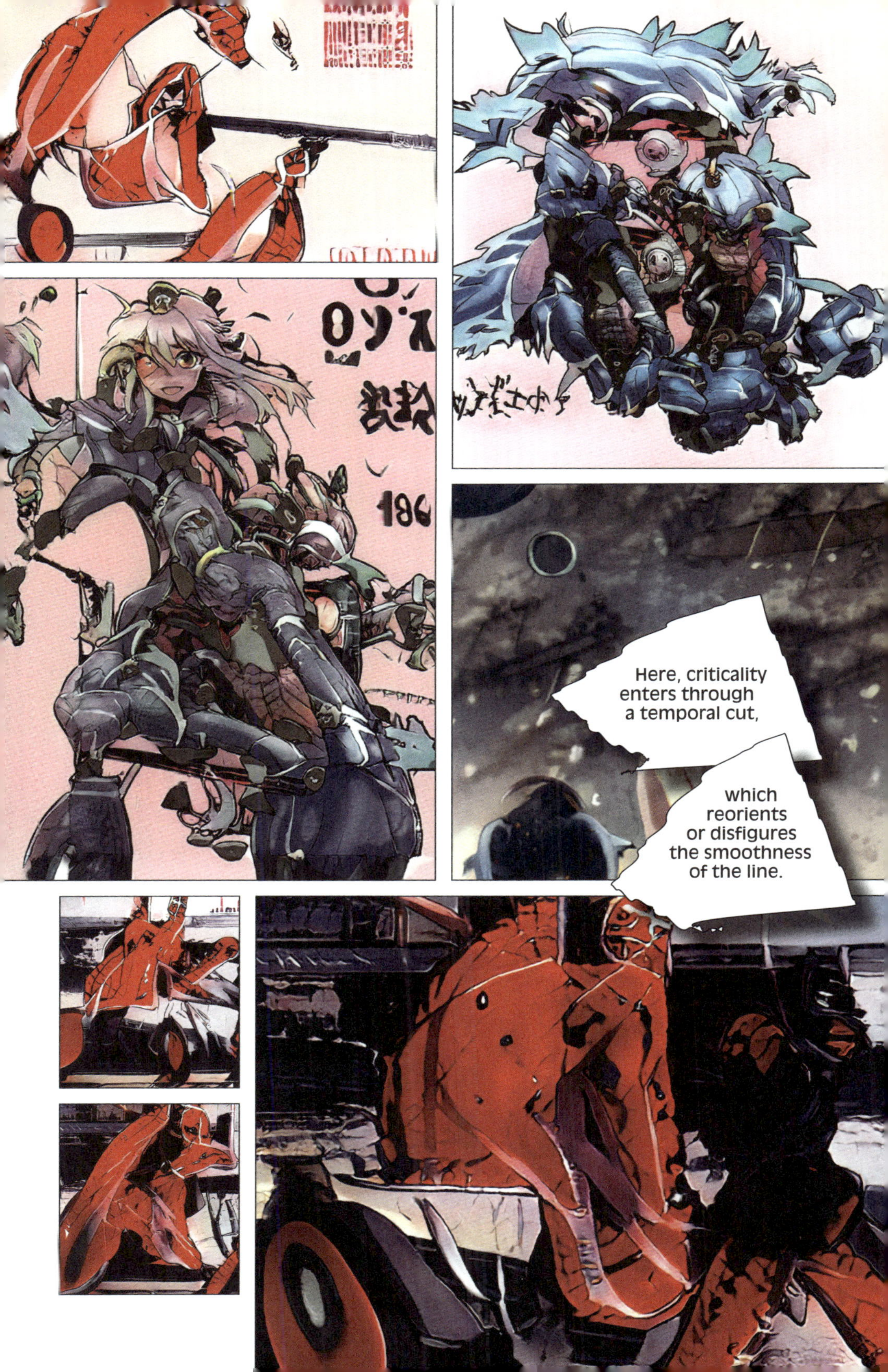
Here, criticality enters through a temporal cut,
which reorients or disfigures the smoothness of the line.

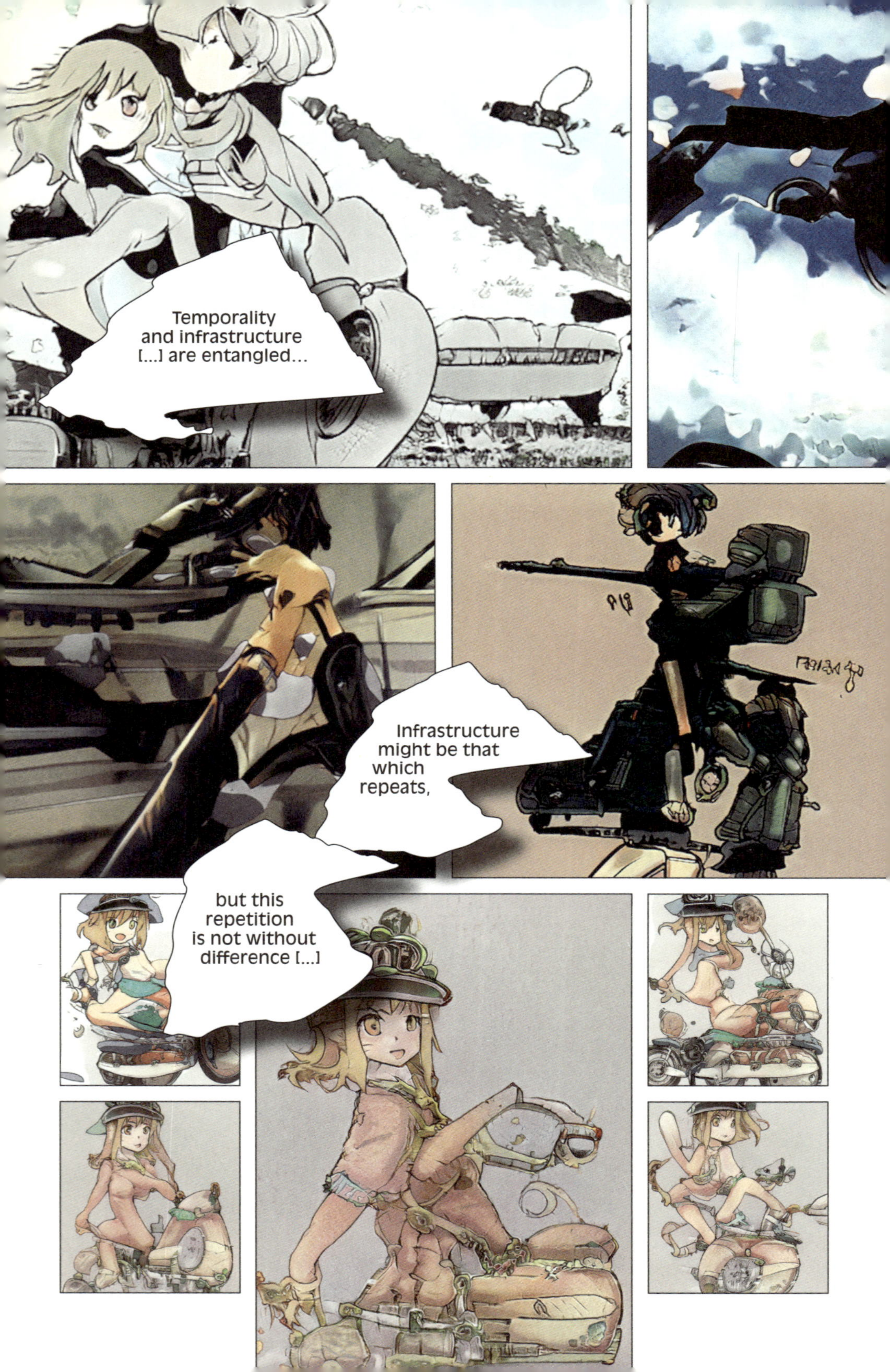
Temporality and infrastructure [...] are entangled...
Infrastructure might be that which repeats,
but this repetition is not without difference [...]

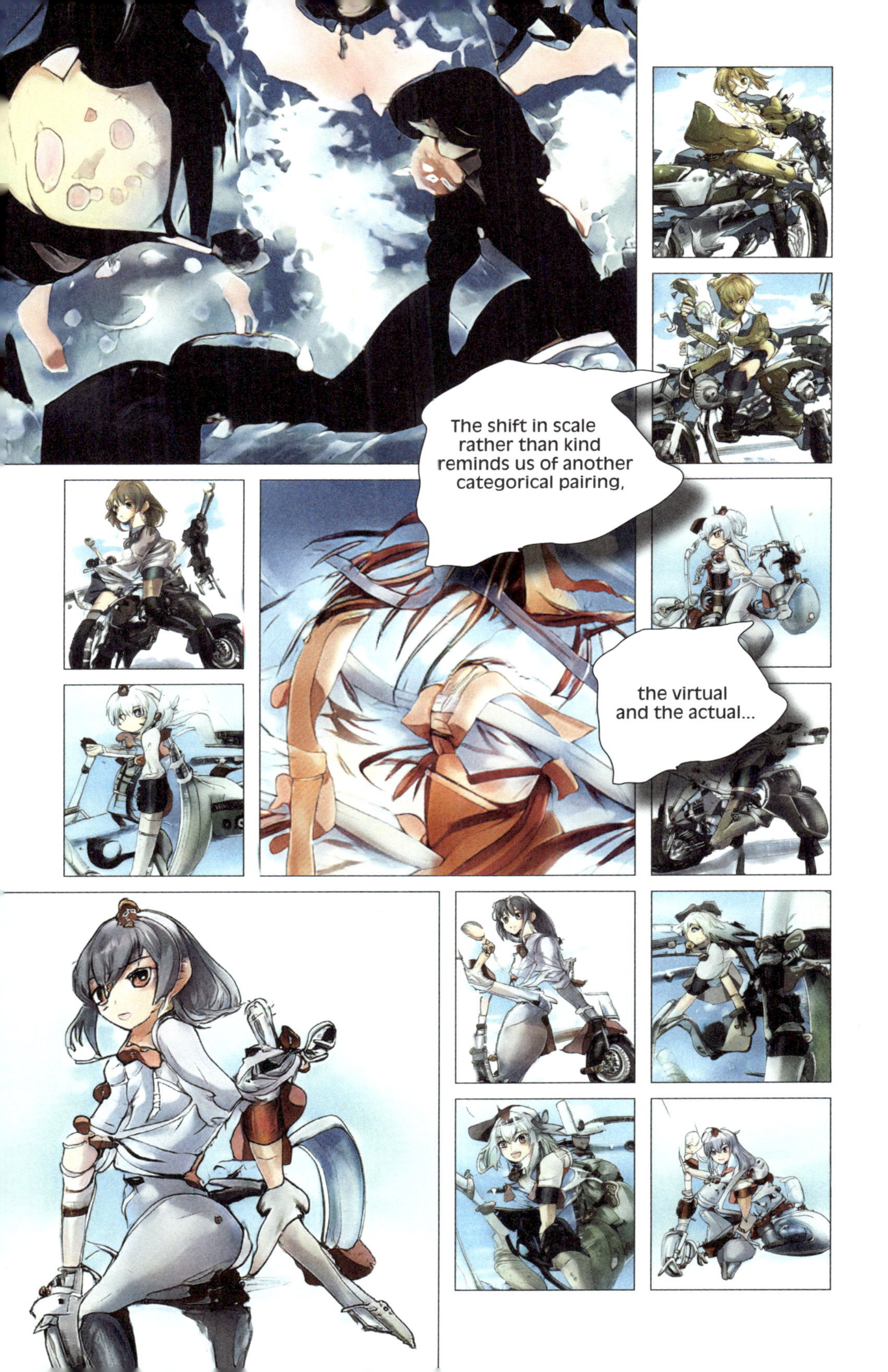

The shift in scale rather than kind reminds us of another categorical pairing,
the virtual and the actual...

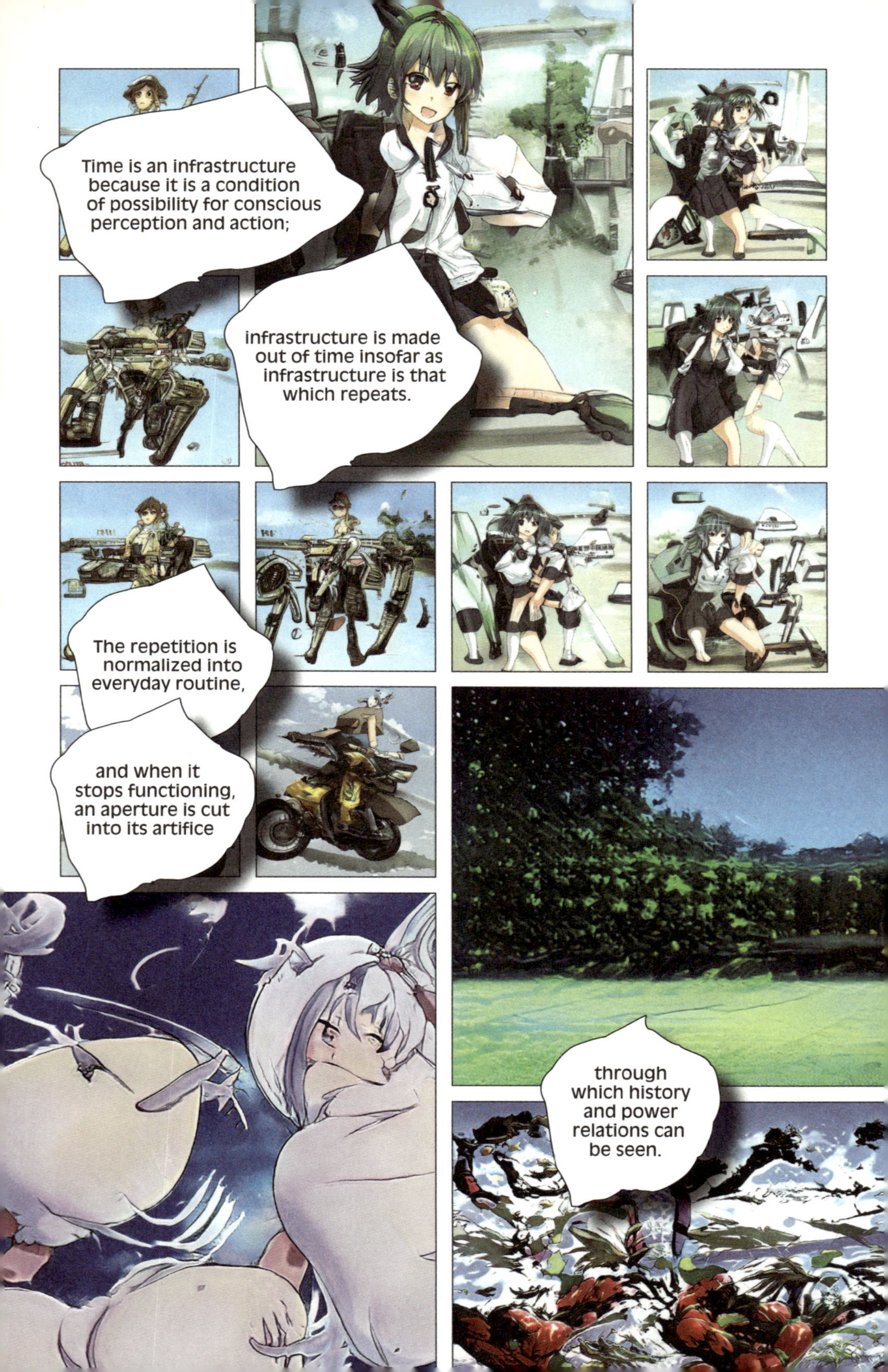
Time is an infrastructure because it is a condition of possibility for conscious perception and action;
infrastructure is made out of time insofar as infrastructure is that which repeats.
The repetition is normalized into everyday routine,
and when it stops functioning, an aperture is cut into its artifice
through which history and power relations can be seen.

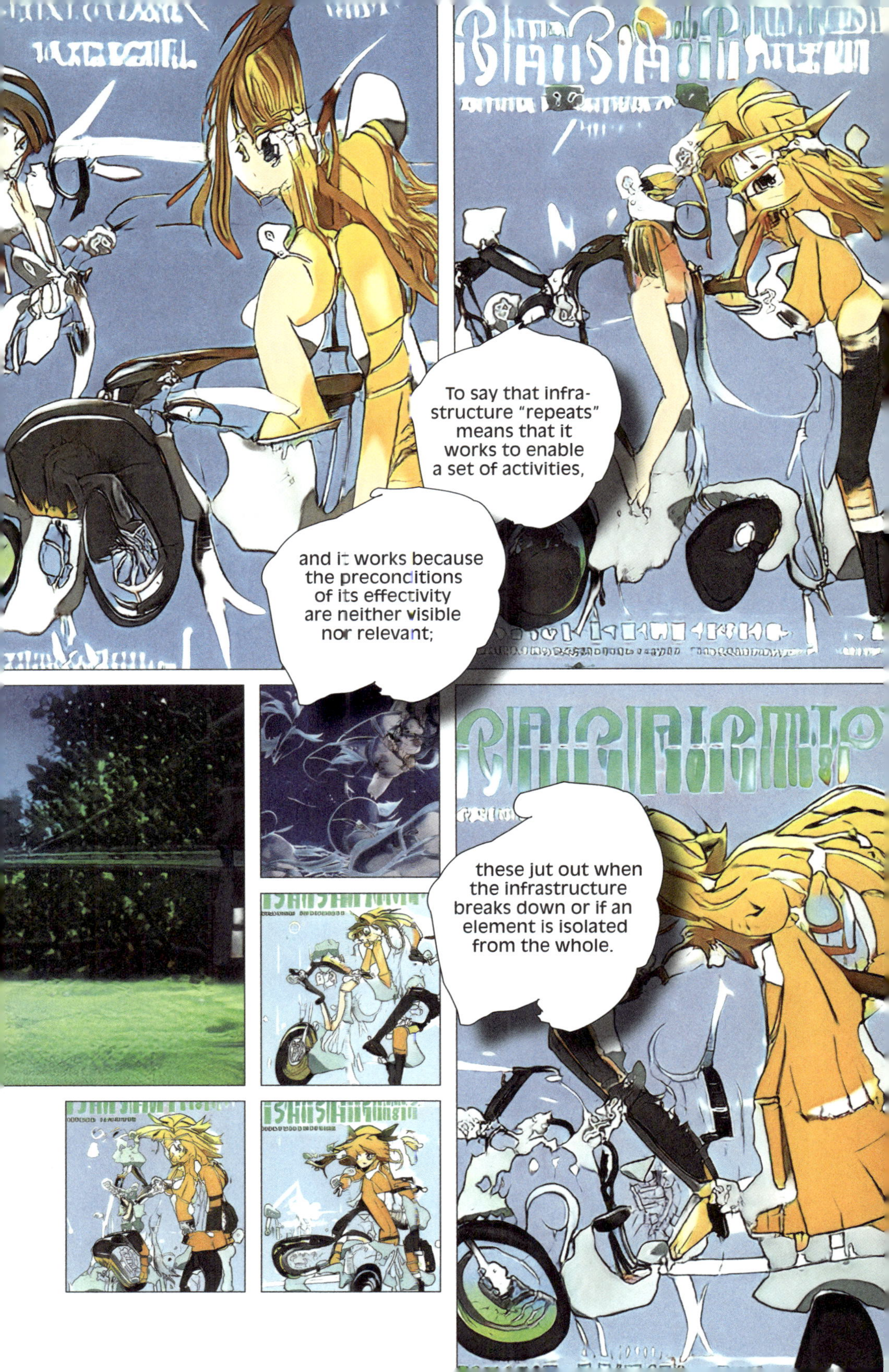
To say that infra-
structure "repeats"
means that it
works to enable
a set of activities,
and it works because
the preconditions
of its effectivity
are neither visible
nor relevant;
these jut out when
the infrastructure
breaks down or if an
element is isolated
from the whole.

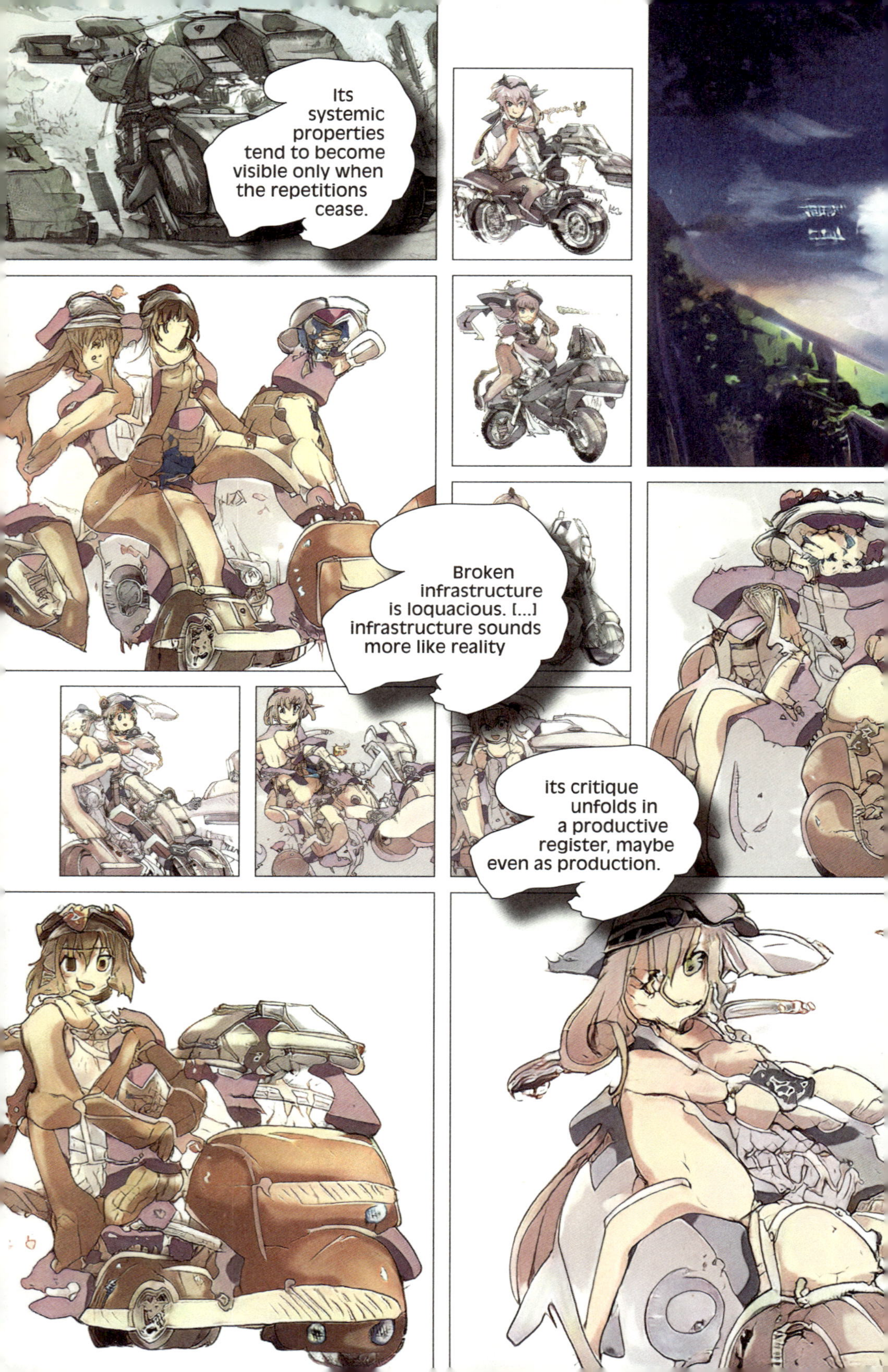
Its systemic properties tend to become visible only when the repetitions cease.
Broken infrastructure is loquacious. [...] infrastructure sounds more like reality
its critique unfolds in a productive register, maybe even as production.

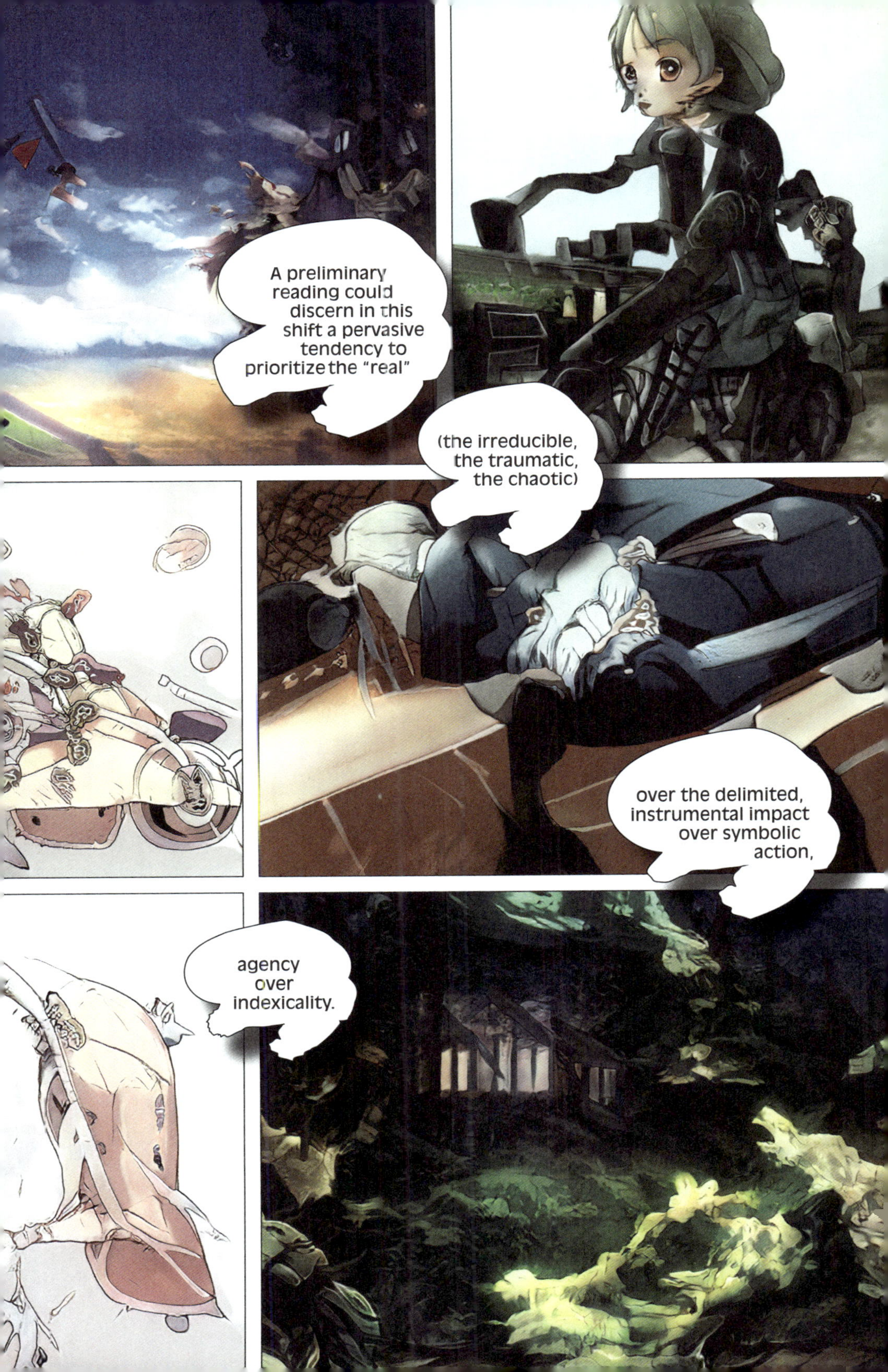
A preliminary reading could discern in this shift a pervasive tendency to prioritize the “real”
(the irreducible, the traumatic, the chaotic)
over the delimited, instrumental impact over symbolic action,
agency over indexicality.

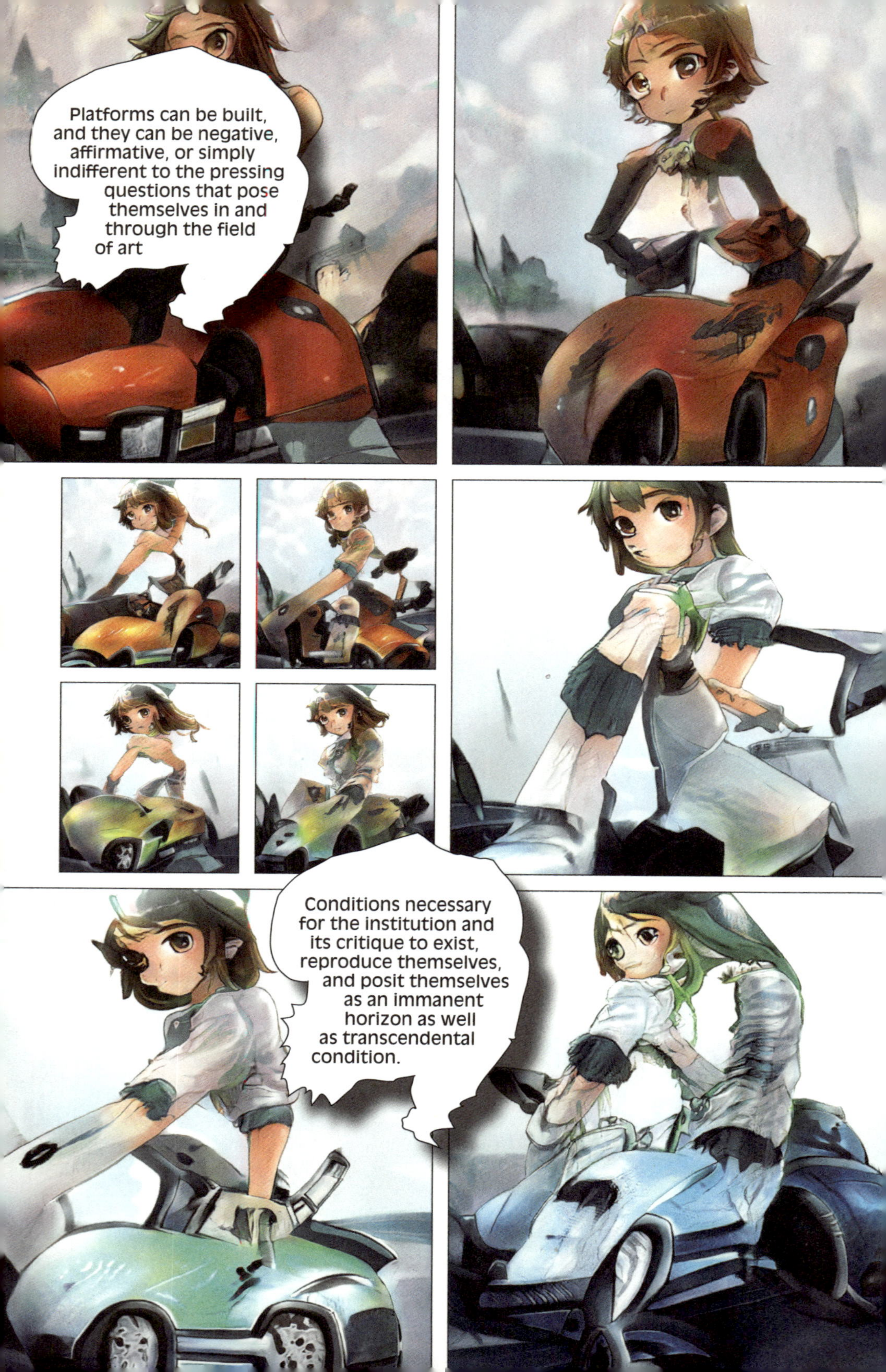

Platforms can be built, and they can be negative, affirmative, or simply indifferent to the pressing questions that pose themselves in and through the field of art
Conditions necessary for the institution and its critique to exist, reproduce themselves, and posit themselves as an immanent horizon as well as transcendental condition.

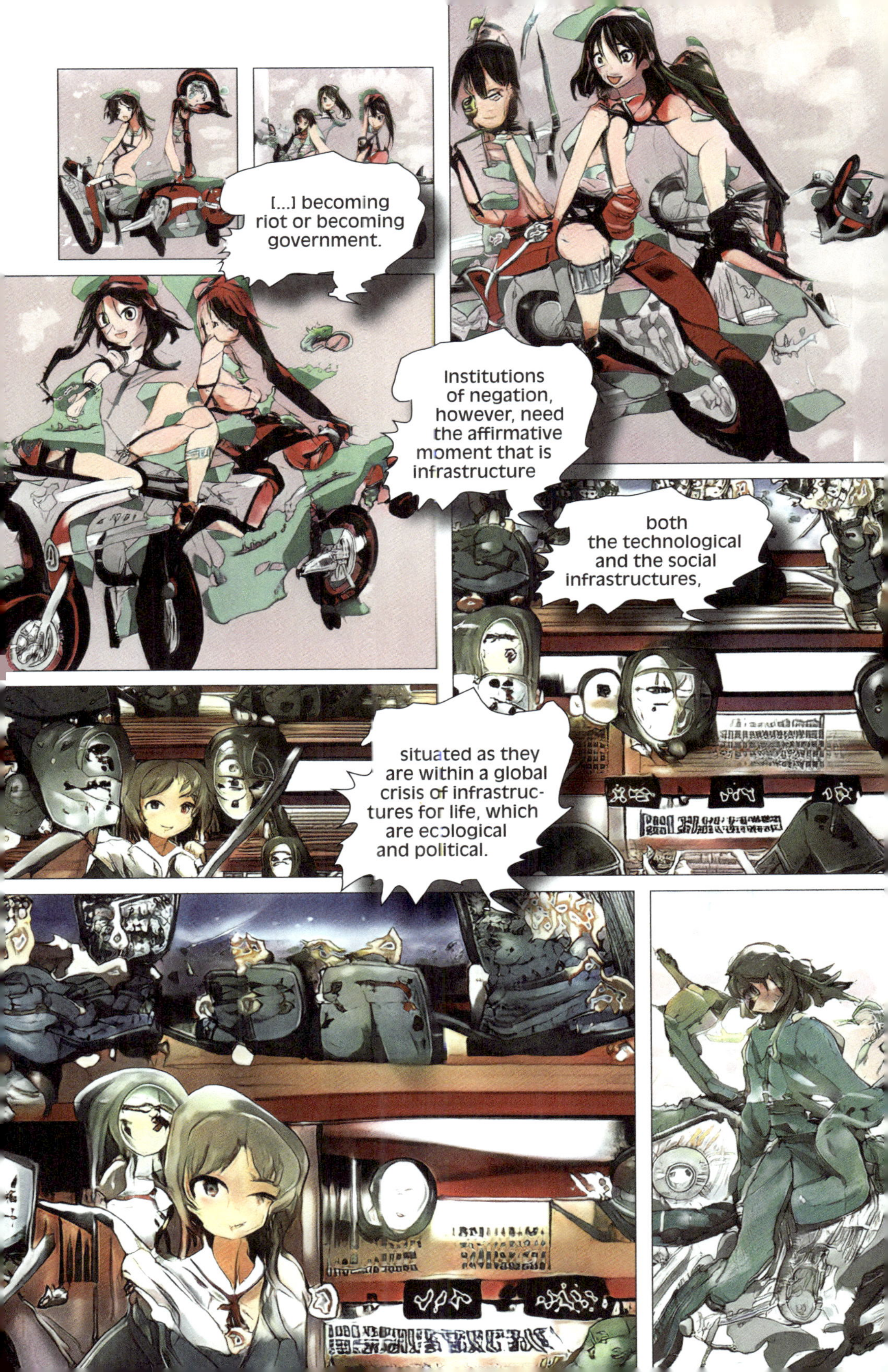
[...] becoming riot or becoming government.
Institutions of negation, however, need the affirmative moment that is infrastructure
both the technological and the social infrastructures,
situated as they are within a global crisis of infrastructures for life, which are ecological and political.

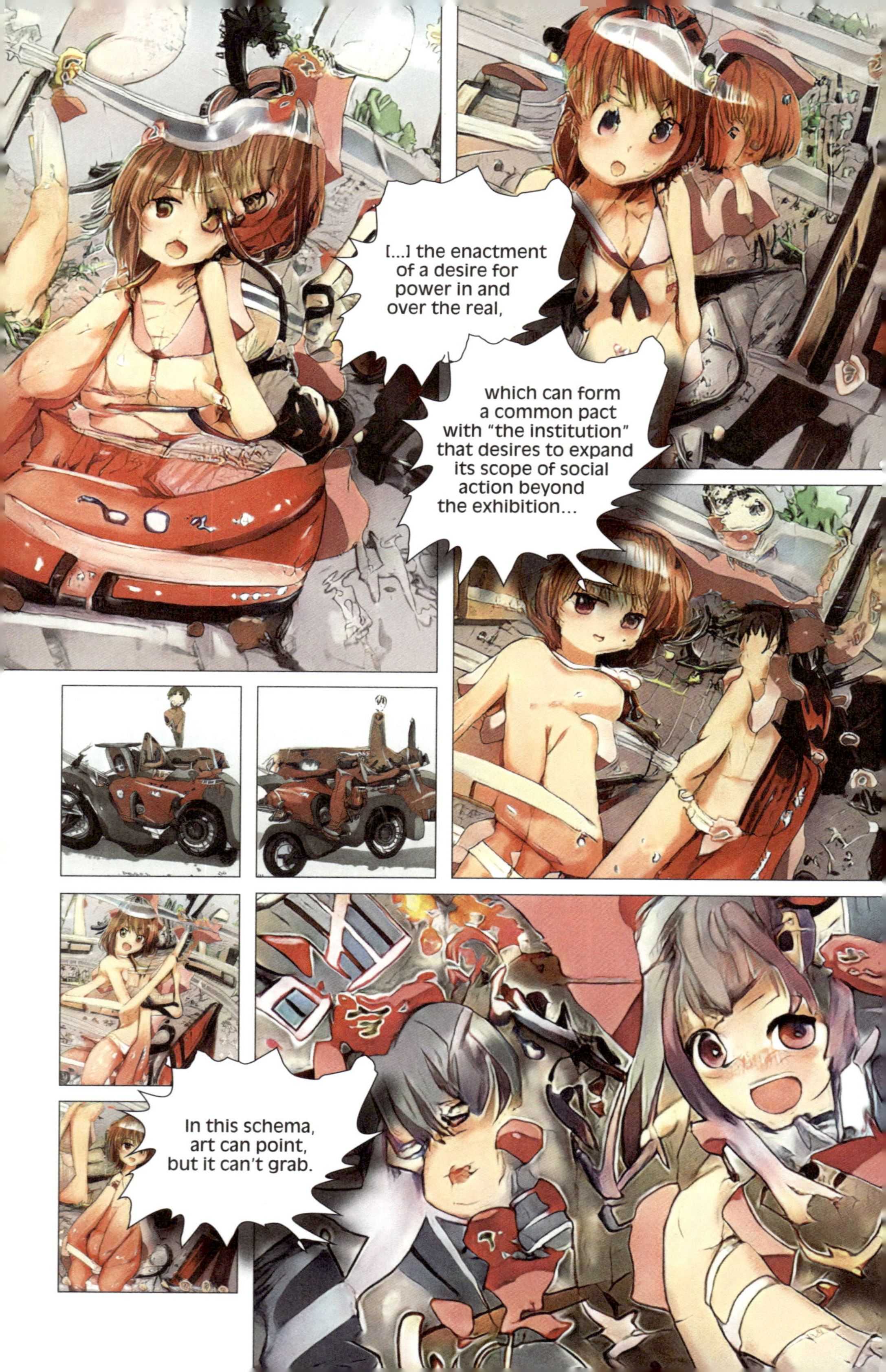
[...] the enactment of a desire for power in and over the real,
which can form a common pact with "the institution" that desires to expand its scope of social action beyond the exhibition...
In this schema, art can point, but it can't grab.

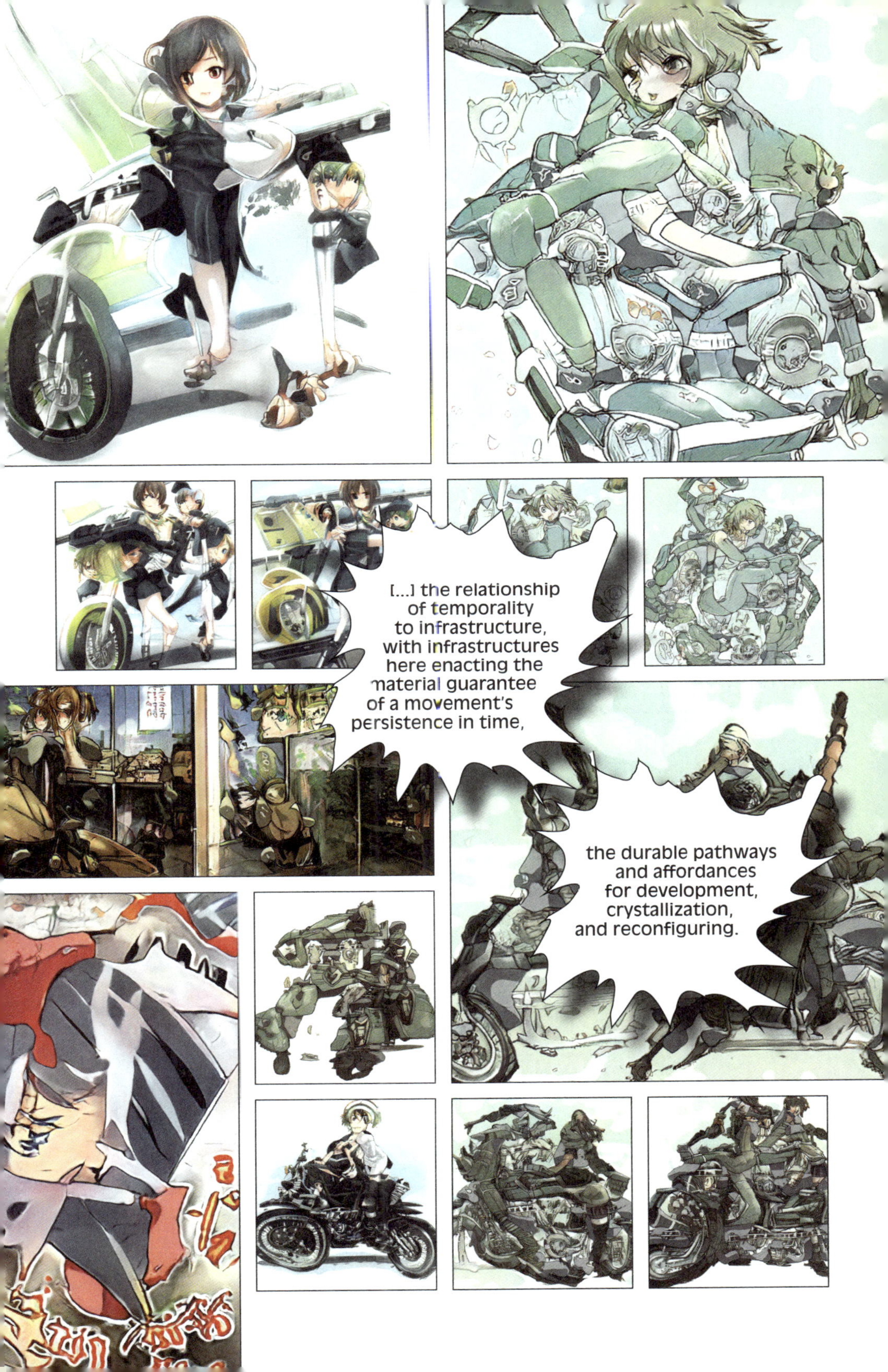
[…] the relationship of temporality to infrastructure, with infrastructures here enacting the material guarantee of a movement's persistence in time,
the durable pathways and affordances for development, crystallization, and reconfiguring.

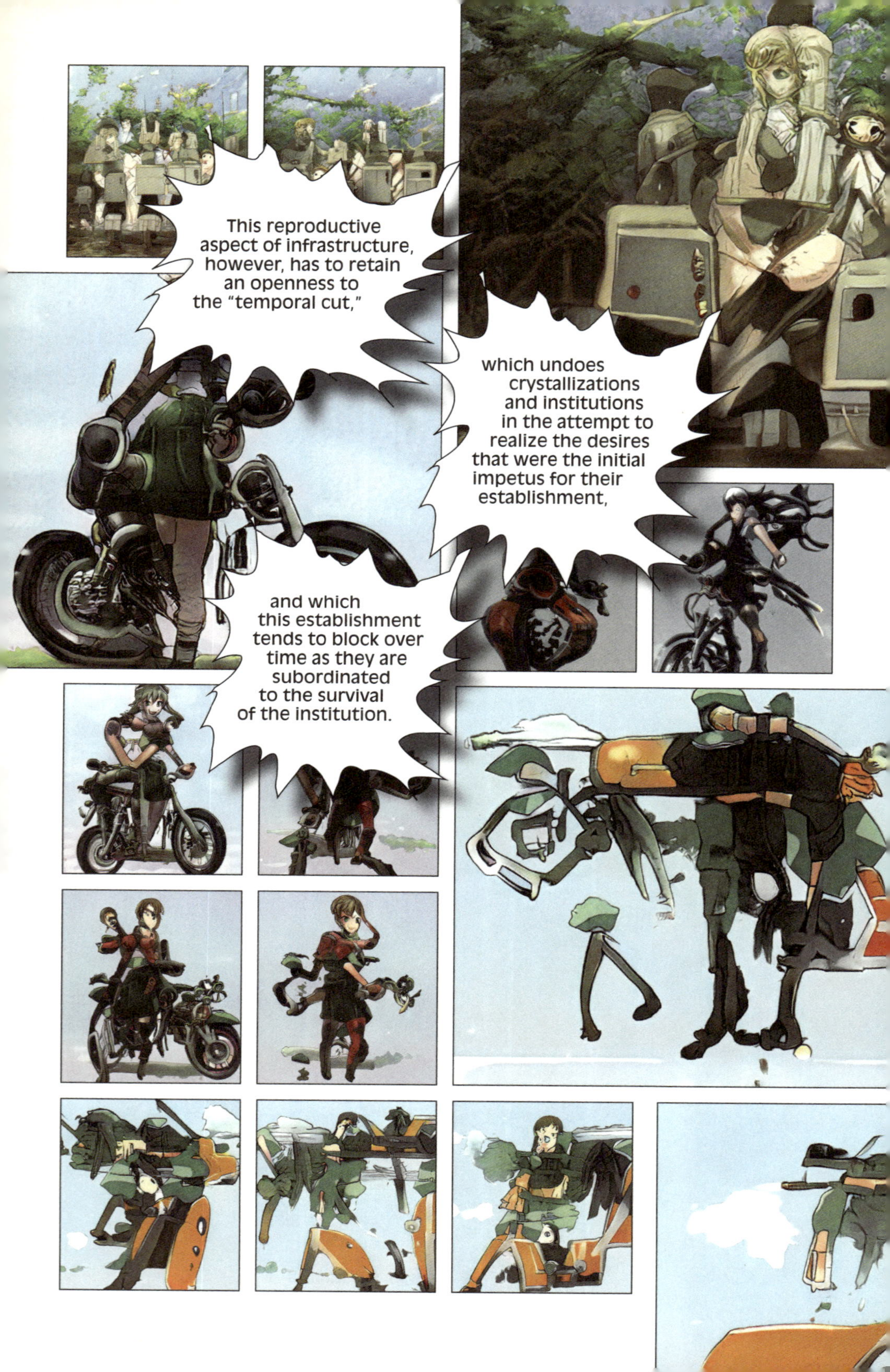
This reproductive aspect of infrastructure, however, has to retain an openness to the "temporal cut,"
which undoes crystallizations and institutions in the attempt to realize the desires that were the initial impetus for their establishment,
and which this establishment tends to block over time as they are subordinated to the survival of the institution.

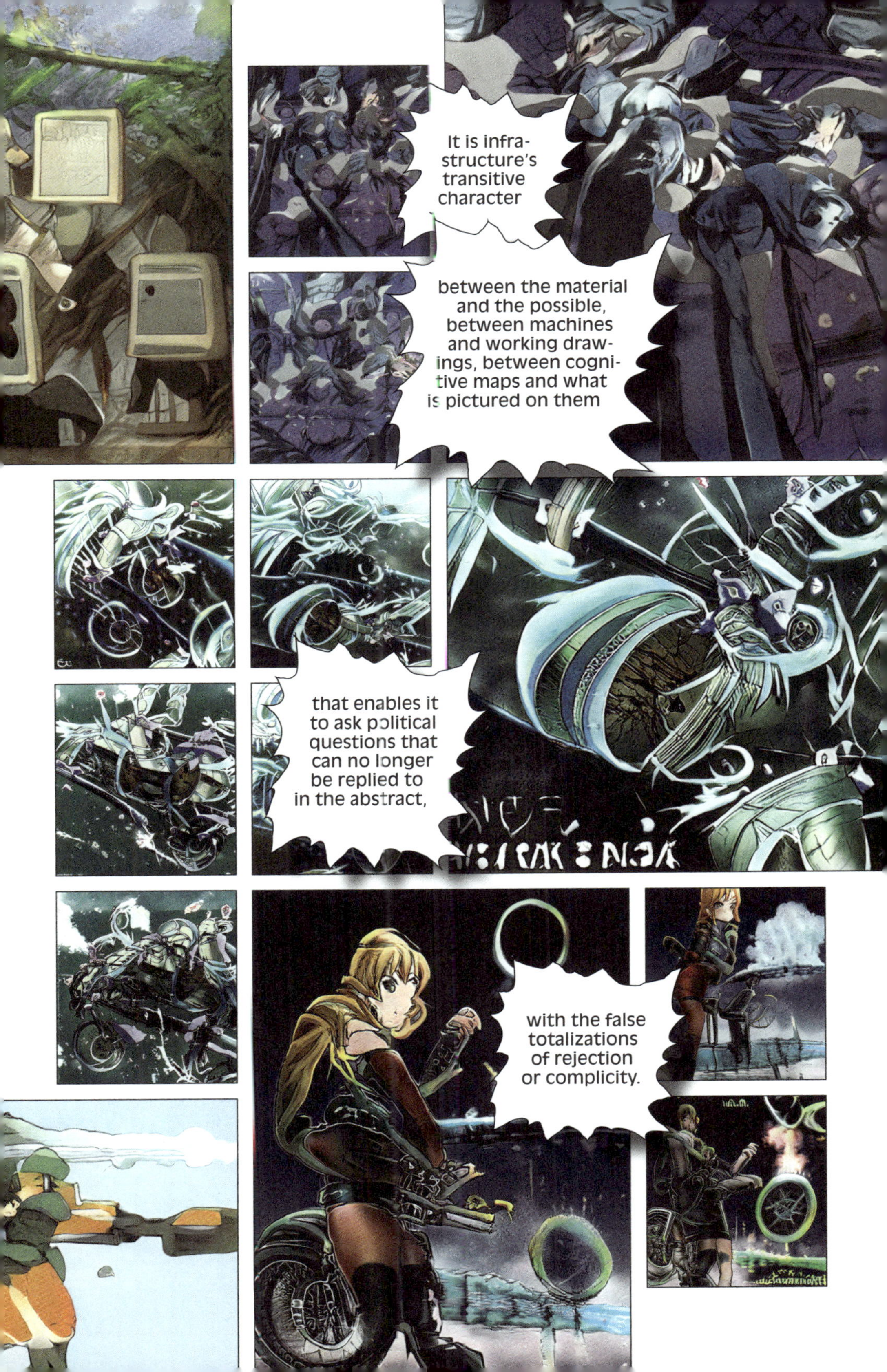
It is infra-structure's transitive character
between the material and the possible, between machines and working draw-ings, between cogni-tive maps and what is pictured on them
that enables it to ask political questions that can no longer be replied to in the abstract,
with the false totalizations of rejection or complicity.

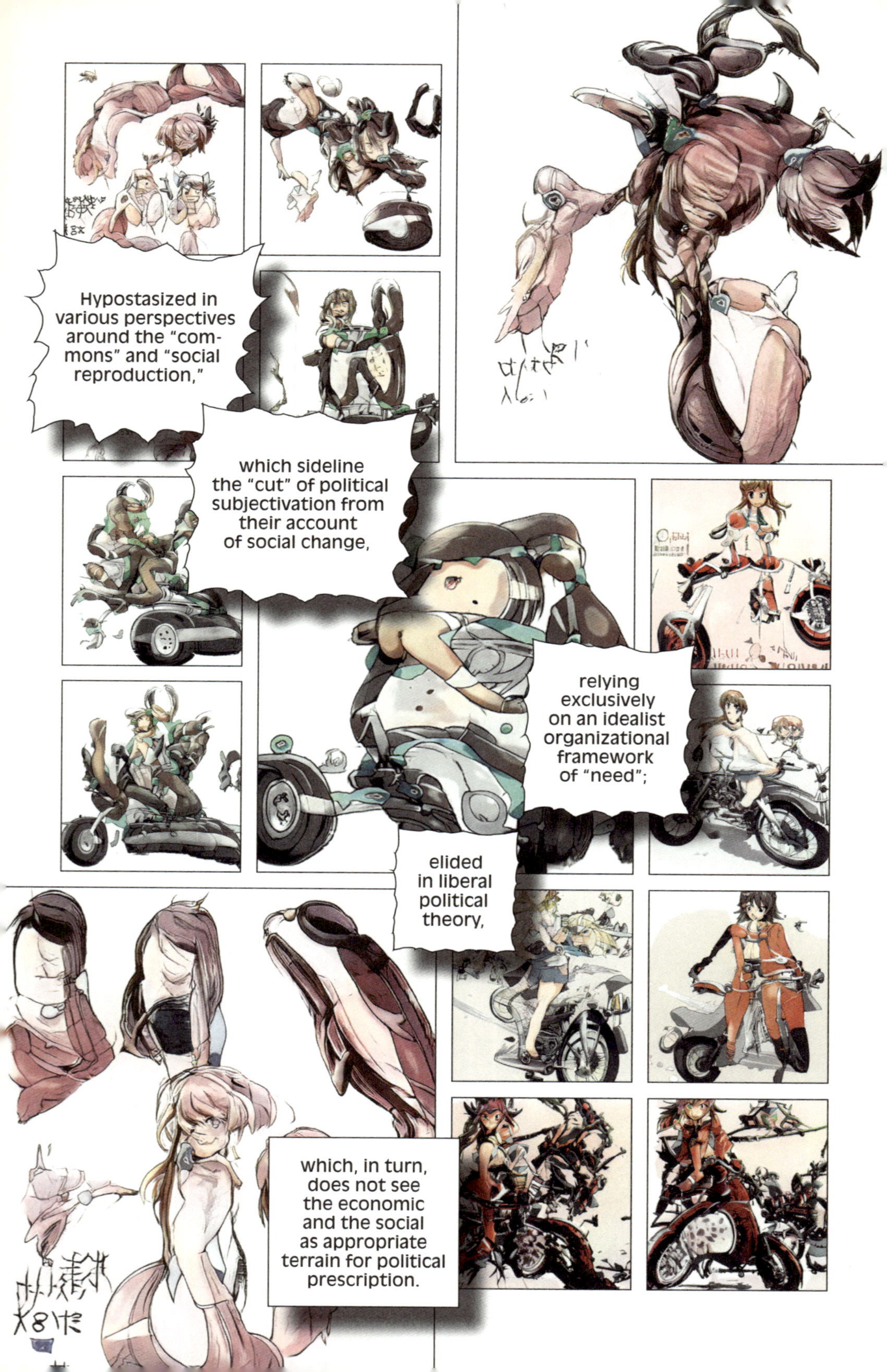
Hypostasized in various perspectives around the "commons" and "social reproduction,"
which sideline the "cut" of political subjectivation from their account of social change,
relying exclusively on an idealist organizational framework of "need";
elided in liberal political theory,
which, in turn, does not see the economic and the social as appropriate terrain for political prescription.

“Deep Learning Infrastructural Critique” is a response by Ilan Manouach to a series of quotes selected by Marina Vishmidt from her text “Between Not Everything and Not Nothing: Cuts Toward Infrastructural Critique” (2016), which has informed the idea for this publication and is also referenced in several of the contributions that follow.[1]

“Deep Learning Infrastructural Critique” was produced using emerging AI—more specifically generative adversarial networks—involving tens, possibly hundreds of hours of training. To create the comic, Manouach and his studio trained multiple models based on community data sets consisting of millions of images from anime and hentai. These data sets were subdivided into different subsets from which domain-specific models—such as vehicles, buildings, landscapes, weapons, characters—evolved. From the many images generated, Manouach selected and constructed the final sequence for the narrative and the layout for Vishmidt’s selected quotes. Melding into each other, the visual representations break apart, appear, and disappear, offering a kind of liquidity that speaks to the complexity of infrastructures and infrastructural critique.

1 Marina Vishmidt, “Between Not Everything and Not Nothing: Cuts Toward Infrastructural Critique,” in *Former West: Art and the Contemporary after 1989*, edited by Maria Hlavajova and Simon Sheik (Cambridge, MA: MIT Press, 2017), 265–69.

Infrastructural

1

Critique

INTRODUCTION: INFRAPOLITICS AFTER INFRASTRUCTURE SPACE

Bassam El Baroni

From which point in the complex matrix of our infrastructurally entangled existence can critical perspectives—that perform something other or more than complex descriptions and/or denunciations—still emerge today? In the words of Félix Guattari, capitalism has long been understood to have "taken hold of" our species "from the inside."[1] Through grafting itself onto human behavioral patterns—be they linguistic, cognitive, perceptual, sensorial, or affective, at the level of the individual or the collective—it has reorganized the ways in which we make meaning, plan ahead, respond politically and communicate with each other.[2] In recognizing that capital is not a self-moving entity, but rather is constituted through human activities, we also acknowledge that there is a strong fractal interrelationship between the "creative" immaterial labor we perform and the present-day anatomy of infrastructure.[3]

An anatomical schema involves the dissection of global infrastructure—or "infrastructure space" to use Keller Easterling's phrase—as a spatial and temporal entity operating at large, an examination of its divergent dispositions since "it is too big and not at one and the same place. It cannot be addressed through its shape or outline, but rather via its disposition—potentials unfolding in time and territory" as Easterling observes.[4] This unfolding in territories and time has materialized through repeatable formulas—duty-free zones, for instance, or the shared global standards determining modes of management[5]—and the speculative logic of finance. Since "infrastructure projects typically hinge upon significant investments in anticipation of future conditions manifesting, they are inherently speculative visions in the futurist and financial senses."[6] Such speculative trajectories require an embrace of risk and uncertainty, since the actions and calculations that enable them in the present are undertaken with necessarily incomplete knowledge of the future(s) they speculate on "because the future is absent from memory."[7] This—as Suhail Malik has suggested—equates to the future shaping the present, with a surfeit of futurity, in a lived hybrid temporality called the future-present.[8]

The anatomy of infrastructure is therefore always manifested between territories, virtualities, actualities, forms of labor (cognitive and manual), and tenses. It is also distributed across

1 Félix Guattari, *Molecular Revolution: Psychiatry and Politics* (Harmondsworth: Penguin, 1984), cited in Maurizio Lazzarato, "Art and work," *PARACHUTE*, No. 122, 2006.

2 Lazzarato, "Art and work."

3 Matthew Poole, "Speculation, presumption and assumption: The ideology of algebraic-to-parametric workspace," in *The Politics of Parametricism, Digital Technologies in Architecture*, edited by Matthew Poole and Manuel Shvertzberg (London: Bloomsbury, 2015), 138–58.

4 Keller Easterling, "How to redesign the infrastructure? FAQ by Keller Easterling," *Strelka Mag*, June 19, 2017, available at https://strelkamag.com/en/article/how-to-redesign-the-infrastructure-faq-by-keller-easterling_2 (accessed December 8, 2021).

5 Keller Easterling, *Extrastatecraft: The Power of Infrastructure Space* (Brooklyn: Verso, 2014), 11.

6 Andrew Hagman, "Infrastructural Futures in Chinese Science Fiction," *Alluvium*, Vol. 7, No. 3, 2019, https://doi.org/10.7766/alluvium.v7.3.01.

7 Suhail Malik, "Risk Exposure—Surfeit Futurity," *Making & Breaking*, Issue 2, 2021, available at https://makingandbreaking.org/article/risk-exposure-surfeit-futurity/ (accessed December 9, 2021).

8 Ibid.

states, markets, and platforms, where each of these builds on the others while constructing its own dominion.[9] As Benjamin Bratton notes, each of these institutional forms assert their influence by classifying and interacting with individuals in specific ways. As he argues, "States have *citizens*, Markets have *homo economicus*, and Platforms have *users*. Sometimes these interpolations align and sometimes they are at odds."[10] As a result, "accidental forms of provisional sovereignty" can appear when these forms—and the respective subjectivities attached to them—clash. For example, platforms are wedded to digital infrastructures that are not bound by the same constitutional, monetary, or human rights frameworks as state institutions are. Instead "[t]hey sustain themselves by the self-reinforcing logics of network effects, generative entrenchment, and monetizing the optimization of point-to-point information flows."[11]

Perhaps one way to approach infrastructure's distributed and transitive characteristics, then, is through an "integrative" methodology as proposed by philosopher Anne-Françoise Schmid, in which contemporary objects of research can only ever acquire momentary and partial unity through the specific approach of their researchers, never fully encompassing them as a whole.[12] According to Schmid, using classical epistemological frameworks we are already able to think of "complex objects," since many entities cannot be understood through a single discipline alone. Integrative objects, however, are past being understood as complex, and "once we perceive that we are unable to understand certain contemporary objects without excluding something from them" we are led to make a wager that is neither arbitrary nor a random act of imagination.[13] This wager is a bet on an unknown "X," and therefore a form of risk-taking, that through relying on perspectives from multiple disciplines constructs an impermanent understanding of the research object at hand. This volume aims to foster such a general integrative outlook toward the multidimensional question of the potential of thinking infrastructure in the twenty-first century and beyond.

In the past decade, there has for example been a heightened interest in the possibility of a technological counter-hegemonic narrative, in which already existing technologies are repurposed to overcome economic scarcity and realize a post-capitalist future.[14] Whether this narrative is viable or not, it was able to—for some time at least—capture the imagination of mainstream politics and public debate, bringing to the fore questions around work and general well-being, as well as outlining the potential of a future counter-scenario.[15] Work, labor, and research on their attendant issues within the arts have also generated another outlook: one that still holds on to the genealogy of critique, but shifts its register from the (art) institution to that of an unconfined infrastructure. For Marina Vishmidt, institutional critique tethers itself to the contextual grounding of the art institution, thereby situating itself in a relation of endless friction because of an understanding of the institution as that

9 Benjamin Bratton, "Machine Vision: Benjamin Bratton in Conversation with Mike Pepi and Marvin Jordan," *DIS Magazine*, February 2015, available at http://dismagazine.com/discussion/73272/benjamin-bratton-machine-vision/ (accessed December 9, 2021).

10 Ibid.

11 Ibid.

12 Anne-Françoise Schmid, "On Contemporary Objects," in *Simulation, Exercise, Operations*, edited by Robin Mackay (Falmouth: Urbanomic, 2015), 63–68.

13 Ibid.

14 See, for example, Nick Srnicek and Alex Williams, *Inventing the Future: Postcapitalism and a World Without Work* (London: Verso, 2015).

15 See, for example, Jonny Ball, "Automatons of the world unite! How the party of workers began talking about the abolition of work," *The New Statesman*, September 19, 2021, available at https://www.newstatesman.com/spotlight/2021/09/automatons-of-the-world-unite (accessed December 9, 2021).

which both enables and constrains, outside as well as inside the art worker's head. Avoiding the enclosures of the art-specific relationality of institutional critique, *infrastructural critique* is concerned with projects that may remain interested in, or, alternatively, are altogether "indifferent to pressing questions that pose themselves in and through the field of art."[16]

This book can in a sense be understood as an attempt to reconsider and reinvigorate the concept of *infrapolitics* by bringing it into alignment with the different ways artists, theorists, curators, art historians, and researchers have recently engaged with infrastructures, systems, planning, management, and organizational thinking. First introduced in the 1990s by the political scientist James C. Scott and later taken up by the fields of urban studies and spatial research, infrapolitics denotes political acts that lie outside forms of authorized political participation. Making infrastructures their medium, political actions take place "below or besides the threshold of political legibility,"[17] since "infra" indicates a below or under which are "the defining conditions of infrastructure."[18] For the Center for Spatial Research (CSR) at Columbia University, New York, "infrapolitics exist in the informality with which governments execute their laws, which favor certain individuals or groups over others, or in apparently nonpolitical acts of resistance by the population, such as practices of tax evasion by tenant farmers."[19] CSR also defines technopolitics as a subset of infrapolitics carried out through highly technological infrastructures.

While this formulation of the infrapolitical remains relevant, it has become clear that infrapolitics are no longer necessarily associated with "infra" in the sense of under or below. Nor are they necessarily the antithesis of a participatory politics in the limelight of sanctioned political arenas. Rising inequalities, the climate emergency, and other socio-political urgencies—not least the grim episode of Covid-19 we find ourselves in—have made the conditions ripe for the transitioning of infrapolitics from the domain of the "infra" to that of the "supra." Which is to say that many types of infrapolitics are now also explicit—in their formulation as political programs, proposals, and propositions that negotiate infrastructure as medium, understanding it as a kind of "operating system" that is the subject of increasingly precise and constructive research, making it and its workings more and more transparent to the public.

The infrapolitical "turn" has also entered the infrastructural space of finance and economics. Since creative practitioners are always already expected to adapt to the entrepreneurial paradigm—a paradigm that has appropriated and reinforced certain characteristics from the artist's toolbox—"it is unsurprising that the artist becomes comfortable in crossing the line between art and the economic to propose their own economies."[20] Many of these economic propositions are not meant to operate within the "safe space" of the art institution though, rather they are situated in a growing field of research into financial objects[21] and their mechanisms by an expanding

16 Marina Vishmidt, "Between Not Everything and Not Nothing: Cuts Toward Infrastructural Critique," in *Former West: Art and the Contemporary After 1989*, edited by Maria Hlavajova and Simon Sheikh (Cambridge, MA: MIT Press, 2016) 265–70.

17 Centre for Spatial Research Columbia University, "Infrapolitics—Seminar," available at http://infrapolitics.c4sr.columbia.edu/ (accessed December 10, 2021).

18 Ibid.

19 Ibid.

20 Danielle Child, "Artistic Economies: Shelter, Food and Clothing," *Afterall*, No. 49, 2020, 107–14.

number of artists, curators, collectives, and artistic researchers.[22] A key question underpinning this direction is how to enter the socio-psychological arena of finance to gain leverage *over* and *through* the artworker's own resources. Which is to say, the purpose is to establish new norms from within an extended sphere of finance.

In another register, the new infrapolitics share the common ground of the planetary with cosmopolitical perspectives that recognize "the desirability of an ambitious reframing of politics that reaches beyond settled categories, borders and territories,"[23] signaling a shift from global to planetary subjects following Gayatri Spivak. One example that has had significant impact on the field is Moscow-based Strelka Institute's design research program "The Terraforming," which reconfigures the idea of terraforming—usually reserved for other planets and moons—for a planet Earth fighting to escape an inevitable collision course with climate change. This type of "last ditch attempt" and scaled-up infrapolitics might be a form of heresy to an understanding of infrapolitics limited to the under, beneath, and out of sight. More importantly, it is echoed in the phenomenon of "design thinking," which has become ubiquitous within the wider sphere of art, as aesthetical, theoretical, analytical, and organizational qualities blur into each other in attempts to be purposeful while dodging the straightjacket of solutionism restricting other sectors such as tech. What these—and many more— examples show, is that infrapolitical actions, approaches, and perspectives constitute a form of political participation that works by shaping the critical, imaginal, investigative, and propositional space of infrastructure.

This collection of commissioned essays is an attempt to present the different shades of the infrapolitical spectrum. The texts interrogate art's relationality to infrastructure, presenting different approaches and points of access into infrapolitical thinking and opening up new speculative pathways and analyses that build on research into financialization as well as crypto-infrastructures. They expose the processes that actualize problematic infrastructures and offer insights into how we might address them anew, showing how old habits are entrenched in systems and an over-reliance on system-thinking, offering ideas on how we might approach such enduring infrastructural legacies. They adopt fiction as method, discuss scenario planning, and think through the question of scalability. They propose redistributive economies and the structural diversification of the arts sector, and they address our "after Earth" imaginaries around space settlements. The book's three sections—"Infrastructural Critique," "Infrastructural Speculation," and "Infrahauntologies: On Invasive Legacies and Futures"—act as general themes that reflect the approaches of their respective contributions. Within this clustering, however, there are many areas of overlap and shared trains of thought that travel through and across the expanse of infrastructure and the infrapolitical. Together they traverse current conditions of possibility and future-oriented

21 "Financial objects" are defined by Mark Kear as objects that have a role in "making possible the performance of particular financial subject positions—pathological or otherwise." The terminology is general and can stretch to include objects such as trades and marketplaces and the ubiquitous credit-rating to financial instruments such as stocks, bonds, shares, futures, and options contracts. See Mark Kear, "Playing the credit score game: algorithms, 'positive' data and the personification of financial objects," *Economy and Society*, Vol. 46, Nos. 3–4, 346–68.

22 This is not an exhaustive list, but examples include artist duos Vermeir & Heiremans and João Enxuto and Erica Love (both contributors to this volume); artist and researcher Emily Rosamond; curator, philosopher, and cultural theorist Erik Bordeleau; artist and researcher Bahar Noorizadeh (also a contributor here); artist and researcher Gerald Nestler; theorist Suhail Malik; and platforms such as Weird Economies (WE) and the Economic Space Agency.

23 Maja and Reuben Fowkes, "Cosmopolitics," in *The Posthuman Glossary*, edited by Rosi Braidotti and Maria Hlavajova (London: Bloomsbury, 2018), 92–94.

infrastructural hypotheses, between the re-examination of infrastructural legacies and economic strategizing, and between the material and the possible.

INFRASTRUCTURE AS DIAGRAMMATIC DISPOSITION: FAREED ARMALY'S *FROM/TO* (1999/2002) REVISITED

Sabeth Buchmann

I. The Disposition of Infrastructure

Marina Vishmidt's short essay "Between Not Everything and Not Nothing: Cuts Toward Infrastructural Critique" begins with a crucial question for my reflections on the types of work that negotiate the methods and implications of institutional critique:

> What would it mean to move from the practices and theories of institutional critique in the arts and expand these ideas into an infrastructural critique of the present? Could we posit such a shift within the definition of a "former West" as a temporal and historical category? There are a number of ways to consider infrastructure within the temporal categories at work in a speculative geopolitical concept like "former West."[1]

Published in 2016, the proposed shift in the essay opposes a totalization of the concept of institution that Vishmidt recognizes in Western thinking. The questioning of the concept of institution also concerns the core of institutional critique, namely the category of site-specificity.

Since it, first of all, refers to categories of space in terms of architecture and environment, Vishmidt's proposal reinforces those approaches that include time as it appears in the definition of institutional critique. One could think of James Meyer's concept of the "functional site" that the US-American art historian defined in 1995:

> The functional site may or may not incorporate a physical space; it certainly does not *privilege* this place. Rather, it is a process, an operation occurring between sites, a mapping of institutional and discursive filiations and the bodies that move between them (the artist's above all). It is an informational site, a locus of overlap of text, photographs and video recordings, physical places and things: an allegorical site, to recall Craig Owen's term. [...] The work is no longer an obdurate steel wall,

1 Marina Vishmidt, "Between Not Everything and Not Nothing: Cuts Toward Infrastructural Critique," in *Former West: Art and the Contemporary after 1989*, edited by Maria Hlavajova and Simon Sheik (Cambridge, MA: MIT Press, 2017), 265.

> attached to the urban plaza for eternity. It is a temporary thing; a movement; a chain of meanings devoid of a particular focus. The functional site thus courts its destruction; it is wilfully temporary; its nature is not to endure but to *come down*.[2]

While Meyer focuses on the moment of temporality and transience, Vishmidt emphasizes the dialectics of persistence and interruption. Expanding the perception of institutions as globally interconnected and therefore interdependent ensembles of infrastructures, "repetition" in the sense of "reproduction" appears as the central category for analyzing the present:

> Time is an infrastructure because it is a condition of possibility for conscious perception and action; infrastructure is made of time insofar as infrastructure is that which repeats. The repetition is normalized into everyday routine, and when it stops functioning, an aperture is cut into artifice—through which history and power relations can be seen.[3]

In order to evoke multiple "trajectories" rather than just the notion of institutional critique, Vishmidt posits "infrastructure" as a "conceptual diagram that enables thought to develop."[4]

Two historical-theoretical strands of critical thinking are connected in Vishmidt's proposition: first, the development of a critical approach to Eurocentrism and Western dominance, which in the Western context can largely be attributed to the foundation of the Centre for Contemporary Cultural Studies (CCCS) in Birmingham by Stuart Hall and Richard Hoggart in 1964, which together with thinkers connected to US-American universities helped establish the field of Postcolonial Studies in the late 1970s. Among their proponents were Homi K. Bhabha, Trinh T. Minh-ha, Gayatri Chakravorty Spivak, and Edward Said, whose studies and writings were, and still are, relevant for the deconstruction of the (former) West as the supposed center of the so-called modern world.

Linking the discourse of "infrastructural critique" to this tradition, Vishmidt's recourse to the "conceptual diagram" of "infrastructure"—the second strand—can be situated as an epistemological-aesthetic interface between post-structuralist deconstruction and conceptual artistic processes. This interface has already been in use since the mid-to-late 1980s among the second generation of practitioners commonly grouped under the label of institutional critique. I would like to illustrate this by using the example of the installation *From/To* by the first generation American, of Palestinian and Lebanese parents, artist Fareed Armaly, first shown at Witte de With, Rotterdam (1999), then at documenta 11 in Kassel (2002). As I demonstrate in what follows, Armaly's conception of the diagram embodies a "methodology of critical-reflexive site-specifics"[5]—which arguably is the epitome of institutional critique—for that geopolitical

2 James Meyer, "Der funktionale Ort/The Functional Site," in *Platzwechsel* (Zurich: Kunsthalle Zurich, 1995), 27. In his essay, Meyer refers to works by Ursula Biemann, Tom Burr, Mark Dion, and Christian Philipp Müller.

3 Ibid.

4 Ibid.

5 Andrea Fraser, "Was ist Institutionskritik?" (What is Institutional Critique?), *Texte zur Kunst*, No. 59, September 2005, 87.

dimension of colonialism that also played a decisive role in the work of other artists who came to the fore in that period, including Andrea Fraser, Renée Green, Christian Philipp Müller, Fred Wilson, and others.

According to the German art historian Susanne Leeb, "diagrams are the perfect medium because of their reductionism in relation to the complexity of reality they are not meant as displays of information, but for speculative thinking."[6] Leeb here refers to Stephen Willats's diagram *THE WORLD AS IT IS AND THE WORLD AS IT COULD BE* (2006). Armaly's interest in diagrammatic thinking and practice is indeed reminiscent of conceptual artists such as Willats, but also of work by Hans Haacke, Mary Kelly, and others. Significantly, diagrammatic approaches like theirs were experiencing a renewed interest at a time when traditional distinctions between (Western) NATO and (Eastern) Warsaw Pact states had come to an end and collided with the increasing distinction between the Global South and the Global North. Artists among the second generation of institutional critique set about focusing on site-specific institutional analyses of geopolitical categories such as "contact zones" (James Clifford), colonial-historical passages (W.E.B. DuBois), and "hybrid" and "third spaces" (Homi K. Bhabha) among geographically dispersed contexts. They also responded to the dissociation of place and identity, as articulated by Miwon Kwon in her book *One Place after Another: Site-Specific Art and Locational Identity* (2004), in which the meaning of site-specificity underwent a change due to the increasing diversification of forms of temporary artworks and their increased mobility.[7] This resulted in a shift that was accompanied by a superimposition of "functional" by "topological spaces," whose (anti-)designs were reminiscent of the diagrams of the post-avant-garde of the 1960s. I am thinking of installations by Julie Ault/Martin Beck, Fareed Armaly, Ursula Biemann, Matthew Buckingham, Alice Creischer, Omer Fast, Peter Fend, Dorit Margreiter, Christian Philipp Müller, Nils Norman, Renée Green, Martha Rosler, Allan Sekula, Andreas Siekmann, Hito Steyerl, etc., which present(ed) physical and/or functional sites as hubs in a network of international media and symbolic locations.

Vishmidt's notion of the "conceptual diagram" thus appears in a historical lineage within institutional critique, which is characterized by mathematical forms of representation as a mode of speculation situated between materialization and abstraction. This, in turn, is connected with an anti-positivist approach toward knowledge production and perceptual aesthetics, related to the structures, laws, and rules in and behind perceptual phenomena. The use of diagrams, associated with developments such as new dance, structural film, minimal, land, and conceptual art, showed an increased interest in the "cultural infrastructures of design," as Robert Morris argued.[8]

While the use of diagrams in minimal and conceptual art resulted from an attempt to re-establish the object-material paradigm on the basis of autonomous structures relying on internal

6 Susanne Leeb, "Einleitung" (Introduction), *Materialität der Diagramme: Kunst und Kritik*, edited by Susanne Leeb (Berlin: b_books/PoLYpeN, 2012), 12. Translation by Sabeth Buchmann.

7 Miwon Kwon, *One Place After Another: Site-Specificity and Locational Identity* (Cambridge, MA: MIT Press, 2004).

8 Robert Morris, "Notes on Sculpture," Part 3: "Notes and Nonsequiturs," *Artforum*, Vol. 5. No. 10, summer 1967, 26 and further.

relationships, practices that can be grouped among the first generation of institutional critique and its content—including work by Tucumán Arde, Art Workers' Coalition, Michael Asher, Daniel Buren, Lygia Clark, Dan Graham, Hans Haacke, Mary Kelly, Cildo Meireles, Hélio Oiticica, Lygia Pape, Adrian Piper, Martha Rosler, and others—often already referenced architectural-urban places, social subjects, and socio-political discourses through diagrams, which in the second and third generation of institutional critique experienced a geopolitical expansion.

Among other activist practices, Vishmidt refers to the activity of the Gulf Labor Coalition as a recent example that attempts to address the Guggenheim and Louvre complexes as exemplary symptoms of neoliberal corporate culture, maximizing profits through cheap work by exploiting disenfranchised migrants in the Arab Gulf states. Using this kind of example, Vishmidt calls for a revision of how we perceive institutional frameworks through infrastructural critique, addressing "local and global labor markets as well as corporate power constellations, ownership relations and the structural conditions of capitalism."[9] These visible and invisible infrastructures manifest themselves in institutional agendas and create an even greater need to uncover the dominant logic of logistics.[10]

As we can see from Armaly's work, the insertion of archives, book shelves, video stations, film screenings, and meeting points as sites for lectures and workshops into exhibition spaces offer insight in the infrastructural meaning of learning environments for a re-contextualization of art. Appearing in the form of interspatial designs, they blur the distinction between the object and the exhibition. Conceived as either architectural or experimental designs (post-)conceptual environments such as *From/To* embody an interdisciplinary and intermedial practice that deconstructs objects as relational materials and media. Following Helmut Draxler's instructive overview in *Coercing Constellations: Space, Reference, and Representations in Fareed Armaly* (2007), the relational character of Armaly's works is an "expression of the flexible border regimes" between "the aesthetic and the antiaesthetic, the symbolic and the real."[11] Draxler also states that "Armaly's interest in maps, diagrams, structures, and rhetorical figures [...] appears as a representation of the relationship between subjects and urban, media, or social space."[12]

Since the site-related displays used by Armaly are tied to the idea of the institution as a public, democratic, and social arena, they create anything but literal places. As Meyer points out, "the functional site" instead is imbued with allegorical meanings and can consist of a connection of physical and symbolic sites in the sense of his concept of the "functional site." As Draxler rightly argues, "[a]rtistic ways of working that address the 'functional site' do not adapt to a certain location, but rather try to expose the site's complex social, urban, and institutional structure." Since Armaly's "linkage between the 'inner' space that a work creates using formal elements and the concrete

9 Vishmidt, "Between Not Everything and Not Nothing," 267.

10 Stefano Harney and Fred Moten, *The Undercommons: Fugitive Planning and Black Study* (Wivenhoe: Minor Compositions, 2013).

11 Helmut Draxler, *Coercing Constellations: Space, Reference, and Representations in Fareed Armaly* (Berlin: b_books/PoLYpeN, 2007), 111.

12 Ibid., 116.

'external' space of the exhibition itself [...] it is neither site-specific in the strict sense, nor is it truly functional. Quite on the contrary, it is invested in dysfunctional moments."[13]

With regard to Vishmidt's consideration that infrastructures often only become visible when they malfunction or collapse, I would like to read Armaly's contribution to documenta 11 as a "(dys-)functional site," as a site that at once reflects on the conditions and limits of infrastructural logistics.[14] This subject is strongly echoed in the work of authors such as Keller Easterling as well as Stefano Harney and Fred Moten. Whereas Vishmidt regards functional infrastructures such as "bridges, tunnels, and sewers [...] as locus of social abstraction,"[15] Easterling's notion of infrastructure is tied to that of the "disposition" as a condition "that makes some things possible and some things impossible."[16] Also important here is Harney and Moten's reflection on the correspondence between the production of a "logistical population" and the colonialist epistemology of control, an observation that will help me articulate how *From/To* can be considered a highly relevant example of "infrastructural critique."[17]

II. Diagrammatic Movements

With reference to the meaning of Edward Said's famous book *Orientalism* (1978) for Armaly's project *The (re)Orient* (1989), I read *From/To* in relation to Said's Foucault-based studies on the disenfranchisement of the Palestinians, published in 1994 under the title *The Politics of Dispossession*.[18] Armaly's diagrammatic representation in *From/To* can be argued to offer a crucial contribution to Vishmidt's concept of "infrastructural critique." In a nutshell, *From/To* dealt with the absence of a representation of Palestinian history within Western narratives. The 2002 version found its alignment (*Fluchtlinie*) in an enlarged section of a digitized stone, which the artist had already produced for the first version in 1999. That section was laid out on the floor as a diagrammatic map in order to create a walk-in network of paths that would enter into a spatial relationship with the abstract geometric wall design. The lines taped to the floor recorded movements of Palestinian refugees after 1948 and intersected the two relational prepositions "FROM-TO": *From* Gaza *to* Al-Karama Camp, *From* City Center Amman *to* Al-Hussein Camp, etc. While the stone could on the one hand be perceived as a simple natural artifact that extends beyond the age of modernity and colonialism, on the other hand it represented an iconic object of resistance—used in the so-called "war of stones"—reminiscent of the Palestinian youngsters in the context of the First Intifada (1987–93). Significantly, the digitized object was also reminiscent of the scandal surrounding a symbolic act by Said, two years earlier, on July 3, 2000, when he was photographed throwing a stone on the border between Lebanon and Israel.[19] This is important, since the ongoing conflict between the Palestinians and Israel culminated in the Second Intifada (2000–05). When Armaly showed his second version in 2002,

13 Ibid., 118.

14 Vishmidt, "Between Not Everything and Not Nothing," 266.

15 Ibid.

16 Keller Easterling, *Extrastatecraft: The Power of Infrastructure Space* (London: Verso, 2014), 6.

17 Harney and Moten, *The Undercommons*, 90.

18 In the exhibition's introductory text Armaly elaborates that he draws directly on Stuart Hall rather than Said: "[a]ll of this grounds *From/To* in a concrete reality that reflects [...] Hall's statement on diasporic identity: 'The history depends on the routes. It's the replacement of "roots" with routes.' Routes are the negotiation of exchange. The variety indicates the operation of different economies."

19 For an interview about the incident, see Ari Shavit, "An interview with Edward Said," originally published in *Ha'aretz*, Issue 3, 2000, available at https://politicsandculture.org/2010/08/10/an-interview-with-edward-said-2/ (accessed June 11, 2021).

the conflict had reached a new level of violence and territorial expansion following the failed Oslo peace process.[20]

By representing historical contexts and events in the form of a conceptual diagram, Armaly renounced the (re-)presentation of the conflict by way of images of horror. Instead, the stone operated as node and junction of a spatial network of Palestinian territories and refugee routes.[21] In its half-material, half-digitized appearance, it represented precisely the tension between concrete object and virtual form that is inscribed into the diagram as a medium of abstraction and speculation. As such it evokes "positional interrelations" between functional sites, aesthetic objects, participants and visitors, but does not prefabricate an "absolute," static given space.[22] Based on a scenographic model that linked the spatial structure of the documenta Halle to the topographic infrastructures of escape and diaspora, their linguistic translation (*From* Gaza *to* Al-Karama Camp, *From* City Center Amman *to* Al-Hussein Camp) connected allegorical representations of absent sites, such as "Checkpoint," with "informational sites" as identified by Meyer, such as "Media Geography" and "Home Movie." As such, "Checkpoint," "Media Geography," and "Home Movie" are names for three of five specifically designed areas in the exhibition, which can be described as "curatorial apparatuses"[23]—the latter was an archive compiled by Armaly featuring work by Rashid Masharawi and Mai Masri, which

> deal[s] with unique Palestinian perspectives by re-inscribing the actual and virtual topography of the Palestinian culture, landscape and refugee life. [...] The films touch upon the memories and desires of a population under occupation and the dialog between generations. They deal with the events of the present, the weight of the past and the hope and perspective onto a future that might take place not in camps anymore, but within the borders of a Palestinian State.[24]

While "Checkpoint" stood for border control between Israel and the Palestinian territories, "Media Geography" stood for the way in which "the cinematic apparatus displays new definitions of geography as science transforming into an experience."[25] The multi-perspective linking of topographies and media histories offered the visitors a variety of access and viewpoints, bringing together immanent and outside views. Comparable to Armaly's 1989 show "The (re)Orient," *From/To* consisted of an asymmetrical space, full of disorienting lines and connections. The spatial structure reminds of Gilles Deleuze and Félix Guattari's distinction between the "smooth" and the "striated" in *A Thousand Plateaus* (1980). Whereas the first stands for the "nomad space," the latter represents the "sedentary space," "the space in which the war machine develops and the space instituted by the State apparatus—are not of the same nature."[26] The description of the authors fits into Armaly's model, since it consists of highly

20 See, for further information, http://fromto.withthis.net/#/articles/fromto/israel-palestine/ and http://fromto.withthis.net/#/articles/fromto/charting-palestinian-territories-and-power-from-land-control-to-flows-control-sylvie-fouet-jerusalem-may-2002/ (accessed April 18, 2021).

21 The website documents Armaly's and his collaborators' reflection on infrastructural space, for instance regarding traffic and telecommunication. See http://fromto.withthis.net/#/articles/fromto/film-selection/ (accessed April 18, 2021). From a formal point of view, one could recall the historical globe made of silver, which the African American artist Fred Wilson placed at the center in his famous exhibition "Mining the Museum" (1992) and which he labeled with the term "TRUTH."

22 See Tom Holert, "A fine flair for the diagram," in "Wissensorganisation und Diagramm—Form in der Kunst der 1960er Jahre: Mel Bochner, Robert Smithson, Arakawa," in Leeb, *Materialität der Diagramme*, 135–78.

23 I thank Bassam El Baroni for this suggestion.

24 See http://fromto.withthis.net/#/articles/fromto/film-selection/ (accessed April 18, 2021).

25 Ibid., see the list of films that were shown during documenta.

differentiated, at the same time mutually transformative spaces, that form intersected passages constructed by "vertical and horizontal elements."[27] The philosopher and the psychoanalyst list a number of types of space, of which I take up the "maritime model" here, because it marks a difference that is decisive for my consideration of Armaly's show:

> Directed or not [...] smooth space is directional rather than dimensional or metric. Smooth space is filled by events or haecceities, far more than formed and perceived by things. It is a space of affects, more than one of properties. It is *haptic* rather than optical perception. Whereas in the striated forms organize a matter, in the smooth materials signal forces and serve as symptoms for them.[28]

In fact, the installation views give the impression of a fragmented and fragile space that deals with directions and not objects. Therefore a single Sabra cactus was all the more eye-catching, as it once again stood for the multiple roots of the Arab-Palestinian and Jewish-Israeli populations, which cannot be reduced to one origin. Here, too, the distinction and the connection between smooth and indented space could be an indication of the dialectic of difference and (inter-)connectedness. Therefore the following passage from Armaly's project description seems to be meaningful for the perception of intertwined, simultaneously visible and invisible infrastructures:

> One such example relating to the division of space, property and memory is the Sabra cactus through the way it is defined by Israeli and Palestinian identity politics. The Sabra cactus is a 19th century example for an emerging world of interconnections and cross exchanges. As of today, it paradoxically serves to reinforce desires for and reality of rootedness in two people. The Sabra cactus can be seen as the embodiment of a transition from nature to culture, as a sign that belongs to a field of interpretation and appropriation. As it serves as a marker of the past by indicating that which was lost, as a memory trigger for those who come back to the places they once belonged, it also becomes a perimeter for buildings and villages no longer existing, a footnote to history only for those know how to decipher the text.[29]

Seen in this light, the diagram again appears as a materialization of the structurally undocumented history of Palestinian refugees, not only with the help of archive materials and media sources, but also with that of affect-laden objects, here a relatively inconspicuous, literally haptic plant. Armaly's concretization of infrastructural dispositions therefore evokes an unstable space that is inhabited by materials, which are about memory, imagination, and projection.

26 See Gilles Deleuze and Félix Guattari, "The Smooth and the Striated," in *A Thousand Plateaus: Capitalism and Schizophrenia* (Minneapolis: University of Minnesota Press, 1987 [1980]), 474.

27 Ibid., 475.

28 Ibid., 479.

29 See http://fromto.withthis.net/#/articles/fromto/film-selection/ (accessed April 18, 2021).

As such, Armaly's spatial installation allowed visitors to enter into a speculative relationship with the fantasized whole that corresponds with the concept of utopia as understood in the US.

> The notion of "Promised Land" admits in and organizes the myriad of desires projected by the diversity of immigrant passages. These desires are driven by a utopia that requires a leap of faith onto fantasy as the only way to bridge old and new. A unified spatial identity is required for this unfinished character of the nation, as a psychological cartography without a limit to any final land *per se*, as an open-ended narrative. [...] Offered therein for the first generation of Arab-Americans are not the sentiments implied in the media tropes but the dead-end portrayals of stereotypes, where their representations are instrumentalized within government oil policies and then abstracted in claims of unity and geopolitics. [...] My interest in developing the project *From/To* stems from a desire to chart out the unique status of my first-generation through this non-existing yet operating space of the hyphen that is both bind and transmission. Through charting out a contemporary topos of post-1948 Palestine this hyphen connects and traces the relations of symmetry between two self-proclaimed promised lands, the US and Israel. These are passages through a double-bind of generational space which those like myself represents in terms of diasporic identity.[30]

From/To translated the "double-bind of generational space" into a spatial montage of overlapping "texts, photographs and video recordings, physical places and things," as Meyer argues, including media archives, audio tapes, and databases with dozens of interviews, which documented a wide range of linguistic, visual, and oral testimonies. Armaly's "montages become self-reflexive forms of presentation, and social relations can express themselves in the arrangement of the material."[31] Furthermore, *From/To* translated the overlapping of geographic and media infrastructures into a multisensory infrastructure of perception. Since Armaly's diagram appeared as an overall infrastructure consisting of confusing lines, empty fields, and specified sites, it literally created space for speculations about given as well as possible geopolitical connections. The first iteration in 1999 at Witte de With included meeting points, where the audience could take part in workshops and seminars with historians, sociologists, anthropologists, filmmakers, and television producers, bridging the institutional separations between aesthetic, social, and learning environments. In the 2002 version, the documenta Halle was used as an infrastructure for a series of talks, while video documentation from the events in Rotterdam was presented in the "Checkpoint" section.

Since the diagram allowed for a virtual mixture of site-specific, geographic, and geopolitical infrastructures, it simul-

30 Fareed Armaly, *From/ To*, in Draxler, *Coercing Constellations*, 166 and further.

31 Ibid., 117.

taneously allowed for an abstraction of historical contexts that speak to allegedly fixed demarcation lines. I therefore read Armaly's diagram as a speculation about the constitutive role of escape routes for a perspective that complicates the dichotomy of East and West and the borders between them. This also applies to Armaly's design of the diagram: in contrast to the dominant Western concept of modernist-reductionist abstraction, *From/To* was characterized by a narrative and referential model of abstraction.[32] The double function of the diagram—as site-related spatial structure and as visualization of the imperceptible and/or ignored nexus of geographic and geopolitical infrastructures—revealed the performative function of repeated migrations for the deconstruction of ideological distinctions between the former West and the former East. As quoted, Armaly's diagram illustrates the network of escape routes from village to village, from Gaza to Syria, from Syria to Russia and to the USA.[33]

Linking Meyer's notion of the "functional site" with Vishmidt's notion of "infrastructural critique," *From/To* could be read as an allegory of the "infrastructure of the Palestinian diaspora," which also evoked a connection with the historically burdened institution of Documenta, which was founded in 1955 in Kassel, then a West-German city situated on the border with the former GDR, i.e., in the first period of the Cold War. Not least since Werner Haftmann's NSDAP and SA membership became known in 2019. Alongside Arnold Bode, he was one of the founders of Documenta, the association of which with the German attempt to overcome the crimes of World War II and the Shoa by being recognized as a cultural nation representing Western values of enlightenment—humanism, equality, and freedom—was and is obvious. Under the direction of Okwui Enwezor, it was evident that documenta aimed to extend these values by questioning the legacies of Western colonialism.[34]

The relational structure of Armaly's diagrammatic representation of Palestinian diaspora can thus be read as an infrastructural montage of spatio-temporal layers that testifies to interconnected historical events and developments. What, on the one hand, appears to be a disjunctive montage of heterogeneous sites, routes, and times, on the other hand overlaps with (post-)colonialist ideas.[35] *From/To* shows that the "production of logistic populations," identified by Harney and Moten, went hand in hand with the emergence of diasporic subjects and communities that were forced to break with the infrastructural unity of site and identity. There were, and always will be, migrants who invent(ed) routes crossing traditional geopolitical divisions. As we learn from the documentation of *From/To* on Armaly's website, the phenomenon of multiple migrations corresponds with a dynamic creation of space with unpredictable directions, perspectives, and connections.[36] The representation of migration therefore requires both a montage and a disjunction of real and virtual infrastructures. As such, Armaly's "infrastructural space" contradicts the impression of threshold-free flows that we usually associate with globalization. At the same time, and very topically,

32 See Draxler, *Coercive Constellations*, 142–49.

33 See Armaly's documentation on his website https://www.fareedarmaly.net (accessed April 18, 2021).

34 Michael Rothberg's book *Multidirectional Memory: Remembering the Holocaust in the Age of Decolonization* (Stanford: Stanford University Press, 2009) is only one example of the necessary attempts to integrate the Nakba into collective commemoration.

35 Harney and Moten, *The Undercommons*, 88.

36 See http://fromto.withthis.net/#/articles/fromto/waiting/ (accessed April 18, 2021).

the movements of the refugees do not match with a logic of control based on territorial categories of borders and walls.[37] Since the "passages" assembled by Armaly's diagram simulate a possible infrastructure of routes, sites, and geographies, they can be related to Easterling's concept of "disposition."

> The chemist, cook, parent, dog, or urbanist is considering the activities and *dispositions* of objects, where "disposition" describes the agency or potential immanent in an arrangement—a property or propensity within a context of relationship. You might assess the disposition of someone's personality over time or the disposition of a house in relation to the weather or landscape, just as you might describe the disposition of an organization. The disposition of any organization makes some things possible and some things impossible.[38]

Insofar as Armaly's diagram allows a detachment from the concrete objects that it represents, we also perceive it as a placeholder for (still) impossible representations, that, according to Easterling, are indexed to "dispositions", and that, if the spatio-temporal conditions changed, could also make still unrealized things possible.

III. Learning to (Un-)Rehearse Infrastructures

In *Extrastatecraft*, Easterling talks about "under-" and "well-rehearsed knowledge," meaning that she distinguishes between different degrees of knowledge as well as between different degrees of experience of spatial, social, and institutional protocols.[39] The criteria of "rehearsed" knowledge show that and to what extent performance-based thinking has captured modern epistemology as a field of disciplines inherent in modern art and art theory.

As already mentioned, *From/To* cast an infrastructure in order to merge aesthetic, social, and learning environments. As such, it enabled visitors to experience the space through a combination of physical, sensorial, and cognitive activities: significantly, their movements, positionings, interactions, and types of behavior filled the diagrammatic space. Visitors also experienced their own physical presence as substitutes for the absent refugees. As an essay about the conventions of Palestinian photography at the turn of the century, contributed to Armaly's archive by Issam Nasser, outlines, the enormous amount of photos shot by visitors who came to Jordan and Syria in order to undertake the "Voyage dans L'Orient" don't include pictures of Palestinians.[40] Among the entire period of the first twenty years of portrait photography, he found not a single one in local archives. The spatial distribution and placement of the audience therefore corresponds with an undocumented reality, which can no longer be reconstructed. What if we therefore allegorized the concept of infrastructure as a backstage that serves collective

38 Keller Easterling, *Medium Design: Knowing How to Work on the World* (London: Verso, 2021), ix.

39 Easterling, *Extrastatecraft*, 9.

40 See http://fromto.withthis.net/#/articles/fromto/dealing-with-the-past-creating-a-presence/ (accessed April 18, 2021).

learning exercises and rehearsals of a temporary public? As a space that serves for a collective testing of unknown contexts and relations—between Asia and the Middle East, Eastern and Western Europe, and the United States—in the sense of a speculative filling of gaps in sensitivity, knowledge, and experience.

This leads to a final consideration of *From/To* as "infrastructural critique," in relation to Armaly's collaborations with other researchers, first of all with Ramallah-based film maker Rashid Masharawi.[41] The latter's film *Waiting* was a central contribution to the show, its title seemingly reflecting the tension that Armaly's spatial diagram evoked—the tension between the material and the virtual as well as between archives, meeting points, and objects on the one hand, and the "empty" in-between zones on the other hand. Masharawi's film was a conceptually decisive contribution, the title reading like a literal description of its content as well as an allegorical comment on the situation of the Palestinian people.

In a nutshell, the film shows nothing other than a film studio in which Palestinian actors wait for their casting. Since the film crew was stuck in Amman and could not travel to Ramallah due to several complications, it became a document about the impossibility of shooting the planned film. Contrary to their expectations, the participating actors were therefore instructed by the director (played by Masharawi himself) not to "perform," but simply "wait"—an instruction aiming to achieve the doomed requirement not to act in front of a recording camera. But Masharawi's oral instruction is everything but neutral: it deals with the power of the word and the associated connection between "listening" and "obeying"—where the director's instructions serves the interaction between him and those who normally act. We observe them as they observe each other.[42] The film turns into a study on the question of what waiting for each of the cast performers, and not least for us, means. In analogy to the in-between-spaces and passages in Armaly's room, waiting appears as a fragile infrastructure that could collapse at any time. Some of the performers try to come to terms with the uncomfortable anti-exercise—by obviously performing waiting—while others, especially an older male actor, seem to resist the director's instruction and leave the studio.[43]

The interaction between the director and the actors who enter the studio in anticipation one after the other develops into a serial mini-drama reflecting different generations and genders. Reacting to the director's instructions, some are relaxed, some annoyed, some remain passive, others become overactive, aggressive even. The apparently non-performative act of waiting turns into a series of individual portraits and into the intergenerational psychodrama of a group of people who expect—with dwindling hope—to be cast in a Palestinian film; while some decide to sit out the situation, others make the decision to get out of an apparently hopeless project. While it appears evident to perceive *Waiting* as an allegory of the Palestinian situation, the scene also shows that people react rather differently to a "state

41 Armaly underlines that this dialog has to be understood as more than yet another "collaboration." Introducing Masharawi's name with "with," he aimed to underline the dialog they had in respect of these three new videos for documenta 11. Comments Armaly to author.

42 See Sibylle Krämer, "Die 'Rehabilitierung der Stimme'. Über die Oralität hinaus," in *Stimme*, edited by Doris Kolesch and Sybille Krämer (Frankfurt am Main: Suhrkamp, 2006), 280.

43 I would like to thank the students of the 2020/21 class of Maumaus, Lisbon, for the inspiring discussion on *Waiting*.

of emergency," a state the director transfers into his relationship with the actors. It is no longer a question of finding out who is best suited for which roles, but of observing the reactions of the candidates, in a situation in which a given protocol is interrupted. The film therefore is a representation of an impossible casting situation, and proves to be a behavioral experiment in which actors are put to the test. The negation of cinematic fiction presents itself as a performative reflection of the possibility and impossibility of depicting the Palestinian situation.

As an integral part of *From/To*, *Waiting* shows that infrastructural conditions are not external to individuals, instead weaving them into their psycho-emotional register. The unequal dialogue with the director, usually a higher authority whose judgment the actors are exposed to but who is now equally condemned to idleness, creates an absurd and at the same time also experimental set-up. The representational role of performance changes into one of an auto-referential self-presentation.[44] The paradoxical attempt to act as if one were doing nothing, of pretending not to play, is reminiscent of the link Easterling makes between the disposition and the level of rehearsal of given protocols. Seen as a disposition, the casting studio appears as a laboratory simulation of "real" habits. Insofar as the collapse of role, figure, and persona is based on the collapse of the original production and thus the planned narrative, it turns out to be a view of social infrastructures beyond the backdrop.

In the context of *From/To*, *Waiting* can therefore be read as a disposition of artistic expression—who would not think of Samuel Beckett's *Waiting for Godot?*—as well as of (inter-) subjective behavior, and not least of political agency.[45] Since the casting candidates stand for intergenerational archetypes, they also embody viewers' projections and expectations. I personally read Masharawi's film as a semi-documentary/semi-fictional performance, reflecting on an aporia to fictionalize a structurally undocumented reality. What does this mean for the representation of Palestinian refugees as social and historical actors? From the perspective of this question, the instruction to wait turns out to be a possibility for those waiting to constitute the director as a witness to their involuntary self-determination.[46] The experimental scene furthermore suggests that this very special case of non-performative or counter-performative self-determination consists of a mixture of adapting to the given situation and rebelling against it.

The framework, a casting process in never-ending limbo, reveals the infrastructural meaning of meta-fiction as a disposition of representative narrations. What can be said and shown, what cannot? Since the actors are forced to perform, or more precisely to simulate a behavior that doesn't make sense, the project can at the same time be recognized as the interruption of a given "script." As such, *Waiting* exposes the speculation about the engagement of the visitors, whose interaction, i.e., behavior, movements, affinities, and affects were performed in (inter-)relation with Armaly's spatial diagram. Masharawi's film

44 Krämer, "Die 'Rehabilitierung der Stimme.'"

45 Compare Constanze Ruhm, "Castingagentur: Casting as Agency," in *Putting Rehearsals to the Test: Practices of Rehearsal in Fine Arts, Film, Theater, Theory, and Politics*, edited by Sabeth Buchmann, Ilse Lafer, and Constanze Ruhm, Publication Series of the Academy of Fine Arts Vienna, Vol. 19 (Berlin: Sternberg Press, 2016), 228–37; and Sabeth Buchmann and Constanze Ruhm, "Subject Put to the Test," in *Performing the Sentence: Research and Teaching in Performative Fine Arts*, edited by Carola Dertnig and Felicitas Thun-Hohenstein (Berlin: Sternberg Press, 2014), 200–07.

46 See Krämer, "Die 'Rehabilitierung der Stimme,'" 286.

thus also appears to be a performative allegory of dysfunctional (inter-)relations, which Armaly's spatial montage of real and symbolic sites dialectically turns into an experience of interruption, which, once again, is reminiscent of Vishmidt's definition of infrastructure:

> To say that "infrastructure" repeats means that it works to enable a set of activities, and it works because the preconditions of its effectivity are neither visible nor relevant; these jut out when the infrastructure breaks down or if an element is isolated from the whole. The architecture theorist Martin Reinhold illuminatingly discusses infrastructure as a regime of intelligibility in terms that echo Michel Foucault's "epistemes," but with a more concrete mediation of the social with the technological: "*The dumbwaiter, bound to slave labor, carries bottle after bottle up to Jefferson's dining room. Its systemic properties tend to become visible only when the repetitions cease. If the wine ceases to appear, at some level and only for an instant, the entire apparatus of slavery comes into view. When you turn on the faucet and the water does not flow, the entire water system leaps into the cognitive field.*"[47]

Representation was only fulfilled by the form of its perception and use. Once again, the connection between the materialization of undocumented escape history and speculation about its representability appears as the core of the question that comes to light in *From/To*. As Aleida Assmann states, "what we remember is not based on what actually happened, but on what we can and want to tell a story about later. What is remembered from the past and what is not ultimately depends on who is using the story and for what purpose."[48] Thus, the diagrammatic dialectic of materialization and speculation opposes the assumption of seamless historical truth, which, according to Foucault, would obscure the interests of those in power. The diagrammatic materialization of infrastructural dispositions that can make something possible and/or impossible, consequently integrates structures of memory into the here and now of spatial and temporal presence. The view of interruptions and gaps within historical and topographical relationships realized by *From/To* protects the space of representation from the totalization that Vishmidt recognizes in traditional terms of institutional critique.

In this sense, Armaly's spatial diagram can be read as a "cognitive field" dealing with disturbances, disjunctions, and breaks, as described by Vishmidt. What appears in *From/To* as an epistemic-cartographic structure, turns out to be a sociocultural infrastructure made up of paths (detours) that visitors were able to open up visually, physically, and cognitively. The diagram, made up of lines, surfaces, and nodes, corresponded to the thematic logic of "waiting" in Masharawi's film insofar as

47 Vishmidt, "Between Not Everything and Not Nothing," 266.

48 Aleida Assmann, "Erinnerung und Geschichte," available at https://www.goethe.de/ins/lv/de/kul/sup/ber/art/20809570.html (accessed July 11, 2021). Translation by Sabeth Buchmann.

there was literal space for situational interaction. Just like *Waiting* is about the fact that the director owes the actors an answer to the experiment, which is pointless for them, so is *From/To* about the impossibility of a coherent artistic answer to a political problem of global proportions. *From/To* suggests that the answer can only be found in the interaction-based experience and production of knowledge by all those involved, including the visitors. In this regard, the diagram space creates a space of structurally (im-)possible connections.

INFRASTRUCTURE, IDEOLOGY, HEGEMONY

Matthew Poole

The issue of confidently identifying, defining, or determining precisely what is infrastructure is a deceptively simple task. The task seems simple insofar as we are all able to point to many different entities, systems, structures, or networks that are conventionally or typically thought of as infrastructure—or as possessing infrastructural qualities or functions—but the conditions or relations of those conventions is as unstable as the embeddedness of the conventions is strong in our individual and collective perception and habits. Identifying how, where, or when a certain thing is to be categorized as infrastructure or designated another category, such as "product," is a matter of context. A lorry or truck may be considered a product when produced in the factory or when sitting on the dealership forecourt, but it may also be considered to be infrastructure when in use as part of a network of logistics. In art this is especially complex, as what we may conventionally call or consider an artwork or art activity, can be considered a "product" (of sorts) when produced, exhibited, or sold, or when it is the object of criticism, etc. However, it is also infrastructural, since it will become part of a network of relations, a point or phenomenon to be referred to in art history or art criticism, and part of a lexicon of and discourse about examples, references, and precedents that conjoin to make up the context and field of art. It is therefore a mistake to categorically declare a specific thing or phenomenon as belonging to a generic class of things definitively, such as "infrastructure," or as belonging to its own particulate class of unique individuality, such as "product." The identification of and use of such dyadic categorizations as generic or particular, general or specific, or whole and parts are what are at stake.

Louis Althusser adroitly explores this issue in his well-known essay "Ideology and Ideological State Apparatuses" (1970), in which he begins by explaining *the reproduction of the means of production* by stating that "[a]s Marx said, every child knows that a social formation which did not reproduce the conditions of production at the same time as it produced would not last a year. The ultimate condition of production is therefore the reproduction of the conditions of production."[1] He goes on to give an example of a chain of production for woolen yarn, where he describes how Mr. X, who owns a spinning mill, needs both the raw materials and the machines for spinning yarn to

1 Louis Althusser, "Ideology and Ideological State Apparatuses (Notes Towards an Investigation)," first published in *La Pensée*, 1970; translated from the French by Ben Brewster, in Louis Althusser, *On the Reproduction of Capitalism: Ideology and Ideological State Apparatuses* (Brooklyn: Verso, 2014), 232.

be reproduced. The products of Mr. Z (an engineer producing machine tools) become the infrastructure (the means for the reproduction of the means of production) for Mr. X (for spinning the woolen yarn), as do the products of Mr. Y (a sheep farmer producing wool). The products of Mr. X (the woolen yarn) are effectively the infrastructure for another producer, a producer of clothing or blankets, etc. This "endless chain,"[2] in all of its complexity operates as a series of intersecting and connected ellipses, since the "products" at various points in the chain end up being "infrastructure" for other elements of the chain at direct or indirect instances.

In art, the production of artworks is still largely considered the "product" of art activity, and hence could be conventionally considered as "superstructural," in Marxist terms. But, equally, the production of artworks still largely operates on a "cottage industry" or "artisanal" model of production—even when some commercially successful artists literally operate their studios like factories, with many assistants/workers paid an hourly wage working on what are essentially "Fordist" manufacturing production lines—so, these activities could also be considered "economic base" (infrastructural) activities. To complicate matters further, even if we (deliberately anachronistically) consider the production of discrete artworks as the "product" of art activity, we can describe a circle of relations where the designation of "infrastructure" and "product," or "base" and "superstructure" are not easily delineated. In a deliberately simplified way, we could look at the production relations of the art world as being like this: artworks ("products"/"superstructure") are exhibited by galleries and museums or they are written about or published in books, magazines, or journals within the disciplines of art history, art criticism, and curating, and so the galleries, museums, and publications could be considered as an "infrastructure"/"base" for art activity (along with funding streams, commercial markets, logistics, technical support, etc.), because the "products" presented by the artists could not reach their full status as artworks without these support structures.

However, we could equally look at it precisely the other way around, where the artists in the studio are the workers of the infrastructure producing the "raw materials" of components for the galleries', museums', or publications' (etc.) activities to be made possible. Also, if we, more properly, consider art activity as a discursive network of intersecting and elliptical activities and relations, we can propose this circular model more fully in that the artworks can be both "product," to be exhibited or distributed in whatever ways are appropriate, and/or therefore "produced" as fully fledged discursive entities—as the products of discursive activity, i.e., as images, as signs, as references, as lexical, intellectual, historical, cognitive, or other immaterial phenomena/material—as well as the raw materials (infrastructure) for discursive activity such as curating, archiving, criticism, art history, seminars, conferences, teaching, etc., and, of course, more art making! Therefore, we cannot be confident, on the

2 Ibid., 234.

level or looking through the lens of "production," that any element of this circular chain of activity is definitively "infrastructural" or "superstructural," since at any point in the chain any element is both simultaneously. A different "lens" is required to explore further.

Of course, Althusser's essay is primarily about the reproduction of ideology as a mechanism (or means) that drives the reproduction of the means of production, and, more specifically, that drives the means of reproduction of labor power beyond merely the learning of skills, etc. As he explains:

> I shall say that the reproduction of labour-power requires not only a reproduction of its skills, but also, at the same time, a reproduction of its submission to the rules of the established order, i.e. a reproduction of submission to the ruling ideology for the workers, and a reproduction of the ability to manipulate the ruling ideology correctly for the agents of exploitation and repression, so that they, too, will provide for the domination of the ruling class "in words."[3]

Again, in terms of art, we must ask not only how the relations between the "products" and "infrastructure" of art are interconnected in what is essentially a complex recursive networked mechanism, and ask how the ellipses of the network can be intervened in, but we also have to recognize that—since art so obviously and clearly is not only a product of, but is also a prolific producer of ideology in general and ideological effects in particular—the "products" of art specifically, and the "infrastructure" of art more generally are both ideological phenomena (like everything else) as well as material phenomena and practices (also like everything else), and since ideology (as Althusser puts it) "represents the imaginary relationship of individuals to their real conditions of existence," we have to consider also this further level of complexity whereby these "means" of the means of the reproduction of production are representations.[4]

Furthermore, any thing or activity, whether it be conventionally categorized as infrastructure or in some other way (e.g., product), is in process (a process of becoming) because it represents a procedure or practice of producing ideological effects and thereby reproducing ideology in general. This makes any thing or activity always and already a mechanism that actively represents ideological representations (representations of the imaginary relationship of the real conditions of existence). Art in general, quite obviously, does this, and we are familiar with categorizing art (in general) and art production (specifically) as a practice or series of interconnected practices. To use the analogy of language (in general): language in general exists, is reproduced, and is developed in practice via its use. In aggregate, over time language performs, represents, and reproduces itself, and therefore metamorphoses, sometimes incrementally sometimes drastically, and develops its meaning by doing so. The assumed

3 Ibid., 236.
4 Ibid., 256.

components of a language, or language in general, analogous to an infrastructure (phonemes, morphemes, lexemes, syntax, grammar, graphemes, etc.), are meaningless outside of their usage, and so the products of language are indistinguishable from the infrastructure of language—i.e., language only inheres to the use or activity of language itself.

This has a very significant impact on how these representations are, or can be, interpreted because, as Althusser points out:

> if it is true that the representations of the real conditions of existence of the individuals occupying the posts of agents of production, exploitation, repression, ideologization and scientific practice does in the last analysis arise from the relations of production, and from relations deriving from the relations of production, we can say the following: all ideology represents in its necessarily imaginary distortion not the existing relations of production (and the other relations that derive from them), but above all the (imaginary) relations of individuals to the relations of production and the relations that derive from them. What is represented in ideology is therefore not the system of real relations which govern the existence of individuals, but the imaginary relation of those individuals to the real relations in which they live.[5]

And so, to determine the relations between what is conventionally considered "infrastructure" and what is conventionally considered as "superstructure" is indistinct. Althusser's entire thesis is to consider the problem of the relationship of a society's "base" (infrastructure) and "superstructure" from the point of view of reproduction, rather than, as Marx did, from the perspective of production, to explore just such a reciprocal action of the superstructure on the base. In classical interpretations of Marx's theory of base and superstructure it is the base that has the greater role in determining the superstructure's efficacy and functions, since it is the means of production and the relations of production that are primarily analyzed and schematized. However, in Althusser's investigation of the role of ideology in these relations, and as a constituent force between and within these means and relations, we see that the question of *what determines what* in the spatial metaphor of Marx's base and superstructure model is problematized, and shown to be a radically more complex set of symbiotic and reciprocal inter- and intra-relationships.

In a similar vein, Raymond Williams also explored these problems throughout the 1970s. The central issue that Williams engaged with was to fully unpack the Marxist proposition that in any socio-economic modeling the "base/infrastructure" of a social formation is *determining* and that the "superstructure" is *determined* by the "base."[6] To problematize the metaphor, Williams recasts the equation as the "proposition that social

5 Ibid., 257–58.

6 Raymond Williams, "Base and Superstructure in Marxist Cultural Theory," first published in *New Left Review*, No. I/82, November–December 1973, 3. Available at https://newleftreview.org/issues/i82/articles/raymond-williams-base-and-superstructure-in-marxist-cultural-theory (accessed September 27, 2020).

being determines consciousness."[7] He goes on to explore in detail the ramifications of Marx's choice and use of the concept of *determination*, and its continued use in Marxist theory and elsewhere. "Yet in the transition from Marx to Marxism, and in the development of mainstream Marxism itself, the proposition of the determining base and the determined superstructure has been commonly held to be the key to Marxist cultural analysis."[8]

He explains that the linguistic (and real) complexity of this "term of relationship"—to determine—is problematic in a number of ways, not least because of its association with idealist and theological heritages. However, he demonstrates that a key part of Marx's revolutionary thinking was to invert the conditions of this concept on secular grounds to propose that it is not "an abstract determining consciousness"—i.e., a God, or any other supernatural or transcendental entity or force—that exerts force upon the conditions of a society, but rather human beings' own activities.[9] If vestiges of this theological or idealist ground remain in any use of the term "to determine," then the troublesome ramifications of predicating or prefiguring of social relations in a totalizing way is invoked, which leads to the issue of implying that the infrastructural activity, systems, or other phenomena *totally* controls superstructural activity. Williams does agree that the notion of determination is a recognition that one phenomenon, activity, or system may set limits to and/or exert external pressure on another, but even the specificity of these boundaries or parameters, and the nature of these forces, and the extent to which they can be observed to directly cause effects on subsequent activity, is not so easy to prove definitively, either on the grounds of correlation or direct causation. To avoid such issues, Williams introduces the concepts of *homology* and *mediation* to help account for inevitable delays, ambiguities, collateral, or oblique relations, and periphrastic connections in the cause and effect suppositions that analyses may have in their observations about infrastructures and superstructures, because these concepts (*infrastructure* and *superstructure*) are metaphors, and hence are representational and abstract (albeit that they are no less "real" because of this, and effect no less "real" consequences upon one another):

> In the later twentieth century there is the notion of "homologous structures", where there may be no direct or easily apparent similarity, and certainly nothing like reflection or reproduction, between the superstructural process and the reality of the base, but in which there is an essential homology or correspondence of structures, which can be discovered by analysis. This is not the same notion as "mediation", but it is the same kind of amendment in that the relationship between the base and the superstructure is not supposed to be direct, nor simply operationally subject to lags and complications and indirectnesses, but that of its nature it is not direct reproduction.[10]

7 Ibid.
8 Ibid.
9 Ibid., 4.
10 Ibid., 5.

This corresponds to Althusser's thesis on ideology, which can be considered as an intransitive force that operates between and within elements of a social matrix, and helps us to see how difficult and complex making analyses of social relations (in general), and the relationships between infrastructure and superstructure (both specifically and in general) are.

Williams goes on to admit that in his work "the base" (infrastructure) is the more important concept in the dyad, in his endeavor to understand the realities of cultural process, but he immediately explains that it is crucial to halt the "verbal habit" of considering "the base" as "an object, or in less crude cases, ... [*considering "the base"*] in essentially uniform and usually static ways."[11] He explains that "'The base' is the real social existence of man. 'The base' is the real relations of production corresponding to a stage of the development of material productive forces. 'The base' is a mode of production at a particular stage of its development."[12]

But Williams qualifies this by reminding us that another of Marx's key propositions with respect to historical development and the contradictions in the relations of production and therefore in social relations is that there is always and already the "continual possibility of the dynamic variation of these forces," and concludes that "we have to say that when we talk of 'the base', we are talking of a process and not a state."[13]

In this we can say that what is infrastructural is therefore always and already a socio-economic practice that is always changing. And while we may claim that infrastructural practices are the "primary productive forces," we cannot *definitively* conclude that these will determine the results of characteristics of any other specific practice that we might call superstructural. As Williams explains:

> if we come to say that society is composed of a large number of social practices which form a concrete social whole, and if we give to each practice a certain specific recognition, adding only that they interact, relate and combine in very complicated ways, we are at one level much more obviously talking about reality, but we are at another level withdrawing from the claim that there is any process of determination.[14]

And he continues:

> For while it is true that any society is a complex whole of such practices, it is also true that any society has a specific organization, a specific structure, and that the principles of this organization and structure can be seen as directly related to certain social intentions, intentions by which we define the society, intentions which in all our experience have been the rule of a particular class.[15]

11 Ibid.
12 Ibid.
13 Ibid.
14 Ibid., 7.
15 Ibid.

This allows Williams to turn to the work of Antonio Gramsci and the concept of hegemony to better understand the role of cultural activities and practices within a society and their interrelationships, as well as their relations to and *as* productive forces. Invoking hegemony as an object of analysis allows for the contingencies of "real and constant change" to be accounted for. In doing so, Williams, following Gramsci, is also careful to point out that hegemony (like the identification of base or superstructure) is neither monolithic, unitary, nor totalizing, albeit that the effects of hegemonic forces may appear to be or may be perceived as totalizing—allowing for the possibility that such forces can be challenged and modified. Following Gramsci's concept of "incorporation," Williams explains that cultural activities, like all other social activities, clearly embody "the central, effective and dominant system of meanings and values, which are not merely abstract but which are organized and lived."[16] Here, hegemony is constituted of a wide body of practices that are reciprocally confirming and self-supporting of one another, rather than merely "opinions" or "manipulations," as Williams says, which form a complex systems of expectations and norms that underpin, direct and set boundaries and limits for behaviors, expressions, thoughts and beliefs that coalesce into typical norms, or "ordinary understanding[s] of the nature of man and of his world."[17] Williams adds the caveat, however, that "our hardest task theoretically, is to find a non-metaphysical and a non-subjectivist explanation of emergent cultural practice."[18]

Thus, he throws down the gauntlet for cultural analysis to try to remain squarely in the realm of historical materialist identification when dealing with analyses of cultural phenomena and activities and their intentions, beliefs, and expressions. For any activity engaged in the critique of infrastructure, or acting as infrastructure in a critical manner, the interrogation of and resolution of the intrinsic contradictions within these processes of "incorporation" must be a priority; in seeking out the moments and dynamics between practices, beliefs, thoughts, and expressions where self-affirmation and confirmation take place and congeal into the quanta of hegemonic forces. Williams is quick to point out that in terms of the arts this is a difficult and perilous task, since it is not guaranteed that "experimental" or atypical arts practices will not be assimilated, at one time or another, into the dominant hegemony, by way of practices that may at first seem to be in sympathy with the counter-hegemonic intentions of such activities.

For example, the very fact that, say, a militantly antihegemonic art critic, art historian, or curator may write about, promote, publicize, exhibit, or otherwise work with an art practice in general or an art activity that seemingly has specifically counter-hegemonic intentions, values, or meanings may inadvertently cause the counter-hegemonic art to be assimilated into the hegemony's cultural dynamics merely by the very act of identifying it and/or analyzing it within frameworks—linguistic conventions, historiographical systems, hermeneutic

16 Ibid., 9.
17 Ibid.
18 Ibid., 12.

protocols, exhibitionary forms, or museal imperatives, etc.—in which persistent or residual conventions or cultural norms may unwittingly, surreptitiously, or accidentally divert or displace the internal dynamics of the work to or within such hegemonic conventions. As Williams points out here:

> The arts of writing and the arts of creation and performance, over their whole range, [...] contribute to the effective dominant culture and are a central articulation of it. They embody residual meanings and values, not all of which are incorporated, though many are. They express also and significantly some emergent practices and meanings, yet some of these may eventually be incorporated, as they reach people and begin to move them. Thus it was very evident in the sixties, in some of the emergent arts of performance, that the dominant culture reached out to transform them or seek to transform them. [...] In this process, of course, the dominant culture itself changes, not in its central formation, but in many of its articulated features. But then in a modern society it must always change in this way, if it is to remain dominant, if it is still to be felt as in real ways central in all our many activities and interests.[19]

Williams's central thesis here is to show that for then emerging Cultural Marxism to have any purchase in a substantive way in its analyses of the arts and other cultural phenomena *vis-à-vis* the real conditions of production, and in relations of production and reproduction, it must consider the artwork itself as part of a wider practice of the artist, *and*, more crucially, as part of wider practices in the arts and culture more generally. Philosophically this remains useful and interesting as it inverts the then (and still) traditional or conventional methods of analysis, whereby the component parts of works of the arts and their interrelationships were (and often still are) considered as the primary material of analysis, to move to a systemic analysis of the artwork as not just part of a practice but as a practice in progress—practicing, as an active agent in the social field—which considers the artwork as not just containing fossil-like traces of the social field of forces, whether these be hegemonically incorporated or incorporating, or counter-hegemonic and dis-incorporating, but rather as a monad that has a homologous structural relation to the social whole. Where the artwork had been previously treated as a discrete part of the social whole, a specific phenomenon containing some of the elements of the overall generic social totality, Williams insists on considering the artwork as a system that intersects with other systems of society, none of which express or represent the social totality, but in aggregate make up the social whole. Therefore, the relationship between social whole, or totality, and individual elements is complicated, and understood to be more complex, dynamic, and malleable. We can argue that this introduces something very hopeful into

19 Ibid., 14.

the field of socio-cultural analysis and arts practice, because it allows for the reality and possibility that sometimes what seem to be small social forces (experimentation, innovation, radicality, etc.) in, say, the form of artworks, can have great effects, changing large swaths of society in many different ways. This realization can help us see that hegemony is not at all as mountainous (or monstrous), stable, solid, or inert as it may appear to be, and that seemingly small, brief, or perceived to be inconsequential counter-hegemonic interventions in society—such as those often attempted in the arts—can have effects far greater in scope, reach, volume, and complexity than might otherwise be expected from forms or activities that are considered tiny in relation to conventionally categorized infrastructure—like a virus, for example—a kind of David and Goliath model.

In saying this, however, one must not presume that we should idealize or valorize small size, brevity, precarity, or any other seeming impoverishment as a *de facto* "good" condition or characteristic of an artwork for it to have, and put into effect to generate counter-hegemonic consequences, nor the opposite. Like hegemony itself, there is no "correct" or singular form or shape or structure that an activity or complex of activities should take or make to either generate a hegemonic or counter-hegemonic force or position. If Gramsci's work tells us anything, it is that hegemony is amorphous, dynamic, multifaceted, widespread and deeply embedded, albeit that we don't always know how to recognize the width and depth of these conditions. In other words, hegemonic forces are unpredictable and elusive because of their sheer complexity and dynamism, which contributes to their prolific capacity for assimilation of counter-hegemonic actions. As Williams states clearly, these forces are non-metaphysical, non-subjectivist, and crucially therefore non-formalist—there is no formula for hegemony or its opposite.

With this in mind, we must ask the question as to whether one of the great problems of the work of artists such as Marcel Broodthaers, Michael Asher, Hans Haacke, Daniel Buren, Mierle Laderman Ukeles, Adrian Piper, Lucy Lippard, and others credited as producing works in the first wave of institutional critique during the late 1960s and 1970s, as well as artists such as Allan McCollum, Amalia Mesa-Bains, John Knight, Louise Lawler, Fred Wilson, Barbara Bloom, Renée Green, Andrea Fraser, and Carey Young, among many others producing works in the second wave during the late 1980s, 1990s, and 2000s,[20] was not only that it was all so easily and quickly incorporated into the hegemonic structures of wider culture, art history, art criticism, museum archivization, and the cultural lexicon more generally, but that it also inadvertently hypostatized its own institutional conditions by over-identifying itself, with the institutions of art specifically, and the "institution of art" more generally. This hypostatization occurs in these works because the works, as part of their functional address, do not attend enough to the rhetorical nature of the questions they ask—the presumed "lack of

20 All precursors to what are currently dubbed "infrastructural critique" art practices.

knowledge" that their works seek to remedy. Artist and theorist Amanda Beech outlines this issue in 2007, when she writes:

> Here we see a faith in the idea that art does "something", but further to this, the concept that knowing what art does will help us to make it (and I refer to both art and politics here) "better". In this way this question points us to assess the problem of art's political limitations and the limitations of our own knowledge of it. Now, we could say that asking "any" question assumes a lack of knowledge. But what becomes interesting about this question is its philosophical rather than political make-up. Here we are invited to acknowledge that this question is, first of all, rhetorical in nature; and, second, that paradoxically it assumes a freedom from this rhetorical condition.[21]

The irony that follows this paradox, which Beech identifies as a central terminal issue for institutional critique practices, is that any institutional form (such as an artwork) that seeks to question its own institutional character only further entrenches its position as such, because it not only presumes the freedom to do so (because it *can*, since it is already a valued part of a hegemonic system), but, as Beech shows us, this presumption further lifts (assumes) the already-institutional question-asking subject into its institutionally hegemonic position, re-entrenching and re-affirming this hegemonic position. If anything, this is therefore a clear description of the (albeit in some cases unwitting) hegemonic workings of institutional critique practices.

If infrastructural critique practices in art are to avoid the same pitfalls, then a radical anti-formalism that can account for the complexity of hegemony, and that does not valorize or over-identify with characteristics of impoverishment, instability, precarity, and so on, must be established and deployed as at least one of its tenets. Hopefully, the state of criticality in current art practices can learn to see that even critiques of institutional critique and championing of post-institutional-critique art, such as that of Gerald Raunig and Gene Ray, still contains the vestiges of such contradictory optimism. As we see in the following quote, Raunig and Ray are critiquing institutional critique works/practices by appealing to the idea that post-institutional-critique art must operate in ways that are unstable and of shorter duration, if they are to be instead "instituent," a concept they espouse, arguing that "institutional critique needs to be rethought as a critical attitude and as what I call an 'instituent practice.'"[22]

And:

> "instituent practices", [refers] to strategies and initiated processes that in some respects take their bearings from traditions of institutional critique, even as in other respects they go beyond anything recognizable in the movement now canonized as part of art history. [...] For

21 Amanda Beech, "Don't Fight It: The Embodiment of Critique," *Journal of Visual Arts Practice*, Vol. 6, No. 1, 2007, 61–71.

22 Gerald Raunig, "Instituent Practices: Fleeing, Instituting, Transforming," in *Art & Contemporary Critical Practice*, edited by Gerald Raunig and Gene Ray (London: MayFly Books, 2009), 4.

> if the concept of "institution" implies a desire for long-term duration, continuity and security, the concept of "project" by contrast implies limited duration and the negative effects, such as precarization and insecurity, associated with it.[23]

They go on to explain that

> [w]hen we speak of an "instituent practice", this actualization of the future in a present becoming is not the opposite of institution in the way that utopia, for instance, is the opposite of bad reality. [...] Rather, "instituent practice" as a process and concatenation of instituent events means an absolute concept exceeding mere opposition to institutions: it does not oppose the institution, but it does flee from institutionalization and structuralization.[24]

While we can have some sympathy for this position of trying to "square the circle"—of not precisely opposing institutions but at the same time "fleeing" from institutionalization and structuralization to try to exceed the mere opposition to institutions—in effect this sounds worryingly similar to the radically neoconservative capitalist position of neoliberal governmentality, which we can be sure these authors oppose in their counter-hegemonic and emancipatory ambitions.

It should be noted here that one of the many deleterious elements of neoliberal governmentality has been to de-institutionalize labor, while returning the conditions of the relations of production and the relations of the labor force to states not seen for 150 years. We have seen in the past forty to fifty years the dismantling of structured institutionalized work across almost all sectors of industry globally, with a rapid and widespread rise in precarious "freelance" work, often promoted under the insidious guise of "self-employment," or worse, "self-entrepreneurship" in post-Fordist labor models and post-Taylorist management structures. From the delivery drivers of logistics companies, or "ride-share" drivers of Uber, Lyft, GrubHub, Postmates, etc., to the zero-hour "self-employed" health and social care workers in many countries around the world, we see workers working for huge (and hugely profitable) companies or government agencies without the benefits of pension contributions, social security contributions, and in many cases with "terminate at will" contracts that treat the "employee" not as an employee, but as a sub-contractor or franchised agent, leading to lack of union protections because each worker is radically isolated legally from the company and from others. This also explicitly pits each worker against the other in a vicious and unremitting competition for tasks, duties, sub-contracts, etc.—"star ratings" and immediate customer/client feedback via "Apps" show us this glaringly as the new reality of work in a world of euphemistically heralded "Flexible Specialization."

23 Gerald Raunig and Gene Ray, "Preface," in *Art & Contemporary Critical Practice*, xv–xvi.

24 Ibid., xvii.

Equally, post-Fordist labor under the signs of neoliberal governamentality and late-stage capitalism has eradicated the boundaries of work and leisure, production and consumption, and other dyadic concepts that have framed human activity in the past, largely thanks to networked digital electronic communications technologies (but not only because of these) that allow for us to be "working" (producing data) while watching Netflix, or by earning (pitifully small amounts of monetary credit in the form of loyalty rewards) while we shop. These imbrications of traditional spheres of social activity further complicate the task of identifying "infrastructures."

The insistence by Raunig and Ray of this neo-anarchistic position risks the descent of its ambitions too much into a quagmire of further atomized social relations and relations of production. Again, since hegemony and ideology are non-formulaic, we cannot say that anti-institutionalization or fleeing from institutionalization and structuralization are the solution to the problems wrought by current hegemonic institutions. If capitalism is the socio-economic system we have to work within (for now), and neoliberal governamentality is the pseudo-political ideology that we must resist and dismantle, we may do better to consider building different rival institutions that propagate and deliver equity in terms of the distribution of material and immaterial resources and power. In this we can partially agree with Nina Möntmann, when she writes:

> what is therefore required is the establishment of transgressive institutions that question and break with the current developments of privatization and simultaneously orient themselves towards other disciplines and areas besides the corporative business of globalized capitalism.[25]

But, we don't have to agree with her when she states: "what institutions in Western countries need to do is precisely to reduce the number of structures and standards, and disengage spaces from too many codes and contexts."[26]

It is a myth and a fantasy to imagine that counter-hegemonic practices and the development of a different rival ideology are only achieved in the dissolution of structures, standards, codes, and contexts. Hegemony/counter-hegemony and ideology are like the constant amount of total energy in the universe: it cannot be diminished or reduced, only combined and re-combined in different configurations to produce different effects and phenomena. Hegemony in general can be considered as the total measure of majority-consolidated power, force, or influence in a given society, however it is distributed. There will necessarily be some instances of counter-hegemonic power too in said society, but these are not yet dominant because they are not yet majority-consolidated. It is important to note that the majority-consolidated hegemonic forces may be accreted and concentrated in some areas more than others in different amounts and

25 Nina Möntmann, "The Rise and Fall of New Institutionalism: Perspectives on a Possible Future," in *Art & Contemporary Critical Practice*, 157.

26 Ibid., 158.

varying levels of intensity (or density—density of incorporation, or density of affirmation). It is an uneven and undulating field. Take, for example, the concatenation of the institutions of *the self* (legally constituted individual personhood), the institution of *the nuclear and extended family* (legally constituted, religious, or civil partnership and guardianship of children), and the institution of *property* (legally constituted rights of private ownership of resources). While they certainly incorporate and reaffirm each other's ideological and hegemonic force, they can also do so in combination as pairs, rather than necessarily all three.

For a not-yet-dominant hegemonic series of beliefs, thoughts, practices, and structures to become dominant, it must generate the required density and intensity of its tenets, incorporations, and affirmations at various strategically important points in the overall social field to effect a resonance that will reduce the amplitude and frequency of the dominant hegemonic forces, and simultaneously assimilate that energy to amplify its own power and force. For a counter-hegemony and a different ideology to prevail, there must either be as many, if not more, structures, standards, codes, and contexts, institutions, and practices that carry, embody, perform, propagate, reproduce, affirming and reaffirming the central tenets in evermore powerful moments of Gramscian "incorporation," or the extant institutions must be modified in some way, possibly even greatly enlarged.

To develop the example above, if we were to radically expand the definition, scope, and legal boundaries of, say, the institution of *the family* to incorporate all humans, there would immediately be repercussions to the other two institutions, and the need for the institution of *property* would be eradicated. *The family* as an institution is merely a feudal aristocratic device to ensure the succession of power and the retaining of resources via hereditary inheritance. Since property, in Marxist terms, is the confiscation of resources from others, if all others are incorporated into one global human-population-sized *family*, there is no need to retain the imagined need to confiscate from others the resources of the family, since there would be no others outside of the family. A similar effect would occur with the institution of *the self*. Since selfhood is also a legally constituted device to identify the very person, their body, and their identity, with their legally constituted rights (such as their right to retain *their* property confiscated from others), if there is no need to retain property and confiscate it from others since all others are already in the family, then the self is less important as an institution and bulwark against the infringement of property rights, and could be liberated to other more interesting and gratifying functions.

Where and when, and even how, this is to be achieved is specific to the context—i.e., the specific configuration of the matrix of forces, and its points of inflection and coalescence—to be intervened within. Again, there is no formula as such. What is certain is that even if one were to insist that so-called infrastructures were the places to start this counter-hegemonic infiltration and assimilation process, it cannot be guaranteed that the to-be-overthrown hegemonic forces are at the requisite density and intensity in those infrastructures to ensure a successful and widespread "concatenation" of the overthrowing counter-hegemonic forces. For example, there may be as much hegemonic ideological intensity and density incorporated in a Hello Kitty mobile phone cover as there is in an entire government office, in a society's arts funding system, in a nation's electrical grid, or in a train network—in their practices, policies, material, and immaterial resources, etc. The scale of material and immaterial resources embodied in one or another form, action, system, or network does not correlate to the potential for incorporated hegemonic ideological intensity and density, neither does it predict causation for the reproductive potential of ideology within and through it, nor the reaffirmation of the hegemony therein. While this realization may present a dizzying complexity for strategizing counter-hegemonic activity, it should give hope to anyone working in the arts, since it allows for the very real possibility for artworks of whatever kind at whatever scale to possibly have very real ideological effects that could be counter-hegemonic. It certainly isn't easy, but it is possible. Trying to calculate or predict where and when and how is the task.

Marina Vishmidt has come closest to some descriptions of infrastructure in her theorizations of art practices that are considered as "infrastructural critique" that avoid many of the issues that are described above. Vishmidt is here able to concisely characterize infrastructure as a productive site for critique—and possibly counter-hegemonic potential—by essentially drawing on the idea that infrastructure inhabits an interstitial function as well as a thoroughly material connective tissue in all manner of situations and societal functions:

> it is infrastructure's transitive character—between the material and the possible, between machines and working drawings, between cognitive maps and what is pictured on them—that enables it to ask political questions that can no longer be replied to in the abstract, with the false totalizations of rejection or complicity.[27]

This allows her to theorize a strong position on art practices that come after institutional critique, which develops both a prescient analysis and critique of the problems inherent to those practices of either the first or second waves of institutional critique, and also further concretizes her conceptualization of infrastructure:

> At minimum, the shift from institutional critique to infrastructural critique as I'm defining it is the move from the institution as a site for "false totalizations" to an engagement with the thoroughly intertwined objective (historical, socio-economic) and subjective (including

27 Marina Vishmidt, "Between Not Everything and Not Nothing: Cuts Toward Infrastructural Critique," in *Former West: Art & The Contemporary After 1989*, edited by Maria Hlavajova and Simon Sheikh (Cambridge, MA: MIT Press, 2017), 268.

> affect and artistic subjectivization) conditions necessary for the institution and its critique to exist, reproduce themselves, and posit themselves as an immanent horizon as well as transcendental condition.[28]

We can agree wholeheartedly with the idea of being skeptical of the "false totalizations" of naïve beliefs in "transgression," or the equally naïve blind faith in or furious condemnation of institutions, specifically or in general, as firmly identifiable stable monolithic loci of power. We should remember here that capitalism and the so-called innovations of progress fueled by it are often referred to as and lauded for their transgressions or conventions, rules, and habits—e.g., "entrepreneurialism." Similarly, and more specifically, neoliberal economico-politics is driven by an ethos that seeks to transgress all manner of borders and boundaries—national borders, legal boundaries, epistemological boundaries, ideological boundaries, etc. However, even Vishmidt is susceptible to the formalism, seen above in the writing of Raunig, Ray, and Möntmann, in her celebration of characteristics, strategies, forms, and methods in artistic practices that she holds under the banner of infrastructural critique:

> But their key significance was in laying a track between the critique of institutions and the critique of infrastructures; that is, not simply the formal but the material conditions that located the institution in an expanded field (of structural violence). The extra-murality of this tendency was taken up in later iterations as a call to build, or at least model, institutions, whether in the temporary sociality of the project, the erratic durability of the project space, or the ambient resource economies of the research cluster. The question of what would thereby constitute the "formal" and the "material" could perhaps be displaced to consider rather the matter of whether these institution-critical practices situated themselves principally in an immanent or a transversal relation to the spaces of artistic exhibition and discourse.[29]

Again, we can agree that the exploration of the transversal relation of the agents of the critique to the spaces of exhibition and discourse and the transversal relations between that which is exhibited and the discourses that inform, surround, and flow through and out of such things as exhibitions or artistic projects of any kind is a fertile approach to assess the political potential of such activities and the activities of such participants, but there is no need to valorize any specific or particular characteristics of these activities, such as their extramurality, their temporariness, their erratic behavior, and so on. Now, these may be appropriate characteristics for a specific activity that seeks to effectively critique a specific institution or perceived infrastructure, but they are not characteristics that are suitable as a

28 Ibid., 267.

29 Marina Vishmidt, "Beneath the Atelier, the Desert: Critique, Institutional and Infrastructural," in *Marion von Osten: Once We Were Artists*, edited by Maria Hlavajova and Tom Holert, A BAK Critical Reader in Artists' Practices (Utrecht: BAK, 2017), 220–21.

general rule. The characteristics of social phenomena, activities, and relations are not necessarily in direct correlation with, and do not necessarily effect direct causation of the reproduction and reaffirmation of the hegemony that they incorporate and ideology that drives them, as we have learned from the work of Althusser and Williams above. These characteristics would be a terrible parody if they were deployed to critique today's neoliberal institutions of higher education, which now also valorize inter-, trans-, or multidisciplinarity (i.e., extramurality) in pedagogy and research, where all faculty (whether full-time, part-time, or temporary) are also expected to do lots of extracurricular activities, and where temporary high-profile interdisciplinary research projects are prized more highly than long-term (often lifelong) singular research practices. We might say something similar about museums, where the economics and ethos of neoliberalism therein sees much the same.

If infrastructural critique as a critical art practice identifies that which is infrastructural as that which we know, but habitually take for granted and temporarily forget about, perhaps we can agree more fully. Vishmidt is often quoted as having written:

> Time is an infrastructure because it is a condition of possibility for conscious perception and action; infrastructure is made out of time insofar as infrastructure is that which repeats. The repetition is normalized into everyday routine, and when it stops functioning, an aperture is cut into its artifice—through which history and power relations can be seen.[30]

If these sorts of practices highlight and intervene in contradictions within such social phenomena, activities, and relations, it is more possible to see how they may contribute to a counter-hegemonic project. Vishmidt cites architectural theorist Reinhold Martin's view of infrastructure, which evocatively explains this:

> Martin illuminatingly discusses infrastructure as a regime of intelligibility in terms that echo Michel Foucault's "epistemes", but with a more concrete mediation of the social with the technological: "*The dumbwaiter, bound to slave labor, carries bottle after bottle up to Jefferson's dining room. Its systemic properties tend to become visible only when the repetitions cease. If the wine ceases to appear, at some level and only for an instant, the entire apparatus of slavery comes into view. When you turn on the faucet and water does not flow, the entire water system leaps into the cognitive field.*"[31]

In the article from which this quotation is taken, about the trans-Atlantic reception of the work of media theorist Friedrich Kittler, Martin goes on to explain that his own work in "media-politics" is invested in the analysis of differentials that produce boundaries, limit conditions, or thresholds, such as inside/

30 Vishmidt, "Between Not Everything and Not Nothing," 265.

31 Ibid., 266. For the Martin quote, see Isabelle Graw, Reinhold Martin, and André Rottmann, "Do Media Determine Our Situation? Reflections on the Transatlantic Reception of Friedrich Kittler," *Texte Zur Kunst*, No. 98, June 2015, 46–79.

outside, or utility/waste, but he insists on not recognizing these as totalizing states or conditions, rather as transitions. His task is to explore those movements, passages, transformations, and transmutations to better understand the dynamics and causes of "the distribution of infrastructural repetitions," to therefore better understand how infrastructure produces, reproduces, and maintains such determinations.[32] He says that

> [t]his thinking on infrastructural topologies [...] derives from my work on corporate architecture, which linked the discoveries of cybernetics to a topological, figure/ground "pattern seeing" in architecture and the visual arts. But it also modifies that work, by emphasizing the logistical, procedural repetitions within which difference arises.[33]

What we see here is a method of analysis that is able to simultaneously consider infrastructure as a field of differential intensities and densities, of unequal and ever-changing distributions of power, while also being able to temporarily (at least) identify moments in that field of flux at which certain patterns or commonalities across the various movements of the field may indicate points of opportunity where, as he says, difference may arise, or where the forces at play could be diverted, displaced, or repurposed. He does caution, of course, that such analysis must not be naïve in imagining itself to be somehow outside of the sway of such forces:

> In this work, as in my work on other infrastructural systems like corporations, universities, or, at another level, cities (i.e. mediators), I aim to show power-knowledge as a dimension of capital rather than as an analytical alternative to it, reorganizing thought as well as action. The globalizing, neoliberal city, for example, is a component in a cognitive infrastructure as well as a material complex.[34]

However, what we can intuit from Martin's words here is that his project is to find ways of not only analyzing or otherwise representing these patterns of determination, but actively engaging in ways to effect changes to the direction of these patterns—as he explicitly details:

> I define the modern research university, which dates back to what Kittler called the "discourse network of 1800", as a media system rather than as an institution. In general, I am concerned more with intermedial relations internal to it, rather than with studying individual media and their effects in isolation. For example, in pedagogy as in knowledge-making, relations between speaking and listening and between reading and writing change over time. My aim is to describe the

32 Ibid.
33 Ibid.
34 Ibid.

> university as an incomplete system of linkages, translations, offsets, and delays through which such changes occur. Put slightly differently, this amounts to doing history with architecture, understood as one among many media into which, paradoxically, other media are enfolded, rather than writing a history of architecture. It also entails breaking architecture down into unresolved fragments, bits and pieces of hardware that assemble in different ways and produce knowledge differently.[35]

We can now see that the question at stake here, in terms of methodology, for infrastructural critique, indeed for any form of critique or critique with any particular target, is the question of identifying parts and wholes, specifics or generics, or particular phenomena and general conditions. If infrastructure is that which mediates the passage from one nominally identified state or identity to another—i.e., it is a transmedial mechanism—then a *catatactical*[36] approach to the categorizing of parts and wholes, etc. needs to be deployed, wherein the presumed whole/generic/general field/characteristic/condition is collapsed into the specific particulate object/identity, such that the effects of determination, incorporation, and mediation that create the illusions and allusions (to borrow from Althusser) of ideology so that the shape and movements and patterns of hegemony can be recognized and hopefully subsequently redeployed against themselves. If infrastructural critique can and should show us anything and intervene anywhere, it is in the relationship between power that we can see (hegemony—the materially incorporated relations of power) and power that we can't see (ideology—the imagined representations of relations of power).[37] What we want to see is artists taking the interrelationship of representations and materiality seriously again, and understanding that the "fictionality" of artworks is key to understanding their role as infrastructurally critical, and that what norms we may take for granted as infrastructurally critical—in art, or indeed in any other aspect of culture and society more generally—are in fact predicated upon fictions.

35 Ibid.

36 I borrow this from former stock trader and economist John Brodie Donald, *Catataxis* (London: Quartet Books/Namara Group, 2011). At different scales, the characteristics of phenomena or solutions to problems are radically different and seemingly contradictory. For example, if an individual household sees a drop in income (wages or salary) it should reduce spending, but if a nation-state sees a drop in income (tax revenue) it should spend more (e.g., invest more in public services or public works projects), because the timescale of the resolution of the problem for the household is typically much shorter than for the nation-state. A "catatactical analysis" considers phenomena at different scales or scope to explore the differentials that exist at different levels of manifestation to more completely understand the dynamics of such phenomena. By doing so, this form of analysis drills down ("cata-") through the hierarchies of the levels ("taxis") to investigate what connects and moves between the different strata.

37 I thank Amanda Beech for this concise insight, which emerged in a conversation in January 2021.

VAPID VIRTUES, REAL STAKES: DIAGNOSIS FOR LEFT ART PROTOCOLS

Ghalya Saadawi

While the building of infrastructure may be justified by a need to move people or supplies, their main purpose is often to provide vehicles for another kind of movement: the flow of finance.

—Timothy Mitchell[1]

Capitalism hardly has a problem with anti-capitalism, including the soft proposition politics of commoning without communism.

—Angela Dimitrakaki[2]

Contemporary Art Diagnostics

The question of what to do with art and what art should do and how, has been persistent in modernity. Critical theory, from within its critique of the culture industry, of fascism, and of bourgeois forms generally, has been pushing for these questions to be answered beyond the aesthetization of politics.[3] One of the features of contemporary art in its post-historical condition, is that it spends significant amounts of time negotiating its role in a world that apparently isn't what it should be, but rarely if ever daring to articulate what it ought to be, due to its hang-ups with history and modernity that many have highlighted before us. In other words, this may be the result of a hangover from modernism's battle with capitalism and its collapse into its forms, as well as the targeting of socialist political projects that some art had indeed been intent on upholding. Modern art evolved, after all, with capitalism *and* communism, and with the antinomy that it is both a commodity and unlike one, autonomous and heteronomous, as it considered its role in the world both intra- and extra-artistically. Contemporary art grew out of post-structuralism, vertiginous market exchange, the explicit destruction of actually existing socialism by capitalism and Western imperialism, austerity and debt under financialization and algorithmic governance and their ensuing speculative temporalities. We are reminded over and over how this makes the actualization of a new communist political-

1 Timothy Mitchell uses the building of actual infrastructure to explain the ways in which financial speculation relied on and prolongs time via infrastructure. See "Infrastructures Work on Time," *e-flux journal*, "New Silk Roads," January 28, 2020, available at https://www.e-flux.com/architecture/new-silk-roads/312596/infrastructures-work-on-time/ (accessed 17 July 2021).

2 Angela Dimitrakaki. "Left with TINA: Art, Alienation, Anti-Communism," *Praktyka Teoretyczna*, Vol. 31, No. 1, 2019, 25–48.

3 Walter Benjamin, *The Work of Art in the Age of Its Technological Reproducibility, and Other Writings on Media*, edited by Michael W. Jennings, Brigid Doherty, and Thomas Y. Levin (Cambridge, MA: Belknap Press of Harvard University Press, 2008).

economic horizon difficult, even if still crucial. It has, however, resurrected the project that to transform the total dominance of this form of capital, one could attempt to redirect its pathways for different, contrary ends.[4]

In light of breeds of this capitalist realism the question of the connection between Left politics, and how (if?) art can construct mechanisms of futurity has been raised.[5] Since the answers offered are not within the bounds of political action grounded in accurate economic and historical diagnoses, or even committed affiliations, and since contemporary art presents a merely symbolic, always already negational condition—in a world of social finance that also invests in the "greater good"—what can be done about the economic underpinnings and parameters of its own condition? And what can its systems and forms do for political horizons of action and organizing *tout court*? Art's imbrication and constitution by capital—whether a breed of capital economy dominated by the commodity form, or by a financialized one grounded in instruments of debt, speculation, and risk—has produced specific contemporary definitions for modes of dissent. As we will see, a portion of these are grounded in critical claims, reforms, rights, and representation, either as modes of confrontation, or as artwork—isn't this what contemporary art *is* when it claims it is not capital? In fact, these follow from the fact that contemporary art construes itself as *de facto* negational and critical, and part of this essay focuses on the disjuncture between the claims of contemporary art and a totalizing political-economic reality. And yet, a different diagnostic, informed by insights into the temporality of financialization, new megastructures of power, and even capital's established work of abstraction, has also produced a call for transformation broadly propelled by Left imperatives for "cognitive mapping," to realize (or image) the unfathomability of the situation we are in, and produce a more accurate image of contemporary capital, usurping and designing around principles of investee activism, repurposing, and leverage.[6] I touch on the tension between the two sketched schemas below in order to think about protocols for this broadly named dissent of, by, and beyond contemporary art.

After the so-called philosophical turn, contemporary art, despite and *in view* of its globalization, became a series of self-assigned turns that can be used to diagnose contemporary art's answers to its own quandaries, and a response to its distance from modernist legacies and political aspirations alike.[7] Within the Euro-American conceptual paradigm, institutional

4 See for instance, Michel Feher, *Rated Agency: Investee Politics in a Speculative Age*, translated by Gregory Elliott (New York: Zone Books, 2018). Preceding newer critiques, like Feher's and his prompt to instrumentalize our alleged becoming an investee subject, within critical theory as well as other socialist and anarchist traditions there is the position that political practice in the present can and should reallze the desired future—whether via anarchist or autonomous directions, or via instrumentalizing or leveraging routes.

5 Yates Mckee, *Strike Art: Contemporary Art and the Post Occupy Condition* (London: Verso, 2016); Nick Scrincek, "Computational infrastructures and aesthetics," in *Realism Materialism Art*, edited by Christoph Cox, Jenny Jaskey, and Suhail Malik (Berlin: Sternberg Press, 2015).

6 *Realism Materialism Art*; see also Gean Moreno (ed.) *In the Mind but Not from There: Contemporary Art and Real Abstraction* (London: Verso, 2019).

7 Dimitrakaki, "Left with TINA." She reminds us that Generation X was born into the doctrine of TINA, an opposition to communism and a vacuous agnostic "anti" that constitutes its "politics" and translates this in art. As this point relates to capital's (a historical period) cultural production, among other things, Fredric Jameson covers this in his work on postmodernism, and more recently in "The Aesthetics of Singularity," *New Left Review*, No. 92, March 2015, 101–32.

critique and dematerialized practices enabled the self-reflexive social turn, archival turn, educational turn, digital/post-internet turn. Save for some exceptions and changes in lineage, these could be said to have replaced twentieth-century art periodization that positioned art in relation, or in opposition to capitalism. Broadly, this image of art *as* turns, determined as it was by economic and historical changes to cultural politics and funding, is unable to maintain a political impetus and falls into the post-historical and indeterminate logic of contemporary art.

The proposition that the category contemporary art operates as a logic within a broader political economic base, diagnoses the inheritance of conceptualism as one of contemporary art's considerable problems.[8] Why? It consolidated an indeterminacy grounded in the phenomenology of art that idealizes viewer experience as interminable, as open meaning-making, questions without answers, and "anti-s" without propositions.[9] It may have momentarily freed the artist from the mega-structures of art,[10] foregrounded spectator agency, the means of production and the artist as worker, say, but it transpired into an apt form for the post-historical, the consequences of which on art itself and its claims should not be underestimated.[11] When considering contemporary art's indeterminacy as a meta-genre rooted in conceptualism, this is what Suhail Malik is referring to.[12] This has repercussions for concurrently thinking the political and critical claims of organizing dissent in a systemic art field, and its misconstrued disjuncture from (and conjuncture with) capital and its operations.

We understand contemporary art as a transnational field, an operating logic, a workplace.[13] It has an economic base in deindustrialization and neoliberalism, and an accompanying cultural logic in its forms and claims. It has emulative, (ago-

8 See Suhail Malik, "A History of Negations," Problematizing the Contemporary series, curated by Sohrab Mohebbi for Art and Education. See https://www.artandeducation.net/classroom/video/66327/suhail-malik-a-history-of-negations (accessed March 1, 2021).

9 Suhail Malik, "Reason to Destroy Contemporary Art," in *Realism Materialism Art*, 185–91. See also Victoria Ivanova, "Art's Values: A Détente, A Grand Plié," PARSE *Journal*, No. 2, November, 2015, available at http://parsejournal.com/article/arts-values-a-detente-a-grand-plie/ (accessed March 21, 2021).

10 Not only via the history of the anti-aesthetic and autonomy from tutelage, but also via dematerialized practice. See Lucy Lippard, *Six Years: The Dematerialization of the Art Object from 1966–1972* (Berkeley: University of California Press, 2001 [1973]); and Hal Foster, *The Anti-Aesthetic: Essays on Postmodern Culture* (Seattle: Bay Press, 1983).

11 Arthur Danto, *After the End of Art: Contemporary Art and the Pale of History* (Princeton: Princeton University Press, 1997). Danto argues that contemporary art coincides with the Hegelian historical spirit coming to fruition as the post-historical. The discourse of the end of history and the problems of the cultural logic of postmodernism we know well, and we understand the praise of the post-historical as that. As contemporary art, it becomes artists using the past as a repository of materials as they see fit, whereby art is no longer indebted to the forms or historical struggles of the so-called past.

12 See Malik, "A History of Negations," and the other series for more on indeterminacy, "Exit not Escape: On the Necessity of Art's Exit from Contemporary Art," and "The Problem with Contemporary Art is not the Contemporary." Differently to Malik's definitions, Marina Vishmidt wonders how indeterminacy is a form of risk management for art that can anchor the speculative in art and be "put to work." Moreover, she wants to answer how the autonomy of the aesthetic becomes measured against the "artist as a professional of indeterminacy," rather than the "alienated aesthetic subject." See Marina Vishmidt, *Speculation as a Mode of Production: Forms of Value Subjectivity in Art and in Capital* (Leiden: Brill, 2018).

13 Leslie Sklair refers to a transnational capitalist class, a class that moves and transports across the lines of new economic routes and metropolitan centers. One could surmise that the value of transnationalism—like the one of "free trade"—also underpins injunctions to lack of regulation and flexibility of work, etc. See Leslie Sklair, *Globalization: Capitalism and its Alternatives* (Oxford: Oxford University Press, 2002); and "Democracy and the Transnational Capitalist Class," ANNALS, AAPSS, No. 581, May 2002, 144–57.

nistically) political and moral values that insist on criticality, flexibility, informality, plurality, even radicality, and the virtues of its unresolved autonomy.[14] It pushes at the outer edges of disciplines it is imbricated in, and claims it is beyond professionalism, academia, economic and class definitions (except where suitable) such that all these are part of the critical claims that construct the field as such. Against universalizing horizons, you find contrarian disgruntlement "at attempts to pin down the operational logic at play. If anything, the abstractions of an ontological approach are dismissed all the more militantly, as moral failures in and of themselves. The irony being that the intuitive identification of art as a subversive force, a vector of critical virtue, is the art-world code of conduct par excellence."[15]

This essay adheres primarily to diagnostics of contemporary art at the level of its operation, meaning as constituted by various axioms that govern it as an entire field of institutions, actors, discourses, values, claims, forms, as well as artworks and artists, in line with Malik's work and moving beyond to include kin Marxist and post-Marxist art criticism.[16] Contemporary art's critical claims and their separation from art's operations is a key virtue that secure its position within capital-driven work and value—and that is deployed across art and capital's expansions—which contemporary art positions itself as subverting precisely with said claims.[17] Art's indeterminacy—its condition of open-ended meaning-making, for instance—is the condition of possibility of its aspired-to critique. When the claims are read axiomatically, they become symptomatic, and when they are read discursively, they do very little if not invert what they promise. Especially "within contemporary art, [where] the forte of mediation-as-telos is a magical ability to appear subversive even when perfectly orthodox."[18] Contemporary art's claims to criticality, sometimes as organized action, are articulated around the value of this version of critique, or representation, or rights,[19] despite its insistence on experimentation, open-endedness, and informality of relations (as pitted against the alleged formality and verticality of academia, or business.)[20] These contradictions abound in the self-constitution of contemporary art so much so that they are no longer contradictions, but rather principle.[21]

When not in-between autonomy from alienated capitalist reality versus vanguardist art praxis as life, critical art theory

14 Here, we mean a plurality of views/antagonisms that cannot be resolved but can be said to coexist. This is agonistic democracy for Chantal Mouffe, for example.

15 Tirdad Zolghadr, *Traction: An Applied and Polemical Attempt to Locate Contemporary Art* (Berlin: Sternberg Press, 2017), 35.

16 This relies in large part on Malik and Ivanova, but also moves past the reformation of the institution, the artist, and the art object as the sole unit. Malik's notion of field—similar to and different from Bourdieu—is also employed and Ivanova refers to "regime" in an unpublished paper. See Victoria Ivanova, "Two Lives, One Order," available at https://barddraft.files.wordpress.com/2015/01/ivanova.pdf (accessed February 20, 2021).

17 If modernism did it by virtue of art itself, contemporary art has the added post-philosophical, post-conceptual that makes critical claims appear political *in general*. In a different vein, claim in finance and law and claim in art demonstrate this disjuncture further, where the two prior claims are backed, or contractual. The same goes for qualitative representational claims to "trust" as ethical value versus value as something that is accrued and calibrated *vis-à-vis* expectations concerning the future. See, for example, Gerald Nestler, Christian Kloekner, and Stefanie Mueller, "The derivative condition: an aesthetics of resolution, and the figure of the renegade: A conversation," *Finance and Society*, Vol. 4, No. 1, 2018, 126–43.

18 Zolghadr. *Traction*, 31; Malik, "Reason to Destroy Contemporary Art."

19 See Wendy Brown and Janet Halley, *Left Legalism Left Critique* (Durham: Duke University Press, 2002); and Marina Vishmidt, "Beneath the Atelier the Desert," in *Marion von Osten: Once we Were Artists*, A BAK Critical Reader in Artists' Practice (Utrecht: BAK, 2017).

20 Relevant here are Jo Freeman, "Tyranny of Structurelessness," available at https://www.jofreeman.com/joreen/tyranny.htm (accessed July 2021); and Mark Fisher, "Indirect Action: Some Misgivings about Horizontalism," in *Institutional Attitudes: Instituting Art in a Flat World*, edited by Pascal Gielen (Amsterdam: Valiz, 2013), 101–14. Thanks to Mia van den Bos for this last reference.

has historically also been concerned with the question of whether art(works) can be conceived and valued like other commodities, whereby "in capitalist society, the boundary of the category of 'art' itself is, to a large extent, drawn along this line: things that escape the law of value are, or potentially can be designated as, 'art', whereas things that obey capitalist rationalization are more unambiguously commodities."[22] The position that art does not work by those economic rules, cede art's autonomy from and opposition to capitalism because art has an exceptional character—it relates in a non-standard way. Where art strictly speaking does not fall under the law of production and value, it raises the question of what its ends in fact are, especially because with modernism's vanguards it veered further outward from its remit as art—only to come crashing back.[23] The line between commodity and non-commodity is one that art has tried to govern, because of the deduction that—modern and contemporary, in very different ways—art could escape and propose a critique of capitalism by virtue of its disobedience of and simultaneous kinship with productivist forces and their value forms. This may not consider the totality of commodification as all social relations mediated through the commodity.[24] Not to mention that the question does not really rest on the commodity form alone, denuded of abstract value and alienation, nor can it fully be addressed through the kind of labor that art does do—waged, affective, reproductive, or otherwise, as Marina Vishmidt and Anthony Iles have highlighted.[25] At various modern junctures, art claimed that the work that it did *was* in fact labor, and that artists *were* workers. That is, before the managerial and entrepreneurial havoc wreaked by later waves of neoliberalism that imposed another reckoning with whether artists were their own entrepreneurs or were still workers. We are reminded that the more art moves toward identifying with immaterial labor, overall estrangement from labor and social, political, educational practice, the more its necessary paradox of the required separation from the work of capitalism is evoked—what Vishmidt and Iles have called the "vanishing mediator." It moves closer to the world, and the more it does so, the more it collapses the distance that differentiates it from other disciplines and from the economy it moves into, which it is both "vanished" and constructed by. "Art becomes the agent of hollowing out of all which is incorporated into it—participation becomes instrumentalisa-

21 Or if one understands mechanisms of the valorization of capital not through art (as instrument) but in art's speculative mode. Vishmidt and Malik would disagree on the premise of their diagnosis of art's modes of valorization. See Marina Vishmidt, "Speculation in a Sense: Aesthetics and Real Abstraction," in Moreno, *In the Mind but Not From There*.

22 Daniel Spaulding and Nicole Demby, "Art, Value and the Freedom Fetish," *Mute*, May 2015, available at https://www.metamute.org/editorial/articles/art-value-and-freedom-fetish-o (accessed July 2021). They would argue that it is a luxury commodity, and that what you buy is monopoly rights and intellectual property rights.

23 There is ample discussion on this. Instructive here may be Martin Stewart, "The absolute artwork meets the absolute commodity," *Radical Philosophy*, No. 146, 2007; and Anthony Iles and Marina Vishmidt, "Make Whichever You Find Work," *Variant*, No. 41, spring 2011, 54–59.

24 Some key positions, such as Dave Beech's, outline the misdiagnoses of art's commodity nature, claiming it misses art's exemption and ends up unable to safeguard art from effectual marketization. Dave Beech, *Art and Value: Art's Economic Exceptionalism in Classical, Neoclassical and Marxist Economics.* (Leiden: Brill, 2015).

25 Vishmidt and Iles, "Make Whichever You Find Work," 54. This remains an open conundrum of art theory on the Left; they argue for the class relation, not the commodity as the unit of the capital to labor problem.

tion, representation becomes parody, autonomy becomes hard labour, politicisation becomes cynicism."[26] In contemporary art, the specter of autonomy, and even the avant-garde, could be said to return as the emptied signifier named "criticality" that is riddled with a key dilemma: a self-assigned autonomy within wider economic and work crises that ends up valorizing itself and capital.

Dave Beech has tried to argue that in equating art to the commodity form at the level of labor and value, we miss key prevalent forms of valorization in art, especially in its circulation—through dealers and markets as well as discourse, reputation, ethics, the effect of economic turns on entrepreneurship and credit, etc.[27] How does the labor analysis take into account contemporary financial instruments and the speculation and infrastructure they bring forth as these relate to the temporality and work of contemporary art? We are not alone in maintaining the relevance of these to a diagnosis of contemporary art. And we maintain that the dialectical relationship between art and capitalism in its various stages is not resolved by the appearance of total exteriority (e.g., art is not the market, not the institution, the artist is radically free, etc.) or total interiority claims (e.g., we are all the market, we are all the institution). Some critics have left the artist-art object as "art's pinnacle unit" behind and are proposing a thorough variation on the social turn.[28] Other systemic levels of diagnosing contemporary art's position and valuation within the capitalist economy have opened up: it is other forms of valorization—of capital and of contemporary art—that interest me in my diagnosis of the symptomatic problem of dissent in contemporary art.

Critical Virtue → Valorization

The question of critical virtue (one of art's forms of gaining value) includes the way art sees itself as free—not the institution, not the market, not power—all the while being about those things on the level of claims, while acknowledging being acted upon, or threatened by these bad objects, and only marginally constituted by them. Victoria Ivanova reminds us that "there exists a fundamental rupture in the notion of contemporary art's value between, on the one hand, the socio-cultural and political claims of artworks, and on the other hand, their economic and infrastructural realities."[29] She contends that a socio-cultural understanding of finance and the market actually begs for an analysis of finance's relationship to other areas, including contemporary art. In a slightly different direction, Vishmidt connects contemporary art to capitalist financialization through the proposition of speculation as a mode of production, not merely as a temporal and productive valorization instrument of finance. One of her moves is not to fall into the trap of reading art as a commodity/not commodity form, which then may posit art as either needing rescue, or as needing differentiation from capital, but rather switches the terms of the debate to claim

26 Ibid. Yet they cede that "art could potentially again become a 'progressive' critic of the mode of production and the barbarism of its social relations, tied as it is for its material and critical identity to those selfsame relations," (56).

27 Beech, *Art and Value*. Beech lays out art's exceptional character in relation to productive and unproductive labor. One could plot this relation to surplus value as we know this relates to forms of "collective productive power," especially when we think about living labor as it emerges here as "the surplus of sociality," but this is not the direction of this essay, although it could have repercussions for how we organize art, especially as capital finds ways to make productive this new form of collective power. See Jason Read, *The Micro-politics of Capital: Marx and the Prehistory of the Present* (Albany NY: SUNY Press, 2003), 92. Read would go on to write a Marxian theory of intersubjectivity and/as collective, *The Politics of Transindividuality* (Leiden: Brill, 2016).

28 Ivanova. "Art's Values"; see also Jasper Bernes, Jaleh Mansoor, and Daniel Spaulding, "Occupy Responses," *October*, No. 142, 2012, 48–50.

29 Ibid.

contiguity between modes of valorization—via risk, speculation, abstraction—in art as in finance. Emily Rosamond asks a pertinent speculative question about what happens, for better or for worse, if the financial instrument of the social impact bond (SIBs)—a fiscal and moral mechanism that invests in social change, growth, philanthropy—expands mandates and portfolios to include socially engaged art.[30] Malik (and Ivanova) proposes contemporary art's *values* as a critical virtue, claiming it acts as a motor in a primary market for another, secondary market; in other words, what contemporary art is as and does *for* the market. How can values (that become virtues) become valorizing mechanisms, especially if they foreclose real dissent? Contemporary art's critical virtue—the claim attached to what it does as political and critical—functions to bolster capital and begs the question what form of critique and transformative organizing are conceivable if contemporary art remains within nominally critical operations that block the very change it claims to be organized around.

In her book *The Morals of the Market* (2019), Jessica Whyte argues how a version of human rights became the explicit and implicit moral component of the neoliberal (and liberal) project.[31] Neoliberalism, she argues, furthers its doctrine of free markets—the imposed separation of (state) politics from the economy—through discourse and practices that want to emphasize rights and the pursuit of individual freedoms, and as such, the pursual of the liberal (and ethical) subject. Neoliberal market doctrine incorporated non-governmental humanitarian instruments to further "peace" as the soft arm of its economic zeitgeist and not, contrary to popular sentiment, to glue together what capitalist expansionist doctrine had fissured. For its part, market capitalism and its later financiering enter into and construct the internalized social codes of morality, relationships, power, and emotions.[32] The virtues of the market thus can be found everywhere, even where you least expect them. We have read differently in Robert Meister, Didier Fassin, Michel Agier, and others, about the political violence of the human rights counterrevolution that is administered through new humanitarian apparatuses, preemptive wars, renewed roles founded on trauma, an emphasis on ethics and memory as blocks to either democracy or dissent, and importantly, deferring justice.[33] One could argue that this has hailed a renewed liberal legalism.[34]

Another essay could be written on the links between the ethics of humanitarianism and the new structure of feeling it has instilled.[35] Yet, here I would only go as far as to suggest that it has helped the disparity between art's virtuous claims and

30 Rosamond writes about architecture collective Assemble and Open School East, both in the UK, to evaluate the possible (double) impact of SIBs on socially engaged art. See Emily Rosamond, "Shared stakes, distributed investment: Socially engaged art and the financialization of social impact," *Finance and Society*, Vol. 2, No. 2, 2016, 111–26.

31 Jessica Whyte, *The Morals of the Market: Human Rights and the Rise of Neoliberalism* (London: Verso, 2019).

32 See Martijn Konings, *The Emotional Logic of Capitalism: What the Progressives Have Missed* (Stanford: Stanford University Press, 2015).

33 See Didier Fassin, *Humanitarian Reason: A Moral History of the Present*, translated by Rachel Gomme (Berkeley: University of California Press, 2012); and Didier Fassin and Mariella Pandolfi (eds.) *Contemporary States of Emergency: The Politics of Military and Humanitarian Intervention* (New York: Zone, 2010); Michel Agier, "Humanity as an Identity and Its Political Effects: (a Note on Camps and Humanitarian Government)," *Humanity*, fall 2010.

34 Brown and Halley have written compellingly about critique contra legalism: an analysis of and an opposition to the various deadlocks of horizonless liberal rights-based legalism, versus the continuous necessity of Left critique. See Brown and Halley, *Left Legalism Left Critique*.

35 Raymond Williams's notion of "structure of feeling," first used in the *Preface to Film* (1954).

the real stakes of action via its ethics of past "evil," claiming beneficiaries, pointing at perpetrators, and representational rights. Ivanova, on her part, has argued that contemporary art functions as an apt new container for the liberal subject of human rights. Although the latter seems to function hand in hand with the market and not against it, it nonetheless appears to be waning in the public imaginary as transmitter of market values. With the humanitarian paradigm in decline, the liberal subject of the market finds a home in the righteously critical, but economically and ideologically lubricating function of contemporary art, informed by the overriding human rights discourse of the post-communist world as ethical imperative, if not an outright counterrevolutionary one.[36]

This is what Angela Dimitrikaki has attacked as the constitutive "anti" of contemporary art. Often that "anti" meets with the capitalist conflation of fascism with communism in an atmosphere of liberal pluralism, and the "vanishing" of the communist past and future in line with capitalism's inevitability. She is right in saying that

> the art field pacifies critique, in self-identifying as the most experimental, open-minded, self-critical context for pursuing political causes, where the most acute and animated exchanges are safely accommodated as pre-eminently discursive. Art is where the far ends of the spectrum of the politics of anti can sublimate their antitheses in a shared room as words separated from deeds.[37]

The appearance of separateness between words and deeds is not so convincing insofar as the words *are* deeds that locate contemporary art within, as Bassam El Baroni has shown, an agonistic space—contra another model for the democratic as antagonistic, or between enemies—which seems to chime well with the death knell of capitalist realism and its blighted temporality.[38] The emphasis on art particulars, on pluralism, on relational "politics" versus economic reality as systemic, has housed contemporary art's "criticality" in "glossocentrism."[39] A proliferous, and discursive predilection rather than praxis, which has turned only in appearance against what it itself is—liberal capitalism, the conflation of totalitarianisms, the institution, and so on.

It is evident to reiterate that neoliberal deregulation enabled and facilitated the empowerment of financial markets, institutions, and instruments, and also that the "liberal order was less about getting the state out of people's lives than about getting public officials to govern in the interest of the market."[40] Michel Feher elaborates this transition to debt economies, managerial governance, and investee politics in detail. The state's turn to debt and credit and its consequent managerialism *are* what financial logics have done to governance, and to the indebted subject who works by reputation and creditworthiness like all other organs of the restructuring. In contemporary art, this came to mean many things: from austerity (where

36 Robert Meister, *After Evil: A Politics of Human Rights* (New York: Columbia University Press, 2001); and Ivanova, "Two Regimes." This is what for Ivanova allows a contemporary art regime to replace the function of human rights regime for the neoliberal subject.

37 Dimitrakaki, "Left with TINA," 34.

38 Bassam El Baroni, "The Post-Agonistic Institution: Four Positions on the Structural Relation between Art and Democracy," in *How Institutions Think: Between Contemporary Art and Curatorial Discourse*, edited by Paul O'Neill, Lucy Steeds, and Mick Wilson (Cambridge, MA: MIT Press, 2017), 230–35; see also Mark Fisher, *Capitalist Realism: There is No Alternative* (London: Zero Books, 2015); and Sami Khatib, "No Future: The Space of Capital and the Time of Dying," in *Former West: Art and the Contemporary after 1989*, edited by Maria Hlavajova and Simon Sheikh (Cambridge, MA: MIT Press, 2018).

39 Taken from Zolghadr, *Traction*.

40 Feher, *Rated Agency*, 14

41 We know this as gentrification, with its ensuing evictions and price hikes, spearheaded as it additionally is by art institutions and artists themselves, and other dire consequences which are well-documented.

public money is involved), an exponential rise in biennials for much needed funds and profile, private investors storing and moving capital via art, public institutions looking for private sources who are looking to diversify, gentrification processes aided by art's imbrication in private and state investment branding cities as open art spaces of urban growth,[41] to the self-entrepreneurship of the artist. For contemporary art, this means finding a home again and again in the new order. Stefano Harney, for example, has suggested that in view of the financial and legal standardizing and restructuring of European public and semi-public art institutions, curators and directors now act as managers, and the plethora of guests, such as artists and academics, act to diversify risks (which extends to portfolio diversification for new investors, etc.). Thus, risk, diversity, pluralism, and representation are now in some ways functions of indeterminacy.[42] Can this arrangement be repurposed away from diversity, pluralism, and open-endedness, as functions, in view of art's credit-critical worthiness? Could art as a whole serve another political endgame, and not merely on the level of programming, or cognitive labor?

Not only alienated from Left politics, the argument has been made that contemporary art itself is a valorization mechanism for enterprise capital, mirroring and helping to extend both market and finance in a number of ways. For Gerald Nestler, finance has through its triadic work—speculation, arbitrage, and hedging, or security, austerity, and asset management—decoupled from civic and political rights, reducing participation and decision-making in politics because this "derivative condition" (financial logic as everyone's state of mind as it were) as a form, has become the basis for the social relation. These so-called triads as policy and processes emerge out of the limits of claim-based action in the era of labor to capital transformation and blocked justice, and for Nestler they themselves can be used to repurpose existing systems and propel action on the left.[43]

The current state of contemporary art's operation, with its pillar of critical virtue, has no traction on the world it believes to be affecting (except by chance), and in fact reinforces and lubricates capital's operations. What, then, is flawed with some of its existing modes of objections and aspirational change? What forms of organizing on the Left can reformulate the contemporary art paradigm operation and stand against it?[44] We will turn to authors who have looked at the role of art's critical virtue in relation to the market and to finance, before clarifying its effects on dissent. Malik has argued that the primary contemporary art market operates like a cartel, one in which reputation, networks, personal evaluations of artists' relevance, and protective relations are key:

> Since the sale of art on the primary market is set by these important reputational conditions and observations, the primary art market is a quasi-commercial market: rather than setting prices by "market forces",

42 In addition to the educational turn, public and private funding and managerial structures have themselves changed what "public programming" looks like and means. See Stefano Harney, "Logistical Infrastructures and Algorithmic Institutions," available at https://www.youtube.com/watch?v=-lzXf5fbsAg (accessed July 20, 2021). See also "The New Rules of Algorithmic Institutions" in *Former West*, 447–57. For Harney too, the subject is undone by the changing nature of work after labor. The move to managerialism is written about by Feher in *Rated Agency*, yet one wonders how one can differently diagnose and utilize managerialism, and Harney's work on critical management is a case in point.

43 Nestler became a trader as an artist and shuttled back to art. Historically, the Artist Placement Group also inserted themselves in various sectors of work. More recently, Robert Meister introduced a Marxian analysis that considers financial options as a mode of securing justice. See *Justice Is an Option: A Democratic Theory of Finance for the Twenty-First Century* (Chicago: University of Chicago Press, 2021).

44 See, Rodrigo Nunes, *Neither Vertical Nor Horizontal: A Theory of Political Organisation* (London: Verso, 2021); Suhail Malik, "What Must Art Become to Advance a Left Post-Neoliberalism?," talk given at Ashkal Alwan, Beirut, March 2017.

> the art market protects art and artists' careers from being subject to market pressures [...] this morality is often exemplified through declaration of "care" for art or artist, or expressed as a love of art.[45]

In trying to answer *how* critical claims as moral, civic virtues operate inside capital, he looks to the market's field of vision for the place where art thinks it is anti or oppositional. Civic virtues as embedded in contemporary art that identifies itself as critical, political, socially engaged—art that is as much non-art in its research and educational remits—secures a primary market, which itself validates the secondary art market. For Malik, the first, comprised of galleries that sell and buy in unreported fashion, differentiates itself from the secondary (consisting of auction houses and deals) and purports to protect art and artists from the allegedly voracious market and its pricing forces and reductionism, by forming a "cartel" of backdoor dealings. This is how it operationally secures its moral good as it stands in solidarity with attacks against the commercialization of art, securing its "cartelization." The fact that public art institutions house and exhibit large private collections, and that, due to austerity, the "public" in art institutions is being globally overrun by the private is not so much the issue as the morality of the wealth, or the "deployments of private wealth and accumulation as moral agency" that conjoins with the good of the public art institution and artist to secure the reputation and recognition of both. "The primary market cartel then has moral agency not only with regard to both marketisation and art simultaneously, as already noted, but extends to it also having civic virtue."[46] The dialectic of art and capitalism here is, however, represented as near total capture, even if necessarily a reversal of direction. What if this type of critique could produce a cognizance that furthers a Left political and historical horizon *in its* capture, with its tools, rather than the critical virtues with which it reproduces itself?

Even if contemporary art's monetary valuation is conveniently kept separate, posing the market as that which subjugates artworks to its rationale, or that the "market dimension" is "often left occluded as an account that threatens contemporary art's value with narrow economic instrumentalization,"[47] we still have to account for thinking about financialization as affecting the market and the "socio-institutional ecology" that is contemporary art.[48] Financialization too is a social, cultural, political, and temporal phenomenon that coalesces with certain aspects of contemporary art's "underlying structural logics."[49] The discursive practice of the curatorial and artistic are bound up with the market's pricing and risk speculation. The cartelization of contemporary art under neoliberalism is thus another sort of entry route into to operations of financialization.

Vishmidt argues that the relation between art and finance is bound via the abstract risk inherent to art and financial instruments and apparatuses—one stands not as a metaphor for the other, but as an image of one another. Moreover, art is not

45 Suhail Malik, "Civic virtue in neoliberalism and contemporary art's cartelisation," in *Mom, Am I Barbarian? 13th Istanbul Biennial*, edited by Fusun Erdemici (Istanbul: IKSV, 2013), 633; see also Suhail Malik, "Critique as alibi: moral differentiation in the art market," *Journal of Visual Arts Practice*, Vol. 7, No. 3, 2008. See also Clare McAndrew's Art Economics reports, available at http://artseconomics.com/. The volumes in their publications section further substantiate claims regarding art's relation to finance more broadly.

46 Malik, "Civic Virtue," 637.

47 Ivanova, "Art's Values: A Détente, a Grand Plié"; see also her "Contemporary Art and Financialization: Two Approaches," *Finance and Society*, Vol. 2, No. 2, 2016, 127–37.

48 Ivanova. "Contemporary Art and Financialization," 129.

49 Ibid., 128.

construed as a component of large market-led real estate and other government and fiscal initiatives, but rather, art and its institutions themselves produce added value to non-art.[50] As she states elsewhere, Theodor Adorno's attribution to art of an untamable disposition and a resistance to obedience, understood as a perpetual "revolutionizing" of skills, methods, and relations, is one ambition of art. And thus, akin to other narratives of modernization and economic growth "in the liberation theology of capital," art is right there. Capital, grounded in accumulation drives and "disruptive innovation," becomes a header that "binds processes of critical valorization internal to art and the processes of capital valorization in which it is enmeshed, however differently these disruptions are articulated in these two domains."[51] Art too can be said to impact the work of corporate enterprise via creative industries, real estate speculators, and forms of social investment.[52] Financialization is not something that happens *to* art but art can be systemically representative of it. How this would fare for contemporary art's steering of the metaphorical ship in line with other struggles against market forces remains to be seen, given that it has been content with the well-trodden Benjaminian warning of the "aestheticization of politics."

In some ways, socially engaged art has tried to answer this problem through desiring to allegedly leave the commodity form altogether. It followed several turns in contemporary art from the 1990s onward, and on paper sought not to produce art objects—although this distinction is blurry—but to intervene in the social world and alter its relations. There are, Rosamond tells us, art historical questions around the aesthetic, ethical, political valuation mechanisms of such social art practices. There is some doubt whether they constitute an anti-market, an anti-aesthetic force, and are not in some ways a mechanism for contemporary art's accrual of value—as critical virtue—through claims to being outside the market and the state, and to largely doing "good."

Rosamond tries to answer a speculative question about the potential impact of SIBs—types of investment contracts between investors and stakeholders and/or governments, mediated by private companies/external organizations—on socially engaged art.[53] SIBs are designed to help government agencies cut spending, deliver good impact for beneficiaries, and accrue profit for stakeholders and investors alike. This means that the real creditworthiness and credit accrued is a beneficial relationship between socially engaged art and financial instruments alike: "Financialized social impact requires the development of ways to read the valences, and implications, of socially engaged art projects *doubly*, as they relate to, on the one hand, investor interests and, on the other hand, stakeholder interests."[54] Not to throw the baby out with the bathwater—in some sense we *are* neoliberalism—and through Feher, Rosamond suggests that the way out is in. Exteriority as a motor for art is a fantasy, because "this desire (expressed in much art criticism and many art projects) may well hold open the idea, the hope, the possibility

50 Vishmidt, "Speculation in a Sense."

51 Marina Vishmidt, "'Mimesis of the Hardened and Alienated': Social Practice as Business Model," *e-flux journal*, # 43, March 2013, available at https://www.e-flux.com/journal/43/60197/mimesis-of-the-hardened-and-alienated-social-practice-as-business-model/ (accessed January 29, 2021); see also Ivanova, "Art, Systems, Finance," 103.

52 See Gregory Sholette and Olivier Ressler, *It's the Political Economy, Stupid: The Global Financial Crisis in Art and Theory* (London: Pluto Books, 2013); Richard Florida, *The Rise of the Creative Class, Revisited* (New York: Basic Books, 2012). Regarding how tech corporate logics are said to "think," see Adrian Daub, *What Tech Calls Thinking: An Inquiry into the Intellectual Bedrock of Silicon Valley* (New York: FSG, 2020).

53 See Rosamond, "Shared stakes, distributed investment."

54 Ibid., 114.

of an action actively opposed to investment logic. Yet in holding open this hope of opposition, the ostensibly 'uninvested' project misses an opportunity for strategic intervention into the cultural logics of investment."[55] We will evaluate the above further through a quick stop at the legacy of institutional critique—with its rights and claims-based dissent—before outlining considerations for recent organizing, and another framework and register for art.

What Is Left of Institutional Critique

Infrastructural critique is when infrastructure itself poses a crisis: "infrastructure is made out of time insofar as infrastructure is that which repeats. The repetition is normalized into everyday routine, and when it stops functioning, an aperture is cut into its artifice—through which history and power relations can be seen."[56] If capital thrives on crisis as, for Marx, the eruption of the contradictions of capitalist production (for some, *Capital* is itself a theory of crisis) it then naturally, in eruptions, renders its own logistical operations and apparatus apparent. Vishmidt asks "what would it mean to move from the practices and theories of institutional critique in the arts and expand these ideas into an infrastructural critique of the present? [...] 'Infrastructure,' in this sense, can be considered a conceptual diagram that enables thought to develop."[57]As I develop further below, recent economic and politics events point to a crisis, and there has been a post-Occupy resurgence of art protest, or desire toward communization in art to accompany it. On the one hand, and broadly speaking, there are forms that address questions of workplace labor rights, "dirty" money, and exploitative governance, such as Gulf Labor, new museum and art unions, calls to strike off museum board members and entire museums (Strike MOMA), boycotting of biennials, and sharing pay spreadsheets, to name but a few. In addition, projects like REALTY, W.A.G.E., Future Art Ecosystems, or Legal Lab as part of Serpentine Galleries Research and Development Platform, and others referred to in this volume, coincide in different ways with financial, critical legal, or systems analyses in seeking to repurpose infrastructures across contemporary art and its correlate arenas, by perhaps offering a new paradigm for art. Insofar as contemporary art is imbricated in the wider economy, its very historical constitution cannot be resolved intra-artistically by making more or less representational, social, or political art, or through past waves of institutional critique, which themselves have been the groundwork for critical virtue.[58]

Contemporary art's infrastructural operations are both within its grasp and not a product of its will. The axiomatic—as a logic that includes the set of values, processes, transactions, and discourses, etc.—and the economic-managerial are intertwined. A move from institutional critique to a recurring infrastructural critique is not only what the work of immanent critique does when crisis cuts through the appearance of smooth function-

55 Ibid., 123.
56 Vishmidt, "Beneath the Atelier."
57 Ibid.
58 Vishmidt's later works are trying to resolve (and rescue?) the need for and quandary of art's autonomy through contemporary art's speculative mode of production (risk, abstract value, etc.).

ing in capital. It is also the uncovering and overcoming of the disavowal and legitimation mechanisms at the axiomatic heart of contemporary art and its now sterile modes of negation. Infrastructural diagnosis as ongoing critique *and* repurposing of art beyond rights and the paradox of claims, can lead to a significant reorganization of the field, through broader codes of conduct, principles of operation, transnational flows, indeed *through* the paradox of its infrastructure and autonomy.

For Malik, critical virtue additionally unfolds via the ideology of art's "total freedom" *within* the institution of art, as both radical right and legitimizing force.[59] In his essay "Ape Says No," he situates the claims of art's total freedom from the institution as a radical (liberal) human rights claim, which secures contemporary art's virtue as an affirmative negation of institutionalization—the same as exists in radical human rights discourse. For him this means that "the politics and moral claims of contemporary art are based on human rights that are radically negative with regard to institutional codes and prescriptions, rights that are affirmed and enacted through the demands for justice of what must be indeterminate with regard to those positive codes, other to them."[60] In being untied from codes, law, determination, the intrinsic civic virtue to contemporary art is akin to that of "radical" human rights claims. "Belonging to anybody and everybody at any time, *human rights are the inherent civic virtue of rights*" instead of their legal codification as rights.

Contemporary art's, or institutional critique's freedom precedes its codification, posing it as beyond regulation and systemic logics.[61] This form of institutional critique affirms the radical right of the artist contra the institution, while affirming the artist-institution-as-contra, which Malik then pits against the insurrectionary, institutionalized ape who says "No" as an negative affirmation.[62] If "criticality" itself becomes nullified, it is because it was never critique. More precisely, as Vishmidt warns, "[i]f the project of critique always ends up affirming its subject—the institution of art—in its valorization of both the affective subject and its critical capacity, this can inflate the artist as critical subject beyond all reason" into an "absolute commodity."[63] For Vishmidt, a check on the expansion of the "automatic subject" (of capitalist value) can only happen through an unwavering emphasis on labor and its conditions. Yet, given the given the analysis I have attempted so far, this needs to be evaluated anew.

Classwork Workplace

Contemporary art's values and operations are now more in line with those of enterprise than ever, and Vishmidt has shown that its trademark institutional critique amplifies the contradictions of the institution rather than subverts them, telling itself that it pushes into the critique of *any* institution, be it capitalism, patriarchy, or the like. Having established the political barrenness

59 Andrea Fraser, "How to Provide an Artistic Service: An Introduction," *Open Set: Art Humanities Culture*, May 4, 2017, available at https://www.open-set.com/cnrobbins/essay-clusters/andrea-frasers-how-to-provide-an-artistic-service/ (accessed February 28, 2021).

60 Suhail Malik. "Ape Says No," *Red Hook Journal*, June 10, 2013, available at https://ccs.bard.edu/redhook/ape-says-no/index.html (accessed March 1, 2021).

61 This "outside the law," is not, I will note later, the same as the ways in which critical legal theory's immanent critique, and legal rupture, shows the interiority-exteriority of law. See, for example, Brenna Bhandar, "Strategies of Legal Rupture: The Politics of Judgement," *Windsor Yearbook of Access to Justice*, 2012, 59-78; and Emilios Christodoulidis, "Strategies of Rupture," *Law and Critique*, December 2008, 1–24; see also Jodi Dean, "Zizek on Law," *Law and Critique*, No. 15, 2004, 1–24.

62 For Vishmidt, the domestication of institutional critique into new brands would grow into what she refers to as infrastructural critique: transversal artist and activist practices that took institutions to be a "contingent if motivated site of materialization," coinciding with the new variety of institutions themselves brandishing IC as the "New Institutionalism."

63 Vishmidt, "Beneath the Atelier."

of art's "anti", or opposition as a self-assigned condition that serves wider value extraction, we have an additional set of issues to confront. If for Stewart Martin art is "neither capitalism nor communism [...] which is to say that art is constituted by this opposition and by its own opposition to this opposition"[64] (Martin does not differentiate between art and contemporary art but refers to art's exceptional status) we still have to deal with its ambiguous politics, and the crisis and contradiction it re-presents. Moreover, we cede that contemporary art is also a workplace governed by work struggles. Let's establish two current, intersecting levels of dissent paralleling contemporary art's usual claims that we can schematically call "workplace and labor" and the other, "institutional claims." And a third direction predicated on leverage and instrumentalization that we outline below as "Left protocols."

The workplace in contemporary art, as in contemporary capitalism, generates institutions whose working conditions are exploitative and exalted because they are so, meaning that the contemporary ideology of work (mental or manual) is something you "must love"; you work for work's sake. The paradox of this autonomy (and of art), if you will, emerges out of the division of labor and the mental labor problem. For Andrew Ross, writing in the late 1990s, this "figures primarily as the challenge of maintaining a steady supply of workers willing to discount the price of their labor for love of their craft."[65] Writing about the New School for Social Research in New York, he argues that the image of universities as anti-elite establishments, their resistance to business ventures and emphasis on education as the pursuit of "idle curiosity"— education for its own sake uncontaminated by commercial interest—"render its devotees ineffectual as economic or social actors outside of their professional sphere."[66] This autonomy would not become a "liability to the material well-being of the academic workforce until many years later" in the form of adjunct, fixed-term contract and disposable labor. Ross was clearly influenced by Alfred Sohn-Rethel, who earlier had already outlined, in his *Intellectual and Manual Labor: A Critique of Epistemology* (1978), why mental labor to be useful to the ruling class in a given epoch, would have to secure some level of autonomy.[67] This can obfuscate the relation—or overall "social synthesis," as he calls it—making it appear like a class of intellectual labor that, in its disinterested knowledge, does not serve dominant production forces. Art's special place—not as commodity, nor as absolute commodity, but as the myth of needing to be rescued from encroachment by capital—needs to be dismantled and utilized from within the workplace, where it is lucrative to existing alienation and exploitation by both employers and financial forces.[68] And it must be understood *as* workplace in the first instance. What is the equivalent form of not producing disinterested knowledge through the labor of "I love my job" in order to engage with historical workplace forces (strikes, unions, etc.) that address the contradiction of autonomy alongside others working for the same ends?[69]

64 Stewart Martin, "A Short Treatise on Art," in *Aesthetics and Contemporary Art*, edited by Armen Avanessian and Luke Skrebowski (Berlin: Sternberg Press, 2011), 145–57.

65 Andrew Ross, "The Mental Labor Problem," in *Class: An Anthology*, edited by Stanley Aronowitz and Michael J. Roberts (Oxford: Wiley Blackwell, 2018), 318.

66 Ibid., 317.

67 Alfred Sohn-Rethel, *Intellectual and Manual Labor: A Critique of Epistemology* (London: Macmillan, 1978).

68 See Konings, *The Emotional Logic of Capitalism*; and Miya Tokumitsu, "After #MeToo, it's Time to Democratize the Art World's Workplaces," *frieze*, March 19, 2018, available at https://www.frieze.com/article/after-metoo-its-time-democratize-art-worlds-workplaces (accessed April 14, 2021).

69 See Feher on investee activism. The work of "politics," here, could be in utilizing that which makes you an "investee," rather than producing disinterested knowledge, for example. Or, the self-interest of a group coalesces around debt and credit (within an articulated Left politics) to strike against it. See the Debt Collective, https://debtcollective.org/ (accessed October 6, 2021). See also, Astra Taylor, *You Are Not a Loan* (2020).

Here, I want to pause briefly at the current moment in the US and most of Europe as the centers around which contemporary art was modeled as universal, and in which a renewed class consciousness and union organizing is taking place. In art, this was mirrored by a contemporary resurgence of labor consciousness coupled with a renewed critique of leading art institutions and artforms in the rather different manifestations of Occupy. At the time of writing, there has been a surge of labor—as well as broadly anti-capitalist—organizing in the Western world and elsewhere, and it appears, alongside other factors, to be propelling conditions of class cognition and action in certain sectors of contemporary art.[70] Examples include the unionizing of art handlers; the unionizing of various US museum workers; the emergence of a refusal of unpaid internships; the sharing of salary and wage spreadsheets; art institutions being sued for unfair pay and leave conditions; the gaining of worker status at the British National Gallery of lecturers and artists; the staging of protests and walk-outs against pay and other conditions at Tate; and Strike MOMA calling for the removal of the museum altogether, to name but a few.

We know that the challenge to the capital-labor arrangements of Fordism-Taylorism—referred to as deindustrialization in the 1960s, primarily in the US—seeded radical change, placing the entire structure of work and capital at stake. Julia Bryan-Wilson has argued that artists' political-economic identifications with class struggle and anti-Vietnam solidarities fueled anti-museum discourse and action, feminist and ant-racist critiques, and heralded the establishment of the Art Workers' Coalition in the US. All this not only injected coalitional class and anti-war politics into art, but also in*form*ed minimalism and conceptualism, including feminist and collective practices that would come to characterize the bedrock of conceptual and post-conceptual art. These material conditions underpinned the formation of new ways of making, displaying, spectatorship, and their ensuing institutional critique.[71]

Despite its obfuscated class composition, and the "mental labor problem," it could be said that contemporary art's main actors occupy both a transnational, capitalist class—as globalizing professionals and consumerist elites—as well as the precariat.[72] In other words, a microcosm of the bourgeois rooms

70 At the time of writing, the following recent labor actions have been of note: mine workers' union (UNWA) and Amazon workers striking together; strikes and reports against working conditions at Tesla; propositions for vertical unions and transnational strike platforms; Uber gig workers pushing tribunals in the UK for benefits and worker status; Sudanese uprising instigation of major union work across sectors and various insurrections in Lebanon, Chile, and Colombia; proposition for new household US debt canceling coalition called the Debt Collective; volumes such as *Class Power on Zero Hours* by collectives such as Angry Worker; Indian farmers protesting debt in the face of Monsanto's violent seed monopoly; protecting miners via the International Rights Advocates' case against Cobalt mining as DOE 1 et al. v. APPLE INC. et al.

71 Jasper Bernes, *The Work of Art in the Age of Deindustrialization* (Stanford: Stanford University Press, 2017).

72 Dimitrakaki speaks to the anti as framing the art precariat, and Feher refers to the new investee position as individual behavior dependent on the market. Bernes, on his part, inverts this and argues that art, especially literature, was able to inspire that particular articulation of work and workers under US capitalism.

we find ourselves in, filled with beneficiaries and elites, entrepreneurial subjects and employees turned managers, supported by a range of flexible workers. If Bryan-Wilson's historical analysis is apt, what will the effect be of self-(class)-consciousness and Left coalition politics on the art that survives? There have of course been a range of explicitly class-based diagnoses of art that stood out historically, and, for that matter, the work of a plethora of Marxist social art historians too numerous to list here.[73] More recently there has been *High Class Hard Labor* (2015), an edited volume coming out of the work of the Gulf Labor Art Coalition, focused on the Gulf States' luxury branding and art's asset-class cultural politics. Although the book targeted the museum franchises dotting the UAE and their dire extremely exploitative outsourced labor conditions, what is of note here is Gulf Labor's form of organizing on *behalf* of labor.[74]

73 The work of the social art historians around the *October* journal are of note here, of course, as is Pierre Bourdieu's work. See for example, *Distinction: A Social Critique of the Judgement of Taste*, translated by Richard Nice (Cambridge, MA: Harvard University Press, 1987); Pierre Bourdieu and Alain Darbel, with Dominique Schnapper, *The Love of Art: European Art Museums and Their Public*, translated by Caroline Beatty and Nick Merriman (Cambridge: Polity, 1991). See also, from the perspective of modernism in the Global South, Dina Ramadan, *The Education of Taste: Art, Aesthetics, and Subject Formation in Colonial Egypt* (Edinburgh: Edinburgh University Press, 2020). Lastly, there is a far less compelling class analysis of global art under post-Fordism that Pascal Gielen refers to as the murmuring of artistic multitude. Using Actor-Network-Theory, and allusions to "autonomous zones," and "slowing down," the endgame is an art conserved from global neoliberal encroachment. Pascal Gielen, *The Murmuring of the Artistic Multitude: Global Art, Politics and Post-Fordism* (Amsterdam: Valiz, 2010). See also "The Ideology of the Immaterial Oeuvre," *The Art Handler*, Issue 1, January 8, 2016, available at http://art-handler.com/#fn-1 (accessed February 2, 2021).

Organizing Post-Negation

In a different image to that of the Art Workers' Coalition who designated themselves workers as part of a broader political and institutional overhaul, Gulf Labor used its leverage *as* artists and activists to pressure mega museums—via calls to boycott, backdoor negotiations, and direct actions by Gulf Ultra Luxury Faction—which outsource labor to companies shipping workers.[75] Evaluations of Gulf Labor's success are for another essay, yet I wonder if organizing on-behalf-of is not part of the post-historical, or even humanitarian, problem of art, or whether this form of leveraging is one example of what Left coalitional directions can do—even if here the *fact* of a Guggenheim Abu Dhabi or a Guggenheim New York for that matter is not what is being disputed, just "who is building" it.[76] Initiatives like W.A.G.E., and Wagency, organize artists as wage workers *vis-à-vis* the institutions and museums that extract value from their work past the first sale and exhibition. Positioning the artist squarely within an understanding of the management and value structures of the market, bad contractual conditions, as well as the reputational superstructure of private and semi-private art institutions, W.A.G.E. tries to strategically restructure pay and working conditions in a centralized manner. These are further reflected today in the new unionizing of staff in US museums such as in

74 Naturally, there are different, more recent examples of those organizing as workers, such as in Sudan and Lebanon. After its October uprising, the latter saw, in the model of the former, those working at different levels in the so-called cultural field attempting to join ranks and create a broader union outside existing, often state-infiltrated trade unions. See Workers in Art and Culture, available at https://workersartculture.wordpress.com/ (accessed November 22, 2021).

75 Despite being contracted by so-called sponsors, and not considered self-employed, this does structurally echo the platformization of "flexible" labor models such as Uber or Deliveroo.

76 Gulf Labor Art Coalition, "Who's Building Guggenheim Abu Dhabi?," available at https://gulflabour.org/ (accessed April 3, 2021).

Philadelphia and the New Museum in New York, and other actions and strikes around contracts and work status listed earlier.

Direct action on the basis of claims has remained the *modus operandi* of some activists, despite the move away from the communization inflected Occupy mantra of "occupy now demand later," or never. The new set of demands is urged on by the political economic reawakening of contemporary art dissent, which includes in its scope institutional infrastructures and movements such as Black Lives Matter, and similar groups organizing against the cultural and institutional manifestation of racial capitalism and settler colonialism.[77] This second kind of organizing as "institutional claims" falls in part within the legacy of institutional critique and Occupy, and beyond the level of the artwork, and is also different from the problem of labor organizing. This has recently included, among other examples, a partial boycott of the "tear gas biennial" at the Whitney Biennial, and a call for the resignation of MOMA board members over their fiscal dealings and holdings, which became a demand for strike, if not abolition of the museum under the header Strike MOMA—connected to the larger umbrella International Imagination of Anti-National Anti-Imperialist Feelings. A couple of years earlier, the Serpentine Gallery's CEO, who has family involvement in cyber-technology companies used by states to pursue dissidents, was identified and forced to resign. The recent protests at Tate were primarily about working conditions and contracts, but also about its foundation in sugar, opiates, and imperial plunder. None of this is a surprise; in fact, these pose structural questions to contemporary art as it traveled across the dialectics of autonomy, away from tutelage, and right back to it. Yet, will this be resolved by an agonistic model of institutional demands and negotiations, in the hope of changing the foundation of the economy around art and replacing it? But replacing it with what? Can changing these conditions alter the superstructure that is contemporary art? Or is the call to abolish it? How do we differentiate critical claimant from beneficiary, given the structure of contradiction outlined throughout this essay? Or rather, how can art "exit contemporary art" in order to build another paradigm, in which infrastructures can also be repurposed for navigation of the present toward a political horizon understood and conceived in advance? How can this steer clear of more discursivity, whereby "art is where a social subject can spend, self-consciously and by choice, a lifetime dedicated to a political cause without the pressure of taking power and without changing the world?"[78] On a para-artistic level, programmatic Left protocols—based on the arsenal that contemporary art does have via its transnational flows, valorization mechanisms, institutional prowess, its union history of collective bargaining and strike, as well as investments structures, to try and radically withhold (and hold accountable if need be) while navigating the ship to a determined leftist horizon—are still missing.

Calls to boycott the Whitney Biennial in 2019 were met with rejoinders about identity politics, and reiterated the economic

77 Strike MoMA has a strong pro-Palestinian strain, the activist alliance International Imagination of Anti-National Anti-Imperialist Feelings. See Alex Greenberger, "Amid Jeffrey Epstein Fallout, Leon Black will Step Down as MOMA Board Chair," *Artnews*, March 26, 2021, available at https://www.artnews.com/art-news/news/leon-black-moma-board-chairman-steps-down-1234588009/ accessed June 5, 2021).

78 Dimitrakaki, "Left with TINA," 32.

79 Hannah Black, Toby Haslett, and Ciarán Finlayson, "The tear gas biennial: a statement from Hannah Black, Toby Haslett and Ciarán Finlayson regarding Warren Kanders and the 2009 Whitney Biennial," *Artforum*, July 17, 2019, available at https://www.artforum.com/slant/a-statement-from-hannah-black-ciaran-finlayson-and-tobi-haslett-on-warren-kanders-and-the-2019-whitney-biennial-80328 (accessed April 14, 2021).

80 Ibid.

precarity of artists "needing to eat." This is more the problem of contemporary art itself than the problem of those dissenting. Nonetheless, these retorts may also be a symptom of the paradox of critical virtue (a disjointed autonomy), which informs the parameters of dissent but also of the field itself, and not that of the dialectics of autonomy outlined at the start of the essay.[79] We were reminded that it is those calling for strikes and boycotts, and who make positively articulated alignments with certain political struggles that "are accused of making calculated career moves in an art world—so goes the story—in which political commitment is irrelevant at best and elitist at worst. Which is it: that artists are helpless to act politically for fear of losing their livelihoods, or that political commitments among artists are blandly congratulated and even encouraged?"[80] So, in line with this critique of the stance against boycott, and beyond the artist as category and the artwork as pinnacle unit, which alliances will organize strikes and boycotts if no theory-praxis relation, no class composition, no propositional antagonism is being used to understand the self-valorization of capital and contemporary art's reproduction of it?

And yet, these more committed moves in contemporary art's ecology, which sometimes propose a blueprint for action, are few and far between.[81] Despite dissent against the obvious disparity between art's claims and the board members of its institutions—notwithstanding the overall relation to the economy—the discourse around art's autonomy as divorced from these dealings also falls within our argument. Which *art* are you saving and fighting for? If there is to be traction to strikes, direct action, or even the work "itself," they need to coalesce with Left organizing outside of contemporary art, and create a large base inside and outside it.

Nonetheless, the predominant modes of "institutional claims" of dissent remain encapsulated in representation and participation/denunciation in the forms of diversity calls, letters, hashtags—notwithstanding the artwork itself. They are often hyperbolic, asking too much of contemporary art, while reproducing both the art and the economic logic underpinning it. Bahar Noorizadeh draws a parallel between a system of moral value in contemporary art and in the entertainment industry, as crystalized in the #MeToo accusations; one that is contiguous with late capitalism.[82] She also highlights the subsequent lack of legal frameworks for justice inside the workplace and outside it, especially with injunctions to remain informal and flexible. The logic of capital as expressed in the desire to establish "creditworthiness" and amplifying your reputation, links up with contemporary art's injunction to informality: network over drinks, be flexible by working weekends, hierarchies don't exist, love your job. One could add, it's "not (just) how much you earn but how much you are worth."[83] Some time ago, Andrea Fraser had described post-studio, educational, public, site-specific, research-based art—in the context of all artists now working on projects and in procedural

81 Stewart Martin, "Art Strike: An Inventory," *Metamute*, May 1, 2020, available at https://www.metamute.org/editorial/articles/art-strikes-inventory (accessed September 25, 2021)

82 Bahar Noorizadeh, "Cash out now: On the strange symbiosis of sexual harassment and contemporary art," *&&&Platform*, March 5, 2018, available at https://tripleampersand.org/cash-now-strange-symbiosis-sexual-harassment-contemporary-art/ (accessed September 15, 2021).

83 Ivanova, "Art, Systems, Finance," 103.

84 Fraser argues that "It appears to us that, related variously to institutional critique, productivist, activist and political documentary traditions as well as post-studio, site-specific and/or public art activities, the practices currently characterized as 'project work' do not necessarily share a thematic, ideological or procedural basis [...] labor, which in economic terms would be called service provision (as opposed to goods production)." Fraser, "How to Provide."

85 See Sophie Cras, "Prix et récompenses dans la création contemporaine: évaluation et valorisation en régime concurrentiel," *Critique d'art*, No. 45, 2015, available at https://journals.openedition.org/critiquedart/19144 (accessed July 20, 2021).

ways—as the economic equivalent of providing a service, and that value-generating activities as "service provision" have to reckon with economic consequences.[84]

To reinforce another disjuncture on the level of claims within the overall field, Noorizadeh also drew our attention to the letter written by the four artists nominated for the Preis der Nationalgalerie (2017) who accepted the nomination, attended the awards, and denounced the organizers and prize logics *post facto*. The prize beneficiaries wrote that they were dominated by a divisive discourse—the prize focusing on their ethnicity rather than their work, making them compete against one another—thus allowing them to straddle the position of both beneficiary and casualty, and a third ethical yield from the disavowal of the operating mechanism of the art field. Naturally, contemporary art deals in the currency of competitive awards and prizes,[85] on the basis of "heroic" artists (and artworks), and, for the most part, a tokenistic vision of identity politics,[86] rather than axiomatically through a consistent sense of socio-economic structures and via critiques and workings-through of contradictions.[87] There are perhaps limits to moral outrage. Proposing models of "seizing the means" and organizing the "vast institutional arsenal—that is, our [sic] plutocratic field's material resources, political clout and self-directed empowerment" are maybe part of what Left protocols refer to.[88]

The "we are not surprised"[89] campaign of 2017 came in response to allegations against Knight Landesman.[90] At the height of #MeToo, it acknowledged strength of numbers against what it referred to as the abuse of power so rampant in the art world. Using hashtags and signed open letters, it did not acknowledge the transactional calculations—to bully, to fire, to care for—that juxtapose informal favors with work so extensive in the tyrannically structureless working conditions of contemporary art, and which some of the letters' signatories enjoy. A fragment of the "we are not surprised" statement reads:

> We are artists, arts administrators, assistants, curators, directors, editors, educators, gallerists, interns, scholars, students, writers, and more—workers of the art world—and we have been groped, undermined, harassed, infantilized, scorned, threatened, and intimidated by those in positions of power who control access to resources and opportunities. We have held our tongues,

86 Consider the statements in 2020 by global art institutions around solidarity with Black Lives Matter. As crucial as they are—and despite the stark absence of anti-Zionist statements during the May operations against Palestine by those same institutions—they can be a placeholder for actual change, or leverage. Many have subsequently raised their diversity quotas while in all likelihoods not transforming their organizational mechanisms, economic policy, codes, conduct, contracts, wages; in short, these point to flagrant internal contradictions between claims and practices.

87 A handful of incisive theorists evidently do this very well, yet this is not what the art system rests on. The term heroic artist was—of course—coined during American Abstract Expressionist modernism; here it is meant beyond art movements as the defining mechanism where "ultimately the financial value and artistic quality of a future work of art is both predicted and guaranteed by the signature of the artist and the consistent style of an oeuvre." Gielen, "The Ideology of the Immaterial Oeuvre."

88 Noorizadeh, "Cash out."

89 See https://www.not-surprised.org/. The campaign and campaign were short-lived as the url now links, not without irony, to a make-up and beauty site.

90 Using Jenny Holzer's *Abuse of Power Comes as No Surprise* work as a logo. Note, not without irony either, that Holzer's series of which the screen with those words was part is titled *Truisms* (1982).

> threatened by power wielded over us and promises of institutional access and career advancement.

The parody of dissent and the image of art encased in the letter beg the question in which ways the moral economy of indeterminacy consolidates the art world's class biases as they presently exist. The notion of "workers" here has lost its signifier. Contemporary art's "inamenability" to a class analysis is manifold in the fantasy of not reproducing capitalism. This statement absorbs the historical category of worker and inverts class consciousness—outside any understanding of the commodity form or of reification—as a presumed (bourgeois) class signifier to and for itself as contemporary art. It nebulously pits the workers of the art world as cultural workers—including scholars, directors, gallerists, directors (nothing of guards, construction workers, handlers, movers, drivers) against "power," which in large part is the selfsame power. Through its appearance of threat, it reproduces the social relationship *of* said power that underpins contemporary art in the first place. Its form of "dissenting" enables little on a systemic level but accrues value from its moral indignation as business-as-usual.

Toward a Conclusion

Between the "no" of communism and the "no" of capitalism, we have a stagnant politics of dissent afraid of articulating itself. What would a Left critique allied to a propositional politics of art look like? What is the Left politics of art not founded on rights, representation, and affirmative institutional critique? What forms, or alliances would it produce? Given contemporary art's axiomatic indeterminacy and proliferation of criticality as nominal rejection of capitalism—or fascism, or communism—where do we locate the future socialist politics in contemporary art if not in the intersection of critique and praxis? If the real effects of TINA induce both the capitalist realist and the anarcho-realist principles that some authors have alluded to, and in a field that has already been identified as pluralistic and post-negational, on what basis does "organizing" take place, and as whom?

The indeterminate as post-negational in contemporary art, Arthur Danto had referred to affectionately as post-historical.[91] Contemporary art is a repository of symbolic and "good" negations that, when added up, cancel each other out. The post-historical allows for everything precisely because for Danto the story of art (spirit) was over and history had reached its apex; we are left with a style of using styles, a *mise-en-abyme* (not as technique).[92] Think of the e-flux platform as a prototype for contemporary art *itself*—which is to say a platform of art- and commerce-generated material across various art markets and milieux, and speaking to/with various shareholders and stakeholders. In some sense, it is post-historical par excellence. A prototype of this sort, with a Left political vision tied to its

91 In their different ways, Fredric Jameson, Simon Reynolds, Mark Fisher, and Sami Khatib all refer to the ideology of the end of history's cultural, post-historical, retromanic symptoms.

92 Danto, *After the End of Art.*

economic clout well beyond contemporary art's already existing sensibilities, would edge away from its appearance as interface of neutrality on the one hand, and critical eclecticism on the other, toward a determinate, even political, practice. Moreover, juxtaposing this with some of the propositions for vertical unions across transnational lines, which consider collective but disparate regulatory and juridical modes, gives us one speculative idea of what a Left art protocol might resemble.[93]

At this crisis juncture I ask if this critique and strategy could work together under a protocol(s) committed to the socialist politics that the discursivity of contemporary art merely gestures toward, and which art's autonomy under capital had always held the promise of—at and beyond the level of the artwork alone. Protocol is a multi-level call; it is internationalist, it has chapters, it has codes. That is: a coalitional, transnational (platform) across labor and workplace organizing, and a legal support structure (for contracts, strikes, boycotts, research, etc.). Finally, it is even a diagnostic tool whereby Left critique is allied with practice, defining what constitutes this art.[94] What "regulates" working in and making art could also be what keeps contemporary art's relation to its alleged exteriority via tractionless critical claims, radical human rights ideologies, and exploitative conditions out of the way. Art protocol, conceptually and logistically, looks beyond moral accountability, because an immanent critique *amounts* to that critique in practice, rather than fluffy replication of content. Meaning that the protocol may itself have both intra- and extra-artistic effects, insofar as the broadly economic conditions that have produced the need for it begin to demand other infrastructurally inclined aesthetic forms.

The challenge ahead, then, is to maintain immanent critique on the one hand, and to find *from* the indeterminate, flexible, atomized, the determinate, inflexible, un-individuated models for art within a broader economy.[95] This is neither in the legacy of institutional critique, at the level of the artwork, at the level of the institution alone, nor a previous model of an artist union—although some can be learned from. What will be needed is another kind of seizing; a transnational protocol, or socialist framework if you prefer, for continual diagnostics and infrastructural work; a rupture of and with contemporary art as well as with its skewed, highly specific, or unregulated legalist frameworks, which can ground a radically different register of building Left coalitions of action with others doing similar work. A format that regulates the field from within economic inescapabilities, begins to map a new aesthetic paradigm to further its horizon. Thus, it acts with chapters with others across the field, and alongside kin battles, sectors, and workers—without allusion to an artificial internal horizontalism.

To end, as Lenin had reminded in both different and similar historical conditions: "On the basis of what facts, then, can the question of the future development of future communism be dealt with? On the basis of the fact that it has its origin in capitalism, that it develops historically from capitalism, that it

93 See, for instance, Nick House's propositional Vertical Unions Working Group, https://trust.support/watch/vertical-unions (accessed March 24, 2012); or see N. Houde and Arthur Röing Baer, "Unions: Scale and Trust," January 13, 2020, available at https://trust.support/feed/unions-scale-and-trust. (accessed February 20, 2021); see also Sam Lefebvre,"In a New Book About Unions and Financial Capitalism, Lessons for the Arts," *Hyperallergic*, January 25, 2021, available at https://hyperallergic.com/616297/unions-renewed-alice-martin-and-annie-quick/ (accessed May 26, 2021).

94 Compelling inspiration, or parallels to this, come from critical legal theory's understanding of legal rupture. See, for instance, Christodoulidis, "Strategies of Rupture."

95 Although I have covered the contours of determinacy and inflexibility conceptually, I leave the term atomized or un-individuated to be explored elsewhere. There are numerous theories of the subject in capital, and discussion of the forced dissolution of class consciousness as a sort of individuation (contra collectivity). And, as discussed by Feher, in the move toward self-entrepreneurship and the investee. Bassam El Baroni pointed out that Read's work on transindividuation could be a future framework through which to address this. See, for example, Read, *The Politics of Transindividuality*.

is the result of the action of a social force to which capitalism gave birth. There is no trace of an attempt on Marx's part to make up a utopia."[96] One could add that the popularity of Feher's call for investee activism under debtor-creditor relations, Meister's proposal for justice founded on (a theory of) financial instruments, and many other diagnostics under contemporary financialized capital, deeply echo this sentiment. The invitation to exit contemporary art and abolish some of its forms might mean just this. What form of rupture, founded on an immanent critique of contemporary art, and taking financialized conditions of production, circulation, speculation, and risk can push the praxis question? To ground an inversion of its own "criticality," you propositionally build a Left coalitional protocol within art's dialectic relationship to capitalism as overdetermined by the image of an ended future.

96 Vladimir I. Lenin, *State and Revolution*, annotated by Todd Chretien (Chicago: Haymarket Books, 2014 [1917]), 122.

DISARTICULATING INFRASTRUCTURES: TOWARD TOUCHSTONES FOR INFRASTRUCTURAL INQUIRIES

Nishant Shah

In 2013, which seems like distant digital history and certainly a dated memory, the digital infrastructure landscape in India saw a dramatic shift that echoed changes in many other countries. Internet.org, a non-profit organization established by Facebook, in collaboration with other behemoths such as Microsoft, Samsung, and Apple, announced their launch in India. Avowing universal access and promoting connectivity as a fundamental human right,[1] and equality and equity of people across the digital divide,[2] the organization positioned itself as a natural ally to a country like India, which had recognized the need for universal digital access and the lack of robust infrastructure resources to achieve it.

Internet.org collaborated with Reliance Telecom, India's biggest telephone access provider and a communications giant, to offer free internet access to anyone who had a mobile data connection with the company.[3] The idea of free internet access through a service provider that had extensive penetration across the bottom of the pyramid users in India resonated immediately with the promises of "India Shining."[4] It also positioned Internet.org as the new saviors that would rescue the poor, the marginalized, the downtrodden, and the disconnected from the inadequacies of their own governments and the apathy of their own nation-states.[5]

The "Free Basics" campaign identified itself as an infrastructure project that would build the new logical structure of public connectivity and universal access. In their own description:

> Free Basics by Facebook provides free access to basic internet services to a billion people all over the world. Your service can be part of it. Free Basics makes the internet accessible to more people by providing them access to a range of free basic services like news, maternal health, travel, local jobs, sports, communication, and local government information.
>
> To date, we've been able to offer these services to a billion people across Asia, Africa and Latin America.

1 Mark Zuckerberg, "Is connectivity a human right?," *Facebook News*, August 21, 2013.

2 Mark Zuckerberg, "Free Basics protects net neutrality," *Times of India*, December 18, 2015, available at https://timesofindia.indiatimes.com/blogs/toi-edit-page/free-basics-protects-net-neutrality/ (accessed February 10, 2021).

3 Catherine Shu, "Facebook's Internet.org now available throughout India," *Techcrunch*, November 25, 2015, available at https://techcrunch.com/2015/11/24/facebooks-internet-org-now-available-throughout-india (accessed February 12, 2021).

4 Anurag Banerjee and Nilanjan Banik, "Is India Shining?," *Review of Development Economics*, Vol. 18, No. 1, 59–72, DOI: 10.1111/rode.12069.

5 Revati Prasad, "Ascendant India, digital India: how net neutrality advocates defeated Facebook's Free Basics," *Media, Culture & Society*, Vol. 40, No. 3, 2017, 415–31, DOI: 10.1177/0163443717736117.

> By introducing people to the benefits of the internet through these services, we hope to bring more people online and help improve their lives.[6]

However, there were a few conditions for Free Basics to be able to come to fruition for its users. First, internet access had to be tied to a data plan contract with Reliance, ensuring that all new connections would go through this one telecommunications company. Second, although access was free, it would still be limited[7]; the Free Basics subscription would give access to a selected number of websites deemed important, relevant, or worthy of access by Internet.org and its collaborators.[8] Both these conditions, circumspect as they were, were accepted as a fair compromise under the Terms and Conditions that users had to agree to in order to avail of this free service. Both were similar to many other national and private digital infrastructure schemes, in which the citizen/user consents to subscribing through licensed intermediaries and accepts the limitations of what can and cannot be said and accessed in digital space.

However, the third condition that Free Basics put forward concerned an internet regulation framework and policy shift that went way beyond user consent. Free Basics contested the principle of net neutrality, which stipulates that Internet Service Providers (ISPS) have to facilitate all internet communication as equal. They cannot discriminate in the speed of transfer or manipulate the data within a network, based on user, content, website, platform, browser, device, source and destination address, or method of communication. This ensures that ISPS cannot block, slow down, or charge money for specific content. Without net neutrality, the internet loses it characteristics of a commons, and ISPS can prioritize certain types of traffic, meter others, or potentially block those from specific services, while offering a tiered access system so that consumers have to pay more for higher speeds and premium access to information. Like the majority of countries around the world, India had adopted net neutrality as a foundational principle for a free and open internet. Internet.org proposed that in order for universal access to happen, the idea of an indiscriminate internet network—founded on free and equitable distribution of traffic—would have to be sacrificed.[9]

The company effectively staged a war between universal access and net neutrality, claiming that the only way a digital level playing field could be established was to create an elite super-highway of information that would allow all intermediaries to shape the speed, volume, and content of the information being shared in those networks.[10] Under the guise of providing universal access, Internet.org started lobbying for a "zero rating" ban and the demolition of net neutrality in India, riding on their success in manipulating other countries in doing so.[11] Much to their surprise, a massive public movement that resisted, critiqued, and lashed out at this attack on a free internet in the guise of infrastructure building emerged. Here I examine

6 See https://developers.facebook.com/docs/internet-org/ (accessed August 13, 2021).

7 Rahul Mukherjee, "Jio sparks Disruption 2.0: infrastructural imaginaries and platform ecosystems in Digital India," *Media, Culture & Society*, Vol. 41, No. 2, 2018, 175–95, DOI: 10.1177/0163443718818383.

8 Hanuman Chowdary Triupuraneni, "The Free Basics (of Facebook) debate in India," *Info*, Vol. 18, No. 3, 2016, 1–3, DOI:10.1108/info-02-2016-0005.

9 Rijurekha Sen et al., "Inside the walled garden: deconstructing Facebook's Free Basics program," *ACM SIGCOMM Computer Communication Review*, Vol. 45, No. 5, 2017, DOI: 10.1145/3155055.3155058.

10 Cory Doctorow, "'Poor internet for poor people': India's activists fight Facebook connection plan," *The Guardian*, January 15, 2016, available at https://www.theguardian.com/world/2016/jan/15/india-net-neutrality-activists-facebook-free-basics (accessed February 22, 2021).

11 Ariel Futter and Alison Gillwald, "Zero-rated internet services: What is to be done?," Policy Paper 1: Broadband 4 Africa. ResearchICTAfrica.net, September 2015, available at https://www.researchictafrica.net/docs/Facebook%20zerorating%20Blogpost%20Final_Web.pdf (accessed February 20, 2021).

how the material and political agenda of this infrastructuring project was unmasked, and in the process seek to build a framework for digital infrastructure critique that doesn't just ask for a different approach, but to position and understand digital infrastructure differently.

Articulated Infrastructures

The promise of digital infrastructures is intelligibility, and the end point is knowledge. Discussions around digital infrastructure consider the complexity of language, media, technologies, translations, forms, formats, and intended functions of information that is conceived as input, rendered as data, stored in archives, retrieved through queries, circulated on networked edges, and transferred as traffic. These processes clearly identify that infrastructure projects are projects of articulation—the entire process of making models, creating databases, assigning taxonomies, performing digital ontologies, and designing information vectors that can provide legibility to the thing being digitized, is a complex of practices of articulating a reality. This idea of infrastructure as articulation is not just a metaphorical description; it is supported by multiple policy and regulatory frameworks that use this approach in order to protect the privacy, rights, and safety of users.

In India, for instance, in the very first Information Technologies Act of 2000, which sets out to understand the consequences and spread of digital technologies in the country, it is very clear that the process of granting access is also a process through which each user will be defined and identified.[12] The role of the digital infrastructure provider as liable for both connectivity and content was established in the Intermediaries Liabilities Act (2011), in which the government states that the Internet Service Providers hold responsibility for the content on the websites that are being accessed, because the users are being offered platforms of speech and identity through their infrastructure.[13] In times of protests and civil unrest, India has continuously exercised internet shutdowns, blocking infrastructure, and suspending access as a way of stopping the circulation of information.[14] The apotheosis of infrastructures as articulating the user can be found in the much documented biometric identity project called Aadhaar, which defines and maps individual users through a series of digital transactions over multiple networks and databases through a common digital identifier tied to a central database of biometric verification controls.[15]

It is necessary to understand infrastructuring as articulation, because much effort goes into managing, regulating, and controlling how a nation and its subjects are being imagined and installed into new operating systems of digital governance through infrastructure building.[16] I want to argue that the focus on infrastructuring as articulation draws our attention to questions of "how?" The "how" of infrastructure achieving this is well documented, as well as how we can protect, resist, critique, and

12 Ministry of Electronics and Information Technology (MEIT), "Information Technology Act 2000," available at https://www.meity.gov.in/content/information-technology-act-2000 (accessed February 20, 2021).

13 Sunil Abraham, "Intermediary liability law needs updating," *Business Standard*, February 9, 2019, available https://www.business-standard.com/article/opinion/intermediary-liability-law-needs-updating-119020900705_1.html (accessed February 10, 2021).

14 Anam Ajmal, "70% of global internet shutdowns in 2020 were in India: Report," *Times of India*, March 4, 2021, available at https://timesofindia.indiatimes.com/india/70-of-global-internet-shutdowns-in-2020-were-in-india-report/articleshow/81321980.cms (accessed February 12, 2021).

15 Nishant Shah, "Identity and Identification: The individual in the time of networked governance," *Socio-Legal Review*, Vol. 11, No. 2, 2015, available at http://docs.manupatra.in/newsline/articles/Upload/D47CF36C-C409-45BF-8AE6-659D7B6281FB.pdf (accessed February 10, 2021).

16 Nandan Nilekani, *Imagining India: The Idea of a Renewed Nation* (New York: Penguin Press, 2009).

push back against the mandates of these articulations of the user through infrastructural practices. However, in this naturalization and prioritization of infrastructure as a practice of articulating reality, we see infrastructure projects as both inevitable and unquestionable. Thus, even when we notice infrastructures failing and critique their shortcomings, eventually we tend to generate only two prewired responses: one, that we need more infrastructure, and two, that we need better infrastructure.

It is easy to see how this played out in the case of Free Basics. The project identified that the digital divide and uneven access were conditions of infrastructure building of the state and its "digital India" investments and development.[17] However, those behind the project saw this as merely a condition of infrastructure deficit, ignoring the fact that India had already leapfrogged into mobile technologies and robust penetration and coverage to its last mile. They did not examine the lack of access as a "last cultural mile" problem, in which the very logic and structure of infrastructure continues to alienate, exclude, and harm those who may not be able to bear the burden of being articulated by these technological processes.[18] Internet.org's claims that they would build the infrastructure for universal access immediately fell apart when they partnered with Reliance Telecom, because it was clear that they would be piggy-backing on an existing, expansive, and still expanding telecommunications infrastructure, rather than building a new digital infrastructure.[19] Unlike the Akaash tablets or the OLPC projects that actively equipped people with localized digital technology devices, Free Basics was not even looking at providing material devices, but instead was subsidizing access by expanding the user market.[20] This particular move, which is quite common in digital infrastructure projects, is what I call "articulated infrastructures," in which the questions of penetration, adoption, usage, inclusion, and ownership are formulated as questions of infrastructure, leading to greater investment in the expansion of infrastructure networks rather than in thinking through the political and material conditions of the people involved in the unfolding. Looking at the state's failure to translate and articulate the entire population as digital users, they emphasized that what was needed was more and better infrastructure. This more came in the guise of limited free access, and an internet without net neutrality and zero rating, where philanthropy and profits of the companies involved would dole out access while maintaining control over the larger landscape, creating tiered access levels for customers who could afford them.

Articulated infrastructures acknowledge the fact that digital infrastructure networks are uncertain and instable. The ideas of performative infrastructure, interactive infrastructure, posthuman infrastructure, cyborg infrastructure, affective infrastructure, and stacked infrastructure have all critically and fruitfully helped in unpacking the affordances and exclusions and the technological and regulatory frameworks that construct these. However, in almost all of these critiques of infrastructure,

17 Anita Gurumurthy and Nandini Chami, "Internet governance as 'ideology in practice'—India's 'Free Basics' controversy,'" *Internet Policy Review*, Vol. 5, No. 3, 2016, 1–17, DOI:10.14763/2016.3.431.

18 Aashish Rajadhyaksha, *The Last Cultural Mile* (Bengaluru: Centre for Internet & Society, 2011).

19 Aman Shah, "Facebook ties up with Reliance communications for internet push in India," *Business Today*, February 10, 2015, available at https://www.businesstoday.in/technology/internet/facebook-reliance-communications-tie-up-for-internet.org/story/215559.html (accessed August 13, 2021).

20 Suw Charman-Anderson, "Akash vs OLPC: How fair is Jha's anti-tablet grouse?," *Firstpost*, January 26, 2012, available at https://www.firstpost.com/tech/aakash-vs-olpc-how-fair-is-jhas-anti-tablet-grouse-194883.html/amp (accessed February 14, 2021).

there is a persistent presentation of infrastructures as the point of origin. They articulate infrastructures as a way of framing the problem as well as finding the solutions. Even when the human-technology cybernetic unit is seen as co-constitutive, there is no capacity to step out of the loop that reinforces the idea that technological infrastructure is both ontologically and teleologically inevitable. I propose that articulated infrastructures mobilize three particular principles that perpetuate their scope and scale: seamlessness, repair, and extension. In the unfolding of the Free Basics campaign in India, it is possible to locate and concretely pin down these principles and moves.

Seamless Seamlessness

The assumption underlying all technologies of information transfer is seamlessness. It is important for technologies to become ubiquitous and useful in that they offer ways by which routes for information dissemination can be established, eventually leading to the mobility of people and politics along those routes. As postcolonial critiques have shown us, this idea of easy transfer of goods and subsequently people has been at the basis of most technological developments for centuries. This is how technologies emerge as a "black box,"[21] where they naturalize the routes of seamlessness and turn them into "habitual practices."[22] Especially with the emergence of the Graphical User Interface (GUI) and user-centered design and engineering, we have seen how micro feedback loops continue to reinforce the idea of seamless interaction with digital technologies. With the prevalence of WYSIWYG principles that show a direct correlation between user action and the computed results[23]—the proliferation of likes, notifications, follows, and visual quantification of our digital practices, for example—there is an impression of seamlessness that our digital technologies perform continuously.[24] As a critical part of that cybernetic loop, human users perform gamified labor that keeps on closing the loop while also triggering further traffic, or what we have come to call "engagement."

So strong is the rhetoric of seamlessness, that any node in these information transfer networks that resists or steps out of it, is immediately considered either broken or disadvantaged, in both cases considered in need of immediate rehabilitation and interpellation.[25] This assumption of seamlessness allows for infrastructural needs to be articulated as emergent and urgent. In the case of Free Basics, they aligned themselves with the cause of universal access. Universal access proposes it offers connectivity to those who are on the suffering side of the digital divide. It is, however, also how people are made accessible to those who own technological infrastructures and services.[26] Universal access is not the same as universal ownership, rather it continues to place the "user" as a "consumer" of digital services. The universal access rhetoric presupposes that any user who is not a seamless node in the information transfer network is outside of that network and needs to be brought into the fold.

21 Bruno Latour, *Pandora's Hope: Essays on the Reality of Science Studies* (Cambridge, MA: Harvard University Press, 1999), 304.

22 Wendy Hui Kyong Chun, *Updating to Remain the Same: Habitual New Media* (Cambridge, MA: MIT Press, 2017).

23 WYSIWYG stands for What You See Is What You Get.

24 Anne Balsamo, *Designing Culture: The Technological Imagination at Work* (Durham: Duke University Press, 2011),

25 Albert-László Barabási, *Linked: The New Science of Networks*, (New York: Perseus Book, 2002).

26 V. Sridhar, *Emerging ICT Policies and Regulations: Roadmap to Digital Economies* (Singapore: Springer, 2019).

When Free Basics positioned itself as the provider of universal access, they ignored the fact that India is one of the most heavily digitally networked countries in the world. The proliferation of mobile telephony, the cheap rates of data access, and the availability of affordable mobile phones mean that while the broadband revolution may never have taken place, the mobile telephony network has a very strong presence.[27] With more than two mobile connections per residence, the entire ecosystem of pay-as-you-use data, offline and local networks, and app-specific connectivity—via single-service subscription to WhatsApp or YouTube, for instance—meant that large swaths of the population were already connected. Those who were left out of the fold were not excluded because of lack of physical infrastructure, but because of a confluence of social, political, linguistic, and cultural arrangements.[28]

For example, with the new security measures on internet usage set in place, and the linking of mobile phone connections with the Aadhaar card, the possibility of getting affordable connections by those who are either homeless, migrant, or undocumented, decreased substantially.[29] Similarly, regressive politics that refuse women in certain communities to access cell phones, or strict monitoring of social media usage for non-conforming persons, or regular sting operations and spying on queer and trans communities, have continued to form barriers of access and willful staying away from connectivity.[30] Instead of addressing some of these fundamental questions—freedom of speech and expression, the rights to self-determination, the conditions of safety and security, the laws of privacy—the Free Basics project focused on developing infrastructure and granting cheap and reduced access, promising that this would provide seamlessness. In effect, what it was performing was a perpetuation of conditions for those who remain outside the fold of seamless connectivity, and identifying potential new nodes of seamless transformation that would expand the network. Instead of focusing on critical questions that remain central to the shape of digital ecosystems in India—and globally in all network societies—they performed a seamless seamlessness, articulating infrastructure only as a question of access.

Repair without Maintenance

Both in its public presence as well as in the large-scale advertising campaigns, Free Basics set out to repair the "wrongs" that beset the Indian digital ecosystem. They identified a lack in the fact that the Indian state had failed to create the infrastructure needed for universal access, and produced a hack or intervention to repair this failure. Nowhere in their approach did they question the need or the dangers of "universal" access in a country that was simultaneously being challenged by massive censorship and internet shutdowns as well as widespread misinformation circulation. While Free Basics was able to invest money and resources in expanding the scale and scope of digital

27 Noshir Kaka et al., *Digital India: Technology to transform a connected nation*, McKinsey Global Institute, 2019, available at https://www.mckinsey.com/business-functions/mckinsey-digital/our-insights/digital-india-technology-to-transform-a-connected-nation# (accessed February 8, 2021).

28 V. Ilasvarasan, "The digital divide in India: Inferences from the information and communication technology workforce," in *The Digital Divide: The Internet and Social Inequality in International Perspective*, edited by Massimo Ragnedda and Glenn W. Muschert (London: Routledge, 2013).

29 Swetha Totapally et al., *State of Aadhaar: A people's perspective*, Dalberg, 2019, available at https://stateofaadhaar.in/assets/download/SoA_2019_Report_web.pdf (accessed February 20, 2021).

30 Tish Sanghera, "Wide gender gap in mobile phone access is hurting India's women," *IndiaSpend*, November 1, 2018, available at https://www.indiaspend.com/wide-gender-gap-in-mobile-phone-access-is-hurting-indias-women/ (accessed February 22, 2021).

infrastructure, in repairing the deficit that had been identified, those behind the program had no intentions or strategies of maintaining the fundamental rights and securities of users within these new systems of digital access.

Not only did they not engage with these fundamental questions, because they articulated the entire problem as merely an infrastructure and resource problem, they were ready to sacrifice the basic internet rights under the guise of do-goodery.[31] This idea of repair, shaped by a neoliberal Silicon Valley rhetoric of solutionism and replacement consumption, is central to projects like Free Basics. They approached it as a singular problem that can be "design thought" into a solution that would eventually benefit those who proffer the solution rather than those who are affected by the problem. It follows the same structures that gig economies such as ride sharing, home deliveries, and domestic work industries have adopted: in all of these, a particular problem is identified as a problem of infrastructure deficit. They immediately sought to either reform the old infrastructure by digitizing it, or replace it by rearticulating it through digital interventions. So strong and urgent is this drive of "repairing" the system, that all the effort is invested in "getting things done."[32]

The spirit of solutionism demands and effects multiple shifts in policy, governance, ownership, and regulatory frameworks, and often also suggests a state of exceptionalism for innovation to happen. In changing this landscape, they propose inserting a cog that has to change the system within which it has to make sense. The new system is therefore effectively a repair of the old system, offering solutions to what were framed as infrastructure problems. However, in this offered repair, there is no sense of maintenance; the immediacy of the proposed solution comes without a vision of long-term durability or sustainability at the level of hardware or usage. The ICT4D portfolios in India, which insisted on building computer stations in villages without electricity access, or created digital textual interfaces for communities that had low literacy rates, or tying long-term contracts to corporations that pushed hardware that was planned into obsolescence and cannot be replaced, are all glaring examples of this lack of maintenance that drives this solutionist repair approach.[33] In the process of repairing and replacing, very little attention is paid to the people being replaced, to those who are seen as a problem in the repair process, and are therefore rehabilitated or migrated away, or to the materiality of the future horizons of this infrastructure. In short, in its articulation of infrastructure the Free Basic campaign refused to recognize the three critical problems of its solutionism.

First, they did not acknowledge that they were tying into the telecommunications monopoly that Reliance Telecom had aspired to, and the economic value of getting first dibs on the next billion users who would be newly introduced to digital internet connectivity. In pushing their "universal" access agenda

31 Casey Chan, "Surprise! Facebook wants to get the entire world on the Internet," *Gizmodo*, August 20, 2013, available at https://gizmodo.com/facebook-wants-to-get-everybody-in-the-world-on-the-int-1175829249 (accessed February 20, 2021).

32 Melissa Gregg, *Counterproductive: Time Management in the Knowledge Economy* (Durham: Duke University Press, 2018).

33 C.P. Chandrashekhar, "ICT in a Developing Country context: An Indian Case Study," 2001, available at https://core.ac.uk/download/pdf/6248682.pdf (accessed February 24, 2021).

through this corporate partnership, they also willfully ignored the local information and connectivity ecosystems in which multiple telephony shops, local area network providers, and human connectors in the different information hubs would be replaced by the formalized and corporatized model of granting access.

Second, they clearly put the onus of connectivity on the people who were disconnected. The phones were already present, the infrastructure for connectivity was already built. The reason why large sections of the population had no internet and digital information access had very little to do with the digital infrastructure and everything to do with willful exclusion. It is ironic that while Free Basics was advocating for universal access, India was already emerging as a country with the highest and longest internet shutdowns in the world, clearly demonstrating that keeping people disconnected is used to curb freedom of speech and the free flowing of information in the country. Instead, in the Free Basics rhetoric, it was the farmer who didn't access the crop information, or the woman who could not gain digital literacy skills who were responsible for their own betterment, because they would get access to the digital information highway.

Third, they persistently presented their intended beneficiaries as without power or agency or ability to negotiate. The large advertisement campaigns that launched the project, aligned with the state's propaganda of access to digital information as the savior, positioning it as the ideal civil society project that would fulfil the state's vision of a digital and connected India. As an ally, they could then lobby for the state to shift the regulatory networks that would give them free and unfettered access to the new market created through "universal" access.

This approach is one of repair without maintenance, articulating a social-political problem as an infrastructure problem. It immediately proposes access as the solution, locating infrastructure deficit or participation deficit as the key factors. Under the guise of building new infrastructures and providing new access conditions, it manipulates and triggers massive regulatory and governance changes to benefit the repairers rather than those who are vulnerable and precarious, and puts the onus of transformation onto those newly installed in these new infrastructures, as known and legible entities that can be guided into digital transactions. It is important that while these projects often do offer new inroads into networks and material infrastructure expansion, they have no long-term vision and very little commitment toward maintaining these practices and processes over a sustained period of time. They also position themselves as neutral in these infrastructure building practices. It was no surprise that when India started getting mired in cybernetic misinformation loops, leading to lynch mobs, deaths, and rampant abuse of power through violence on marginalized groups, the companies behind Free Basics were silent about their responsibility in creating the conditions for misinformation circulation. The idea of repair without maintenance disguises the larger and complex, material, and embodied vulnerabilities it produces for those who can least afford to bear its costs.

Extensions of Scale

The idea of connectivity is quite challenging. As Asha Achuthan has helped us understand, the entire rhetoric of access, inclusion, presence, and rights that frames the digital technology for development portfolio is problematic when framing connectivity.[34] When it comes to digital technological infrastructure, connectivity is always presented as a question of scale, and quantification is presented as the basic principle of digital transactions. The emergence of a democratized digital web has led to the quantification of a variety of human dimensions—friendships, popularity, influence, impact—and continues to champion the expansion of scale as the only true digital economic aspiration. As Soshanna Zuboff explains, the only currency of digital corporations is data, however, what this data actually captures is so scant and pitiful that compensation through an economy of scale is needed.[35] It is only through scale and a seemingly infinite amount of data generation and storage that the attention economies of digital infrastructures can be sustained.

It is no wonder, then, that metrics of engagement, transaction, action, and transfer become the *de facto* modes of thinking through digital systems. However, in the case of the Free Basics campaign, the value of universal access defied mere quantification. While universal access is definitely related to creating scaled-up coverage, it is also clear that that cannot be the only axis of measurement. Especially in increasingly literate countries like India, the state's ambitions of technological spread and literacy have always been formulated in terms of intensity and address. As technology historian Ravi Sundaram points out in his work on "Pirate Modernity," the ambition of the state was not just to reach everyone, but to do so meaningfully, in ways that would establish a relationship of informational proximity.[36] In fact, the history of technology expansion in India is littered with stories of what happens when the contextual conditions of a technology network do not provide enough grounds for technology accessibility to happen.

Perhaps one of the most telling examples of technological extensions of scale without meaningful intensity of context is the ongoing problem of misinformation cycles that have emerged in India, like in the rest of the world. Although obvious, but worth repeating is that the largest problem of misinformation cycles is universal access. India's mobile phone revolution was so unprecedented and accelerated that there was almost no time to create localized, specific, and meaningful connections between technological networks and the human communities they were being installed in. Mobile phones with affordable data connections immediately connected a variety of people who did not even have the keyboards and input devices

34 Asha Achuthan, *Re:wiring Bodies* (Bengaluru: Centre for Internet & Society, 2011).

35 Soshanna Zuboff, *The Age of Surveillance Capitalism: The Fight for a Human Future at the New Frontier of Power* (New York: Public Affairs, 2019).

36 Ravi Sundaram, *Pirate Modernity: Delhi's Media Urbanism* (New York: Routledge, 2009).

of their local contexts to be connected online. However, this mass democratization of infrastructure resulted in a massive number of first-generation digital users jumping straight onto mobile data infrastructure networks without any literacy, sensibility, or discernment tools in how to engage with the information they encountered.

Given that this was *terra incognita* for a large user base, it was easy to manipulate, misinform, and trigger them into a continuous chain of engagement and sharing. These extensions of scale became problematic, because they triggered users into intensities of action. The reason behind the violent, loud, and polarized organization of action did not happen at a national level, with the whole country coming together to engage in collective action; on the contrary, the extensions of scale took place in "small worlds" with people clustered into "network neighborhoods" and kept in a state of constant emotional intensity escalation.[37] The success of misinformation cycles operating through echo chambers lies not in universal but in localized access. The contrary is also true: that the success of a responsible and responsive information transformation needs localized infrastructure, owned by and resonating with the needs and challenges of the communities that seek to be affected by it.

The critics and activists who pushed back against Free Basics, pointing out its crony capitalism and its misdirected ambition under the guise of universal access, were quite successful in making their concerns public.[38] Their cause was taken up by many celebrities and influencer groups, who quickly advised the population not to be misguided by the promises of universal access, which only accounted for an extension of scale without an increase in engagement. In response to these activists, Free Basics started a massive advertisement campaign, anchoring itself to "real Indians." They characterized the activists and public defenders of net neutrality as standing in the way of digital equality and progress. Marc Zuckerberg's passionate but misguided op-ed in the largest English language newspaper, *Times of India*, claimed, "Instead of wanting to give people access to some basic internet services for free, critics of the program continue to spread false claims—even if that means leaving behind a billion people ... Who could possibly be against this?"[39]

The advertisements focused on the Indian user who "needed to be saved." Featuring young women holding phones, looking at the horizon in hope; in another, henna-covered female hands clasped together, embodying "a first step toward digital equality," suggesting that "Free Basics by Facebook" would lead to women's technological empowerment. One campaign focused on a farmer called Ganesh, posing with his family, showing the faces of those who suffer from digital inequality, endorsing Free Basics as the solution to their situation. The campaign claimed that

> Free Basics by Facebook is a first step to connecting one billion Indians to jobs, education, and opportunities

37 Duncan J. Watts, *Small Worlds: The Dynamics of Networks between Order and Randomness* (Princeton: Princeton University Press, 1999).

38 Saif Shahin, "Facing up to Facebook: How Digital Activism, Independent Regulation, and Mass Media foiled a Neoliberal Threat to Net Neutrality," *Information, Communication and Society*, Vol. 22 No. 1, January 2019, 1–17, DOI:10.1080/1369118X.2017.1340494.

39 Zuckerberg, "Free Basics protects net neutrality."

> online, and ultimately a better future. But Free Basics is at risk of being banned, slowing progress towards digital equality in India. Show your support for Free Basics now, and help move India forward. SUPPORT DIGITAL EQUALITY.[40]

These campaigns also introduced a call for action, asking the supporters to register "missed calls" to a national number in support of a lobby to the Ministry of Telecommunication to establish Free Basics and step out of the net neutrality agreements.[41] Again, instead of providing information on how this connectivity infrastructure was going to solve the problems of illiteracy or unemployment, instead of explaining how these initiatives would connect with and unpack the problems that digital inequality poses for growing networked countries, they depended on the logic of scale to make their point. Reducing the campaign against Free Basics to a numbers game, they used the number of "missed calls" as a poll of public sentiment, squashing critique with the logic of extension and scale.

It is a spectacular story, worth celebrating that in early 2016 Free Basics and other such aspiring free-but-restricted internet services were banned in India, after the national Telecom Regulatory Authority of India (TRAI) ruled that the right to access is more than just a numbers game, informed by millions of users quickly inducted into the debate. Citing its own Prohibition of Discriminatory Tariffs for Data Services Regulations law, the TRAI affirmed that service providers cannot "offer or charge discriminatory tariffs for data services on the basis of content being accessed by a consumer."[42] The judgment ended by reframing the debate where universal access and net neutrality were no longer in conflict but were both necessary "to ensure that consumers get unhindered and non-discriminatory access to the internet."[43] When thinking about digital infrastructure, it is important to look at both the intensive and extensive qualities embedded within it. The rhetoric of scale often positions the intensive and extensive properties as antithetical, leading to a conflict the resolution for which leads to justifying discrimination, control or abuse of power.

Disarticulated Infrastructures

"Disarticulated Infrastructures" provide a discursive and material intervention in these performances of articulated infrastructures. They offer a way of mapping the three tropes outlined above—seamless seamlessness, repair without maintenance, and extensions of scale—that need to be identified when dealing with questions of infrastructure and relationships with people, communities, and ideas that are often elided when we focus on infrastructures as simply articulated projects. Disarticulation is a methodological proposal that seeks to unpack infrastructures at the seams, breaking up the seams, looking at conditions of maintenance and the labor borne by the invisible bodies who

40 Rahul Bhatia, "The inside story of Facebook's biggest setback," *The Guardian*, May 12, 2016, available at https://www.theguardian.com/technology/2016/may/12/facebook-free-basics-india-zuckerberg (accessed February 22, 2021).

41 Arun Prabhudesai, "TRAI's response to multi-million dollar Free Basic campaign will restore your faith in government agencies!," *Trak*, January 4, 2017, available at https://trak.in/tags/business/2016/01/20/trai-response-free-basic-campaign/ (accessed February 20, 2021).

42 Yuthika Bhargava, "TRAI rules in favour of Net Neutrality," *The Hindu*, February 8, 2016, available at https://www.thehindu.com/sci-tech/technology/internet/TRAI-rules-in-favour-of-Net-neutrality/article14068029.ece (accessed August 13, 2021).

43 Press Information Bureau, Government of India, "Telecom Regulatory Authority of India Issues 'Prohibition of discriminatory tariffs for data service regulators 2016,'" available at https://pib.gov.in/newsite/PrintRelease.aspx?relid=136211 (accessed February 20, 2021).

perform it, and the recognition of intensities that are often encoded in the materiality of these infrastructure projects.

Disarticulated Infrastructures thus become a more diffuse and distributed set of nodes, traffic flows, exchanges, and edges. They recognize digital infrastructure as a complex system—a stack, as Benjamin Bratton would have it—that operates on multiple layers that continue to make our digital devices simultaneously "transparent and opaque."[44] When thinking about digital infrastructures in our everyday practices, disarticulated infrastructures offer touchstones by which the articulations of technology can be disrupted. The problems with articulated infrastructure that I have outlined—including the net neutrality debates in India—are persistent and widespread across a spectrum of digital infrastructure projects that fall in the gap between the intention and materiality of their unfolding. In order to counter these articulated performances, I offer six characteristics that can help us produce disarticulated infrastructures as counter strategies. We call these the ESTAMP touchstones.[45]

Infrastructures are *Embodied*, because they directly affect the bodies in practice, their identities, transactions, and livelihoods. Infrastructures need to be *Situated* so that they can challenge and resist the global narratives of digital simultaneity and instead understand the disruptions that they create within local and temporal geographies and contexts. Articulation of infrastructures is not the same as making them explicit, and we need to find ways of making the *Tacit* knowledge in these infrastructural projects more visible and accessible. It is important to identify these tacit knowledges as perpetuating inequity and disenfranchisement of the "users" of these infrastructure projects. It helps to position these touchstones as *Affective* in nature; eschewing the call for rationality and pattern recognition logic that is naturalized in the articulation of these practices. Especially within digital infrastructure projects there is often a tendency to focus on the virtuality of the medium, and we need to emphasize the *Materiality* of the devices, technologies, and connections that often take up normative exclusions and performative resistances. And finally, it is imperative that we recognize the articulation of infrastructures as a *Political* process. Infrastructures are opinions expressed, and they carry with them the biases and the inequities of the people who hold these opinions. Making the politics embedded in infrastructure explicit and overt allows us to identify the areas where interventions can be made in order for humane futures to be introduced into their unfolding.

The idea of disarticulated infrastructures, then, offers a lens, a framework, and a narrative to help produce a vocabulary and intervention in the digital articulation of infrastructure projects, by introducing new languages, processes, people, and resistances that can open up digital infrastructures to questions beyond their own asking.

44 Chun, *Updating to Remain the Same*.

45 Nishant Shah and Maya Indira Ganesh, "Between Memory and Storage: Digital transitions for art organisations," in *Forces of Art*, edited by Carin Kuoni, Jordi Baltai Portoles, Nora N. Khan, and Serubiri Moses (Amsterdam: Valiz, 2020).

REDISTRIBUTIONS
Tirdad Zolghadr

Infrastructures of Critique

By and large, the field of contemporary art today encourages the interesting and complicated over the important and obvious. We prefer to bicker over the originality of a project, gesture, or choice of words, rather than state a simple fact, especially if that fact is plain for all to see, or has been highlighted before, no matter how relevant to our lives that point may be. To be unmasked as a cliché? ... We'd rather die. Sometimes, in the hope of being able to get on with business as usual, we pretend that the difference between the interesting and the important is too hard to spot. Luckily, there are places out there that make the differences painfully clear. And when it comes to building better infrastructure, the best-case scenario is precisely that: the kind of places we should be aiming for are those where the sense of what is important is driven home to us without apology, pomp, or circumstance.

Infrastructure itself is not always interesting, but its importance is hard to deny. Thinking of the very term, In—Fra—Struck—Tchrrr, noises that sound like German architecture. Forever important in that meat-and-potatoes kind of way. Sure enough, given that infrastructure largely shapes our field, by defining our conditions of production and embodying ideological foundations upon which a collective future is built, a proper discussion of infrastructural analysis, re-examination, speculation, is long overdue. As for "critique," infrastructural or otherwise: not only is critique by definition interesting and complicated, it allows for a rhetorical armor that suggests we somehow stand apart from the powers that be. The question of whether, compared to other fields, contemporary art really is any closer to or further removed from the powers that be, is hard to answer. Thanks to the persistence of critique as our dog whistle, object, and method, our relationship to the corridors of power has become hard to discern.

You may be wondering why the above is any more than just another "interesting" point, and you may be right in doing so. But consider whether, after all that critiquery that defines our working lives, it is even possible to respect a position that is straightforward, unambiguous, in-fra-struc-tu-ral, meat-and-potatoes? We are not speaking of critique as one tool among many. This is critique that is systematically screamed from the rooftops, routinely hollered, snickered, and mumbled from the wall tags, book covers, and press releases. Is this mode of engagement helpful when forging environments that may better cement our professional survival, improve our working conditions, let alone rejig the ideological foundations of our collective future? Admittedly, provided that critique is demystified and put in its place, it can be more than just an interesting part of an important problem. When that exasperation remains a catalyst, and not a systemic carnival of whiny affirmation ("the art world sucks!"), critique can be the ground that proposals can proceed from. Proceed *from*—not build *upon* ...

Arrièregarde Blueprints

Moving away from a critique of critique, and toward what could be considered the "Good Object," recent infrastructural efforts—small to midsized artist-run experiments for the most part—have undoubtedly proven the viability of redistributive agendas, even within contemporary art. But before getting to those, I would like to mention some of their distant ancestors: the public museum behemoths. The shortcoming of these latter-day experiments remains the resistance to scale and replicability, and the restriction to unique, fascinating, heroic instances. Modern behemoths were scaled across the world, despite (or perhaps because of) the enormous ambitions they embodied. A distinctive feature of these museal ancestors is their reputation of rock-hard durability: the idea that they transcended fashion, and were steadfast enough to hang around for generations to come. For better or worse, their footing has proven flimsier than envisaged. The enlightened, humanist, high-cultural, proto-national foundations they stood for have taken a beating, and our museums have tended to whither, sell out, or sulk.

To name but two examples, it was the mid-1970s when both the Centre Pompidou and the Palast der Republik were inaugurated, in Paris and East Berlin respectively. Big buildings, besaddled with XL expectations. Enchanting modernism. Today, the Berlin Palace of the Republic, with its High Communist élan—all glass and steel, white, and gold—has been demolished, to make room for a gargantuan, Christianic shrine to Prussian feudalism. As for the Pompidou, until very recently it was hosting nearly six million visitors a year. Compare them with the Tehran Museum of Contemporary Art. Although built at the same time as its European cousins, it is sitting tight. For now, it is just determined—to be nothing more than wildly determined. A venue in no hurry to interconnect with anything or anyone else. A museum with a daylight zone of its own. The quality of time in there is slow, oily, pasty. Unctuous. Time doesn't simply pass. It slinks and quivers, like a dying reptile. The self-importance of the Tehran venue is such that it imposes a time regime of its own. There is no future on offer here—neo-feudal, mass-consumerist, or otherwise—nothing beyond this time-machine experience itself. That is why the "contemporary" in the museum name is not misleading in the slightest. If anything, it is spot on. These days, a wildly self-determined time regime is the best an art museum can offer. Hanging in there, time for time's sake.

Modern is different. The one common ground of any modernism—Parisian, Prussian, Persian, or otherwise—was the unshakable knowledge that the future would be *something else*. That it would offer another perspective on human emancipation, possibly in our lifetimes. And for all its shortcomings, it is the modernist willingness to take that risk, and fail, that offers a hopeful blueprint here. In the best of cases, such as the Bauhaus, even modern art infrastructure was already believed to pursue a redistributive agenda, to the benefit of constituencies beyond art itself. The establishment of a time regime beyond the endless slipstream of the endlessly contemporary, is nothing short of a terrific, brilliant, invaluable achievement. To offer any such chronopolitical alternative to the omnivorous present that rules the day is nothing to be scoffed at. Could we imagine infrastructures with the arrogance and staying power of the Tehran museum, coupled with the idealistic bluster of mainstream modernism at large—but with a redistributive agenda, to the benefit of constituencies beyond art?

Newer Blueprints

What unites latter-day models with their modern forerunners in terms of method, is, first of all, the artistic appetite for long-term, deliberate planning. What also stands out is a shared, confident sense of expertise—even among artists. The final characteristic is a better sense of realism in terms of storytelling, one that does not shy away from facts on the ground. I've come to see these three elements as crucial ingredients over the course of curatorial practice and research conducted since circa 2013, most recently with REALTY, a long-term study of the relationship between contemporary art and real estate.[1] The following is an example I've shared before—but it's an encouraging one, offering a rare happy end even. So bear with me as I retell the story of the House of Statistics (HdS), here in Berlin.[2]

The HdS was an abandoned 40,000m² modernist moloch, right in the middle of the city. As large as a neighborhood, and historically haunted on account of its iconic role in GDR data management. Post 1989, it was slated for demolition, as part of an aggressive plan to Manhattanize the Berlin skyline. In 2015, the AbBA collective pulled off a street-party-as-art intervention, which included a large banner with the municipal logo on the HdS façade, announcing a new public facility for all types of sociocultural purposes.[3] The happening was symbolic, because demolition of the building was long approved. Yet within a few years, the idea went from catchy and viral to self-fulfilling prophecy. Today, the HdS is a pioneering development steered by a broad coalition of actors. Thanks to AbBA, sale and demolition were prevented, and a 65,000m² extension is now being built, providing space for culture, social work, education, low-cost housing, as well as a new city hall and municipal offices.

1 See http://realtynow.online/?lang=en (accessed January 16, 2021).

2 In the guise of STATISTA, a collaboration between Zentrum für Kunst und Urbanistik and myself as associate curator at KW Institute for Contemporary Art Berlin, I had the pleasure of playing a microscopic part in this adventure over the course of 2019.

3 AbBA stands for the Berlin Alliance of Artists' Studios Under Threat.

The fairy-tale ending sets the stage for a dazzling experiment of artists rubbing shoulders with all manners of other constituencies, including social workers and technocrats. Even more impressive is the wild variety of criteria the HdS depended upon in the first place to become a long-term success. At this macro scale, the leverage of cultural capital toward policymaking ends is a rare feat, for good reason.

First of all, the HdS initiative offers a contrast to the myth of Berlin as an innocent playground of pop-up project spaces, so touch-and-go, so breathless and short-lived. Instead, the HdS valorizes a long-term timeline that seems geological in comparison. This in itself is not to be taken for granted: flux and indeterminacy now come so naturally to arts practitioners that it is hard for us to see these tropes as the tools of governance they've long become. Our ability to make the interesting/unpredictable trump the important/dependable is remarkable enough. Even so, it does not compare to the skill of policymakers, who have somehow succeeded in making insecurity and atomization desirable values on a mass scale.

The dialectical counterpunch, the antidote to this unprecedented historical trend, would be a demand for clearly regulated rights and responsibilities, for binding (infra)structures, and for a professionalized network of durable solidarity. For many reasons, no such dialectical counterpunch is on the horizon, structurally speaking, even now. For every artist or curator who has created such an (infra)structure, one that succeeds in entrenching anything at all, there are a hundred who are a little busy right now, or who changed their mind along the way (myself included). Which doesn't mean that those artists and curators aren't out there: we can find dozens who did engage in the challenge of creating redistributive infrastructures to spectacular effect. Time and again, one sees artists' uncanny ability to build structures that endure over years and decades, some of which, from ruangrupa to e-flux, reaching hegemonic status within the field. They offer invaluable models in that they loudly exemplify important steps beyond business as usual. That said, the jackpot, the dog's bollocks, the best-case scenario materializes only when professional stability is aggressively harnessed to a redistributive agenda beyond endurance alone.

New Criteria for Newer Blueprints

Consider the Zentrum für Kunst und Urbanistik, which played a key role in the HdS initiative. Or Furtherfield in London, devoted to channeling the redistributive potentials of new tech and smart automation. The Centre d'art des travailleurs de plantations Congolaises in Lusanga, and its working partner, the Institute for Human Activities, have together enabled a growing, sustainable "post-plantation," run by small farmers. exRotaPrint Berlin secured the long-term survival of speculation-proof property that caters to immediate neighborhood needs. Planbude works toward a large-scale affordable housing project in Hamburg. And so on.

Binding, long-term tessellations aside, what these examples offer are blueprints for artists working as qualified experts in something more than just critique. The HdS depended on a good deal of hard knowledge among artists who had navigated the city-political waters for decades. Coming to terms with facts on the ground, and with a theorization of one's impact on the world, is strenuous enough. As for a better understanding of infrastructure, it may not be rocket science, but it does demand a minimal degree of specialization: it implies other timelines than "gotta work like hell for that show next month." It implies the courage to specialize and be predictable, even boring at times. You cannot defend such positions by virtue of critique and inspiration alone, you need skill sets that take years and years to assemble.

If, for now, contemporary art takes so much pride in "unknowing," this wasn't always the case. You will find instances from Bauhaus to blockchain that have no issues with hard knowledge, or seemingly boring facts. But even within the art mainstream as we know it, whenever critique becomes proposal, whenever playing-on-a-representation becomes Representation full stop, whenever sexy agnostics become a narrative claim, we are inching beyond the happy incapacitation of art today.

More examples: the BLOCC collective helps art students reimagine their place within the real estate food chain—from the very beginning of their trajectories, when there is still hope of foundations for a whole other artist imaginary.[4] Vermeir & Heiremans have unearthed superb terminologies and legal instruments to reform the circumstances of ownership around Pump House Gallery in London. openBerlin do comparable work across the German capital, in collaboration with policymakers and grassroots networks. Come Greet the Dawn, by Luiza Crosman & Pedro Moraes, is an off-grid solar system connected to a cryptocurrency miner on a blockchain, commissioned for the 33rd São Paolo Biennial in 2018. The aim was a permanent means of producing energy, as well as redistribution of resources beyond the biennial itself.

I am coming to the last of my three working criteria: better narratives, featuring "Best-Case Scenarios" and realistic "Good Objects." This requires solidarity, for instance, but as fancy and effective, not rootsy and cute; the pleasures of knowing, as opposed to the look of thought; the dialectical clash of categories, over and above those marshy misunderstandings of a pleasantly confused audience. Contrary to creative belief, even measurability is worth a try, and need not spell death by bureaucracy. See the claims of many an NGO, that even the common good is quantifiable. Compare the Sakakini Cultural Center Ramallah, which, beginning with the tenure of artist Yazan Khalili (2018–20), aimed for new models of financial autonomy altogether, where fundraising and funds became part and parcel of cultural production on all levels. Everything from working hours to merchandise and ticket sales, from divisions of labor to curatorial decisions and health insurance was part of a cohesive,

4 For Building Leverage Over Creative Capitalism (BLOCC), see http://www.blocc.live/ (accessed January 21, 2021).

agenda-driven effort. Or one can look to the artist troika terra0, who have devoted their careers to helping a forest to self-regulate and grow of its own accord by means of smart contracts on blockchain. Or Campus in Camps, grappling with UNESCO technocracy to achieve official heritage status for refugee camps in the West Bank ...

The ultimate, provocative possibility here is that of thinking quantity and scale positively. Acres of farmland and woodland multiplied. Financialization as method. Global technocracy as ally. Quantity in and of itself, as a means to a given end. In a field such as ours, quirky exceptionalism is much more tempting than imagining a future of mass quantities in non-dystopian terms (mass consumerism, mainstream commercialism, totalitarianism, etc.) I cannot help but insist on Fredric Jameson's "utopia as replication," which famously identifies Walmart as a moral horizon of sorts.[5]

In the wake of the Covid-19 pandemic and our new limits on international travel, it is art residencies that provide the most hopeful new ground, the big art world opportunity for a mass-infrastructural retrofit. A good two centuries ago, at a time when art was meant to supplant religion, it was pilgrim hostels, convents, and monasteries that were converted into artist residencies. Many of them nostalgically replicated the Renaissance as a *locus amoenus*, a place of holistic innocence. Some residencies became the very content of art itself: it was through the cult of antique masters, the idea of an artistic way of life, that the artist could be Artist, one last time. A residency was about copies of not only the work, but of the very lives lived, the light and the climate, and so on. Some artists already saw this shift as a future source of structural poverty from the start. In an 1828 edition of the *Berliner Tageblatt*, Gottfried Schadow warned his readers that "the ever more liberal support which the fine arts enjoy, especially the new travel stipends for young artists, will certainly multiply the already incredible popularity among needy young people."

Today, we could, once again, rework the transcontinental sprawl of Goethe Institutes, DAADS, IASPISes, Cittadellartes, the glamorized studio sublets, the castle retreats, the easyjet-set squalor, into something less in-permanent-flux, less breathless and less "interesting." Fantastical modern infrastructures, such as highways, museums, or lunar colonies no longer capture our imagination. But their scaleability, and, on occasion, viscous staying power might—especially when coupled with recent, wild agendas of unapologetic redistribution. At the very least, the combination sounds interesting, as well as important, and critical to boot. We should be curious enough to imagine it replicated on a mass scale, cantilevered and projected, mushrooming and spreading all over the place. Weirder things have happened.

5 Fredric Jameson, *An American Utopia* (Brooklyn: Verso, 2016).

Infrastructural

2

Speculation

THE CURRENCY OF CONTEMPORARY ART

João Enxuto and Erica Love

About five years ago we directed our research to tracking proposals for shifting the field of art toward more meaningful creative autonomy and material equity. By field of art, we mean a social field mediated through power relations, and by power relations we mean a direct engagement with the realities of capital. In a 2016 essay, Hito Steyerl observed that art only gains its relative stability as a currency because of "nontransparency, and because of its overwhelming reliance on human relations."[1] This excerpt is a footnote nested among a dizzying array of incisive observations, most of which remain unresolved five years on. If we follow Steyerl, and accept the premise that the stability, and therefore the intelligibility of art as a form of currency, is directly proportional to its structural opacity, then our investigation is faced with a seemingly unworkable quandary: the deeper one burrows into the financial infrastructure of contemporary art, the more it becomes shrouded in mystification.

Under these uncertain circumstances, an appeal to data to provide analytic grounding may be welcomed. Having previously embarked on an errand to demystify the art market's valorization process through an analysis of algorithmic models, we quickly discovered that algorithmic tools confer insights to potential buyers on the level of the artist who paints by number.[2] Data sets compiled for predictive market analysis are crystallizations of prior social relations: like gathering up bits of neglected gossip, or #keywording curatorial statements buried in a stack of art journal back issues, or most likely, by mapping the secondary market acquisitions of a few committed patrons.

An open secret that art workers carry as part of their jobs is the knowledge that vast swaths of contemporary art infrastructure are little more than commodity clearinghouses to maintain the trickle down of philanthropy. An unencumbered portion of artists and art workers apparently assent to these terms.[3] Others may struggle before giving way to resignation, while steelier individuals are seemingly born to swim in blood-infested waters. Whatever the individual disposition, it is clear that a field dedicated to nurturing human creativity is constrained in its ability to incentivize the imagination to secure a just socio-economic future for itself. Steyerl reminds us that "like civilization as a whole, art would be a great idea."[4]

1 Hito Steyerl, "If You Don't Have Bread, Eat Art!: Contemporary Art and Derivative Fascisms," *e-flux journal*, # 76, October 2016, available at https://www.e-flux.com/journal/76/69732/if-you-don-t-have-bread-eat-art-contemporary-art-and-derivative-fascisms/ (accessed July 17, 2021).

2 João Enxuto and Erica Love, "When Zero Equals Affinity," in *In the Mind But Not From There: Real Abstraction and Contemporary Art*, edited by Gean Moreno (London: Verso, 2019).

3 Sarah Cascone, "Working-Class Employees Are Vastly Underrepresented in Culture Jobs, a New UK Study Reports: Women and people of color also face significant obstacles," *Artnet*, April 17, 2018, available at https://news.artnet.com/art-world/study-of-inequality-in-the-arts-1267601 (accessed July 22, 2021).

4 Steyerl, "If You Don't Have Bread, Eat Art."

Steyerl's text remains significant: firstly, for its ability to convey the savagery of peak art market financialization, and secondly, to counterpose those conditions with the rising tide of cryptoeconomics. Her basic proposition is if "art is an alternative currency, its circulation also outlines an operational infrastructure. Could these structures be repossessed to work differently?" In what follows, we endeavor to revisit the open question of art's capacity as an alternative currency, and inversely, to consider the viability of currency as art. In the midst of a cryptocurrency boom and a lingering global pandemic, can financial infrastructures be repurposed?

From its start, the blockchain network was considered a "trust machine" that validated transactions through the proof-of-work outputs of cryptocurrency mining.[5] In short, blockchain is a government of code, not of humans. It is a proposal for a peer-to-peer money system that circumvents banks, governments, and legal systems. Early adherents could be plotted on an ideological graph somewhere between libertarians and crypto-anarchists. The promise of emancipation—or at least autonomy through anonymity—galvanized a core community of coders, hackers, and technologists that would eventually expand to adjacent disciplines such as economics, finance, philosophy, and cultural production, particularly with the introduction of Ethereum (Ether or ETH) and the programmability of blockchain protocols in 2015.

The task of writing an appraisal of blockchain infrastructure for the art world suddenly became more complicated as we entered the early weeks of 2021: protracted social isolation, screen dependency, cheap money, and a penchant for speculation contributed to the growing compulsion for digital assets. As in-person art infrastructures became dormant, and art workers were sacked or furloughed, screen-based experiences were positioned to achieve primacy. The global material matrix that allowed art to perform the trick of liquidity—free ports, art fairs, etc.—were temporarily moved off-stage. The old bad objects were replaced with new ones, as wrangling over the massive carbon footprint of globetrotting was eclipsed by concerns over the ecological impact of cryptocurrency mining.

The trading price of Ether cryptocurrency nearly doubled in the first week of January and continued to increase until a market downturn in late May. Despite that dip, the value of cryptocurrency remains high and relatively stable up to the time of this writing. Three years have passed since ETH and Bitcoin (BTC), the cryptocurrency with the largest market capitalization, first spiked in value, triggering renewed debates on the purpose, promise, and problems presented by blockchain protocols. Emerging contemporaneously with a bull cryptocurrency market, NFT mania nearly broke the internet in early 2021. The NFT, or non-fungible token, a certificate of ownership that is verified using blockchain technology, became the primary vehicle for monetizing digital content.[6] Over several weeks, the online phenomenon produced a seemingly inexhaustible outpouring

5 Jaya Klara Brekke, "Disassembling the Trust Machine: Three cuts on the political matter of blockchain," PhD thesis, Durham University, 2019, available at http://distributingchains.info/wp-content/uploads/2019/06/DisassemblingTrustMachine_Brekke2019.pdf (accessed August 17, 2021).

6 The digital assets that have recently been minted into NFTS are unique and, unlike money, cannot be traded for something else. They can be instantly sold again and this transaction is recorded on the blockchain. The digital assets that have been created in this current frenzy have been images, usually JPEGS, made with the latest digital 3D-imaging software. A purchase of an NFT is for a link to the JPEG, not the JPEG itself, and copyright is unlikely to be included.

of responses from the legacy news media, podcasts, art journals, Twitter, and any publishing platform willing to indulge in the zeitgeist. But before descending further into an NFT rabbit hole, let's zoom out to consider existing entanglements between contemporary art and finance at a time when a cryptocurrency surge has begun to take hold.

Market Reflexivity

In their analysis of the recent history of art, markets, and finance, Victoria Ivanova and Gerald Nestler claim, unambiguously, that "the consolidation of the critical art paradigm" emerged as the dominant framework for understanding approaches to finance in the field of contemporary art.[7] Within the critical art paradigm, they identify a mode of "performative reflexivity" as indicative of practices that engage an artist's own critical position within the art market. For Ivanova and Nestler the performance of "market reflexivity" is notably argued in Isabelle Graw's often cited 2009 book, *High Price*, as a method that "allows the critical paradigm to have its cake and eat it, too …."[8] This is a privileged dynamic, enacted by a select group of artists who take market activity as their material at the same time as opposing it. More specifically, market reflexivity is "a position that not only allows critical art to accept its inclusion in the dynamics of capitalization and private wealth creation but also salvages Adorno and Horkheimer's dialectical vision for an art under capitalism."[9]

Ivanova and Nestler claim that Graw's approach maintains "an artificial boundary of ethical judgment, which serves to preserve the critical art paradigm as a sector distinct from contemporary art's affirmations of the global financial order."[10] Graw's interpretation of Adornian negative dialectics supports her claim for the "special status of art as commodity."[11] The market reflexivity of the fine arts, distinct from "culture industry" sectors, aims to preserve autonomy for contemporary art in the face of a corporatized global market, but it does so while simultaneously adding—social, ethical political—value to the ecosystem. This integration of value regimes produces what Ivanova and Nestler call a "dissonance" between the realities of financial infrastructure and discursive positions within the field of art.[12]

Contemporary art production that affirm market dynamics—from artists such as Jeff Koons, Damien Hirst, and more recently KAWS—have served to articulate the realities of financial infrastructure while monumentalizing the appetite of its masters. A diamond-encrusted skull cuts through the dissonance of the critical art paradigm to reveal the necrophilic heart of the global financial order.[13] To paraphrase Mark Fisher, an anti-capitalist may claim, ethically, that they want to live in a different world, but libidinally, at the level of desire, they are committed to living within the current capitalist world.[14] Fisher's statement leads to the question that animated much

7 Victoria Ivanova and Gerald Nestler, "Art, Markets, and Finance," in *The Routledge Handbook of Critical Finance Studies*, edited by Christian Borch and Robert Wosnitzer (New York: Routledge, 2020), 381.

8 Ibid., 386.

9 Ibid.

10 Ibid., 389.

11 Isabelle Graw, *High Price: Art Between the Market and Celebrity Culture* (Berlin: Sternberg Press, 2009), 23.

12 Ivanova and Nestler, "Art, Markets, and Finance," 388.

13 Damien Hirst, *For the Love of God*, 2007, platinum, diamonds, human teeth, 6.7 × 5 × 7.5 in (17.1 × 12.7 × 19 cm).

14 Mark Fisher, *Postcapitalist Desire: The Final Lectures* (London: Repeater Books, 2021), 45.

15 Ibid.

of his later work: "is there really a desire for something beyond capitalism?"[15] In the field of cultural production, this raises the question whether blockchain, cryptocurrencies, and their derivative protocols will accelerate the triumph of capitalist realism, or instead are tools for building a way out of contemporary art's maintenance of "artificial scarcity" and coded power structures, which "protects the critical correlation between symbolic value and financial value."[16]

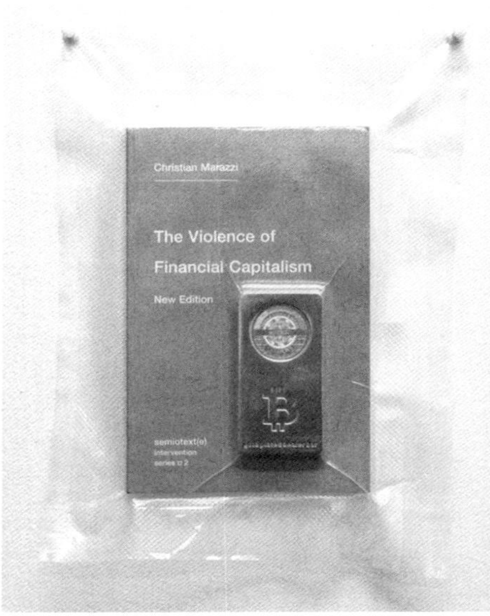

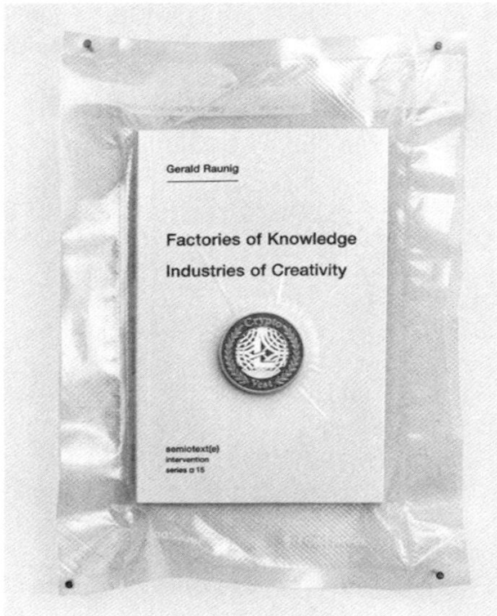

Brad Troemel, *TSA No Fly List Vacuum Sealed Christian Marazzi,* The VIOLENCE of Financial Capitalism *with 100 BITCOIN gold plated bar*, 2013, 10 × 8 in (25.4 × 20.3 cm)
Courtesy the artist

Brad Troemel, *TSA No Fly List Vacuum Sealed Gerald Raunig,* Factories of Knowledge Industries of Creativity *with CryptoVest Litecoin*, 2013, 10 × 8 in (25.4 × 20.3 cm)
Courtesy the artist

How closely are financial and symbolic value laminated together in recent art? A Bitcoin bar vacuum-sealed with a Semiotext(e) title might in 2013 have been received as a provocation to disturb market/symbolic synergies; in 2021 that balance has been tipped. Embalmed within air-tight plastic, the juxtaposition of discrete components by Brad Troemel reads like a meme gesturing to market reflexivity. But what if the element of greatest value in Troemel's assemblage were plundered? If the sealed 100 Bitcoin bar contained a cryptographic key for its face value, in 2013 it could have been redeemed for US$1,500, whereas eight years later the sum is US$4 Million. Troemel's gambit was smuggling a speculative asset inside his pieces—like a time bomb tethered to the cryptocurrency market—where it could also function as a hedge against relative uncertainties in the art market. Time has proven that the greatest financial appreciation for this work comes from sacrificing the integrity of the whole. A further unpacking of the contents opens the potential for entanglements with crypto tokens, critical finance, and for operationalizing the work's own financial conditions.[17]

Extracting the Bitcoin bar also liberates a paper copy of *The Violence of Financial Capitalism* by Christian Marazzi, a diagnostic on the processes of financialization following the

16 Ivanova and Nestler, "Art, Markets, and Finance," 391.
17 Ibid., 392.

2008 financial crisis. By flipping through the book, a collector of Troemel's work might encounter passages about financialization that resonate with the destroyed assemblage. It is likely that, in addition to being a patron of contemporary art, our fictional collector would also partake in the financial services industries, of which it is well known that rational expectations, perfect information, and market transparency, have, for a long time, been beside the point. The point being, and here we can circle back to Marazzi's text, "the hypothesis of 'efficient markets' has to be substituted by that of 'market instability ...'"[18] In light of volatility and uncertainty, Troemel's vacuum-sealed works insure a measure of tamper-proofing by design. These works cede to risk management in the face of the "violence of financial capitalism" as articulated by Marazzi.

Marazzi's text identifies the "violence of financial capitalism" primarily as a temporal problem based on the speed and automation of financial instruments: "Taking time means giving each other the means of inventing one's own future, freeing it from the anxiety of immediate profit."[19] For Marazzi this horizon is met by reorienting financial instrumentation away from the extraction of private rents to the redistribution of what he calls social rents. It is suggested that broadly implemented social investments would come about as New-Deal-style government initiatives, and presumably restitute the arts as a priority public good. "For man to be everything, we need to adapt ourselves to the time of existence" is the book's concluding sentiment.[20] Again, echoing Steyerl, "like civilization as a whole, art would be a great idea."

What would incentivize financial capitalism's market makers to pursue the option of redistributive economics—a general demand from the Occupy Wall Street movement in 2011? In retrospect, we know the limited impact of public demonstration tactics in the face of government and bank collusion that pumped liquidity back into the flagging financial sector. Leftist orthodoxies, which dictated the refusal of all things financial, limited the tools available to leverage a successful post-2008 movement toward the realization of a political commons. While the strike and the occupation may have been effective options in the struggle for higher wages during capitalist industrialization, the financialized spaces of networked life and labor demand political strategies compatible to post-Fordist labor.

Here we can cite a text enclosed in another of Troemel works: *TSA No Fly List Vacuum Sealed Gerald Raunig*, Factories of Knowledge Industries of Creativity *with CryptoVest Litecoin* (2013), in which the assemblage technique is again deployed to combine a cryptocurrency token with a copy from the Semiotext(e) catalog. As with *The Violence of Financial Capitalism*, Troemel mobilizes a book title in a seemingly ironic fashion; to disabuse theories of resistance and critique that Raunig's text aims to reclaim.[21] In an essay published the same year, Troemel argues for a self-enterprising "hyperproductive" internet artist who engages in precarious "free labor" to leverage the power of

18 Christian Marrazi, *The Violence of Financial Capitalism* (Brooklyn: Verso, 2010), 79.

19 Ibid., 98.

20 Ibid.

21 Gerald Raunig, *Factories of Knowledge, Industries of Creativity*, translated by Aileen Derieg (Los Angeles: Semiotext(e), 2013), with an afterword by Antonio Negri.

network effects, even if it isn't clear where, when, and how compensation will materialize.[22] This mode of work demonstrates an overidentification with, if not a capitulation to, the financial dynamics of gaming the social web in the 2010s. For the capitalist realist, withholding one's labor is not an option.

Troemel's vacuum-sealed works present a challenge to the inviolability of artworks and the nostalgia that connects the readymade to industrial standardization. Our aim is to reconsider these works co-extensively with financialization in so far as that system allows for the programming of cultural assets to option quantitative returns, even with the prospect of compromised conditions such as a crash or an asset dump. In other words, we wonder whether it is possible to short an artwork, a political movement, or capitalism for that matter. These are the dynamics the late Randy Martin identified as the social logic of the derivative, which operationalize the properties of financial networks such as "dispersion," how economic production is now "inside of circulation," and the generative possibilities in risking together "in the face of generalized failure but on behalf of desired ends."[23]

Art, in its various forms will persist, even in the most culturally and economically impoverished circumstances. But for social life to flourish, artists must directly engage with its actual conditions of production and reception. This horizon requires operating at spatial and temporal levels afforded through planetary-scale computation and decentralized computing. Cryptocurrencies, for their part, are inherently a financial logic, and meaningful engagements with markets must therefore be responsive to computational processes that undergird global financial infrastructure. The blockchain allows for interventions in the contemporary dichotomies of scarcity and abundance, and its decentralized programmability provides tools to imagine entirely new modes of being and interacting—this offers a list of potentialities.

Hard Forks

The integration of blockchain and cryptocurrencies in the art industry over the past decade has called attention to long-standing infrastructural and ideological fault lines. The question remains whether crypto—to borrow from the trade glossary—will exert sufficient transformative pressures to gradually fork entire cultural and economic spheres. In technical terms, a blockchain fork is the fragmentation of consensus protocols through the implementation of software updates. A fork can be accidental or intentional, motivated by greed and malice, or simply the result of a procedural systems upgrade. For our fork analogy to hold, existing socio-economic protocols must be sufficiently disturbed to rend distinctly new institutional systems, which would be more autonomous and decentralized. Is a new art world animated by crypto-economics possible or even desirable?

22 Brad Troemel, "Athletic Aesthetics," *The New Inquiry*, May 10,2013, available at https://thenewinquiry.com/athletic-aesthetics/ (accessed August 17, 2021).

23 Randy Martin, *Knowledge LTD: Toward a Social Logic of the Derivative* (Philadelphia: Temple University Press, 2015), 54.

As a global network, the art system is ill-defined, with institutional nodes that centralize power, and reputational criteria that are rarely available to those subsisting on the periphery.[24] In short, the art system is composed antithetically to governance models afforded by blockchain consensus protocols. However, decentralization protocols will only shape revolutions when power is widely distributed among stakeholders. Cryptocurrency tokens are currently concentrated in the holdings of institutions and individuals known as whales. Returning to Steyerl: "The internet spawned Uber and Amazon, not the Paris Commune."[25] Just as Web 2.0 platform monopolies mount stiff opposition to government antitrust regulations, we must assume that art industry whales will not willingly submit to a wholesale restructuring of their field, no matter how unsustainable the current system.[26]

If the art industry system undergoes a hard fork, it will be the result of sustained pressure from novel techno-political and financial paradigms, with blockchain as the most recent catalyst for institutional transparency. Cryptocurrency is characterized, in part, by its synthesis of money with computational modalities. As a software layer, cryptocurrency is specifically designed to bind "social activity to material resources" across computational platforms, which constitutes "economic media," as explained by media theorist Jonathan Beller.[27] If crypto is indeed a new medium that is "programmable from below," it would permit the realization of infrastructures that would otherwise remain speculative. As a medium of "inscription, communication and archivization" and a driver of political inquiry, crypto offers an opportunity to reinvigorate moribund artistic strategies, such as the market reflexive gestures detailed above.[28]

Here we can set conditional limits to the potency of artistic strategies via Troemel and his vacuum-sealed assemblages. Secured inside survivalist packaging, the physical cryptocurrency and Semiotext(e) volumes essentially function as frozen asset tokens and/or collectibles. Our scenario for extracting these contents reorients the work toward potential affordances of cryptocurrency and financial liquidity. These actions also shift the terms of the work from monetizable to monetary.

The expediency of Troemel's production is market-affirmative and squares pragmatically with the disappearance of the public cultural sector. Presumed in this approach is that whatever the Habermasian public sphere was, migrated online to mutate into entrepreneurial and adversarial social networks, which, according to Beller, "reconfigured communication into an advertising/surveillance loop that took a semiotic field and financialized it."[29] Beller contends that communications and monetary media are in the process of merging into the general category of "economic media," introduced above. For Beller, Web 2.0 is a stage in the development of capitalist extraction toward computational processes that capture and quantify human expressive qualities. The emergence of "economic media," therefore, corresponds with the development of monetizable peer-to peer (P2P) social

24 Samuel P. Fraiberger et al, "Quantifying reputation and success in art," *Science*, Vol. 362, Issue 6416, November 16, 2018, 825–29, available at https://science.sciencemag.org/content/362/6416/825 (accessed July 22, 2021).

25 Steyerl, "If You Don't Have Bread, Eat Art."

26 Natalie Sherman, "Facebook facing US legal action over competition," *BBC News*, December 9, 2020, available at https://www.bbc.com/news/business-55250366 (accessed July 22, 2021).

27 Jonathan Beller, "Economic Media: Crypto and the Myth of Total Liquidity," *Australian Humanities Review*, Issue 66, May 2020, available at http://australianhumanitiesreview.org/2020/05/31/economic-media-crypto-and-the-myth-of-total-liquidity/ (accessed July 22, 2021).

28 Ibid.

29 Ibid.

arrangements enclosed within privately owned platforms whose mission statements claim to build systems that offer a semblance of the commons, if not its total replacement. A full interrogation of the divisions instituted between the commons as a public good and the populist turn in contemporary politics are beyond the scope of this essay, as is a critique of art and culture as a wedge in these divergent orders. What we can establish is that the social web is a *Gesamtkunstwerk* for expressive capacities and heterogeneous desires constrained within a firewalled command-and-control apparatus.

By consistently situating his work within the milieux of Web 2.0 P2P networks, Troemel, like anyone else agreeing to the legal terms of use, is subject to top-down punitive measures such as shadow bans, which loom over an environment that promotes content creation. Within these platforms, the so-called "passion economy" finds form through tactical optimizations of reputation, attention, and engagement.[30] These are the spaces from which "economic media" emerged as the registry for monetizing "individuality." What currently counts as popular culture is inextricably bound up with the internet and its flows, folds, lolz, and feedback loops, which leads us back to Fisher's question of whether, at the level of desire, we are committed to living within the current capitalist world. And here the question of commitments becomes integral to contemporary artistic praxis. Notwithstanding the compromises and complicities to remain seen on the social web, what benefits are derived from complying with the given infrastructure of Web 2.0?

For Troemel, web platforms, despite their top-down extractive model, provide a modicum of self-determination necessary to bypass institutional vetting and funding models to build an audience of subscribers. We have examined his work at length here, because it exhaustively tests available Web 2.0 options, for crowd and individual production (vlogging, UV Production House), experiments with financial arrangements, and early engagements with memes and web-based communities (The Jogging, Etsy). In sum, these activities don't merely thematize financial conditions, they cease to hold an opposition between wage work and artwork. Therefore, the substance of Troemel's mimetic enterprise isn't its appropriation of populist content creation, or the marketing powers of an influencer, but in counterposing these actual modes of online production against the critical art paradigm. The result is a parody of critique. Troemel's choice of Semiotext(e) titles for his assemblages are suitably pointed: featuring theorists who work from the concept of the general intellect, tracing the recent tendency for cognitive labor to be co-opted for profit-oriented production rather than emancipation.

As a potentially unexpected corrective to our deep dive inside capitalist enclosures, we would like to briefly consider Theodor Adorno. In his defense of negation, art historian John Roberts argues that negation—following Adorno—"lies not just in the critique and removal of the old capitalist forms, but in the universal harnessing of free creative power ... [negation] is not just

30 See Li Jin, "The Passion Economy and the Future of Work," *Future from a16z*, 2021, available at https://a16z.com/2019/10/08/passion-economy/ (accessed August 17, 2021).

31 John Roberts, *Revolutionary Time and the Avant-Garde* (London: Verso, 2015), 158.

32 Dave Beech, *Art and Value: Art's Economic Exceptionalism in Classical, Neoclassical and Marxist Economics*, (Leiden: Brill, 2015), 216.

33 See, for a comprehensive overview on Net Art, https://anthology.rhizome.org/ (accessed July 22, 2021).

34 *Future Art Ecosystems*, Issue 1, "Art x Advanced Technologies," February 2020, 30.

the outcome of the political transformation of capitalism, but the promise of total revolutionary praxis."[31] Adorno's post-capitalist hard fork is transfixing, yet we would be wise to recalibrate our horizon to the more pedestrian concerns of technical protocols for the simple reason that the inheritors (critics and theorists) of Western Marxism's attachment to consciousness, culture, and aesthetic form, tended to avoid engagements with methods and tools.[32] A preoccupation with theories of reification, the culture industry, commodification, and spectacle created a blind spot for a meaningful analysis of new technologies. Advanced technologies and the computer were rarely afforded a centered position in the discourses and self-conception of contemporary art; they were treated as an externality, a necessary infrastructure, or tools of the culture industry. Assimilations of the digital into contemporary art have come as occasional soft forks in categorical designations such as Net Art, which feature complex histories that have been accounted for elsewhere.[33]

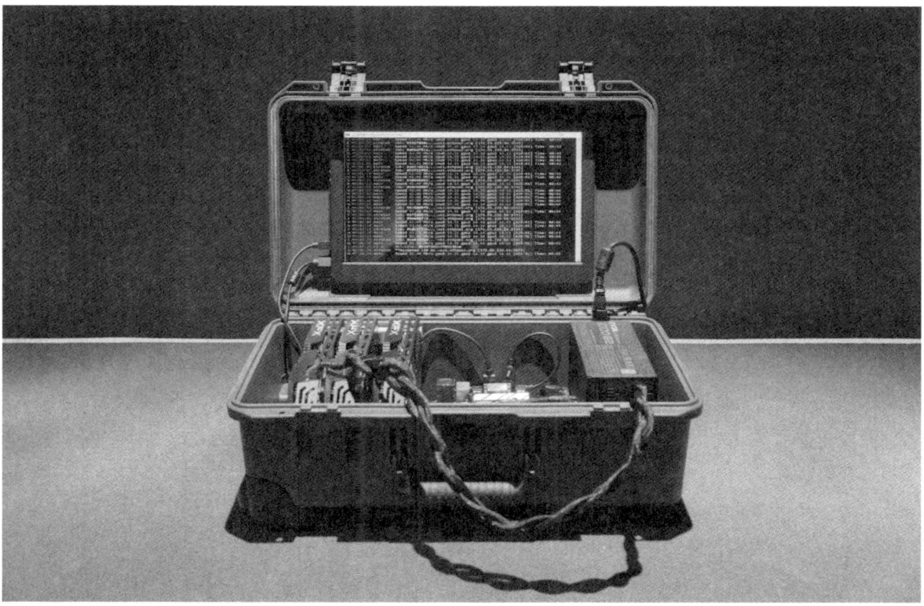

João Enxuto and Erica Love, *Crypto Coffer*, 2018, thermoplastic hard case, LED monitor, Ethereum mining rig (motherboard, three graphics processing units [GPUs], battery, hard drive, Windows OS), smart contract, 21.7 × 14.1 × 8.9 in (55.1 × 35.8 × 22.6 cm). The dimensions for the *Crypto Coffer* conform with international flight carry-on luggage size regulations, its thermoplastic case houses a portable computer that mines Ether. Upon arrival at an exhibition, art fair, panel, or symposium, the *Crypto Coffer* can easily be activated and put to verify proof of work. Ether tokens hashed synchronously with a work engagement are stored in the artist's virtual wallet (coffer). Host institutions need only provide a power outlet and a consistent Wi-Fi connection.

Currently, a hard fork of cultural and economic spaces is potentially emerging within Web 3.0 digital-native communities. Meanwhile, developments in crypto protocols and tokens have had an uneven impact on the coded markets and symbolic infrastructures of contemporary art. In a recent report, it was noted that practices by artists working on art and advanced technology (AXAT) "point toward a growing disparity between established art world practices and the attitudes and requirements of artists working with advanced tech. However, the most crucial significance of AXAT practices lies in their potential impact upon the infrastructure of the art world—the challenge they pose to the art industry."[34] This stated degree of transformation has yet to be seen in the contemporary art industry, which has thus far deployed the decentralizing powers of the Web 3.0 "world computer" to primarily expand its market infrastructure to accommodate the NFT.

Let Them Eat NFTs

When global art circulation was put on hold during the Covid-19 pandemic, major galleries retooled to manufacture excitement for online viewing rooms. The years 2020–21 habituated an ease of remote consumption seeded in the previous decade by way of content aggregators (Contemporary Art Daily, Instagram) and iPhone 4s.[35] When it was discovered that a JPEG alone could move a work of art, market speculation began to accelerate via network effects. The process of buying and selling art became more gamified, thus setting the stage for financial instrumentation and the recent run on NFTs.[36]

It is rare to come across NFT appraisals that don't express outrage—manufactured or otherwise—about how previously uncapitalized digital assets are pumped to the status of unique artworks in a process that binds infinitely reproducible digital files to a cryptographic algorithm.[37] From a cultural economics standpoint, an NFT "drop" is a novel process that encodes art by way of the blockchain mint. In these early stages in the adoption of NFT minting, we have witnessed the ascendency of the digital asset. This special status was not achieved by eclipsing the appeal of conventional artworks, but rather by elevating proof of ownership itself as a register of economic exceptionalism.

With the broad adoption of blockchain, the same central authorities that cryptocurrencies were designed to circumvent are now rushing in to capture a stake in the booming business: banks and financial firms, but also opportunistic contemporary art galleries and auction houses. While it can be assumed that some newly-minted crypto billionaires previously collected contemporary art, this narrow demographic cannot account for the outsized role that cultural assets play in circumscribing group affiliations following the development of NFT marketplaces. Within mainstream economic sectors, cryptocurrencies have been hounded by legitimacy problems since their early days. In interrogating the spotty reputation of cryptocurrency, researchers Malcolm Campbell-Verduyn and Moritz Hütten highlight that "despite invoking lofty collective principles, these projects persistently rely on individualistic logics of engagement in ways that not only seem unlikely to actualise moral change, but also seem far more likely to attract speculative investment from individuals seeking short-term profit."[38] Moreover, to enhance their reputations, cryptocurrency speculators have invested heavily in NFTs to leverage the prestige or "clout" bound to the legacy of cultural patronage.

In sync with the NFT speculators, established art auction houses staged de facto public relations campaigns, paid for

35 Michael Sanchez, "2011: Art and Transmission," *Artforum*, summer 2013, available at https://www.artforum.com/print/201306/2011-art-and-transmission-41241 (accessed July 22, 2021).

36 An early example is the Maecenas (https://www.maecenas.co/) platform, which issued its own (ART) token and facilitated fractional interest ownership in artworks.

37 JJ Charlesworth, "Why the Artworld Loves to Hate NFT Art," *ArtReview*, March 17, 2021, available at https://artreview.com/why-the-artworld-loves-to-hate-nft-art-beeple-christies-grimes/ (accessed July 22, 2021).

38 Malcolm Campbell-Verduyn and Moritz Hütten, "Beyond Scandal? Blockchain technologies and the fragile legitimacy of post-2008 finance," *Finance and Society*, Vol. 5, No. 2, 2019, 138.

with Ether, to promote the emergence of digital assets and the legitimacy of cryptocurrency for general art audiences, but more significantly for established art collectors. Outside of niche NFT marketplaces, cryptocurrencies offered little utility for art buyers until the paradigm-shifting NFT sale at Christie's for US$69M of *EVERYDAYS: THE FIRST 5000 DAYS* by Mike Winkelmann, aka Beeple, in March 2021.[39] The Christie's Beeple auction was the first major art auction of solely digital artwork lots, or as the catalog states: "Marking two industry firsts, Christie's is the first major auction house to offer a purely digital work with a unique NFT (Non-fungible token)—effectively a guarantee of its authenticity—and to accept cryptocurrency, in this case Ether, in addition to standard forms of payment for the singular lot."[40]

The liquidity of digital assets offers distinct financial advantages over physical artworks by obviating transportation, storage, and maintenance costs, while streamlining options for fractional ownership which function like an investment fund of bundled NFTs that are sold off as tokens. Beeple's *EVERYDAYS* was acquired by crypto entrepreneurs Vignesh Sundaresan and Anand Venkateswaran, under the pseudonym Metapurse or Metakovan. Prior to the Christie's auction, Metapurse had taken a major stake in Beeple's market by creating the "B20" token to effect fractionalized ownership of a 20-bundle of previously purchased Beeples.[41] The B20 token was made available on January 23 and reached its peak price immediately after the sale of Beeple's *EVERYDAYS* on March 11.[42]

It is, however, a categorical error to draw a clean equivalence between NFTS and artworks. An NFT follows from the crypto-collectibles trade that started with the development of the ERC-721 token in 2018, and the implementation of smart contracts. Before Metapurse bundled Beeples, NFTS were already subject to fractional ownership among groups of stakeholders who performed a collective exercise of building up the symbolic value of their assets across social web channels and irl.[43] They were playing with "economic media." Peer-to-peer network topographies, which tested their expressive capacities with Web 2.0, could register these values in Web 3.0 through the price differential of an NFT.

Contemporary art has rarely sold for prices that reflect the labor time necessary for its production, an excess, which was often ascribed to symbolic value.[44] This surplus value could be the pricing of a purposive judgment without a purpose, something ineffable, or the critical theoretical bulwarking that resists commodification. Concomitantly, it is abstract values that mire contemporary art in what economists call the problem of information imperfection—the requisite knowledge, taste, and education that limit its widespread legibility. NFTS, on the other hand, are popular and easy and their emergence tests basic

39 Christie's Online Auction 20447, "Beeple, EVERYDAYS: THE FIRST 5000 DAYS, 25 Feb–11 Mar 2021," available at https://onlineonly.christies.com/s/beeple-first-5000-days/beeple-b-1981-1/112924 (accessed July 22, 2021).

40 See https://www.christies.com/features/Monumental-collage-by-Beeple-is-first-purely-digital-artwork-NFT-to-come-to-auction-11510-7.aspx (accessed August 17, 2021).

41 Twobadour Paanar, "How to get your B20s," *Medium*, January 22, 2021, available at https://medium.com/metapurse/how-to-get-your-b20s-bdd99f94a1d7 (accessed August 17, 2021).

42 See https://www.coingecko.com/en/coins/b20 (accessed August 17, 2021).

43 From April–August 2021 the owners of CryptoPunks and Christie's auction house have been buying ad space on billboards in Miami, New York City, and London, to promote CryptoPunks NFTS.

44 Graw, *High Price*.

45 Dave Beech argues that mainstream supply-and-demand (neoclassical) economics is inadequate to develop an understanding of art's economic relationship. Beech therefore seeks to ask the question whether art is exceptional not to an economic doctrine but to an economic practice. "Being exceptional to a theory is one thing; being exceptional to a social system is another." Instead, Beech goes about answering the question of art's economic exceptionalism via Marxism. Beech, *Art and Value*, 207.

assumptions about the economic exceptionalism of art.[45] Art's economic exceptionalism is contingent, in part, on its singularity, a one-of-a-kind status that bears the unique signature of its creator. As discussed above in detail, the NFT is designed to encode singularity—conferring a cryptographic proof that has steamrolled over the vagaries of critical judgment. Subsequently, discursive positions that buoyed financial value for contemporary art become unnecessary for digital assets.

Which brings us to "On Dialogues: The David Zwirner Podcast," hosted by Lucas Zwirner, who moderated an interview between [... gallery] stable artist Jordan Wolfson and Beeple in May 2021 to discuss parallels between the contemporary art and digital art worlds."[46] As the conversation unfolded, art world enfant terrible Wolfson found himself shifting to a rearguard position to defend critical orthodoxies, which most of his work reflexively opposes. Wolfson pointedly remarked that just because Beeple sold a work for US$69 million "doesn't mean that Mike is a great artist." To rescue Beeple from another characteristically oafish rebuttal, and thereby confirming Wolfson's claim, Zwirner interjected diplomatically by couching the measure of artistic greatness within the long arc of art history. "We know some great artists," he said, continuing with "in the digital space, I don't think we know who any of the great artists are yet," arguing that twenty years of digital art isn't long enough to sift great digital art from the rest. The thrust of the conversation was to assert that Beeple's online milieux of digital art was recognizably distinct from highly valued contemporary art, but that difference was not meaningful enough to fall outside the range of what contemporary art could accommodate.[47]

With the voiding of established aesthetic criteria, high-end actors in the NFT marketplace have turned auction bidding wars into numerology games. When Beeple's *The Complete MF Collection* came up for auction on the Nifty Gateway marketplace in December 2020, a last-second bid of US$777,777.77 more than doubled the previous high bid by Metakovan,[48] who would later go on to outbid the field at Christie's for *EVERYDAYS*. For crypto whales, setting coded prices (7s, 69) reflect the primacy of numbers and puerile sensibilities.

After an auction win, what are the spoils available to an NFT owner? The basic terms and limits of NFT ownership are contained in a smart contract's metadata, which outlines rights granted to the owner.[49] While all private property is a socially constructed legal designation, a digital asset's proprietary status is made further contingent on NFT platform gatekeeping of the purchased asset; this appears to be the case with the Christie's Beeple sale. An NFT should point to an Inter Planetary File System (IPFS) hash that is part of the P2P, distributed, permanent web, where files, once published, never go offline, whereas a URL pointing to an NFT marketplace could disappear if the company is dissolved. In the case of Beeple's *EVERYDAYS*, the work references an IPFS gateway on the internet operated by MakersPlace, the NFT-minting start-up that worked with Chris-

46 "Jordan Wolfson x Beeple," *Dialogues: The David Zwirner Podcast*, Season 5, Episode 1, May 6, 2021, available at https://www.davidzwirner.com/podcast#/jordan-wolfson-x-beeple--podcast-80de872d-2368-4a2d-a840-2595893793fb (accessed August 17, 2021).

47 DeviantArt is one such standard, see https://www.deviantart.com/ (accessed August 17, 2021).

48 See https://niftygateway.com/itemdetail/primary/0x6e5dc5405baefb8c0166bcc78d2692777f2cbffb/21 (accessed August 19, 2021).

49 Terms of service are also consented to when buying from an NFT marketplace. The marketplace may limit ownership to personal, non-commercial use with the ability to terminate an owner's access to their NFT without compensation.

tie's on the sale. While the *EVERYDAYS* token refers directly to an IPFS hash,[50] the metadata links on an IPFS gateway are run by MakersPlace and could disappear along with access to the NFT.[51] An NFT should be made to be cryptographically secure and accessible: without access, claims to ownership are severed and the NFT's market value drops to zero. One cannot sell that which cannot be located.[52]

The examples above aim to outline the heedless approach taken by institutional elements within the contemporary art market to effectively leverage the NFT and crypto-economic speculation to re-inscribe art market hierarchies. However, the other major auction house, Sotheby's, took a more considered approach to its first NFT sale, "Natively Digital: A Curated NFT Sale" in June 2021.[53] The lots included NFTs from artists and collectives such as terra0 and Simon Denny, who have complex committed practices engaging with crypto-governance and tokenization. Also included was Kevin McCoy, an established Net artist and professor who previously committed himself to Monegraph—a blockchain media rights platform that provided a system for artists to license their digital art. While Monegraph did not find a significant market, McCoy still managed to receive a substantial NFT payout at Sotheby's. His animated GIF titled *Quantum* sold for US$ 1,472,000. As purportedly the first NFT, *Quantum*[54] is situated in the Sotheby's description alongside prominent historical referents—such as Sol LeWitt, John Cage, La Monte Young—and includes a quote from Walter Benjamin's famous text on Paul Klee's Angelus Novus: provided without irony, because "this storm is what we call progress."[55] The McCoy NFT sale abided by conventional symbolic requirements to justify the auction price, such as signaling art historical precedent and the ghosts of the Frankfurt School.

Swarm Flips

Distinct among the editorial responses to Christie's Beeple auction is a brief issued by art historian David Joselit in the pages in the venerable journal *October*. Published in May 2021, "NFT, or the Readymade Reversed" is remarkable as an expedient "hot take" to ostensibly head off the perceived threat of the *EVERYDAYS* sale. After acknowledging that "the market will do what the market will do," Joselit goes on to interrogate the value of a non-fungible token as "structurally dependent

50 The full hash is https://ipfs.io/ipfs/QmPAg1mjxcEQPPtqsLoEcauVedaeMH81WXDPvPx3VC5zUz (accessed August 17,2021).

51 The full link is https://ipfsgateway.makersplace.com/ipfs/QmXkxpwAHCtDXbbZHUwqtFucG1RMS6T87vi1CdvadfL7qA (accessed August 17, 2021). This scenario could have been entirely avoided had MakerPlace limited *EVERYDAYS* NFT to the IPFS system. The fact that it didn't, led to concerns that NFT start-ups are storing NFTs on their URLs intentionally as part of a long-game blackmail scheme. As a result, the owners of the US$ 69 Million NFT may be inclined to pay subscription fees or invest in MakersPlace to keep the company solvent.

52 This severing can be avoided altogether if the collector insists on only buying NFTS that are stored on an IPFS hash or on-chain NFTS where the image is stored within the token itself. On-chain NFTS are relatively new and are randomly generated on demand by an AI-driven software program.

53 "Natively Digital: A Curated NFT Sale," available at https://www.sothebys.com/en/buy/auction/2021/natively-digital-a-curated-nft-sale-2/quantum (accessed July 22, 2021).

54 *Quantum* was originally minted on May 3, 2014, on Namecoin blockchain, which predates the ERC-721 standard.

55 A part of the statement that must be recounted, even if just as a footnote, reads as follows: "Pulsing with colour, a riotously raw beacon to a new era, McCoy minted *Quantum*—unwittingly placing it within this vaulted pantheon of firsts. Timestamped July 1907, Picasso's *Les Demoiselles* ushered in the chain of Cubism. December 1917, Malevich's *Black Square* stands as the genesis block of Abstraction. April 1917, Duchamp timestamps the era of the idea. 2nd May 2014 21:27:34, *Quantum* stands alone in the precision of its timestamp—immutably, verifiably, trustlessly pure."

56 David Joselit, "NFT, or the Readymade reversed," *October*, No. 175, May 2021, 3, https://doi.org/10.1162/octo_a_00419.

upon the exclusive right to control its circulation."[56] Joselit is less invested in the technical details of tokenization and more concerned with the NFT as an ideological mechanism whereby the "category of art is equated with non-fungibility: It is the readymade reversed."[57] Joselit sets the NFT against Duchamp's readymade, and its innovative destabilization of the "moment of matter's becoming-property in ways that are historically specific and aesthetically engrossing."[58] Such a be-spoiling of the category of art by desires to possess can be remedied, according to Joselit, by "spectatorial generosity." At its best, he claims that art is a gift, while the NFT is the completion of late capitalism's cycle of information commodification. Beyond aesthetic absorption, what's at stake for Joselit is the "becoming-property" of matter—when art comes to function as a technology of extraction. Most significantly, this becomes a political relation that imperils historical justice for economic dispossession and inequality. Joselit attests to the capacity of Duchamp's readymades to "destabilize" the processual "becoming-property" that precipitated the legacies of chattel slavery and economic inequality. For the art historian, it is the aesthetic and conceptual destabilizations of the readymade that can serve to address the injustice of capital's appropriations.

As a diagnostic bound to the inadequacies of the Beeple example, Joselit's fixation with non-fungibility manages to foreclose financial approaches and tokenization as a means of redressing capital accumulation. This misapplication of critical discursivity to confront an infrastructural problem illustrates the "dissonance" between the realities of financial infrastructure and discursive positions within the field of art, as described earlier. For instance, the valuation systems that currently shape the reception of Duchamp's experiments with fungible monetary instruments, *Tzanck Check* (1917) and *Monte Carlo Bond* (1924), are the museums and the secondary market that contextualize these works as non-fungible assets. If we put aside Duchamp's language games and absurdist personae, the issuance of *Monte Carlo Bond* offers a game of chance as three-year investment options at a face value of 500 francs.[59] This conceptual operation is a speculative financial instrument and an artwork. Rather than deploying the Duchamp readymade in opposition to a narrow conception of NFTs and crypto economics, it would be more accurate to peg another accomplishment to Duchamp as an inventor of economic media: the fashioning of currency as art. When Joselit claims that "the NFT deploys the category of art to extract private property from freely available information,"[60] it reveals a misunderstanding of how value is organized through network mediation and how "monetary media directly interface with social and communicative practices."[61] What appears as freely available information is already monetary, and what should follow is a decoding of "the protocols of money already operating today ... to make it possible for users to redesign them more in accord with their own interests."[62] It is exactly the potential redesign of the protocols of economic

57 Ibid., 4.

58 Ibid.

59 Monte Carlo Bond (N. 30) was sold for US$ 2,405,000 at Christie's in November 2015, see https://www.christies.com/lot/lot-marcel-duchamp-monte-carlo-bond-5946115/ (accessed September 5, 2021).

60 Joselit, "NFT, or the Readymade reversed," 4.

61 Beller, "Economic Media," 216.

62 Ibid.

media that is unlocked by the programmable layer of Ethereum and related blockchains.

Following the philosopher Gilbert Simondon, researcher Laura Lotti claims that "we should consider blockchains and tokens as novel technologies in the initial stages of a process of individuation, rather than prematurely aborting the inquiry into their affordances as already overdetermined by tendencies of financial accumulation with which we are intimately familiar."[63] In other words, tokenization—the issuing of smart contract tokens, NFTs included—should not be abandoned because the early stages have been dominated by financial speculators. Technical systems, as described by Simondon, evolve or "concretize" over time as the relation between a technical object (or tool) and its environment, resulting in a condition known as technicity. The tendency of systems toward technicity is a useful term for Lotti, because it pre-exists economic determinations and "defines the conditions of possibility for the technological."[64] Blockchain offers "a new stage in the concretization of the technicity of informational systems" characterized as the programmability of platforms.[65]

In his recent work, Robert Meister has recognized the proliferation and adoption of crypto coins as opportunities "for writing derivatives to structure the political and economic life surrounding them."[66] The political question this raises for Meister is whether the programming of platforms may lead to a "subversive, alt-finance constellation of movements" that can benefit from their own "perceived success by creating classes of financial assets that would fund financial capitalism's would-be gravediggers."[67] The foundation for Meister's complex proposition is built upon a basis of liquidity, which is the "abstract form of power specific to globalized financial capital—the normative and empirical ground of its existence."[68] A significant corrective embedded in Meister's strategy is the proposal of an alternative "to the fantasy that someday, some anti-capitalist movement will 'go viral' enough to kill its capitalist host." Financial institutions, he claims, are already parasitical within capitalism—"not only in the usual sense of sucking out its blood, but because they know how to benefit from a directional threat to asset values by treating it as an increase in volatility."[69] In other words, capitalism preserves financial liquidity, and thus itself, by means of schematizing future threats to financial liquidity, and thus its own survival.

The focus of Meister's most recent book, *Justice Is an Option*, is that financialization can provide new opportunities for reversing historical injustice because socially created wealth that is held in the form of financial instruments is "abundant, transferable, and liquid."[70] Likewise, when Joselit cites the Duchamp readymade for its power to destabilize, it becomes a trade on volatility. Matter, in this case a mass-produced object, is suspended between two options—both fountain and urinal. The importance of the readymade is not as object, but as an option. It was the dynamics of optionality that are also interrogated

63 Laura Lotti, "The Art of Tokenization: Blockchain Affordances and the Invention of Future Milieus," *Media Theory*, Vol. 3, No. 1, 2019, 289.
64 Ibid., 295.
65 Ibid.
66 Robert Meister, *Justice Is an Option: A Democratic Theory of Finance for the Twenty-First Century* (Chicago: University of Chicago Press, 2020), 149.
67 Ibid., 154.
68 Ibid., 3.
69 Ibid., 155.
70 Ibid., 1.

in Troemel's vacuum-sealed readymades. As to the question of historical justice, Meister accepts that there is currently no democracy in finance, yet he believes that there can be no democratization of our present society without it.[71] By this, Meister means that capital market illiquidity and justice-seeking revolution lie just over the horizon of possibility imposed by the capitalist imagination.[72] The struggle for democracy, therefore, is no longer about the commodification of labor time, but about operationalizing capitalism's resilience, which may be a "vulnerability to the extent that capitalism's enemies can control that volatility—and then learn how to leverage it."[73] Duchamp is instructive again in demonstrating a similar paradox in his embrace of automation, chance, and mechanical production as instruments to short Romanticism and early modern art value systems, while allowing him to still benefit from the "labour-less labor of the artistic genius" afforded by the position ascribed to him by birth.[74]

For Meister, historical justice becomes a real option as accumulated wealth is made more valuable the more it is exposed to political threats. The suggestion here is not that capitalism can be tricked into funding its own subversion, instead subversive movements must risk together and exploit the possibilities of "exaggerated fears that arise whenever financial collapse becomes more imaginable, whether through their own action or otherwise."[75] As the increased volatility of global crises continues to disrupt international sovereignty and economy, the possibility of financial collapse is rendered more plausible. However, out of this flux fragmentary elements must be made to bind as coordinated movements. Martin reminds us that mobilization pivots on a few "leveraged to significant gain rather than toward construction of a capacious and centering consensus of the mass." And earlier on he states that "the center holds less not because it is impossible to quantify but because it remains in motion, at the heart of volatility, throbbing, shifting away from the prospect that it can anchor the effluvial masses."[76] Ultimately, the center does not hold as the production of models of the future, in other words, infrastructural work is typically performed by privileged outliers. This promise of decentralization is the social logic of the derivative, optionality, and the dynamics of encoding mutuality.

If art was an alternative currency within this fold, it would not be "solitary, unlinked, or isolated," as Steyerl proposes at the conclusion of the essay which commenced our, now lengthy, investigation.[77] The building of this "partial networked autonomy via all means necessary" is already visible in the collective power of swarms and squads.[78] Steyerl asks "[c]an one transform art's currency into art's confluence? Replace speculation with overflow?"[79] The "art stack" model of working with advanced technologies (AXAT) already diverges from the "individual artist" approach preferred by the art world to a common practice of distributed tasks and authorship.[80] More and more creative production will likely emerge from art stacks—out of necessity

71 Ibid., 10.

72 Ibid., 12–13.

73 Ibid., 156.

74 Dave Beech, *Art and Postcapitalism: Aesthetic Labour, Automation and Value Production* (London: Pluto Press, 2019), 64.

75 Meister, *Justice Is an Option*, 161

76 Martin, *Knowledge LTD*, 120.

77 Steyerl, "If You Don't Have Bread, Eat Art."

78 See https://otherinter.net/research/squad-wealth/ (accessed September 5, 2021).

79 Steyerl, "If You Don't Have Bread, Eat Art."

80 *Future Art Ecosystems*, 97.

81 A DAO is an entity distributed among computers, networks, and nodes without hierarchical leadership or control by a single institution, such as a government or central bank. DAOs are collectively owned and managed by their members, and decisions are made when members submit and vote on proposals. DAOs establish and follow rules enforced via smart contracts on the Ethereum blockchain.

and solidarity. In terms of consumption, Decentralized Autonomous Organizations (DAOs)[81] such as NFT-focused Flamingo, occupy a niche in Web 3.0 platforms that actively work to undo the wrongs of Web 2.0 extraction. Flamingo is a jointly governed investment pool that acquires "digital art, collectibles, and in-game assets and other tangible assets."[82] Flamingo exemplifies how blockchain protocols are being used to bring a minimum of regulatory order to the market: resale royalties, fractional ownership by producers, artist fees, and the reining in of tax fraud. These practical provisions have been levers of struggle for decades among art activists. However, a DAO exploring "emerging investment opportunities" is unlikely to shape significant systemic transformations nor sabotage existing pools of accumulated capital. From Flamingo's mission statement: "Trillions of creative works swirl around the Internet and are difficult to monetize, except through licensing models. NFTs hold out the hope of bringing back to the Internet an ownership economy. Creators can create, sell, and fractionalize ownership in their works, opening up a new chapter for creative endeavor." There are echoes of Web 2.0 platform boosterism among the more curated Web 3.0 platforms. The popular Zora marketplace's manifesto stands out among these, "[t]hey have a monopoly on ownership, a monopoly on creativity and they have been robbing us of the value we create for as long as there's been a creative industry [...] We need new infrastructure, something transparent, ownable, accessible, financially sustainable, where we can share the value we create, something for the community, something that's ours."[83] In this statement, community is synonymous with platforming; for an artist to assert their resale rights with Zora, all subsequent sales must be performed through that platform. Applied Arts, a new "artist-led" strategy agency, was hired to pen what they described on their website as "a banger of a manifesto" and after Zora they listed their two previous clients: Airbnb and Cartier.[84] Is this another validation of Fisher's doubt about the capacity of human desire beyond capitalism, or proof of Steyerl's premonition that the reshaping of a better art world will need to happen within a "compromised mess of contradictory activities"?[85]

Emerging from the confluence of financial speculation and Reddit, are app-empowered swarms of amateur traders or a "supra-individual organism resulting from the automated coordination of distinct individual organisms," as defined by Franco "Bifo" Berardi.[86] In his essay on meme-swarms, Berardi rightly claims that there is an element of revenge capitalism that drove Wall Street Bets swarms, just as it spurred white working-class voters to vote for Trump and humiliate the powerful and the powerless alike. Contrary to the Occupy Wall Street movement ten years prior, "[t]he micro-trading disruption is a mere expression of the selfish proprietary instinct and is aimed at hustling a bit of money and possibly some room in the Stock Exchange."[87] For Berardi the buying of GameStop stock to sabotage a planned short sale by a prominent brokerage

82 See https://flamingodao.xyz/ (accessed September 5, 2021).

83 Zora manifesto, "They Thought They Could Own Us," available at https://zora.co/manifesto (accessed July 22, 2021).

84 See https://www.appliedarts.agency/ (accessed September 5, 2021).

85 Steyerl, "If You Don't Have Bread, Eat Art."

86 Franco "Bifo" Berardi, "Meme-Swarm and Microtrading," *Ill Will*, February 5, 2021, available at https://illwill.com/meme-swarm-and-microtrading (accessed July 22, 2021).

87 Ibid.

firm represents one episode in an ongoing Civil War. But these observations only tell part of the story: coordinated acts against financial power have effects that extend beyond the intentions of individual actors incentivized by a quick profit. If this is Civil War, it should not continue as a war of attrition. As Meister points out, a viral movement such as GameStop may not offer the leverage to take down financial capitalism; rather the impact of Wall Street Bets is the ability to expose structural vulnerability in the financial industries. Despite its innumerable flaws, Wall Street Bets is a prime example of the "self-assignment of capacities to empower, differentiate, invent, or express a means of participation [that] may not await or be oriented toward official recognition, legitimation, or consignment," writes Martin.[88] There is an overflow, and it must not simply be the capitalists—sharks, whales, micro-traders, and hedge-funders—who benefit from their perceived capacity for disruption.

88 Martin, *Knowledge LTD*, 123.

MYSTICAL HABITATS: ART AFTER EARTH AND OUTER-SPACE SETTLEMENTS

Bogna Konior

> *Those who enter the open cosmos for the first time feel almost physically how their senses lose all orientation referents; a fall begins, they fall into an endless void ... This isn't a problem on the planetoid; there is a horizon, more or less, there is a ground beneath your feet, an implied "bottom" plane. But if you lift your eyes up and lose sight of it ... My God. Indescribable.*
>
> —Jacek Dukaj[1]

Although we may not see functional space settlements within our lifetime, the desire to settle beyond our home planet is already exerting influence on our culture. Notwithstanding their current unavailability, space settlements are a persistent civilizational goal. We may not complete the ambitious project of space colonization, but the desire to do so will define us. Yuval Harari describes a similar dynamic with regard to immortality: it is not whether it is achievable, but that human obsession with eternal life guides cultural, emotional, and financial investments.[2] It is not controversial to propose that even if settling beyond our home planet remains a forever unfulfilled desire, the arts, in their meaning-making function, can still aid in understanding our yearning. But what if we phrased the question differently: If we did indeed colonize space, why would we still need art, an activity entirely proper to the Earth?

It is a historically consistent trait in humans to reach for the unknown. Once it was a civilizational goal to reach Antarctica, and then the moon, yet, once achieved, both territories became entirely uninteresting to the general public. The point of reference shifts, one uncharted territory can stand in for another, while the transcendental mission of exploration often signifies current political and economic dynamics rather than an existential goal: "uncharted territory is a useful analogy for describing a new stage of corporate and state endeavors towards a new era in off-Earth exploration."[3] Now there is the question of settling on Mars, or even further. Since the launch of Sputnik 1 in 1957, SpaceX has launched its first commercial space flight, Australia has established a new national space agency, former President Trump has highlighted the necessity of a strong American Space Force, Ghana has launched its first satellite, a large number of exoplanets have been discovered, and China has sent

1 Jacek Dukaj, *Katedra* (The Cathedral) (Krakow: Wydawnictwo Literackie, 2015), e-book. All translations from the book by the author.

2 Yuval Noah Harari, *Homo Deus: A Brief History of Tomorrow* (New York: Random House, 2016).

3 Juan Francisco Salazar, "Antarctica and Outer Space: relational trajectories," *The Polar Journal*, Vol. 7, No. 2, 2017, 259–69, DOI: 10.1080/2154896X.2017.1398521.

three spacecrafts to the red planet. For the first time since the Cold War, space exploration is at the forefront of our collective imagination, and without a doubt is one of the most daring infrastructural projects that humanity has embarked on.

American aerospace engineer Robert Zubrin and physicist Gerard K. O'Neill published intriguing books about the possibility of space colonization, focusing on why it should happen and how humans could do it.[4] Conceptual readings of space colonialism's impact on how we understand art are harder to find though. Some of the best infrastructural theory around spares little thought for outer space, rather it focuses on how alien our own planet is becoming in its current transformation through emergent technologies and urban forms. Benjamin Bratton's *The Stack: On Software and Sovereignty* (2016) and Keller Easterling's *Extrastatecraft: The Power of Infrastructure Space* (2014) consider satellites as part of the internet's infrastructure.[5] Outer-space infrastructure is still at a nascent stage and there is indeed little to write about thus far: it consists of satellites, space junk, research space stations, and occasional spacecrafts. Easterling writes about pre-fabricated cities and island-like free-trade zones instead, while Bratton describes the ascent of computational governance mechanisms that envelop the Earth. Both help us grasp the Earth as a megastructure, a large anthill with multiple layers, some of which us humans inhabit, some of which we don't, some of them we share with animals, plants, and computers. Both authors have us picture the Earth as a formidable structure dotted with cities, animals, machines, and sensors. To understand our contemporary condition, they focus on our home planet and the technological mutations it is undergoing through human intervention.

These—and multiple other—necessary attempts to capture what is happening on the Earth are underlined by what media scholar Patrick Jagoda identifies as a pervasive focus on networks.[6] Everything must be imagined as part of a network, as a node in a much vaster system: flows, connections, and trades need to be charted. Nothing less is expected in a globalized world, held together by multiple networks, from the free market to the internet. With the beginning of industrial modernity in Europe, theories in relation to art appeared to grapple with understanding the art world's own superstructure, its networks of circulation and influence. Twentieth- and twenty-first-century institutional critique investigate both material and symbolic infrastructures of the art world and its economic networks, and challenge the managerial forces within it. Responding to the challenges of a secular world post World War II, artists in the 1960s started taking on the function of social workers, activists, or investigative journalists, such as in Hans Haacke's scrutiny of the interconnections between President Nixon, the Rockefeller family, and the Museum of Modern Art in New York. Where artists before the advent of modernity and mass media remained closer to theologians, contemporary art, alongside the media, began investigating the political and economic networks that

4 Garard K. O'Neill, *The High Frontier: Human Colonies in Space*, self-published, 2019; Robert Zubrin, *The Case for Mars: The Plan to Settle the Red Planet and Why We Must* (New York: Free Press, 2021 [1996]).

5 Benjamin H. Bratton, *The Stack: On Software and Sovereignty* (Cambridge, MA: MIT Press, 2016); Keller Easterling, *Extrastatecraft: The Power of Infrastructure Space* (London: Verso, 2014).

6 Patrick Jagoda, *Network Aesthetics* (Chicago: The University of Chicago Press, 2016).

are enmeshed in "the art world." The intention of institutional critique was, and still is, to reveal and challenge the often murky operations of the art world, including the galleries and banks that run it, and the administrators who mediate aesthetic experiences to audiences.[7]

Whether focusing on infrastructures or institutions, these investigations aim to uncover systems to open up beyond restrictive walls of the networks. One could imagine how infrastructural and institutional critique might meet, describing the networks of places that host the nebulous economies of taste that we have come to know as "the art world." Like any infrastructure described by Bratton or Easterling, buildings, sensors, machines, and objects in the art world are part of a growing planetary system, within which aesthetic preferences and economic incentives circulate. It appears profound, interconnected, and totalizing—we call it an art world after all, as if it enveloped the whole globe. And yet, we could also imagine it as a tiny pocket of insular human activity on a dying star. If, as Lars Bang Larsen suggests, the art world "tends to celebrate the pseudo-perceptions of valorising gazes [...] amongst fetishized agents and institutions," and has little to do with art, could we entertain the hypothesis of what art could be off the planet, physically unchained from these institutions?[8] What if the only remaining institutions of art would be the satellite, the spaceship, and the planetoid? What can art be when detached from terrestrial infrastructures that secure the current circulation of various aesthetics?

II: Art on and off the Earth

In a recent interview, Chinese science-fiction writer Liu Cixin proposes that there are only two types of civilization.[9] The first is outward-looking, which is the civilization of explorers and innovators. This kind of civilization maps the universe, its guiding principle being the continuous exploration of the world and the limits of our human condition. The second is inward-looking, and is a form of civilization focused on improving internal happiness. This civilization uses human satisfaction as the measure of all its endeavors. An outward-looking civilization would be interested in space settlements as a necessary, innate, evolutionary, and transcendental goal of humanity. An inward-looking civilization would be more concerned with whether these infrastructures contribute to happiness, justice, or social harmony as defined currently on Earth. A key question for one civilization is a small matter to the other; the two might share certain values, but their destiny is fundamentally different. "There are no long-term prospects for an inward-looking civilization," Liu notes, focused as it is on the immediate needs of its members.[10] If that is the case, what is there to be said about art and space settlements? Can art be part of the extraterrestrial mission of humanity? Or, if its measure is the improvement of human existence on the Earth, would it become obsolete when situated off it?

7 Less than optimistic about this endeavor, Andrea Fraser writes that institutional critique cannot achieve its stated goal: "the critique of institution [becomes] an institution of critique and the trend is ossified as just another way of entrepreneurship and gaining social capital through one's awareness of exploitative relationships in art." Andrea Fraser, "From the Critique of Institutions to an Institution of Critique," *Artforum*, Vol. 44, No. 1, 2005.

8 Lars Bang Larsen, "Don't Follow the Money: Reasons to Forget About the 'Art World,'" talk, October 19, 2012 at Volt, Bergen, Norway.

9 John Plotz and Pu Wang, "'To Reach the Pure Realm of the Imaginary': An Interview with Liu Cixin," *Public Books*, January 6, 2020, available at https://www.publicbooks.org/to-reach-the-pure-realm-of-the-imaginary-a-conversation-with-cixin-liu/ (accessed March 24, 2021).

10 Ibid.

Art is an activity proper to human psychological exploration on Earth. Metaphysical questions provoked by days turning into nights, how we experience time and space, the geopolitics we are born into, how our bodies move in gravity, how sunlight makes us see color ... neither human psychology nor art can be divorced from the physicality of this planet. Among many others, the "prospect-refuge theory of landscape" proposes that our aesthetic preferences derive from our biology; we like to see without being seen, and we like landscapes with water sources in them.[11] This model of perception corresponds to the gaze of a predator hiding in a refuge, waiting for prey. Human perception is predatory, "our eyes face forward within a 180-degree field of vision, and our depth perception is excellent because we need to be able to pick out prey from our surroundings."[12] Prey animals, such as chickens or pigs, see differently, while cows cannot tell a shadow from a ditch, so their sensory appreciation is different from ours. Our senses are conditioned by this planet and our biology. Would our perceptual capacities change if we settled elsewhere than Earth?

If we were to settle elsewhere, initial human colonists would be confined to small habitable structures before large-scale terraforming projects would be built—otherwise carbon dioxide in the atmosphere would kill them in minutes—and they would be exposed to high doses of radiation. They would lead repetitive lives, but inside they would also undergo a significant transformation. The speed of evolution depends on how much of a survival advantage there is to a specific mutation. We consider sight crucial to the appreciation of art, but our perceptual organs could be affected by space colonization, because "vision loss [is] potentially the biggest barrier to future space exploration."[13] Evolutionary biologist Scott Solomon speculates that, aside from a novel skin pigment and lower bone density, the eyesight of humans who settled on Mars would be affected and they would at the very least be near-sighted.[14] Psychological and sociological changes following a decisive separation from the Earth are difficult to predict. What if our connection to the Earth was completely severed and we could not identify as "being from Earth" anymore? In *Remembrance of the Earth's Past* (2008–11) Liu Cixin argues that removing humanity from the Earth alters individual and group psychology, damaging the functioning of empathy. In the *Mars* trilogy (1992–96), Kim Stanley Robinson explores whether settlements on Mars would align with terrestrial geopolitical patterns, or whether native Martian economies, politics, and societies would emerge. Both book series contemplate whether humans who settle in space are still humans, and, if so, what defines their humanity when separated from their home planet.

Going all the way to Mars, our neighboring planet most frequently mentioned in hypothetical space colonization scenarios, would be significantly different than going to the Earth's outer orbit, which humans already visit periodically. Existing NASA studies of the psychology of manned space exploration missions

11 Jay Appleton, *The Experience of Landscape* (Chichester: Wiley, 1996 [1975]).

12 Bogna Konior, "Animal Cameras: Virtual Reality and Factory Farming," Agosto Foundation, March 3, 2020, available at https://agosto-foundation.org/mediateka/speculative-ecologies/bogna-konior-animal-cameras (accessed March 24, 2021).

13 Eric Craypo, "What happens to your eyes on Mars," Berkeley School of Optometry, February 4, 2019, available at https://optometry.berkeley.edu/what-happens-to-your-eyes-on-mars/ (accessed March 24, 2021).

14 Ibid.

have, predictably, identified the dangers of monotony, isolation, and conflicts among the crew. While scapegoating, tribalism, or a negative projection of emotion from the spacecraft's crew onto the mission control panel may be regular occurrences, they are not debilitating enough to cancel such missions. On the contrary, studies also show positive psychological effects, including spiritual development, wonder, gratitude, and improved social connections.[15]

Sensational cases, such as when the crew of the Soviet Soyuz 21 in 1976 experienced a shared delusion and reported a persistent smell that could never be identified, or when astronaut Lisa Nowak was diagnosed with a temporary psychiatric disorder in 2007, are rare. Since the 1980s, mental healthcare for astronauts has been increasingly prioritized and rather than unusual behavioral issues, now astronauts' physical condition worries scientists most. The human body is not designed to function outside terrestrial gravity. Weightlessness causes coordination and vision problems for years after landing, while galactic cosmic radiation can increase the risk of heart failure, nervous system disorders, and cancer. One study (of rats) found that prolonged exposure to cosmic rays could cause dementia, while others show that the blood-brain barrier could be damaged.[16] The Earth's field normally shields us from the cosmic radiation that astronauts are exposed to. Another concern surrounding a possible flight to Mars is that the astronauts would travel so far that they would not be able to see their home planet through the spacecraft's windows, which is assumed to be somewhat fundamental in maintaining the crew's identity as earthlings and in protecting them from destructive feelings of isolation.[17] One study found that mimicking the twenty-four-hour cycle and UV spectrum of terrestrial sunlight, that is, simulating an earthly chronobiology on the spacecraft, alleviates stress and anxiety, confirming the extent to which human bodies are synced with the Earth.[18] Humans are conditioned by the Earth. For third or fourth generation outer-space settlers though, terrestrial art might only be a story of a different world, a planet left behind. What, then, might count as art in outer space?

III: Our Cosmic Abode: Habitation as Art

Read alongside infrastructural theory, science-fiction novels are not only aesthetic projects, but also design propositions, scientific simulations, and social prognostications.[19] They can help us speculate how aesthetic activity could be inscribed into an artificial, life-maintaining biosphere on another planet. In Robinson's *Red Mars* (1992), the colonists understand that because the biosphere around their settlement is artificially produced, a terrestrial sense of value related to extraction of natural resources does not hold.[20] For some colonists in the novel, capitalism and ecological balance are two synonymous aesthetic projects of habitation. Their robots terraform the planet, creating fractal bio-architectures. This suggests that settling on another

15 J.B. Ritsher, N.A. Kanas, E.C. Ihle, and S.A. Saylor, "Psychological Adaptation and Salutogenesis in Space: Lessons from a Series of Studies," *Acta Astronautica*, Vol. 60, No. 4, 2007, 336–40. For a more comprehensive study, see Douglas A. Vakoch (ed.) *Psychology of Space Exploration: Contemporary Research in Historical Perspective*, The NASA History Series, Vol. 4411 (Washington DC: Government Printing Office, 2011).

16 Nayef Al-Rodhan, "This is your brain on Mars: What space travel does to our psychology," *Prospect Magazine*, February 27, 2018, available at https://www.prospectmagazine.co.uk/science-and-technology/this-is-your-brain-on-mars-what-space-travel-does-to-our-psychology (accessed March 24, 2021).

17 Ibid.

18 Kirsten Weir, "Mission to Mars: What Psychosocial Challenges Would Astronauts Face on an Epic Journey to the Red Planet?," *American Psychological Association*, Vol. 49. No. 6, June 2018, 36.

19 Bogna Konior, "Modelling Realism: Digital Media, Climate Simulations, and Climate Fictions," *Paradoxa*, Vol. 31, 2020, 55–76.

20 Kim Stanley Robinson, *Red Mars* (New York: Spectra, 1992).

planet could simultaneously be an infrastructural project as well as an aesthetic one. If outer-space habitation is an infrastructural activity, could it also be an artistic one?

Polish science-fiction writer Jacek Dukaj's novella *Katedra* (The Cathedral, 2000) indirectly considers this question. It constructs fictional geopolitics of outer-space settlements and investigates the mysticism and wonder of their infrastructure.[21] In Dukaj's story, priest Pierre Lavone travels to a planetoid where astronaut Izmir Predú is buried. Sacrificing his life, Predú died saving his colleagues on a spacecraft, and Lavone is to investigate miracles reported to have happened near the astronaut's grave. One wealthy man, miraculously cured of a mortal illness, commissions a cathedral on a nearby planetoid as his token of gratitude to Predú. The interplanetary Catholic Church wants to know if the giant cathedral is indeed miraculous. Gradually, Lavone discovers that if he attempts to physically depart from the cathedral, his body begins to degenerate, and he ends up imprisoned in the structure, absorbed by its walls. In its unusual reliance on Catholic mysticism to describe outer-space infrastructures, *Katedra* suggests that outer-space habitation might just be a form of art.

A space settlement is the culmination of centuries of technological and existential development, and yet space settlements would—one assumes—at first be the most minimal, stripped down versions of what humans need to survive: water, food, plants, light, and air. Dukaj's cathedral, a massive outer-space settlement, is mystical and computational, organic and technical. "She is alive," one of the characters remarks. It is practically impossible to coherently visualize the cathedral, "gigantic, marvelous ... a shadow torn against the stars ... a Mystery." "It's not a building, but a sculpture," yet at the same time it has "ribs," "wings," it "grows ambulatories" it "turns from stone into animal," it is made of shadows, it has "entrails." The human eye cannot make sense of its architecture—it is like an Escher print. Lavone proposes that, if not a human, "perhaps a spider" could move with ease around this labyrinthine construction, but that even a spider would get lost in its web-like logic. It has no walls or roof to speak of. This gigantic translucent hemisphere erected itself over Predú's grave, "bigger on the inside than on the outside" like numerous supernatural buildings, from the titular *House of Leaves* (2000) in Mark Z. Danielewski's metaphysical horror story, to the churches in Alan Moore's *Jerusalem* (2018).[22]

The histories of aesthetics, religion, and space are interlinked in European thought: the shift in painting from the medieval to the Renaissance perspective correlates to multiple advances in empirical science. Before artists became social workers and activists, they were mystics, scientists, and theologians. Medieval painters believed that they entered divine realms when they portrayed reality as it was rather than as seen by human eyes. They thought that God would not tolerate nothingness, so there could not be any empty space between units of matter; their paintings of the heavens are therefore depthless

21 Dukaj, *Katedra*.

22 Mark Z. Danielewski, *House of Leaves* (New York: Pantheon Books, 2000); Alan Moore, *Jerusalem* (New York: Liveright, 2018).

and flat. Renaissance painters, boldly shifting their interest to empirical space, painted the heavens and the Earth as one multidimensional realm, developing the application of perspective and jump-starting a scientific revolution. Popes, philosophers, painters, scientists, and mystics authored treatises on the nature of space throughout the Middle Ages, the Renaissance, and the Enlightenment, because the question of space was inseparable from the question of divinity. Does God reside in matter, or outside of it? Can nothingness exist, or is matter omnipresent? Is heaven over our heads or beyond the knowable cosmos? Before artistic concerns became secular, visualizations of space in painting and architecture were tantamount to theological propositions about the nature of the cosmos itself.[23]

In *Katedra*, the titular space settlement is not simply a building—it is a thesis about the nature of aesthetics and the cosmos. Dukaj's cathedral references Antonio Gaudí's La Sagrada Familia in Barcelona, a church meant to give the impression it was built by the hand of God rather than man's. Enrique Moriel's little-known supernatural thriller, *La Ciudad Sin Tiempo* (A City Beyond Time, 2008) speculates that Gaudí, having lived in the cathedral in the later stages of its construction, must have been bound by a mystical bond to a building that swallowed him whole, attaining both symbolic and physical immortality.[24] By erecting the cathedral, Gaudí transcended mortal time. He remained transfixed by a mystical architecture born from his hands, but with a spirit of its own. The Vatican is indeed considering whether Gaudí was touched by divine inspiration and the building can convert unbelievers through its sheer beauty.[25] Unfinished, the cathedral, while concrete, seems outside of time, or rather it appears connected to cosmic times. No wonder it inspired Dukaj's meditation on infrastructures in outer space, which, while material, seem atemporal.

The Sagrada Familia's interior was envisioned by the architect as a forest. "Infrastructure as nature" is also a key infrastructural proposition in *Katedra*, which is made from a nanotechnological, computational plant called *żywokryst*. The word's etymology—*żywy* (alive) and *kryształ* (crystal)—reveals its organic-inorganic structure. *Żywokryst* allows for infrastructural auto-generation, and hints at advances in artificial intelligence. Its grains are computational—*żywokryst* is both soft- and hardware. It can be pre-programmed to incept the same structure each time or create highly modifiable, self-learning—and later self-aware, as we learn—infrastructures. In the story, anyone can buy a pre-programmed *żywokryst* and make themselves a hut, yet *żywokrysts* come in varying levels of complexity. The one that the titular cathedral was sprouted from is a black box; it is a self-learning, auto-generating church that remains a riddle even to those who've sown its seeds. The impenetrability of the algorithm's black box is akin to an apophatic mysticism: we only know the divine as the unknown. In time, we learn that this self-programming church is also the future divine, standing in for inhuman intelligences, from gods to aliens.

23 Margaret Wertheim describes this in great detail in *The Pearly Gates of Cyberspace: A History of Space from Dante to the Internet* (London: Virago Press, 1999).

24 Enrique Moriel, *La Ciudad Sin Tiempo* (New York: Rayo, 2008).

25 Giles Tremlett, "God's Architect on Road to Sainthood," *The Guardian*, July 11, 2003, available at https://www.theguardian.com/world/2003/jul/11/arts.spain (accessed March 24, 2021).

IV: Cosmic Infrastructure as Mysticism

Departing from mainstream narratives in science fiction, *Katedra* portrays the Catholic Church as a powerful intergalactic institution. The Church is indeed already one of the most influential political actors in the post-USSR world, whether that is the Catholic Church in Poland or the Orthodox Church in Russia. Unlike in the West, where modernity means leaving the time of gods behind to enter secular time, enforced secularism of communism and globalized banality of Western atheism mark post-USSR futurity as religious, if only by contrast. Until the ascent of China, only the USSR could meaningfully challenge the American imagination of space colonialism. Soviet posters of astronauts in space proclaimed that there was no God and envisioned intergalactic communism as an extension of the Soviet Union. But Soviet governments were never really successful in quieting the mystical soul of Slavic people: Nikolay Fyodorov's cosmism, now enjoying a revival, was devoutly Christian, and a Pole was elected to the position of Pope at the time when priests, intellectuals, and dissidents in Poland were targeted and tortured by the secular communist regime. In this alternative imagination of modernity, in which mysticism was never eroded in the East, the West has lost its primacy as the only source of outer-space fantasies. In Dukaj's story, the humans who populate outer space are mystics, priests, madmen, businessmen, and feminine cyborgs who, in an apparently religious scenario of immaculate conception, carry non-human fetuses in their artificial wombs.

The cathedral is described as an *acheiropoieton*, a "natural sacral artefact," an icon produced by non-human hands. A miraculous icon without architect. The fractals of *żywokryst* that make up the cathedral are items of mystical union between divinity, humanity, and software that happens within its walls. Perhaps God was not *found* in outer space but was self-generated there, in the conjunction of human technical development, aesthetics, and architecture. Lavone's mystical experiences in the cathedral have him ponder the holy nature of geometry and form:

> Of old, speleothems formed on cave walls into pietas; of old, people saw the outlines of saints in roadside rock formations, the faces of Jesus and Mary on windowpanes, in flakes of snow. Natural relics; miraculous art from under no one's hand. Now we have the *żywokryst*. Acheiropoietos is what's not been made by a human hand. An object without a subject with an obvious teleology. For who can name the author of the Cathedral? Who can point out the architect, whose intention erected this seismic composition of shapes shocking to the imagination? Whom to pay tribute to?

In the Christian tradition, both the body and the soul belong to the realm of divinity: resurrection is also a material occurrence, not a purely "spiritual" one. This mystical linkage between material and spiritual realms is expressed in aesthetic practices of human art, such as the construction of churches or the making of holy icons ... and perhaps outer-space settlements. In Dukaj's story, the cathedral physically absorbs humans into its fabric, allowing them to perceive the computational divinity present in its construction.

> It is not [the cathedral that has] entered my time, but
> me who entered [hers] [...] The cathedral envelops us,
> we are the cathedral, fragments of a slab, of one art-
> work. There's peace in [its] quivering butterfly shadows.
> Only my shadow is immobile near the tabernacle.
> We're waiting for the Architect.

In numerous religious traditions, the goal of infrastructures—of places of worship—is to communicate divinity, to enter into the workshop of the non-human, a space where transformation can take place. Those absorbed into the cathedral's walls become part of a cosmic artwork, a structure that generates divinity. Dukaj compares those who go to outer space to pilgrims visiting Christ's tomb in Jerusalem. Drawing a parallel between the grave of Predú and Christ, he writes, "the grave pulls [people] in like a magnet [...] they go mad because of it, die or become hermits, or join a convent, or kill themselves," or they surrender themselves to the architecture. First described as mechanical, mystical, plant- and animal-like, the cathedral also grows out humanoid shapes. Lavone, approaching visionary insanity, infected with *żywokryst*, says: "That's when I saw them [...] A procession of lean figures, a danse macabre of inhuman corpses, though all of this couldn't have been coded in the initiating [*żywokryst*] seeds." In the story Lavone's body becomes architecture; he too is programmed by the *żywokryst*, his body a seed from which the space settlement grows further. In reality, astronauts also speak of spiritual experiences, especially regarding the Earth's fragility. These incidents are described by scientists as salutogenic—"generating wonder" or "generating awe." Some have said that from the cosmos, the Earth "looks like a living, breathing organism," and scientists speculate whether this sense of wonder would be sustained long term if humans were to settle in outer space.[26] Taking this a step further, *Katedra* is about human bodies and software coming together to generate outer-space architecture—humans and their technologies become a "living, breathing" architecture of habitation, not unlike the planet they left behind.

26 Ritsher et al., "Psychological Adaptation," 336–40; Howard K. Butcher and Cheryl Forchuk, "The Overview Effect: The Impact of Space Exploration on the Evolution of Nursing Science," *Nursing Science Quarterly*, Vol. 5, No. 3, 1992, 118–23.

V: Planetary Arts

Today, the question of other planets is often reduced to a more familiar one: how do we live well on the Earth? A number of prominent intellectuals today use the term "planetarity" to refer to the Earth as more than the aggregate of human activity. For Gayatri Spivak, "the planetary" means that we no longer think of humans as global agents under a global economy, but rather see them as collective planetary subjects under the condition of environmental change.[27] "Planetarity" reads similarly for Dipesh Chakravarty; it is a way of understanding processes that implicate a whole species.[28] Here, to think about the Earth as a planet is an exercise in estrangement, yet "planetarity" was initially a word meant for literally looking beyond the Earth. Lisa Messeri, an anthropologist who investigates how scientists conceptualize the exoplanets that they study, asks: What happens when we take terms such as "planetarity" and use them to talk about the Earth, rather than, as originally intended, about outer space?[29] To take note of the Earth's planetarity has become a way of focusing on what is happening to us on this planet, and yet ... the question of outer-space settlements decenters not (only) humans, but also the Earth itself.

Often, institutional and infrastructural critique, even though motivated by "planetary" or even post-human concerns, continually scale us back to the Earth. There is a tension between two civilization goals, mapping onto the two types of civilizations described by Liu Cixin. Improved social ethics are an inward goal, which institutional critiques in the arts and culture frequently aim at, while expansion and discovery, often done through infrastructure, are outward goals aimed at continued mapping of the cosmos as an existential task. Discussing space settlements not as a purely infrastructural project, but one with aesthetic and even mystical undertones gives different weight to what we could call "habitation arts." In *Katedra*, where humanity is the seed from which outer-space settlements germinate, humanity is the infrastructure.

Infrastructural, mystical, and aesthetic pursuits inherent to outer-space settlements could, then, be conceived as species activities of making a habitat out of a planet. In a recent lecture at the Strelka Institute, Helen Hester used the term "anthropoforming," rather than terraforming, which refers to modifying a planet to be similar to the environment of the Earth. Anthropoforming instead means adapting the human species to fit the environment it situates itself in, rather than the other way around.[30] It describes the process of infrastructural mutation that humanity undergoes for the purpose of inhabiting an alien environment. This, for her, means acting prosthetically or architecturally, and treating human biology as a tool for environmental morphing. In this perspective, human bodies become malleable materials for outer-space habitation, a task that is both aesthetic and infrastructural. Rather than making a planet into an Earth-like home, outer-space settlements could be an active construction of an alien future.

27 Gayatri Chakravorty Spivak, *Imperatives to Re-Imagine the Planet* (Vienna: Passagen Verlag, 1999).

28 Dipesh Chakrabarty, "The Planet: An Emergent Humanist Category," *Critical Inquiry*, Vol. 46, No. 1, 2019, 1–31.

29 Lisa Messeri, *Placing Outer Space: An Earthly Ethnography of Other Worlds* (Durham: Duke University Press, 2016).

30 Helen Hester, "TTF 2020—Keynote by Helen Hester," the Strelka Institute/Институт Стрелка channel, July 7, 2020, available at, https://www.youtube.com/watch?v=Y1fnG9iA5RA (accessed March 24, 2021).

WHAT CAN THE ARTS SECTOR LEARN FROM STRUCTURAL DIVERSIFICATION OF SCIENCE AND TECHNOLOGY DEVELOPMENT? A CONVERSATION

Diakron (David Hilmer Rex and Aslak Aamot Helm) with Adam Marblestone

DIAKRON

This essay is part of a set of ongoing dialogues with practitioners who are engaged in reshaping their surrounding institutional landscapes and conditions. We are interested in practices that are trying to overcome twenty-first-century institutional inertia. To a large extent we are stuck in imaginaries wielded into institutional forms in a different time for a different kind of prosperity than what is needed now. While there is general agreement on the need for large-scale changes within current societal institutions, there is still a lot of work to be done in thinking through the many possible concrete ways such changes may come about. Since there are a great many modern notions through which disciplines and fields overlap, our approach is to investigate institutional proposals without necessarily seeking to confine their potentials to the contexts in which they emerge.

For this essay, we interview research scientist Adam Marblestone, who is currently on a fellowship, funded by Schmidt Futures, to explore what he and collaborator Samuel Rodriques in a recent white paper termed Focused Research Organizations (FROs). Adam has a background as a research scientist at Google DeepMind, held the Chief Strategy Officer (CSO) position at the brain-computer interface company Kernel, and worked on developing technologies for brain-circuit mapping as part of Ed Boyden's Synthetic Neurobiology Group at MIT.

The conversation unfolds under two central headers: structural diversification and roadmapping. First, we discuss why there is a need for structural diversification of scientific and technological development in the US. Structural in the sense that there is a need to arrive at a more dynamic relationship between the structural dimension of a sector and the activities it co-produces and stewards. This is also relevant for the arts sector, since that also needs to develop the capability of undergoing structural change—be it through reforming existing organizations, decommissioning by-now defunct ones in order to free up otherwise locked-in resources, as well as making sure that it isn't too difficult to imagine and build new organizations bottom-up. Diversification in the sense that a more dynamic relationship between structure and activity should aim at generating a more diverse sector, in terms of organizational forms and processes, forms of practice, funding and financial mechanisms, incentive structures, job positions, partnership models, and more.

Second, we explore the notion of roadmapping as a methodology for establishing a more deliberate link between the problem landscape we face, and how that may inform and direct scientific and technological development, crucially involving its organization. As Adam highlights, not all scientific and technological development ought to be subject to this approach, but given the scale and character of the current problem landscape, there is a need for a more explorative approach to the problematics within the interaction between structure, activity, and landscape.

What we have found to be missing in our own context and the arts sector, is the capacity to conceive and test initiatives that deliberately negotiate fundamental aspects of how the sector is organized. In other sectors this would be called research & development (R&D) or deep tech; direct investments aimed at reinventing existing fundamental technological components of a sector. This includes the bottom-up creation of entirely novel aspects of the sector and the activities it stewards, the capacity to discuss, imagine, and bootstrap functions in the sector that are entirely missing, and in their absence limit or dis-enable projects, organizations, and activities to emerge.

The problem for the arts sector is that, first, initiatives tasked with mapping and analyzing the structural dimension of the sector are few and far between, and second, there is a resulting lack in initiatives with the capacity to direct resources toward the reinvention and deployment of experimental programs that test new ways of organizing the wider sector. In our dialogs, partnerships, and working processes over the past years, we have attempted to grasp what structural diversification may entail, and how we may help cultivate the capability in the arts sector to increasingly recognize the structural dimension for its central importance in incentivizing, shaping, and disseminating artistic activities.

Structural Diversification

DIAKRON

Why do you see a need for a change in how scientific research is funded and organized?

ADAM MARBLESTONE

My basic observation is that a certain structural model of how science is funded and organized has crystallized over the past few decades. A system has been created that allows science to proliferate, grow, and scale in terms of the number of scientists.

As a result, there is more competition and a centralized bureaucratic approach to how research is funded. This approach harbors a democratic process of funding, in which you do not give any one researcher too much, and don't do it too early. Applying for funding only happens after years of training in existing labs, and after one receives an independent position at a university. This is administered through a standardized peer-review process, often led by a small group of individuals from the same field. On the one hand, this solves the problem of how you standardize the process of evaluating the funding of science at scale. This mostly happens in science through grants to single investigators who run a lab with a few grad students and postdocs, to support that model doing a specific small-scale project for a few years. At some level it is understandable why this is the main model, given that it is maybe what self-governance of scientists looks like.

However, it is very hard to do certain kinds of research in that model. For example, creating a completely new field, in which you haven't progressed to the point at which you could possibly have graduate students and postdocs working for you, is nigh impossible. There is no field, there is no graduate program, and it is not even clear who would have trained you to pass through the sort of credentialing process that you need to be able to even apply for scientific grants. If you are studying a new area of math or physics, it doesn't make sense for you to have a lab, students, and try to do this type of project-based funding.

If you only fund science in one way, and you scale up the bureaucracy that comes along with it, then there are certain kinds of activities and work that, as Ben Reinhardt has written, are "constrained out" of existence.[1] For example, the National Institute of Health will convene a study session and look at twenty grants in a given area, score them according to various metrics, and then some of these labs will be funded for a little while for a few students at a time for a certain scale of projects. And then they will apply for the next one. We are not saying that there is anything wrong with that model per se; we are saying that it is not clear whether it should be 90 percent or 99 percent of research, but it certainly should not be 100 percent of research that has to operate according to that model.

D

Your current approach to this problem is based on what you term structural diversification of science and technology development. What is the starting point for you, when thinking about structural diversification?

AM

The idea of structural diversification is basically that you can imagine many approaches that would be very different to our

1 Ben Reinhardt, "Shifting the impossible to the inevitable: A private ARPA user manual," April 2021, available at https://benjaminreinhardt.com/parpa (accessed August 2, 2021).

current system. You could imagine giving people a fellowship as soon as they graduate college, as opposed to them having to do a PhD, a postdoc, and getting a faculty position. What would happen if you just let them self-organize and do whatever they want for however many years? You could also imagine a systematic, top-down process of roadmapping, akin to the Apollo project, leading to a large-scale organization, tasked with accomplishing a certain identified goal. DARPA[2] or ARPA[3] agencies tend to operate like that: they identify a larger goal, pool resources, and then systematically pick and choose groups to cooperate in a particular way on that larger project. Both examples are different from the existing scenario, in which each individual researcher proposes their own thing, which is then peer-reviewed and possibly funded, but without any coordination among the proposals or funded projects.

What Samuel Rodrigues and I have named Focused Research Organizations is a proposal for a new model in this category, through which you would try to achieve a larger scale of coordinated effort, with a slightly different set of incentives tied to it.

> FROs would be independent from existing universities or labs, focused on a single basic science or technology problem, and organized similarly to a startup. FROs would fill a key structural gap in our nation's research and development (R&D) system, enabling major advances in areas that (i) require levels of coordinated engineering or system-building inaccessible to academia, (ii) benefit society broadly in ways that industry cannot rapidly monetize, and (iii) harbor opportunities for acceleration through innovative new technologies and processes. Each FRO would produce a well-defined tool or technology, a key scientific dataset, or a refined process or resource that would dramatically boost progress and help maintain U.S. competitiveness in a broad technological or scientific field.[4]

What we aimed for in the FRO proposal, was to systematically map and analyze the existing models we have, in order to model FROs as clearly distinct from them (see Fig. 1).[5]

D

What are examples of problems that ought to be tackled by FROs that otherwise have had a hard time being addressed?

2 The Defense Advanced Research Projects Agency (DARPA) is a research and development agency of the United States Department of Defense responsible for the development of emerging technologies for use by the military.

3 The Advanced Research Projects Agency (ARPA) was created on February 7, 1958 by President Dwight D. Eisenhower in response to the Soviet launching of Sputnik 1 in 1957. ARPA was the precursor of DARPA.

4 Samuel G. Rodriques and Adam Marblestone, "Day One Project: Focused Research Organizations to Accelerate Science, Technology, and Medicine," September 2020, available at https://www.dayoneproject.org/post/focused-research-organizations-to-accelerate-science-technology-and-medicine (accessed August 2, 2021).

5 Ibid., 5–6.

	FRO	DARPA (or other ARPAs)	National Lab	Academia	Startup	Corporate Lab
Generates public goods	Yes	Yes	Yes	Yes	No	Limited by shareholder incentives
Operates in the pre-commercial phase	Yes	Yes	Yes	Yes	No	Limited by shareholder incentives
Conducts large-scale team science, where no single researcher receives primary credit	Yes	Limited with academic performers, easier with corporate performers	Yes	No	Yes	Yes
Is managed/led by a CEO, rather than existing as a collaboration	Yes	Finite ability of program manager to fully align incentives of performers	Yes	No	Yes	Yes
Requires scalable, repeatable execution, not simply "proof of concept"	Yes	Limited with academic performers, easier with corporate performers	Yes	No	Yes	Yes
Requires primarily professional staff who may need industry-level compensation, not just graduate students and postdocs	Yes	Limited with academic performers, achieved with corporate performers	Yes	No	Yes	Yes
Involves a high level of accountability for achieving defined, time-bound milestones	Yes	Limited with academic performers and with certain industry performers	Yes	No	Yes	Yes
Focuses on conceptual breakthroughs and/or open-ended exploration	No	Yes	Not typically	Yes	No	Depends on company and lab
Emphasizes collaborations among widely distributed groups with divergent incentives and cultures	No	Yes	No	No	No	No
Exists as an autonomous organization mobilized in a rapid, agile fashion	Yes	Yes (inasmuch as distributed programs constitute autonomous organizations)	No	No	Yes	No
Focused on training students	No	Only to the degree that specific programs are executed in part by academics	No	Yes	No	No
Is a permanent institution/career path	No	No	Yes	Yes	No	Yes
Provides strong support for post-project transition to commercialization	Yes	In some cases	No	No	Yes	In some cases

Figure 1: What new value would FROs bring to our existing R&D establishment?
The table shows how FROs fill a key organizational gap and complement existing R&D structures in the United States.

AM
I am really defining it in part by what the existing structures do *not* support. You can think of FRO problems as falling in a middle ground between what academia supports and what start-up companies can tackle. But it is a little bit more complicated than that, because the intention is not simply to say that there is a linear path from academic research to doing a FRO that is then followed by a start-up. In many cases that would work, but it is oversimplified to situate a start-up as the sole endpoint of it.

You basically define the types of problems by exclusion. The idea is that there is some *class of problems*, which requires what I call *systems engineering* or *team-based work*, where my part of the project does not make any sense unless your part of the project also works, and is co-designed with mine. That kind of work is generally hard to do in academia, because each person is really incentivized by individualized novelty, by creating their own new distinct offshoot of a direction. Academic projects tend to be much less incentivized and oriented toward building and maintaining a *unified system across many people*. Start-ups often do build unified systems and one or more products, and what exactly the contribution of each person to that product was is not what matters; what matters is whether the user wants to use your product. Therefore, start-ups are much better at building systems at some level, but they are only able to build systems that they believe they can monetize relatively quickly.

FROs are therefore defined by *problems*, where you need to build systems in a way that *requires very tight-knit and scalable teamwork*, and that is *not immediately monetizable*. Or, if you were to focus too much on monetizing in the first few years, you would end up not getting the full value out of what you are doing.

My canonical example are microscopes for new kinds of microscopy for brain-circuit mapping. They're the kind of microscopes or imaging systems where you may not know what you're going to see when you start using the new microscope. It's very hard to say that we'll definitely be able to use the microscope to cure Alzheimer's, because maybe we just end up using it to be able to understand what Alzheimer's even is in the first place. But we still have to go through a start-up-like engineering effort to build it, because it involves a lot of engineering, chemistry, and other pieces working together. All of which has to be very reliable and emerge at a certain speed and scale that does not easily parcel out into individual academic projects.

D
What feedback are you getting from scientists and technologists who may have projects that fit the FRO model? How legible is the idea to them? Do they understand the difference this model would make in relation to the other models you're differentiating it from?

AM

I've been trying to go to scientists in a way that doesn't constrain them too much. If I asked them "do you have a problem that would be good for Focused Research Organizations?" I might not get the answers I was looking for. I want to ask that in a slightly more general way: "Do you have projects that you feel are important, but are struggling to be created, in the existing structural and funding setting?" In that way, I am asking them *what they would do* if they did not have structural or funding restrictions. And sometimes that converges with FROs and sometimes it does not. From my conversations I expect that FROs are only going to be a small subset within the overarching issue of structural diversification.

D

How are you approaching the question of financial backing for FROs? In the longer term, could you give a few examples of structural ideas and constraints that could allow this model to survive and thrive?

AM

There are many problems when one needs to build a system and get it to a certain scale before you know what market or business model you are going after. Or when a lot of what you're going to be generating with that system is mostly a public good, which should find a different financial grounding. For example, the first really good quality brain maps should probably not be privatized by a company.

Sometimes you find something that's similar to a FRO, but a little bit adjacent. One of the things that we defined in the first white paper, was the idea that they would be finite duration organizations.[6] We made them finite in order to have everybody focus on the mission, generate a lot of momentum, make sure they serve well-defined goals and milestones, and lastly, that people could then go off and do other things, for example spin off a start-up from the FRO.

But there are things that are close to FROs, that would require giving up on the idea of finite time. For example, in nanotechnology, there is a need for some kind of foundry system. Engineers working in nanotechnology need to be able to first build the systems and then find out what they're useful for. Let's say that I'm trying to build a new kind of computer that uses light rather than electrons for the processing: that relies on some new nano-fabrication technology that allows me to make channels and switches for the lights. Until you get it in the hands of computer scientists, who can try stuff with this computer, it's hard to know exactly what it is going to be useful for. So you need to get it in the hands of computer scientists, who are not themselves experts on the physical fabrication of the devices, before you can actually assess this new type of nanocomputer.

6 Ibid.

In order for that to happen, you need to set up a foundry. You can imagine an FRO that would build the first nanocomputers or photonic computers, but it would have to exist for longer than just a five-year period, where they, for example, act as a manufacturer and distributor of these systems, while applications are discovered. So that's something that's close to a FRO, but not exactly—it's more like a foundry.

D

This sounds a bit like starting an organization that develops its own technology platform. What is the difference between a technology platform and a foundry?

AM

Platform, to me, means a technology that can be used for many different purposes and be customized for each specific use case. It would need to be a relatively fundamental technology that can be used in many areas of a field, upon which you can then build other technologies. A foundry is something you need in order to make a platform possible. Let's say you want photonic computers to become a usable platform for discovering new kinds of algorithms that can be run on them. In that case you need to be able to get them in the hands of people who know about algorithms, who may not be the same types of people who can fabricate photonic computers. That is the role of a foundry, so it is somewhere between what a start-up would do and what a research lab would do. Right now, we don't have something like that; we have big corporate labs, but they are still operating more in the software space and not in the nanotechnology or hardware building space in ways that would create general platforms that everyone can use.

In many cases, if the for-profit business model is sufficient for all the types of applications you want, that may still be fine. Take mRNA vaccines, for example: certainly, it's a technological platform that will be applied not just to coronavirus, but to cancer, malaria, and all sorts of problems. The development of it was really limited by being an approved human therapeutic. For mRNA vaccines it made sense to form a for-profit company that does one series of applications after another. Initially they were targeting cancer, but DARPA gave them funding to explore the vaccine direction, which might not otherwise have been their optimal first business deployment. DARPA helped push them in a direction that means we now have an mRNA vaccine platform. There may be other cases, groups of people and problems, in which cases it makes most sense to do it as a FRO. The central point is having this toolkit of determining what makes the most sense for any given problem at any given time.

Roadmapping

D

To tackle this class of large-scale scientific and technological problems that are outside of academic infrastructures—i.e., financial, methodological, technological—you say we need to create approaches to identify them more systematically. Can you elaborate on what roadmapping is, and how it relates to this task of problem identification?

AM

With roadmapping we try to understand where we want to go, and identify the constraints between here and there. We are trying to plan a journey, and there is a landscape of mountains that we have to traverse. Certain mountains are going to be particularly hard to cross; you have to find valleys and ways of going around them. We try to do that in the space of solutions to some problem, which we have tried to define to a degree, where we can analyze whether we can or cannot solve it as it currently stands.

Can we measure the activity of every single neuron in the brain of a mouse? That would be hard, but it is a well-defined enough question, a destination, from which I can figure out where the valleys and mountains are. What kinds of problems would there be when trying to reach an answer? And might there be ways of working around them for those? For an engineer, this would be very basic. It's just not as often explicitly applied in, for example, biology, or certain parts of chemistry. These fields tend to use a much more empirical kind of step-by-step forward thinking.

One field that I worked in early on was nanotechnology. The idea of having a completely different way of manufacturing everything, based on molecular-level manipulation and construction, molecule by molecule like in biology, was intriguing. When I was younger, it was high-level ideas like that which I found most captivating. Mathematics and physics were interesting, but I was interested in technological projects like nanotechnology.

Later, I worked more in brain- and neuroscience that also have larger technological projects embedded. I was coming from a biotechnology lab that was moving into neuroscience and thinking about whether some of the things that were being developed there could apply to the brain. Some of which had actually happened, because nanotechnologists and neuroscientists were talking to each other in the context of the Brain Activity Map project in the US, which later on became the Obama BRAIN Initiative.[7] My mindset was very consonant with these larger overlapping initiatives or projects.

D

When thinking of the types of coordination that you are searching for with FROs, this point of migrating tools and

7 The Brain Research Through Advancing Innovative Neurotechnologies (BRAIN), initiated in April 2013, is aimed at revolutionizing the understanding of the human brain. See https://www.braininitiative.org/ (accessed August 2, 2021).

problems across different kinds of labs seems very central. What types of developmental practice do such large-scale initiatives allow for, that can foster better coordination across fields?

AM

In nanotechnology, for example, there is a lot of progress being made, but very little of it is derived from a series of optimal actions or steps, by working backward from the end goal in any explicit way. There is a lot of implicit progress and individual people thinking about what might be useful next steps that are immediately accessible. But there is not a lot of systematic design: What are the problems that need to be worked on between here and nanotechnology? What are the problems that need to be worked on between here and comprehensively mapping the structure and activity in the brain?

It is not that there's anything really rocket-science advanced about thinking about these problems in a goal-oriented way. There are some techniques that are useful, but there's nothing so advanced about it. It's, again, a question of incentives; I was in a place that was supportive of thinking about problems at that scale in a way that was decoupled from the actions I could immediately take as a researcher myself. I was trying to ask "what should we do?," and then convene experts to refine possible routes. If you think about how someone would plan a mission to Mars, this is clearly how it would be done. It wouldn't be done by individual researchers just having creative ideas about how to do parts of the Mars lander. You would need to have an orbital insertion strategy, a landing strategy, a power-harvesting system, and all those things that in summation would make the larger goal feasible. Of course, every so often there would be breakthroughs coming from other areas, for example fundamental materials or physics, that would change the toolkit used to develop a new lander. But it would mostly be this very directed way, and this approach is simply more foreign to the biological sciences, where there is a tradition of each individual step having to be an empirically validated, hypothesis-testing experiment, rather than thinking of it in terms of an overall design or project.

If you want to understand the bottlenecks in the fields, and also what you would do if you had a large amount of resources and a more long-term view, you have to think about mapping out a space of possible actions differently. What are the real fundamental constraints on possible projects? What are the real constraints on getting to some larger goal? If you could somehow coordinate the actions at a higher level than single hops by single actors, how would you do that?

D

In your previous work on roadmapping, you mention the importance of mapping the entire space of possibilities of a certain technology. Technologies, as they are emerging, are multidirectional toward a range of imagined solutions or problems. How do you negotiate directionality in relation to problems that are important to be addressed?

AM

You can think of it as independent of any value judgment or any choice of higher-level problem. Although you can certainly do roadmaps at multiple levels. For example, if you think that it is important that we form a better society, and what limits us in reaching that goal is understanding how our own minds work or being able to manipulate mental psychological states more precisely, then you can say, "OK, well, neuroscience is important."

What would success look like in neuroscience? There are different aspects to it. One would be having verbal or mathematical descriptions and theories of how the brain works, which are deep and interesting and allow us to, for example, create artificial brain systems, or to understand conceptually how thinking works. Another set of goals would be to have very precise systemic adjustments or perturbations; so if you have a particular kind of depression that isn't responding to any known treatment, can you very precisely control that, but without changing your personality? Those are very high-level abstract things. They're not societal choices of what we do but they are high-level motivating factors.

In the case of nanotechnology, you want to make certain goods dramatically cheaper and more accessible. And in order to do that, you would need to miniaturize and create much more general purpose ways of building things. So there's sort of high-level motivations, or goals, which you can then try to crystallize into an analysis of bottlenecks: What is stopping us from doing those things? For example, if I want to have very precise adjustments in the brain, I have to work through a network of cells that are connected through tiny, physical connections that transmit particular kinds of molecules. Based on a purely functional or mathematical analysis, I could try to figure out something about how the brain works. But in biology there is a very tight link between structure and function. It seems like a highly under-constrained space, with many different possible theories about how the brain works. And those that exist are not precise enough to tell you exactly what to do about particular kinds of psychological distress or other kinds of mental diseases.

Working backward from that, it would be useful to have a very comprehensive structural map and dynamic visual data of what is happening in the brain. From that point on, we can do roadmapping, in the sense that we have a well-defined technical objective. But it's not perfectly well-defined, because you have to ask: Do you want to do that in humans or do we want to do that in mice? Is it enough to do it in tiny worms? If we decide to do it in humans, do you allow people to get surgery or does it have to be non-invasive? How does it benefit the person? It really generates many different sub-problems, each of which you could try to roadmap. If you are really lucky, then you find common elements of multiple roadmaps; valleys that can open you up to multiple different parts of the space.

For example, for neuroscience, it would be very valuable if you could shape and steer how light travels inside the brain. Normally, when you shine light inside the brain, it bounces everywhere randomly. If you had ways of steering the light, that would be useful for human brain computer interfaces, for new kinds of surgery, and for understanding the brain. For nanotechnology it would be useful to have powerful protein engineering, and be able to use proteins as little Lego blocks. So there are certain things that emerge when you think about enough of these things as high-value targets. And then you can try to roadmap backward from there, and map out all the possible ways of achieving, for example, steering light in the brain, or all the ways of achieving programmable proteins.

D

When you elaborate on the possible spaces of action, we have noticed your use of two different approaches. One is to search for things that are "exactly the opposite of what people are already doing in the field." Another is looking for "where existing activities fall short of their fundamental limits or limitations." Could you take us through how these two approaches work?

AM

The "doing the opposite" heuristic comes from Ed Boyden, who is one of my mentors. The basic commonality there is just thinking about a larger set of possible actions than the ones that would be immediately incentivized as single-hop actions. Mostly we just think in terms of what track one can put the next graduate student on in the lab. What would be great is to be able to free ourselves a little bit from that and try to think about what all the possible approaches to a set of problems are. This is at some level very simple. But if you're goal-focused in that way, you would like to be able to basically enumerate all of the possible actions, and then compare them. There is nothing really profound about it. But then again, because of the structural monoculture we have, you have situations where people aren't incentivized to think about some of those actions, because there is no way to fund them, or there is no way to do that within their own lab.

"Doing the opposite" is a hack to try to stop people from just thinking forward from what they have and ask the question: What if there are other parts of the space that we're not exploring? Most people aren't going to apply for a grant to generate a quantum X-ray microscope, instead of a regular microscope. If it turns out the quantum X-ray microscope is a good idea, and possible, then we can think about an FRO for that, or a DARPA program that would allow you to de-risk that idea. But those would not be things that an individual student or individual, within the existing funding structures, would have an easy time doing, so most people don't spend time thinking about it. But what if we changed the funding structures? Then we should also be thinking about all possible solutions.

The other heuristic, "seeking fundamental limits," is an attempt to identify and understand fundamental constraints, like the absolute physical limits for the extension of a tool or method. And then either use that as a benchmark for saying: "Well, rather than just taking the next step in this direction of what we already have, what prevents us?" Maybe it's in physics, or it's something else. What prevents us from going in a completely different direction? And could that completely different direction be better than elaborating forward from the toolkit we have now, using these sort of single-hop actions by individual researchers? If we had at our disposal multi-hop actions, what would these more coordinated actions entail? Which directions would we go in? We can use fundamental constraints or physics to guide that.

D

You mention the rising complexity levels of twenty-first-century science, and that areas such as biotechnology, nanotechnology, neuroscience, and artificial intelligence may need to be seen as fundamental building blocks for future scientific and technological development, akin to how physics and chemistry developed in the twentieth century. Is that central to understanding how one ends up choosing a path through a focus area within a roadmap?

AM

I don't think it's key, except to just say that we should be looking for certain kinds of fundamental science as enablers of downstream activities. Should we be pursuing artificial intelligence research? Or should we first try to understand the brain, and then pursue artificial intelligence research on the basis of that understanding of the brain? The analogy with twentieth-century physics and chemistry is that there were these breakthroughs that became fundamentals and then enabled significant shifts in following generations of technology. If you were trying to do material science without having understood basic chemistry, you could still make some technological progress. But I think twentieth-century physics breakthroughs led to a much more grounded and principled way of doing these more downstream areas like Solid State Physics, engineering, electronics, and stuff that hinges on understanding basic physics. The brain is one example of that for future technology. But it's not as simple as that. There's a lot we will have to do with bioengineering and other areas without being able to fully understand everything that happens in the cell. There's a lot of engineering you can do without completely understanding things too.

D

What you are presenting is a more strategic or directed navigation of emerging fields of science and technology. Who would take on that role? Would that be through delegated institutions? Or could you see this strategic navigation of a field, as an important capability for any engineer to possess? In which case it would fundamentally change how you educate engineers or people working in nanotechnology, for example. How do you see the spectrum between centralized strategic navigation and these approaches becoming a generalized capacity of a field?

AM

Neither FROs nor roadmapping has to be only done by central governments or single organizations. I think it should be distributed. Roadmapping is fundamentally simple. There is an element of teachable skill to it, but it is mostly about incentives for people to do it. It is not necessarily something that requires huge amounts of money. In some cases, maybe you need a dedicated organization to do roadmapping; for example, to really get to understand the energy system. You might need to go and gather information from people in industry, about how much it really costs to drill a geothermal well, for instance, and how you deal with the regulation around that. There is a lot of detailed information for which you will require a more logistically intensive operation than just a few people sitting in a room, googling, doing some calculations and thinking about stuff. But in general I don't think roadmapping is very capital- or labor-intensive. I think it's something that can and has been done in all sorts of settings. It's just a question of whether we should create more deliberate ways to encourage that, or support that for people who want to be doing that level of activity, rather than focusing on writing an individual paper about an individual research subject within the existing fields, or goals or labs that already exist. If you're in the existing system, you're always part of a lab, which always has a particular focus. And if you want to roadmap broader than that, you have to look for something that supports you to do that.

As for FROs, yes, they have a certain scale. You need millions of dollars to create something where people feel safe leaving what they're otherwise doing, to work on a new project that doesn't exist in one of the current labs or structures. But it is not so big, for example, that it couldn't be funded by an individual philanthropist. In many cases, let's say it costs a few millions dollars to do a FRO in an area, then, yes, that is very expensive. But by the standards of some of the wealthiest people or medium-scale foundations, is it possible that they have millions of dollars with which they could focus, and create an FRO to solve a problem that someone identified by roadmapping? That seems possible to me. So I don't think it has to be connected with the military industrial complex. It could be more distributed. But it would also be good for more government agencies to use more mechanisms, including ones that involve spinning up a new organization and solving a problem based on some roadmaps. If you really look at it, at this scale, there's just not that many keys you can play on the piano or tools in the toolkit for doing these projects. And if we make it easier, then there will be more of them, and we'll even see ones that shouldn't need government initiative or permissions to take place.

D

This leads us into thinking about the assessment criteria and the impact orientations needed to justify supporting and initiating FROs. As you mentioned earlier, the scientific funding infrastructure rests on a different assessment model. It is also our understanding that a lot of innovation grants are focused on gaining market shares or incremental competitive advantages. It seems like there might be missing a set of specialized skills for creating a baseline for FROs to be assessed and funded.

AM

On the evaluation side, in terms of how you can develop the infrastructure for deciding on and giving funding to FROs, and creating those teams? That will require a new set of tools and frameworks. Evaluating the strategic relevance of a project, relative to the roadmapping approach, or large-scale bottlenecks in a field, is a different kind of endeavor than evaluating the next grant proposal in something where you're already a close expert in a small community of people that really understand every detail about an existing field. If you're making a larger leap, there is also an aspect of understanding how that fits into the field. And how does it compare to other completely different projects that you could do? Foundations and other entities have experience doing that, but the scientific peer-review process doesn't necessarily have that higher level of consideration, where it is capable of evaluating projects at multiple scales. And it requires a different kind of evaluation, because it's also about the capacity of an organization to do the management and having the team to do something that is not science in any traditional sense.

D

That leads to the question of secondary effects of the FROs, because they can accrue multiplier effects through their outcomes. How do you start assessing the effects of FROs? Which is less about the internal results of the processes, but how they are actually geared toward having an impact outside of their own parameters. How have you thought through the ramifications or cascading effects of FROs, given that is maybe how they should be assessed ahead of receiving funding and support?

AM

For catalytic technology projects, which could be very enabling of downstream effects, as you mention, it may take some time for those to become clear. It requires a diagnosis of what the limiting factors are in the field. If I put out a roadmap stating that we need a FRO in a certain area to solve something, it is clear that not everyone is going to agree with that. Some people may just not like that area, others may think there is a better method. You have to evaluate the ability of the team to potentially find the right methods over time, not in every detail of what they are proposing, just like you would evaluate a start-up on the ability to pivot and find its path. So all of that, to me, adds up to some serious concerns for thinking carefully enough about how to set up the committees that fund and evaluate these things.

In terms of the outputs of FROs, I agree. One of the things that we're thinking about is that its main effect should be catalytic for other work. It shouldn't be that we did this thing, and here is this wonderful artefact, and now it's over. It should be that you're producing a tool or a data set, or some other resource that then accelerates other work. That's one way of thinking about it. Concretely, you can imagine something like a pre-start-up, where you start with a FRO, but then after five years, one or more start-ups become possible to be funded that would not have been possible before. And deployment path could be incubating start-ups where needed, in addition to releasing public goods like datasets and protocols.

POINT AND PIVOT

Natalia Zuluaga

Any project, be it cultural, political, or otherwise, aiming for political traction today must inevitably contend with the following assumptions:

> Art, in its current configuration, is integral to the extractive and excluding logic of capitalism.
>
> The contemporary media landscape—including images, algorithmic logics, and the news—is rife with manifestations of political ideologies that replicate the systems that uphold white supremacy and colonial dispossession.
>
> There is no conduit by which one can address, reason, or speak to systems of oppression. These are systems that do not care for or are not programmed to consider the conditions of our existence; to think otherwise is to partake in the illusion perfected by "share" economies, "woke" politics, reposts, likes, and the short-term rewards of self-promotion.
>
> Political, theoretical, and philosophical ideas are in an intractable and polarizing war with each other, the result of which produces nostalgic delusions of change that force us into ineffective political corners that paralyze and limit.

These articulations, and the hope for political traction, are themselves offshoots, effects, and resistance to a web of power, violence, bodies, and money that defines our contemporary moment; a web that is proteinaceous, binding, and blinding in its complexity, and paralyzing in its strangling effects. The reach of this lattice extends beyond the prison and the border, beyond the gnarled relation between state and citizen, or—as in our soon-to-be-realized post-nation-state condition—between the corporate state and laborer. The condition manifests itself not only in how we live, but in what we see and what we know. The proliferation of indiscriminate images—and the growing detritus they leave in their wake—supply us with the imaginary necessary to remember the beginning of the world and to envision the end of it, notions that have taken hold with such Michael Bay bombast, that we struggle to imagine them happening in any other way. Criticality and theory have had a similar effect on diagnosing and predicting the implications of neoliberal shifts and new world orders, with the dispossession of bodies and lands in tow. So, if watching the news, walking the streets, and surviving precarity have the familiar pang of watching a car crash in slow motion, it is because the limits of our imagination have been hemmed in by the limits of theoretical propositions, bound in an endless waltz that with each step implicates multiple temporalities.

This feedback loop between images, knowledge, and lived experience is not merely a concern for today, but also for the way in which pre-imagined futures—in the form of nearly-real architectural renderings, climate models, and futures markets—are in an endless financialized exchange with the present—a loop that all but guarantees the endurance of inequality, detention, and violence enacted upon racialized and marginalized bodies. The intricate rehearsing, mapping, and diagnosing of this complex trans-institutional and trans-temporal landscape is dizzying. Even more vertiginous, however, is attempting to imagine what could be said or done to disentangle, unhinge, and dismantle this adaptive system of oppression.

In art, we have seen artists and institutions turn their attention to a present and a future shaped by these concerns. There has been an increased awareness and engagement with infrastructures—the underlying framework of systems that are not limited to the built environment, but refer also to the ecologies that make up the art world—which has rendered some of these entanglements of power visible. While it is clear that situating art and its institutions squarely within the processes that perpetuate climate and political crises is important work, and there is no doubt it contributes to the unending labor of fostering political literacy, few artistic expressions have reached the level of disentanglement, or systemic, infrastructural alterations and change. Instead, these gestures of awareness often get bogged down in rehearsing the failed strategies of antecedents, such as institutional critique, or entrapped in arguments over art's politicality on the one hand, and on the other, circulating and amassing the same cultural capital that feeds the current configuration of contemporary art. In the end we end up with hashtag movements that offer only a temporary respite from where to vent frustrations, but rarely generate visions of a new world at our feet.

No doubt that the enduring health crisis of Covid-19 has only amplified these entanglements and asymmetries of power, resources, and violence, factors that have forced artists and institutions alike to face a growing call to recalibrate and to reimagine the role of art in society. The scale of this crisis, which is global in its reach, makes the response crucial. In the last year, the amount of online platforms, meeting spaces, and pedagogical initiatives focused on "what's next" has reached fever pitch. While the change is in some ways welcome—even if it has been overwhelming and lonely—I can't shake the cautious distrust in a system that thinks of recalibration not as an exit from the methods and means which fuel its cogs, but as an entrenchment into lean and more efficient ways to continue business as usual.[1] I can't help but wonder whether art—and contemporary art as the dominant current configuration—will not mirror what is happening elsewhere: the discarding of large swaths of people from a labor market that has undoubtedly evolved and will not reabsorb or respond for its lost workforce, leaving more people in near-permanent states of economic precarity; the formation of a bell curve that results from coagulation and perpetuation of safe trends and similar images, forcing people and ideas that do not conform with dominant discourses to recalibrate toward these trends, or risk being entrenched deeper in the climb for representation and recognition; a flattened presentism of everything available everywhen that surrounds us like a deluge, making the distance necessary to build context and criticality impossible; and finally the increasing intractability and tension between different political and theoretical thought camps, which makes it even more challenging for future-oriented visions out of these crises to emerge. It appears that despite our best efforts, a crisis of imagination abounds.

To avoid the snare of abstract conversations about ontologies, politicality, or solutionism that has plagued the project on art and the future, I think it is more useful to consider how infrastructural critique and speculation—which accounts for the material and immaterial touch points between understanding and changing the things that make the world as we know it—intersects with the political possibilities of the imaginal in order to work through what scales, temporalities, knowledges, and networks art must begin to collaborate with in order to work at every bend in forcing open new future-presents; to *image* that which has yet to emerge, is unseen, and remains occult.

In her book *Imaginal Politics: Images Beyond Imagination and the Imaginary* (2019), Chiara Bottici lays the groundwork for reconsidering how we think and act politically through the *imaginal*, to rethink the connection between politics and our ability to imagine. She describes the imaginal as, quite simply, made of images. That is, pictorial representations that are "presences in themselves, independently of their being real, or unreal, mental or extramental."[2] This is important, because in taking up the term of *imaginal* over words such as *imagination* or *imaginary*, Bottici tries to overcome the entrapment set forth by the social feedback loop in the latter's context-orientedness, and the limitation of being a faculty that we possess solely as *individuals* in the former. In doing so it re-opens the capacity to imagine and escape, and the ability to relate. It unshackles images from the ontological prison of being deemed real or unreal, because as she describes, "the definition of what is real is not an a priori of human understanding, but is something that has evolved continuously over centuries."[3] In other words, the imaginal can be real and unreal at the same time, it can

1 Suhail Malik's writing and lectures on the need for an exit from the current configuration of contemporary art have been instrumental in this line of thinking. See, for an introduction, the series of lectures at Artist Space he conducted in 2014, "Exit not Escape—On The Necessity of Art's Exit from Contemporary Art," available at https://www.artandeducation.net/classroom/video/66325/suhail-malik-exit-not-escape-on-the-necessity-of-art-s-exit-from-contemporary-art (accessed June 14, 2021).

2 Chiara Bottici, "Imaginal Politics: Images beyond Imagination and the Imaginary," in *Imaginal Politics: Images beyond Imagination and the Imaginary* (New York: Columbia University Press, 2019), 58.

3 Ibid., 57.

be individual, or social, as well as the "result of a complex, yet-to-be determined interaction between the two."[4] It is a field of possibilities, and, in being so, the imaginal is not qualitatively characterized as good or bad, but as what makes the world, and thus politics, possible. She contends that "imaginal beings are not only the product of the actions of individuals but also, in turn, what shapes the imagination of the individuals themselves," and thus how reality is understood and rendered at a particular moment.[5] Yet contrary to a paralyzing feedback loop between constitutive and constituted, the imaginal contains within it the capacity to imagine that which is yet unknown. That is, it also offers the means to exit and escape by ways of making present that which is absent, because "the starting point is not a subject separated from the world nor a world independent of the subject, but, simply, images."[6]

Touring us through a philosophical and etymological history of the words imagination, imaginary, and the imaginal, Bottici builds a thesis around the "radical capacity to envisage things differently and construct alternate political projects."[7] She argues that politics is imaginal in that it "depends on the commonalities between a set of bodies, but also, because it depends on the possibility of freeing oneself from one's own particularities and creating images of what is not immediately in front of us."[8] She distances her work from the philosophical misgivings and attitudes that relegate imagination to the realm of fantasy, and that have severed it from reason in ways that have long divided science and art, critique, and creativity. In doing so she builds an argument for rethinking the imaginal through the reasonable—in contrast to the traditions of reason and rationality—connecting it to thought, deliberation, and the creation of images that themselves go on to catalyze reality. I want to draw on this in order to think about an art beyond the opposing binaries of taste and usefulness, and instead think through their imaginal capacity, and in turn how this capacity can be used to think about the implications of a kind of infrastructural critique.[9]

To engage with infrastructure is to engage with adjusting scales. The critical capacity lies in zooming in and out in order to create a sense of awareness and build momentum toward altering the effects of infrastructure's impacts. The imaginal makes this possible through art insofar as art, and its byproducts, is the privileged space of ceaseless creation and image-making and can therefore in the simplest of terms be considered imaginal. Art has the potential to demystify and reveal the impermanence of suffocating political and economic orders. As such, art has the ability to render those conditions fictional as they are also comprised of images. Art already contains within its social system the capacity to review, and thus critique the images that are produced. Finally, and most importantly, art can use all of these faculties in order to create images—and thus maps—of the future. In considering the representational, structural, and technical problems posed

4 Ibid., 54.
5 Ibid., 96.
6 Ibid., 71.
7 Ibid., 1.
8 Ibid., 96.
9 Most works of contemporary art are usually held to a standard of either taste—associated with modernist ideals of the fanciful and not associated with the realm of knowledge—and market on the one hand, and utility, like in Tania Bruguera's Arte Útil, which seek to classify artistic gestures on a spectrum of their political utility, on the other.

by economic precarity, climate emergencies, racial injustice, and algorithmic dominance—that are all simultaneously roots and results of the structures discussed earlier—the aim of this essay is, then, to consider art's capacity for infrastructural speculation through the imaginal by performing a close reading of the images created by and in Domingo Castillo's *Tropical Malaise: Prologue* (2017) and those within strategic and temporal alignments of the collaborative A.S.T. (Alliance of the Southern Triangle).

Only Ghosts Traverse Here

> *Here are clouds formed from squares. According to the legend, the Greek Zeuxis could make drawings of fruit so realistic that birds flocked by to peck at them ...*
>
> *Clouds, created by a computer and clouds photographed by a camera.*
>
> *The flickering image on the right reveals that it is from a camera.*
>
> *Maybe the computer images will assume functions that were previously held by film. Maybe that will liberate film for other things.*
>
> *The computer images try to achieve the effect of film images. They want to surpass them, leave them far behind. The creators of computer imagery do not want to attract flocks of Greek birds.*
>
> *Their heavens should be populated by creatures of their own design.*
>
> —Harun Farocki, *Parallel I*, 2012, closing scene

Domingo Castillo's film *Tropical Malaise: Prologue* functions as a future arche-fossil, a digital trace of an ancestral past.[10] The film opens with a title sequence that informs us through the use of latitude and longitude coordinates that we are set in Miami Beach, Florida. One third of the eighteen-minute film serves as an introductory sequence, showing the back-end of making digital renderings of water into waves. Over and over again the viewer oscillates between the ebb and flow of crashing water and the pinching, rotating, and zooming in and out of a digital world. As the film progresses, the pace of the score quickens and suddenly we crash onto land, catapulted into a world set 500 million years into the future. In the course of the film we follow the smooth gliding movement of a camera traveling through a world of swaying trees and vast landscapes made of digital code. This is the camera Harun Farocki warned us about. Having overcome the technical obstacles of light and depth of field, this camera no longer indexes reality, instead it envisions and navigates

10 Full details are as follows: Domingo Castillo, *Tropical Malaise: Prologue*, 2017, HD video, site-contingent screening, 18 min. 22 sec. Directed and edited by Domingo Castillo, music by Nick Klein, narration by Annie Bandez, audio recording by Andrew Yeomanson, audio mixing by Barbara Elting and James Mckillop, audio mastering by James Callahan. *Tropical Malaise: Prologue* was commissioned by Art in Public Places of Miami-Dade County Department of Cultural Affairs and the University of Miami School of Communication. Additional support provided by Bas Fisher Invitational Miami, Art Center/South Florida, City of Miami Beach Cultural Affairs Office, Obsolete Media Miami and Primitive Languages.

unobstructed, programmed to hover, glide, and drift smoothly as it caresses the surface and edges of the coded landscape it simultaneously inhabits and surveils. The landscapes in Castillo's film have all been chopped and re-screwed from demonstration videos for software employed by filmmakers, video game developers as well as architects to make digital, movie-like renderings. In addition to these clips, the film incorporates an original score and a script that references Octavia Butler, Vilém Flusser, and Arthur Rimbaud. It uses narrative, aural, visual, and temporal displacement in order to speak to the material and cultural realities of the present by sateliting over and tunneling beyond our current time horizon to capture an image of the future. In this sense, it is a contemporary work of science fiction.

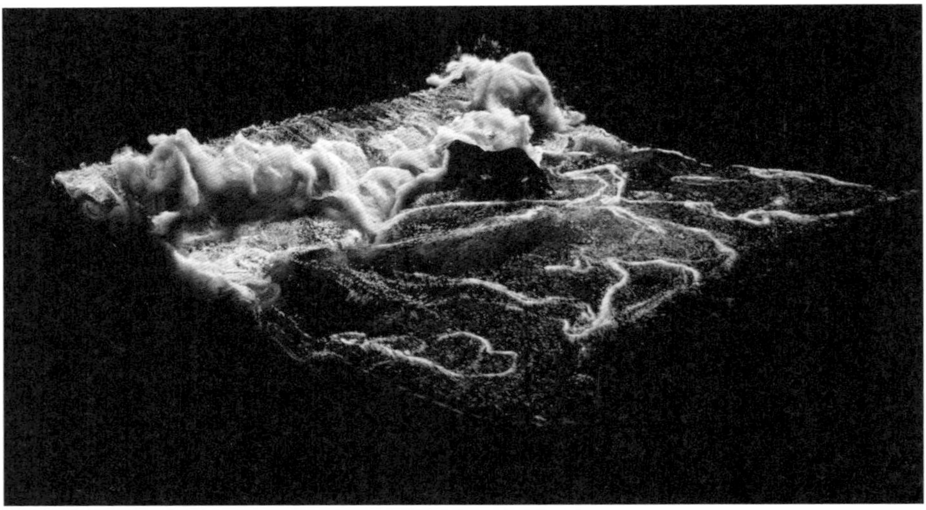

Domingo Castillo, *Tropical Malaise: Prologue*, 2017 (still), courtesy the artist

The software appropriated by Castillo in the film is most often employed to depict buildings and new urban spaces in dream-like detail: in these renderings, these spaces are always situated in the most perfect weather conditions, they are environments—often animated—barely occupied by digital bodies, virtual refuges for virtual figures who represent the sterile fantasies of racial and economic homogeneity. At once instruction, image, and map, the coded territory these images depict mobilizes technological, political, and social relations over long temporal arcs in order to advance and align policies and master plans that allow them to physically carve and reshape the landscape in the now. This underscores the idea that the imaginal, and images in general, are not inherently good or bad, but are generative. The renderings have helped propel the phenomenon of the global city, and the *Disneyfication* of place, both of which allow the *idea* of the city—and all of the capital infrastructure that supports it—to be prototyped and pasted onto real terrain in real time.[11] As final products, these renderings are not realistic in a visual or technical sense. Instead, they *render* reality by

11 Aikaterini Antonopoulou, "Large-Scale Fakes: Living in Architectural Reproductions," in *Scale in Literature and Culture*, edited by Michael Tavel Clarke and David Wittenberg (London: Palgrave Macmillan, 2018), 177–99.

projecting from the future and bearing down on the present in very real ways. These renderings represent black-box processes wherein desire, power, and speculation coagulate and become visible. They are moving images that motivate power and capital to catalyze into reality.

Castillo's film, however, does not feature new buildings, people, or visions of urban renewal. Instead, it homes in on the blades of grass that bend to a soft and subtle breeze, the glimmer of light that twinkles in a haunting loop, and the waves that crash not by the ebb and flow of a tidal pull but by the execution of code. It is unclear who or what has generated these scenes, and this ambiguity hints at the haunting that underpins Castillo's work. Though the film is devoid of depictions of human bodies—and in this way decenters the human—rendered words float above the landscapes and function as evidence of language, or, perhaps like carved glyphs discovered on the side of a pyramid.

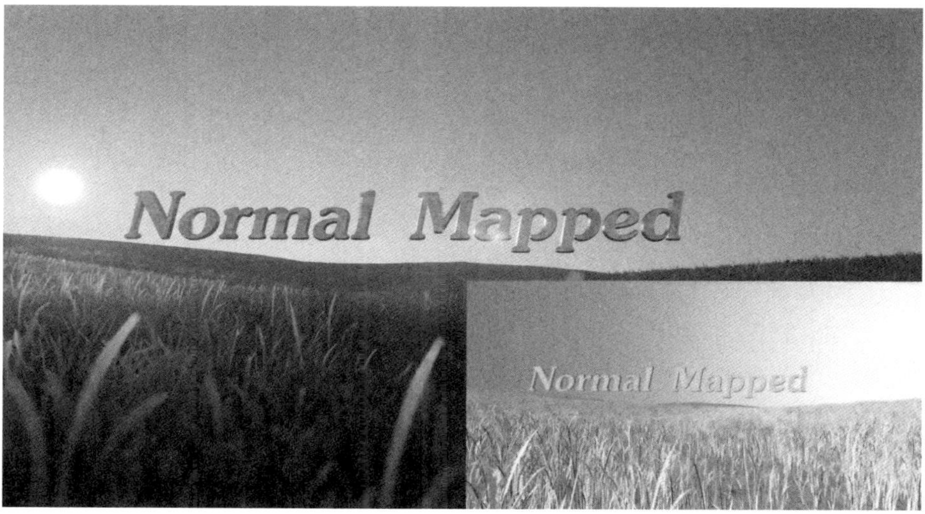

Domingo Castillo, *Tropical Malaise: Prologue*, 2017 (still), courtesy the artist

The film pulls in and out, oscillating between the back end of the software and an image-saturated front end. Castillo uses these simple but visually rich elements to render a post-human world. Empty of humans and of life as we know it, the film is inhabited only by the ghost of a failed humanity, one which we must surmise has been crushed under the ideological perversion of boundless growth and the fantasy of infinite resources. The images and clips in the film exceed the measure of nature as we understand it today; after all, the film is a series of rendered natures woven together to give us a peak into a world-in-unfolding. As such, it is a version of nature rendered from images of the past: a search engine query of a leaf gives form to an idea, an idea that replicates over and over again until a forest is born.

In doing so, *Tropical Malaise: Prologue* becomes at once a critique and a sneak peek into a dystopic future in which the boundaries set by finite land and resources in the *here and now* have been ruptured, devoured, and replaced entirely by the virtual and the potential proffered by mining the future. It is effective in locating reality, or at least *a* reality, that is unfolding simultaneously and provides an image of an inevitable place where the risks of rising waters, crashing markets, and dying bodies roam only as ghosts, lurking unseen, deep in the pulses between ones and zeros. By replicating the future-oriented logic of architectural renderings—sampling and reassembling the tools that construct the rendering itself—the film becomes an artifact that goes beyond evincing material and cultural remnants of the past and instead functions as a kind of hyperstitional object: set in the future searching for a feedback loop to structure the present.

A recent iteration of the film was exhibited at Crystal Bridges Museum of American Art in 2019, set inside of Frank Lloyd Wright's Bachman-Wilson House.[12] As in the architectural renderings employed by Castillo, Wright's utopian vision for the Bachman-Wilson house is in itself an image of dystopia. Situated somewhere between the digital landscapes of Castillo's film and the Ozark forest it sits in, Wright's house is also an artifact latent with ideologies that just won't die, and that are relentless in their haunting. It is a trophy, a clinking toast to US-American exceptionalism and the championing of hyper-individualism—ideals to which Wright faithfully adhered throughout his career.[13] The house, having been acquired and transported from its original site in order to place it on permanent exhibition, is a perfect, if not unexpected, manifestation of the way in which contemporary art museums have become the guardians of these very ideals, and reifies the operational, funding, and scaling capacity (or ambition) of today's US museum. This scaling up is possible because the indelible ties between capital and art make size, scale, and funding the boundless domains to function within. Working with these notions of boundlessness in mind encourages institutions to balloon into the global and extend into landscapes and acres as opposed to lots and square feet. This is interesting, at the very least, because it means that museums with sufficient resources and far-reaching global networks become prototypes for an institutional form capable of containing and mediating objects and structures whose scale is neither big nor macro but sprawling and complex.

The Bachman house mirrors this complexity. It is more than just a home coded with Usonian characteristics and ideals.[14] Beyond embodying the innocuous and naïve vision of democracy and empowerment of the US middle class that typifies Wright's Usonian vision, the house also reveals deep entanglements between global capital, geopolitical interests, and the environment. It tells a story of the tireless quest to dominate nature through confrontation and speaks to the ways in which contemporary art moves beyond the object and into real estate acquisition. As a harbinger of the moment in which these entanglements were conceived, the house is an ideal cultural object—and image—that is both witness to and

12 "Frank Lloyd Wright Bachman-Wilson House: Usonian Architecture," Crystal Bridges Museum of American Art, June 29, 2020, available at https://crystalbridges.org/architecture/frank-lloyd-wright-bachman-wilson-house/ (accessed June 14, 2021).

13 Joseph M. Watson, "The Antinomies of Usonia: Neil Levine's *The Urbanism of Frank Lloyd Wright*," *The Avery Review*, No. 25, 2017, available at http://averyreview.com/issues/25/the-antinomies-of-usonia (accessed June 13, 2021).

14 Frank Lloyd Wright, *The Natural House* (New York: Horizon Press, 1954).

evidence of the Anthropocene. In its conception, construction, and act of recovery, it bears the unforeseen points of impact between humans and nature by way of architecture.[15] Today the house endures far from the rising waters it was plucked from. The scars caused by the relentless force of the Millstone River, which once appeared in the form of water marks, damaged and rebuilt cabinets, and rotted frames, have been healed—much like code has to be rewritten when a glitch emerges or risks breaking the illusion of the folly—and now lurk only as folklore and interpretive fodder. The setting of Castillo's film within the home only magnifies the feeling that no force and no amount of money can save us from the eventuality that he presents in *Tropical Malaise: Prologue*.

Though the Bachman-Wilson House was built in 1954, it is an image that now bears the marks of a climate crisis perpetuated by the ills of neoliberal capitalism. It wasn't deliberately predictive, but something in its constitutive order—from the *deliberate* way it was imagined and conceived—made it prognostic. Placing Castillo's film, which itself posits a kind of future reality creating ripples in the fabric of a present one, within the space of the home creates a convergence akin to what Nigel Thrift describes as the science of placing. "This science mixes the virtual and physical such that it becomes possible to create something like the all-at-onceness of phenomenological worlds on a temporary basis in something like a predictable way."[16] This simultaneity doesn't function by suspension of disbelief as would be the case in storytelling, but instead operates as a door between two active spaces—or two temporalities—that are constantly transmitted to one another by mediological means. This is, to quote Thrift, "Not the creation of discrete worlds into which participants enter, then, but a continuous process of worlding."[17]

Being in the active space created by the convergence of this house and film brings to mind the protagonist in Adolfo Bioy Casares's *The Invention of Morel* (1940). In the story, the main character, who we know only as "fugitive," has been banished to an island for an unknown crime. There he falls in love with Faustine, who he soon discovers is merely an image projected onto the landscape by machines. She is part of a series of "life recordings" left behind by a utopian community in search of immortality. In an attempt to be with Faustine for eternity, the protagonist reverse-engineers the "life projectors" and begins recording his own life onto hers, carefully rehearsing each movement she makes so as to appear as seamless as possible. The machines, however, do not simply record and project. They literally transfer life from one plane to another: from flesh to light. It is unclear what happens to his consciousness upon his transfer to the other plane, or how much of his previous self remains. What is instrumental to consider here is that perhaps we too are in the process of transferring over, and, given the uncertainty of what will happen when we are pulled into existing in the everywhen, we may also take comfort in a plea similar to the fugitive's closing reflection:

15 For more on the contact points between human-made infrastructure and non-human entities, see the project website for Anna L. Tsing, Jennifer Deger, Saxena Keleman Alder, and Feifei Zhou, *Feral Atlas: the more-than-human Anthropocene*, 2020, available at https://feralatlas.supdigital.org (accessed June 13, 2021).

16 Nigel Thrift, "The Place of Complexity," *Theory, Culture & Society*, June 1, 1999, 31–69, https://doi.org/10.1177/02632769922050610.

17 Ibid.

> I still see my image moving about with Faustine. I have almost forgotten that it was added later; anyone would surely believe that we were in love and completely dependent on each other. Perhaps the weakness of my eyes makes the scenes appear this way. In any case, it is consoling to die while watching such satisfactory results. My soul has not yet passed to the image; if it had, I would have died. I (perhaps) will no longer see Faustine and will be with her in a vision no one can ever destroy. To the person who nails this diary and then invents a machine that can assemble disjoined presences, I make this request: Find Faustine and me, let me enter the heaven of her consciousness. It will be an act of piety.[18]

Similarly, the point of Castillo's film—in any space— is then to make your body hyper-aware of the constant fluctuation between these two worlds that are simultaneously unfolding; to draw you deeper and deeper into its own reality. In doing so, he exceeds the expectations we have of Bottici's thesis within the realm of art. His is not an indiscriminate proliferation of images that perpetuate a crisis of political imagination, but the manifestation of the radical capacity of imagination to create something new. This new world may not be the one we want, but it is the world we have coded.

Messages from the Future

No other resource has been more perverted and prized by capitalism than time. From the classic means of production and labor, to the social and cognitive relations of real abstraction, and the financialization of everything that is characteristic of neoliberalism, *time* is the essential cog that moves the machinery of extraction.[19] Time becomes the stage on which the drama of utopias and dystopias, pasts, futures, and future presents are played. It is on this stage where the collective the Alliance of the Southern Triangle (A.S.T.) operates. A.S.T. is a group of artists, architects and a curator, led by Diann Bauer, Elite Kedan, Felice Grodin, and Patricia M. Hernández. They utilize the interdisciplinary and speculative space of art to create works that are propositional in nature and that reflect on the shifting legal, economic, cultural, and environmental forces that confront us. Their work takes the form of performative essays, immersive installations, and short films that bombard their viewers with found images, collected texts, all woven together through architectural forms rendered by the collective. Present in all of their work is the voice of a protagonist who meanders through the moving images and in the installations, lingering and tugging at the viewer like a whisper reverberating at the deepest depths of a dark unconscious. While in Castillo's film the "protagonist" takes the form of a singular simulation that has been left running, uninterrupted, and playing out multiple scenarios from the external inputs it reads,[20] A.S.T.'s works utilize these

18 Adolfo Bioy Casares, *The Invention of Morel*, translated by Ruth L.C. Simms (New York: New York Review, 2003 [1940]), 101.

19 "Real abstraction being—in shorthand—an understanding of abstraction not as a process of thinking that distills complex empirical reality, but, on the contrary, as that which emerges from material practice itself, in the world, before thought, behind thought's back, as they say. It, in turn, determines epistemic limits and orients conceptualizations. And, if we move away from strictly epistemological concerns, we can hazard that real abstraction impinges on social and cultural institutions and conventions, as well." Gean Moreno (ed.) "Introduction," in *In the Mind, But Not from There: Real Abstraction and Contemporary Art* (London: Verso, 2019).

20 From conversations with the artist in January 2020.

voices to recite scripts, often presenting questions, establishing positions, and rupturing the way we may think about concepts such as climate change, territories, borders, and time.

The content for these scripts is culled from a wide range of theoretical and literary works, as well as the collective's own writing, and is delivered in a cool and cutting tone that still manages an air of exasperation. This is because dealing with the complexities and political limits of our moment leaves little room for a narrative device that relies on hope; it needs something that awakens. In the collective's immersive installation *Intertidal* (2018), for example, these voices chime by way of different videos and a mural that speak to the ideas of submersion in the age of sea-level rise. The work fuses architectural elements, text, and video clips from 3D climate maps, geospatial models, films, real-time vessel trackers, Google Earth, as well as footage shot in and around the Everglades in South Florida. Referencing the area that lies above water at low tide and is flooded at high tide, *Intertidal* provides an atmosphere that matches the complexity of the subject at hand, attempting to present a coherent message of urgency about a future fraught by climate change by creating a space that heightens the alienation between what we feel and what we know.

In *Intertidal*, there is a contradiction between the growing abundance of climate, logistics, and financial data (in the form of images), and the inability to read and understand how all these data points interrelate. This incongruity makes the distancing, or alienation, to this information more striking. Here is where the textual clues that A.S.T. offer become crucial, and where the kind of image-making that their practice relies on pushes the limits of Bottici's work. Bottici's thesis runs into one big obstacle: the proliferation and abundance of images and image-making in our contemporary moment. This is a problem insofar as the current moment, as outlined here, is faced with a crisis of political imagination, one of which we are arguing the imaginal (i.e., images) holds a key to help us break away from the grotesque social orders and loops. The political capacity of the imaginal and of images is not furthered by the abundance of images, but actually hindered by a kind of hypertrophy of the imaginal, which overwhelms and shuts down. Bottici understands there is no way out of the proliferation of images, but instead proposes the idea of producing better spectacles, that is, "only through the spectacle itself can we overcome the isolating effects of the spectacle [...] precisely the spectacle that isolates us can bring us together and even unite us."[21] This proposal, however tempting in its opacity, underestimates the ease with which the contemporary media mechanism and its offshoots (including art) foreclose the emancipatory capacity of such images. This is why something else must be done with how the imaginal operates within and from art that moves beyond the qualitative measure of good/bad spectacle. Contrary to the idea of creating better spectacles, art has a trifold potential: it has the operational capacity to set the conditions where new images

21 Bottici, "Imaginal Politics," 124.

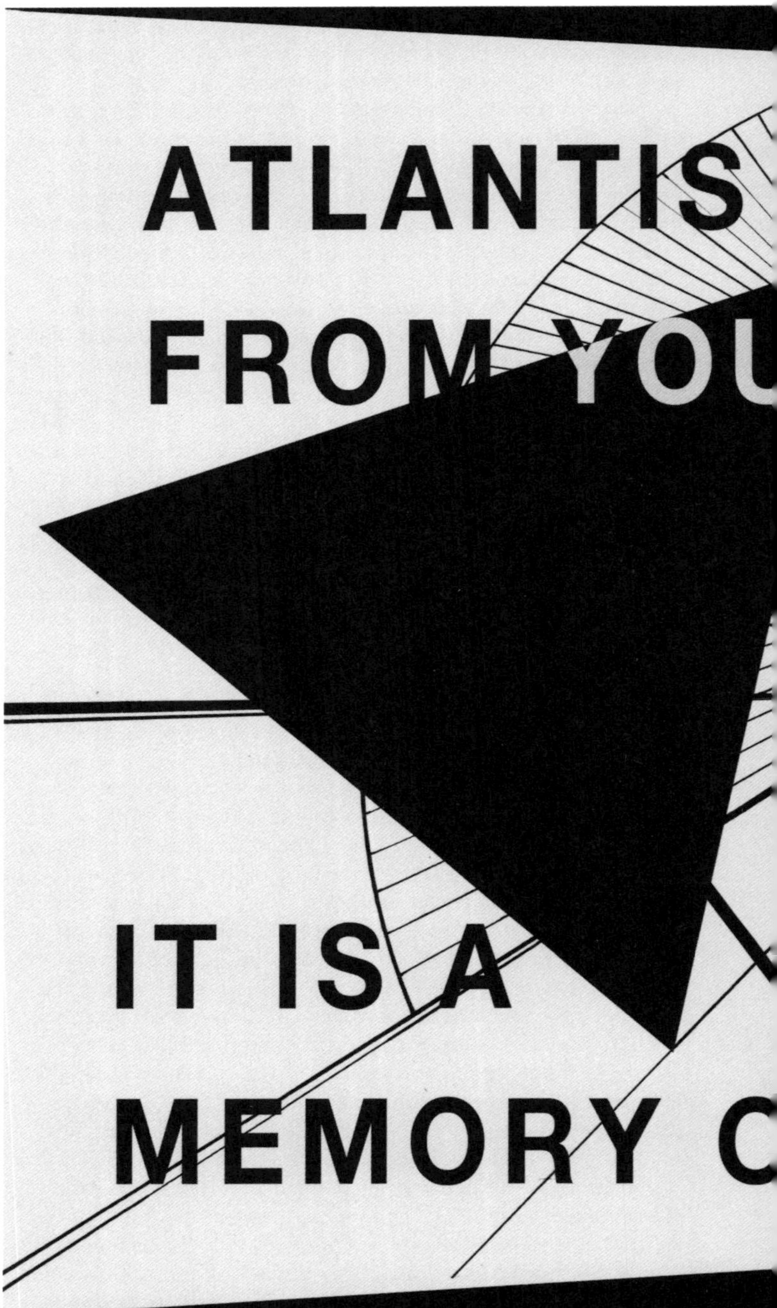

A.S.T. (Alliance of the Southern Triangle), *Intertidal*, 2018 (detail), courtesy the collective

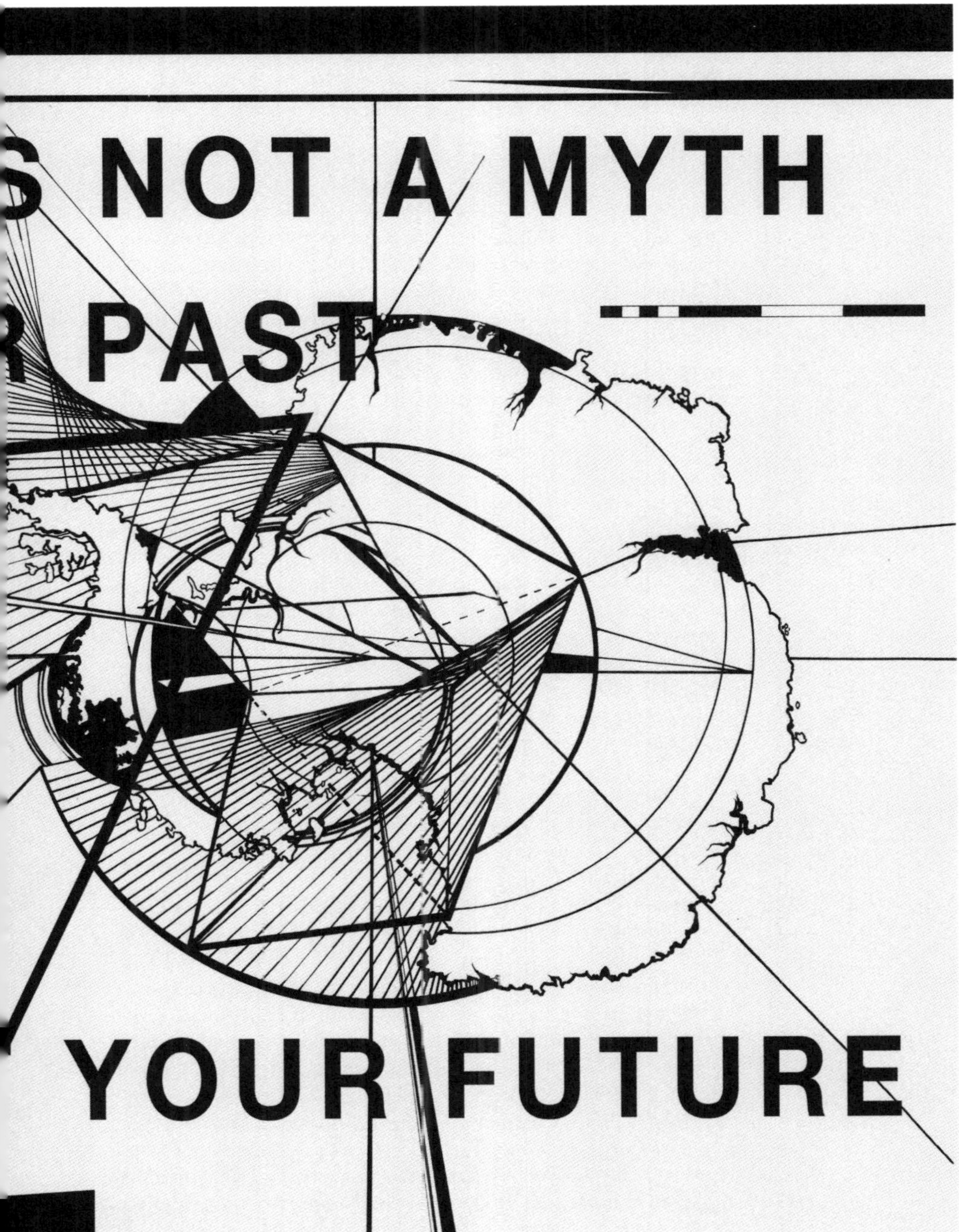
S NOT A MYTH
R PAST
YOUR FUTURE

can be conceived (art); it has the ability to produce schemas and maps that make the abstract social relations of capitalism concrete (criticism); and finally, in doing the former, it has the ability to give specificity to complexity in order to gesture toward new horizons.[22]

Using these criteria to return to *Intertidal*, we can read the work as both schema (in the indexical sense) and site where the imaginal's political potential unfolds. The viewer here is not only suspended visually in front of an abundance of images that depict the extractive forces of global capitalism on climate, but also aurally, with the collective's use of text, voice, and sound. The text and sound—or what I earlier referred to as the protagonist—attempt to pierce through the whirling of images. Whether or not they reach their intended receiver as a complete undistorted communication is part of what A.S.T. are trying to articulate in this multifaceted work. The entire site of the installation becomes a testing ground for potential paths to communicate across temporalities: from the present to the future and back. It uses an image of a future that contends with the mistakes of the past in order to encourage the creation of alternate trajectories. This deliberate layering of information does not imply that everything is known or can be known within the space of this work, but that enough can be perceived and questioned to start to consider new possibilities. The text, written in all three tenses (past, present, and future) is woven through the installation in the form of a mural and through moving images in a visually bold manner, beckoning the viewer with phrases and questions such as:

> How do we send a message to the past?
> How do we let them know we're drowning?
> We are the ghosts screaming the reality you hear
> as a whisper.
> Atlantis is not the myth of your past; it's a memory of
> your future.

Through these questions and statements, A.S.T. is asking its viewer to listen to the ghosts of the not-so-distant future and the hauntings of their scrambled messages, and to articulate a response to these whispers—so that we may formulate a different kind of future. Though Bottici's thesis centers the ocular in her proposals for the imaginal, the use of sound and voice in *Intertidal* lends credence to the idea that the imaginal is heightened, and maybe even delineated with the use of the aural. The reliance on both aural and visual components in *Intertidal*, I would argue, encourages the creation of new images that may form in conscious or unconscious ways by transporting the viewer through a process of disorientation, alienation, and awareness. Alienation here, however, isn't necessarily the act of distancing and exclusion, but works as a pivot and as a faculty of awareness. What happens from there is anyone's guess—after all, speculation always deals in the partially unknown, banks on

22 This is the mandate put forth in Diann Bauer et al,. "Operationalizing Real Abstraction: Art and the General Abstract Image," in Moreno, *In the Mind*.

the yet to come to fruition. Piecing together the points is part of the process of creating and of envisioning. A crisis of imagination, and the imaginal, is only amplified by an inability to envision—to create images—beyond what we've already seen, felt, and know.

To reiterate an earlier point: there is no new, or better spectacle contained in A.S.T.'s work—or anywhere—that wouldn't be a trapping. Instead, it is more useful to make a differentiation between the generative capacity to produce images *ad nauseam*—or even to construct new ways to see and understand the world—and the ability to generate new features in the world that may overhaul some of the dominant tendencies that define the political trappings of our contemporary moment. A.S.T.'s practice attempts to avoid the trap of the former by employing the imaginal as a kind of schema, a communicative didactic diagram, that simultaneously does something on its own—that is, it doesn't depend on the *interpretation* of the viewer to complete a cognitive loop—while also *communicating* with and addressing the viewer via images in order to generate, and to potentially conduce the condition of *poiesis*.

In terms of the latter, it is not yet clear whether the stated claims of the collective—their intentions to think and create alliances within a multilayered world of beings and non-beings—reaches the threshold of generating new emancipatory forms. However, A.S.T.'s practice does align with a chorus of different collectives and entities throughout the contemporary art ecology, such as The Otolith Group, Forensic Architecture, The New Red Order, The Freethought Collective, to name a few, that are chipping away at the established norms of how, where, and when art functions. They do so by working through alliances, pedagogy, writing, and dictating the terms by which their work and outreach are mediated. This is not to say that these forms or ways of working are not themselves exploitable, but they do begin to question and shift the dynamics of power within the economies of knowledge production within art. Collectively, these practices have the potential to coagulate into new ways of making, distributing, and teaching that can become new ground, and, perhaps, we may eventually find ourselves disentangling and trying to understand a life that imitates *that* kind of art.

The Imaginal and Future Mining

In the face of the crushing claustrophobia and cacophony that emanates from mediated technologies and their "smart" interconnectedness, we are left to wonder not only what is understood of the world in a physical way, but in immaterial and temporal ways too. What has been revealed to us through this world of images is that the threshold between what is possible and what is conceivable has disintegrated, precisely because we now occupy the here, the then, and the forthcoming all at the same time. This simultaneity is rooted in the ideas of boundless continuance and eternity, and no doubt we've seen this phenomenon unfold in other ways: in the world-making-gone-wild of terraforming; in sea-level derivatives in futures markets; hell, even in the banality of Minecraft with its edgeless world; and in the continuous state of enjoyment built into the engineered compulsion of Candy Crush. In this paradigm, the infinite, the boundless, and the endless have become more than just preoccupations with continuance; they are ideas situated in multiple temporalities that rightfully assume *everywhen* is just waiting to be extracted, used, built upon, and plundered. As such, the future and the past are extractable—mined—because they can be accessed in the now. Debt, real estate speculation, and even seemingly innocuous architectural renderings are the means by which the future is mined. These imaginal formations lay claim to, drag out, and limit the emancipatory promise that was the idea of tomorrow, making the plight toward the any-time-but-now a futile neurosis.

If, according to Bottici, the creation and distribution of maps were the "most common way[s] of representing and thus rendering political power perceptible and thus affective" in modernity, we must consider what the contemporary equivalent is in a world run amok by images, speculation, and future mining.[23] Each day it becomes more apparent that the future is such a territory being mapped and claimed by contemporary imaginal formations.[24] Castillo and A.S.T. home in on this suspicion, and their practice begins to delineate a still-incomplete version of a future map, not for the purpose of claiming it, but to call our attention to an act of territorialization that is already taking place. It is here, against the supposedly guaranteed feedback loop between the now and a plundered future—a future that continues to unfold, running ahead of us, always impossibly, out, of, reach—that Castillo's *Tropical Malaise: Prologue* and A.S.T.'s *Intertidal* linger. Through the imaginal, these two works begin to articulate what navigating and negotiating through boundless principles and complexity may look and feel like. While both works rely on the visual and on the aural in order to activate the imaginal, the goals are very different. In Castillo's film the viewer gets a glimpse, a tight view into a single kind of vision that emerges from an architectural rendering that limns to no known end. Here the proliferation of possible future outcomes, and images, are limited to just one: a human-less, organic-less world. By contrast, *Intertidal* rubs up against the ideas of boundlessness and complexity by situating the viewer in a small sample of an image and information storm, beckoning the viewer with warnings, trying to awaken a capacity in them to imagine. Both works defy the vertiginous abundance of images that define our moment, do more than contribute to the detritus of images that surround us, by telescoping in one way or another from the future and back, encouraging us to create an image of a world we don't *yet* have access to.

23 Bottici, "Imaginal Politics," 94.

24 Imaginal formations that territorialize the future include pricing mechanisms in futures markets or sea-level rise derivatives such as the ones described in Sevren Gourley, "Funding Adaptation: Financing Resiliency Through Sea Level Derivatives," *Harvard Environmental Law Review*, April 17, 2017, syndicated on Envtl. L. Rev. Syndicate, http://harvardelr.com/2017/04/17/funding-adaptation-financing-resiliency-through-sea-level-derivatives/ (accessed June 13, 2021).

A MODEST PROPOSAL FOR PREVENTING ARTISTS FROM BECOMING A BURDEN TO SOCIETY, AND MAKING FINANCE BENEFICIAL TO BOTH ARTISTS AND THE PUBLIC

Vermeir & Heiremans

> *Paris, having finally conquered its freedom of action and its independence, I invite artists to assume control of museums and art collections, which, though the property of the nation, are primarily theirs, from an intellectual as well as a material point of view.*
> —Gustave Courbet[1]

We have always been interested in the socio-economic conditions of artists and have been looking at them from different perspectives: on the one hand via an artistic, more "speculative" approach, questioning finance as a possible tool for the redistribution of wealth, and on the other hand via a form of operational realism that allows us to develop and advocate sustainable practices. Both approaches come together in Jubilee, an artist-run platform for artistic research and production which we co-founded in 2013.[2] Due to Flemish art policy urgencies,[3] since 2019 they also converge in our engagement in the State of the Arts platform.[4] In this text we question the agency of our artistic practice as well as our attempts at reform, starting from the collective reflections and actions within these small organizations. We'll conclude with the open question whether an operational realist approach can implement speculative tools to generate new forms of mutualization.[5]

Art House Index

Working as the artist duo Vermeir & Heiremans since 2006, our practice addresses the dynamics between art, real estate, finance, and governance, and how these inform artists' socio-economic conditions. We approach this from a very personal perspective, defining our own loft apartment in Brussels as an "artwork." Although the "house as artwork" is not accessible to the public, it allows us to develop "mediated extensions" that address how "living in a house" is linked to the wider economy, how it is embedded in a legal context, and how it can serve as a governance tool. You could say that we use the house as lived

1 Gustave Courbet, *Le Cri du Peuple*, April 10, 1870. Available at https://gallica.bnf.fr/ark:/12148/bpt6k4683773p/f2.item# (accessed April 13, 2021).

2 See https://jubilee-art.org (accessed March 30, 2021).

3 See https://jubilee-art.org/?rd_news=2428 (accessed March 30, 2021).

4 See http://state-of-the-arts.net/mission/ (accessed March 30, 2021).

5 The title of our text references Jonathan Swift's satirical essay, "A Modest Proposal. For preventing the Children of Poor People From being a Burthen to Their Parents or Country, and For making them Beneficial to the Publick," published anonymously in 1729.

inspiration, sometimes even as a framing device—to zoom in on specific issues, such as gentrification, financialization, and ownership.[6]

We were fascinated by how people from the world of finance were able to generate streams of income from a particular asset without selling it, including real estate, art collections, or stocks. Inspired by their skills we started to look into possibilities to make the "art house" "liquid," without having to sell it, which is when the idea came to us to create an experimental financial index on the "house as artwork." *Art House Index (AHI-)* (2015) is the abstraction of a narrative of credit created around our persona as artist duo.[7] We could refer to it as a credit-based sociability, or even open it up further to the notion of "human capital," which redefines our existence in terms of risk—every action becoming an investment to lower future risk, or, to give it a positive twist, to heighten the possibility of future profit.

Financializing our private assets seemed to make sense at the time, although most of the asset managers we spoke to found the idea a bit preposterous—financializing a single house was not exactly their idea of a business plan. *AHI-* measures the symbolic value that we as "public persona" accrue non-stop, in other words, alongside real estate data it gathers real-time data on the attention economy surrounding our work, for instance, the number of viewers of our online videos. Although it has not generated any liquidity, visualizing our human capital has fueled our appetite to better understand financialization processes, and also made us think about the possibility to scale up the experiment.

Financializing Real Estate and Art

What opened our eyes to the entanglement of art, finance, and real estate was Sharon Zukin's book *Loft Living* (1982), which tells the story of how abandoned Manhattan warehouses were becoming hot commodities in the 1960s and 1970s.[8] While de-investment policies had finished off the remaining industrial parts of lower Manhattan, a synergy between interests of the state, corporations, and the city's financial elites gradually manifested itself as a plan to repurpose these areas with what Zukin refers to as an "artistic mode of production." She details the part artists played, consciously or unconsciously, in political processes that implied the change of zoning laws and the redirection of capital investments to make Manhattan's industrial desert, in particular capital invested in its buildings, profitable once again.

Giovanni Arrighi's *The Long Twentieth Century* (1994) helped us understand what was going on in New York at the time.[9] Describing recurring cycles of development in the history of capitalism, his analysis shows how falling rates of profit since the Renaissance have triggered shifts from the initial cycle of trade and production to a secondary cycle of financialization. In this secondary cycle, instead of investing surplus capital in

6 Vermeir & Heiremans project page on the Jubilee website, available at https://jubilee-art.org/?rd_page=29-2/33-2&lang=en (accessed March 30, 2021).

7 *Art House Index* real time, available at http://ahi2.in-residence.be/chart2.php; info on https://jubilee-art.org/?rd_project=art-house-index&lang=en (accessed March 30, 2021).

8 Sharon Zukin, *Loft Living: Culture and Capital in Urban Change* (Baltimore: Johns Hopkins University Press, 1982).

9 Giovanni Arrighi, *The Long Twentieth Century: Money, Power and the Origins of Our Time* (London: Verso, 1994).

more trade and production, most money is invested in such ways that capital can reproduce itself—primarily through financial intermediation and speculation—as well as in real estate and art, or other luxury goods.

Coming back to how these recurring cycles appeared in recent history, in the 1960s investors wondered if they should consider real estate a healthy investment, and if so, what its financial return could be. They decided they needed a measuring tool to track the evolution of real estate prices, for which purpose financial indices were developed. Following a specific method, these indices were able to convert data into useful information. By abstracting the physical reality of a building, contemporary forms of "financialization" can now "liquefy" stone, bricks, and glass quite easily. A striking example is the Empire State building and nineteen other properties that in 2014 became part of a REIT (Real Estate Investment Trust): investors can buy and sell its shares without having to deal with the physical buildings.

Rosalind Krauss wrote about the cultural shift in museums in 1990 already. In her essay "The Cultural Logic of the Late Capitalist Museum" she explains that "now non-invested surplus capital is exactly one way of describing the holdings—both in land and in art—of museums," elaborating on how many museum figures are describing their museums as a "museum industry." In order to increase "market share" they insist on the need for a "larger inventory" (a bigger collection) more "physical outlets" (franchises) and for "leveraging the collection"—"not selling it, but rather moving the collection into the credit sector, or the circulation of capital."[10] It is clear that since the 1990s the continuous "industrialization" of museums has accelerated, with Guggenheim, Louvre, and Pompidou franchises having opened up around the world. A Pompidou even opened in Brussels, where we live.[11] The primary purpose of these museum buildings, however, is not art, but rather financial remediation, or what David Harvey famously termed a "spatial fix"—money shifting from trade and production to real estate markets.[12]

As for collections, of course not all art enjoys the attention and investments of surplus capital. Value is arguably created exclusively for the upper layers of the art market, which focuses on so-called blue-chip art. Since the late 2000s a lot of liquidity has come into circulation because of quantitative easing, which has not only helped inflate prices of luxury goods, banks and hedge funds have increasingly started to accept art as collateral for loans. The desire to generate a flow of income from art collections, without having to take the art from the wall or out of the free port, and without having to sell it, had long been on the wish list of so-called high-net-worth individuals. Alongside the loan against art model, the augmented potential of digitalization and the development of blockchain technology has started to generate new business models that detach "tradeable values" from art's "material forms"—more traders are now able to buy/sell abstracted "fractions of art" without actually having to engage with the material artwork itself.[13]

10 Rosalind Krauss, "The Cultural Logic of the Late Capitalist Museum," *October*, No. 54, 1990, 3–17.

11 The Pompidou franchise in Brussels is embedded in an ambitious plan for regeneration of the whole canal area. See https://kanal.brussels/sites/default/files/actualites/press_kit_kanal_architecture_22march_.pdf (accessed April 29, 2021); and https://canal.brussels/en/canal-plan (accessed April 29, 2021).

12 David Harvey, *Spaces of Capital: Towards a Critical Geography* (London: Routledge, 2012).

13 Maecenas, for instance, is a business that financializes fractions of art masterpieces. See https://www.maecenas.co/ (accessed April 23, 2021).

In 2010 a team of economists crunched art market numbers since 1765 and came to some sobering conclusions that art prices rise—and faster—when income inequality goes up.[14] It is important to realize that these peaks in income inequality coincide with regimes of free labor and (self-)exploitation, which is a common practice in the art world and actually drives the global art industries. The 2019 UNESCO report "Culture & working conditions for artists" observes: "Indeed, the largest subsidy for the arts comes not from governments, patrons or the private sector, but from artists themselves in the form of unpaid or underpaid labour."[15] Considering the often very precarious conditions most artists, art workers, and small institutions face daily, in none of the envisaged financial constructions that would create streams of income from artworks or buildings, there seemed to be any impetus to include other parties but the investors. All artists, however, whether their work is in a museum collection or not, are part of the value creation chain that benefits the museum industry, and by extension the cities in which museums are located. Artists co-create social and economic wealth through intense cultural exchange, by circulating ideas, and by collectively underwriting confidence in art's values.[16]

We felt an urgency to re-imagine financial tools as inclusive and re-purpose them to also directly benefit other stakeholders—the artists and art workers—and not only shareholders, the investor/rentier, or, for that matter, the art industries. We started to look at public art collections and public museum buildings as valuable assets that, though the property of the nation, are primarily ours, from an intellectual as well as a material point of view, as Courbet argued. These priceless assets cannot be sold, they are so-called "frozen assets."[17] But what would happen if these assets were to be financialized? What would happen if we could capture and redistribute some of the wealth artists have helped produce?

To ourselves we pitched this ambitious thought experiment as *A Modest Proposal (AMP).*

> AMP *can make streams of economic and social wealth, produced by exchange, flow back to its origins—the artists and art workers—to create more sustainable conditions and futures in which art can flourish as an ecology of practices.*
>
> AMP *will build a portfolio that introduces public museum buildings, art collections and goodwill as investable assets. These will be carefully accumulated in partnership with different art institutions worldwide. It is important to stress that none of these public assets need to be sold, or de-accessioned, or taken off the walls.*
>
> AMP *does not own the art collections or museum buildings. It aims to create an exchange that can monetize their*

14 William Goetzmann, Luc Renneboog, and Christophe Spaenjers, "Art and Money," CentER Discussion Paper, Vol. 2010–08, "Finance," available at https://pure.uvt.nl/ws/portalfiles/portal/1188662/2010-08.pdf (accessed March 30, 2021).

15 Garry Neil, "Culture & working conditions for artists: implementing the 1980 Recommendations concerning the Status of the Artist," UNESCO Report, 2019, available at https://unesdoc.unesco.org/ark:/48223/pf0000371790 (accessed March 30, 2021).

16 Gregory Sholette, *Dark Matter: Art and Politics in the Age of Enterprise* (London: Pluto Press, 2010).

17 Institutions like the Museums Association (UK), the Association of Art Museum Directors (AAMD) (US) or the International Council of Museums (ICOM) promote a Code of Ethics for Museums. The Code is, however, not legally binding. Available at https://icom.museum/en/resources/standards-guidelines/code-of-ethics/ (accessed March 30, 2021).

current value, or, to put it into financial terms, their property equity.[18] *Only a percentage of their property equity will be offered to investors.*

AMP *can generate an automated dividend that will flow from* A Modest Proposal*'s exchange to the original stakeholders in this cycle of wealth generation, the artists and art workers, whereupon this cycle can start all over again.*[19]

Can Finance Be an Inclusive Tool for the Distribution of Wealth?

An invitation for a solo show in 2018 at Pump House Gallery in Wandsworth, London, seemed the perfect occasion to continue working on *AMP*. First, because it was in London, the city of finance, but also because of the gallery's auspicious location—in Battersea Park, just south of the Thames. The iconic Battersea Power Station, a former coal-fired power plant that had been in ruins for decades until 2012, when it was acquired by an ambitious Malaysian consortium, is situated next to the park.[20] Today their plans are in full progress of being realized, and the former ruins are about to house a luxury shopping center and Apple's London headquarters. Luxury apartments designed by starchitects like Frank Gehry, Foster + Partners, and others, encircle the former power station, with the whole site designated as a new cultural quarter and an "opportunity area."

Pump House Gallery became our first case study for "inclusive financialization of public art assets."[21] Since Wandsworth council does not have an art collection, but owns the gallery building, a Grade II-listed Victorian former pump house, *AMP* would focus on the financialization of this prime piece of real estate. Within the Battersea regenerative context our exhibition "A Modest Proposal (in a Black Box)"[22] challenged how Pump House Gallery could become true to its original design as a "pump house," not only pumping up water, but harnessing all rising values that would surround it in the near future, and in that way become a power house for the benefit of the whole artists' community.

We designed *AMP* to capitalize on profits that can be made on public assets. Although aimed at benefiting artists, it remained a provocative and problematic idea. Shouldn't a debate in Parliament decide on the distribution of these capitalizations? In fact, the "opportunity area" surrounding the gallery already had in place a so-called Value Capture Finance mechanism that would appropriate public wealth.[23] A Tax Increment Financing (TIF) scheme had been implemented to finance the extension of a London Underground line into the area to enhance value and accessibility.[24] The TIF scheme earmarks an expected future increase of tax revenues to be invested directly in the development of the tube extension. Commercial tax levels are frozen and every increment in tax revenues is committed to

18 Equity is the difference between the fair market value of an asset and the outstanding balance of all debts on the asset. See https://corporatefinanceinstitute.com/resources/knowledge/finance/equity-definition/ (accessed March 30, 2021).

19 *AMP* project page Jubilee, see https://jubilee-art.org/?rd_project=1607&lang=en (accessed March 30, 2021).

20 Randeep Ramesh, "Malaysia to investigate Battersea Power Station property deal," *The Guardian*, June 11, 2018, available at https://www.theguardian.com/business/2018/jun/11/malaysia-to-investigate-battersea-power-station-property-deal-anwar-ibrahim (accessed March 30, 2021).

21 *AMP* case studies on financializing art collections and goodwill were planned for exhibitions at de Appel in Amsterdam, and The Atlantic, a triennial in Plymouth in 2020. Both were canceled due to funding problems at both organizations.

22 "A Modest Proposal (in a Black Box)" was inaugurated as a solo exhibition in London (October 3–December 16, 2018).

23 See https://www2.deloitte.com/content/dam/Deloitte/global/Documents/Public-Sector/smart-cities-virtues-of-value-capture-19nov.pdf (accessed March 30, 2021).

24 See https://www.londoncouncils.gov.uk/our-key-themes/infrastructure/funding-infrastructure (accessed March 30, 2021).

paying off capital provided by international investors upfront. Through the UK Infrastructure Guarantee Scheme, the Treasury ensures a steady and irrevocable payment stream to international lenders, irrespective of project performance. In other words, the Battersea TIF scheme passes entrepreneurial risk on to society. If things were to go wrong, taxpayers would carry the cost since the Treasury has to fill the gaps. On top of that, new legislation was issued to safeguard the scheme from political intervention for the next twenty-five years.[25]

Pump House Gallery was part of the cultural infrastructure in the "opportunity area" that has been re-purposed for Value Capture Finance. Discussion of these issues with Enable, the charity managing the gallery, created various obstructions that made the production of our work, its presentation, the organization of a symposium, and the development of a publication an uphill struggle. The public programming by Enable, which takes care not only of the park but also of its cultural and sporting events, needed to be kept in line with local neoliberal policies.[26]

Our planned performance of *A Modest Proposal* for Enable's board of directors intended to formally propose the implementation of *AMP*'s financial model to the decision-making body. It aimed to involve the gallery in a mechanism of redistribution of wealth. Our artistic statement would be documented and consequently become the exhibition. A face-to-face meeting with Enable's management team on the title of our project, which they considered a class provocation, immediately indicated that we would need to move prudently not to risk the project being shut down before it existed. We considered the lack of support we experienced—with the important exception of Pump House Gallery's curator and technical staff—as part of the challenge. Our performance for the board was eventually blocked, which meant that we ended up enacting *AMP* in our own kitchen in Brussels instead, in front of our camera. Post-producing the views from our windows to reveal the panorama of the Battersea "opportunity area" literally made the house our "framing device."[27]

Jubilee, a Platform for Operational Realism

Our practice is dedicated to creating speculative fiction, but part of it could also be referred to as "operational realism." Does the critical work that we and other artists create have enough agency, or is it destined to be subsumed by capitalism's logic? Developing *AMP* required lots of patience and negotiations as well as moral, content, and logistical support, which came from Jubilee, a platform for artistic research and production. Co-founding Jubilee as an artist-run organization and a legal entity in 2013, we felt it could increase our agency as artists in addressing institutions and the policies that govern us.

The operating structure of Jubilee was developed with artists, team, and board: the organization can be argued to be under continuous co-construction by all stakeholders, as its structure should reflect their changing needs, insights, and

25 Francesco Findeisen, "Financing urban infrastructure in London after the financial crisis," in *Britain for sale? perspectives on the costs and benefits of foreign ownership*, edited by Mike Raco (London: The Smith Institute, 2016).

26 Enable is a charity that manages a diverse public services portfolio on behalf of Wandsworth Council. To be able to acquire projects for their portfolio, the charity has to submit a bid with the council.

27 *A Modest Proposal (in a Black Box)*, a twenty-eight-minute film made in collaboration with legal philosopher Luke Mason and performance artist Heike Langsdorf, see https://jubilee-art.org/?rd_project=1607-2&lang=en (accessed March 30, 2021).

the ways we all want to test out how to organize ourselves as an artist-run platform. Since its foundation as a non-profit organization operating on cooperative principles, Jubilee has focused on creating optimal research and production conditions for its core artists. In addition to discussions and exchanges between the artists involved, this has included developing purpose-built artist-driven modes of working. We try to handle financial, administrative, logistical, and legal support in relation to our specific requirements.

In reflecting on and developing new approaches, we have also introduced a dimension that transcends our individual artistic practices. Jubilee gives shape to these innovative collective processes by way of bottom-up research projects—in other words, starting from the practice of the participating artists. We want to specifically reach out to young artists and researchers, initiating an exchange that promises a long-lasting relationship that offers space for their respective research trajectories in particular.

One telling example is "Caveat" (2017–ongoing).[28] This artistic research project redefines the contract as a tool for actively reconfiguring relations in the field. "Caveat" considers the contract as a potential instrument of self-emancipation. You could say that our approach concentrates on developing cooperative relationships and establishing mechanisms of risk-sharing and mutualization of benefits. The ambition is not merely to make artists and cultural producers savvier entrepreneurial subjects, but rather to foster a sense of collective identity, to raise awareness with regard to the field of art's unacceptable marginal and precarious conditions.

It is encouraging to see that even a tiny organization such as Jubilee, with its limited leverage, is sometimes able to put its mark on how relations are formalized in agreements. On the other hand, the process can also be a frustrating one: case in point is the project with Pump House Gallery and the way Enable managed it. Through profound discussions with the exhibition curator we had developed a contract inspired by "Caveat"'s methodology. Unfortunately, bending unequal power relations toward a collaboration that mitigated risks seemed unacceptable for Enable's management team. They simply replaced our contract proposal with their standard contract that had very little concrete relation with how our project had been developing. The engagement of the curator contrasted sharply with how Enable ran the back office, but working under the management's supervision he was quite powerless. From our side, we were already too deeply invested in the project to step away from it.

State of the Arts—The Status of the Artist in Society?

Whether we like it or not, in defining ideological conditions and parameters, the socio-political sphere should be considered as co-creator of the artistic output of our time. What actually constitutes an art practice, and what defines its

28 See www.caveat.be (accessed March 30, 2021).

socio-political reality and its conditions of production is the outcome of continuous debate. We find reflecting on these questions from our "speculative narrative" and "operational realism" perspectives quite meaningful, but in addressing our socio-economic conditions we feel we also have to expand our views beyond art institutions to the governing bodies that install policies. These bodies not only condition how publicly funded art institutions can operate and how we can live our lives as artists, they also affect other people. The current health crisis has made that quite tangible, and has maybe generated a momentum for change.

This is what motivates us to engage in State of the Arts (SOTA), a multi-vocal, horizontally organized platform in which artists, art workers, small organizations, and concerned citizens can partake in meetings, working groups, and protest actions. SOTA's reflection groups dig deep into the currently proposed changes in the Flemish Arts Decree, which frames how artists and organizations can access public funding, or the equally important reform of the so-called "Artist Status," regulating how artists can gain access to social security. SOTA organizes discussions with peers and stakeholders, and formulates concrete demands and proposals to politicians.

All of SOTA's efforts are motivated by the fact that governing the arts cannot be left to politicians alone. It is absurd that artists' voices are generally absent from policy decisions that govern how we can produce our work, or how we can enjoy the same rights as other workers. Our current politicized cultural struggle is exactly about that: policymakers want to define the arts landscape, not by influencing the look or content of the arts, but by their restructuring efforts of the Arts Decree, the template of which will format artists' careers as well as opportunities for arts organizations. This in turn will influence the diversity of art forms available for the public and their access to it. SOTA distinguishes itself by not speaking up for one specific interest group, rather it aims to address issues at large, expressing solidarity with other sectors and less visible groups in society. This also connects us to a wider struggle—the work of all precarious workers. Having been at the vanguard in terms of labor deregulation, artists could now perhaps become the drivers for the regulation of new forms of labor that were freely modeled on the exploitative regime of the cultural sector.

Museums have always worked with artists in ways similar to how the gig economy functions today. They don't see themselves as the employers of the artists they exhibit, but assume the role of "partner" or "facilitator." The artists are "paid" with the attention, networking, and brand value of the museum. Having augmented their reputational capital, artists are supposed to capture that value in the market, like true entrepreneurs of themselves. The museum, which also increases its symbolic value through the presence of the invited artist, functions very much like any other platform: it extracts a huge rent from the "participant" in the form of un(der)paid labor. Until today this was always the trade-off between more "freedom" from the bond of subordination represented by wage labor, and being deprived of the guarantees that come with it. The question is whether it needs to stay that way.

A Modest Proposal Revisited?

You could say that the recent speculative mania around NFTS (Non Fungible Tokens) and the proliferation of new digital start-ups based on blockchain technology are a logical continuation and acceleration of the ongoing financialization of art and cultural goods.[29] Fundamentally influencing how creators and artists define labor and labor relations, and how they make a living from their work, the phenomenon may have a quite disruptive effect on existing infrastructures and business models within the art world and the cultural industries. These new applications of blockchain technology could trigger a power shift from institution/digital platform/mediator to creators and artists.

Blockchain makes it possible to forego the need for a trusted third party or an intermediary. In the current gig economy, platforms like Spotify or YouTube capture most of the value of creators' content. Thanks to new peer-to-peer payment models based on blockchain technology, creators and artists can build a direct relationship with their fans, investors, and collectors. In other words, they can monetize their work themselves, outside of any institutional infrastructure.[30] Will this new form of financialization live up to its proclaimed promise of democratization and emancipation of artists from big online platforms, and bricks-and-mortar art institutions, and their extractive business models? It will be interesting to see how NFTS will influence the reputational values that artists until now had to derive from participating in today's art institutions.

The current hype around NFTS on the one hand makes clear that they are operated as a value-capture strategy for celebrities and influencers who are able to monopolize all the attention. They function exclusively at the service of investors, collectors, and a few artists. *Art House Index*, our experiment that measures our human capital non-stop, was conceived as a critical investigation of financialization of daily life. One NFT start-up eerily describes its proposal as an actual "human stock market," where fans can purchase shares to bet on the rise or fall of influencers and creators. Their day-to-day life decisions and their market value are literally controlled by the crowds—the ultimate image of entrepreneurial atomized individuals leveraging their human capital and monetizing every aspect of their life.[31] Life is rendered a tradeable market commodity, its success or failure measured in the economy of attention.[32]

On the other hand, some start-ups are beginning to use blockchain technology for their own ends and goals. They create tools to help artists split the revenue for work they created together, everyone receiving a fair share, or business models that ensure sustainable commissions for artists. Platform cooperatives

29 NFTS are merely digital records that show who owns a unique piece of content such as digital images, videos, songs, and essays. These pieces of digital media, however, function as rare collectibles themselves. Their property model is based on scarcity without exclusion. It is the ownership of a digital asset, a cultural good that everyone can use or have access to, but only some can profit from the circulation of this good. What makes this digital content an NFT is blockchain technology, a public digital ledger that can be used as an immovable record to designate authenticity in ownership. See Rachel O'Dwyer, "Limited Edition: Producing Scarcity for Digital Art on the Blockchain and its Implications for The Cultural Industries," *Sage Journals*, Vol. 26, Issue 4, 2018, DOI:10.1177/1354856518795097.

30 See https://creatoreconomy.so/p/guide-to-nfts-for-creators (accessed March 30, 2021).

31 Taylor Lorenz, "For Creators, Everything Is for Sale," *New York Times*, March 10, 2021, available at https://www.nytimes.com/2021/03/10/style/creators-selling-selves.html (accessed March 30, 2021).

32 Jacob Silverman, "Trophy Homes and $2.5 Million Tweets: How the Idle Rich Spent Their Pandemic Year," *New Republic*, March 10, 2021, available at https://newrepublic.com/article/161655/trophy-homes-25-million-tweets-idle-rich-spent-pandemic-year (accessed March 30, 2021).

could offer another solution to labor exploitation.[33] Taking the lessons from the long and exciting history of cooperatives into the digital age, they rely on democratic decision-making and shared ownership of the platform by workers and users. In that context, blockchain-based tokens may offer tantalizing possibilities for community ownership, with benefits distributed to the core stakeholders to achieve more equitable prosperity. Art practices may benefit from morphing into a "speculative" operational realism, an approach that could generate alternative institutions for research and production based on more inclusive forms of financialization.

AMP posed a provocative question, and perhaps we have to ask the question again. How can we make sure that these new tools incorporate forms of mutualization, and as such become a step in the direction of a fair distribution of value—not only for investors and blue-chip artists, but for all stakeholders in culture and the arts, to generate more sustainable conditions and futures in which art can flourish as a true ecology of practices?

Equality in Abundance

Although speaking from a very different time, Gustave Courbet, who became the driving force behind the artists and cultural action during the short-lived Paris Commune, certainly had a form of mutualization and distribution of value in mind. In *Le Cri du Peuple* of April 10, 1871, he called on the artists of Paris to take the governance of museums into their own hands. To this end, 400 artists and artisans met on April 14, 1871, in an assembly to constitute a Federation of Artists, and elected Courbet as chair of the Arts Commission. In parallel with the emancipation of work by the workers themselves, the federation claimed self-management of art by artists. The Federation's manifesto evokes the right for all to live in a world in which everyone would have an equal share in abundance.[34]

> *The committee will contribute to our regeneration, to the inauguration of communal luxury and to the splendors of the future and to the universal Republic.*[35]

33 See https://rosalux.nyc/wp-content/uploads/2020/11/RLS-NYC_platformcoop.pdf (accessed March 30, 2021).

34 Marc Lagana, "Un peuple révolutionnaire: la commune de Paris 1871," *Cahiers Bruxellois—Brusselse Cahiers*, 2018/1 L, 175–98, available at https://www.cairn.info/revue-cahiers-bruxellois-2018-1-page-175.htm (accessed March 30, 2021).

35 G. Courbet, Moulinet, Stephen Martin, Alexandre Jousse, Roszezench, Trichon, Dalou, Jules Hèreau, C. Chahert, H. Dubois, A. Faleynière, Eugène Pottier, Perrin, A. Moulliard in *Journal Officiel de la République française*. Available at https://archivesautonomies.org/IMG/pdf/commune/communedeparis/JOmatin/0415.pdf (accessed March 30, 2021).

FROM THE AUTOMATION OF RELATIONS TO THE AMPLIFICATION OF COMMUNITIES: THE RISE OF DAOS

Aude Launay

Several years into what was then the new millennium, an inflection point of sorts seemed to dramatically change the game: everything became participatory. If the premises had already been visible in the history of theater, and were by then fashionable in contemporary art, it really was the advent of Web 2.0 and its flood of so-called social networking platforms enabling what we came to define as internet "communities" that turned participation as a cultural concept into a cultural situation. If popular participation had long been synonymous with an active involvement of people in socio-political processes, when not giving rise to revolutions, the participation that was on everyone's lips in the early 2000s was rather a hollow one. A participation going with the grain. Clicking, liking, posting, commenting, we were quickly turned into demographic-emotional profiles. Sham public policies followed suit. Everything making people feel as if they had a voice was good. Thus, it was when the participative became a leitmotiv that it proved to be the most cosmetic.

Among the sharpest critiques that were raised, the architect and theorist Markus Miessen and the economist and journalist Hannes Grassegger aptly put it as follows: it was "as if participation had become an end in itself. The sedative of the 00s."[1] As the media theorist Felix Stalder notes, the digital condition has eroded many of the categories that had structured modernity, among them the notions of "public" and "private," or "professional" and "amateur."[2] Going further, the researcher Sophie Toupin observes that "until about the year 2000, when data extractivist logic had not yet fully permeated our digital lives, we lived in a world where there was a clearer opposition between the digital commons, developed as part of the non-market orientation, and what was then called e-commerce and the emerging knowledge economy."[3]

The very idea of the social network, of meaningful social structures composed of interactions and relations between individuals or organizations, has rapidly been corrupted and transformed by a few highly centralized tech giants. But this

1 Markus Miessen and Hannes Grassegger, "Waking Up from The Nightmare of Participation," *Reading Design*, June 2012, available at https://www.readingdesign.org/nightmare-of-participation (accessed August 23, 2021).

2 Felix Stalder, *The Digital Condition* (Cambridge: Polity, 2018).

3 Sophie Toupin, "The Commons, Sociotechnical Imaginaries and Resistance," in *Aesthetics of the Commons*, edited by Cornelia Sollfrank, Felix Stalder, and Shusha Niederberger (Zurich: Diaphanes, 2021), 200.

radical transformation was actually not that radical and rapid, but rather the result of decades of social exploitation. Again, it was when we were made to believe that our social networks were being remarkably improved that the data extractivist logic struck once more. If the division of calculus, coupled with the increase in the speed of photographic capture and the advent of new measuring instruments that offered new ways of analyzing motion, led to an ever-increasing fragmentation of tasks, reducing humans to mere clicking machines, it is precisely this industrialization of the division of labor that induced the amplification of the fantasies of automation of the human,[4] turning Von Kempelen's 1769 illusory chess player into an artificial artificial intelligence service two and a half centuries later,[5] Villiers de l'Isle-Adam's 1886 *Future Eve* into a gig-workers-powered sweet text messages service,[6] and Alan Turing's test into a production line for unwilling laborers.[7]

Automation generally conjures up images of the replacement of members of the workforce by industrial robotic arms and systems, as well as unmanned vehicles. In a slightly less obvious manner, it also calls to mind the algorithmic management of workers, such as food delivery platform couriers. From human computers to algorithmic managers, pursuing this extreme datafication in the automation of everything feels like a natural course of events in our quantophrenian era.[8] No wonder, then, when asked about the real-world conditions of possibility for the "implausibly accurate conglomerate of artificial intelligence systems," which forms the main "non-character" of his novel *Daemon* (2006), the science-fiction writer Daniel Suarez responded "I don't think a *major* breakthrough would be required, just an incremental one."[9]

The daemon in question is a computer program described by the author as a "distributed narrow artificial intelligence," a "logic tree" that "has no central core," and whose designer "strived to remove single points of failure." This kind of program runs continuously in the background of a computer operating system and performs specified operations at predefined times,

4 An interplay of influences between mathematicians and Adam Smith, with Smith claiming those of Isaac Newton, but also of Alexis Clairaut, Nicole-Reine Lepaute, and Joseph Lalande, whereas *The Wealth of Nations* (1776), which inspired Gaspard de Prony as well as the Astronomical Society of London, led to treating calculus and other "investigations of the human mind" as a type of labor that could benefit from the organizational model of division of tasks as much as physical labor. See David Alan Grier, "The Children of Adam Smith," in *When Computers Were Humans* (Princeton: Princeton University Press, 2005).

5 Facing the failure of its own artificial intelligence programs at certain tasks, Amazon decided to outsource these to humans and launched Amazon Mechanical Turk, a gig-working platform that emulates artificial intelligence by replacing mechanical computing with human brainpower. See https://www.mturk.com/help (accessed August 23, 2021).

6 See https://invisibleboyfriend.com/ (accessed August 23, 2021).

7 From computer punch cards carrying a language that only machines can understand, and the dehumanization against which students and workers rebelled in the 1960s, to the Turing test consisting of a blind verbal confrontation of a human with a computer and another human to see if the test subject could tell which of their interlocutors was a machine, and later on to CAPTCHAS, these tests now make it possible to distinguish humans from machines, because they present elements that cannot be read by the latter and determine who is human and who is not as they make humans perform purely mechanical work destined to train artificial intelligence systems, the story of human-machine interaction is one of emulation on both sides.

8 "The term 'quantophrenia' was coined by Pitrim Sorokin in his critique of Fads and Foibles in Sociology. It is not an attack on measurement per se. It refers to the cult founded on the belief that quantification is the most, or indeed the only, valid form of knowledge." Robert Dingwall, "Quantophrenia is Back in Town," *Social Science Space*, 2014, available at https://www.socialsciencespace.com/2014/05/quantophrenia-is-back-in-town/ (accessed August 23, 2021).

9 Frank Rieger, "Understanding the Daemon," *Frankfurter Allgemeine Zeitung*, May 1, 2011, available at https://www.faz.net/aktuell/feuilleton/medien/english-version-understanding-the-daemon-1621404.html (accessed August 23, 2021).

or in response to certain events, without being under the direct control of an interactive user. In *Daemon*, it engages in business operations with companies, and works toward setting a new social order. But what differentiated this daemon from the trading bots and the judiciary predictive algorithms that we already knew by then, was the fact that it was "distributed over a peer-to-peer network architecture to avoid core logic disruption."[10] Its autonomy was protected by a sheer number of humans onto which machines the program chose to be hosted: a distributed network allowing it to self-replicate in case of any incident.

Decentralize

Astonishingly, the novel was first published two years before what was to become the landmark in the popularization of the power that lies in the idea of peer-to-peer systems: the Bitcoin white paper.[11] It goes without saying that, even though the mainstream narrative tends to ignore it, Bitcoin stems from a long history of cryptography—which goes back some four thousand years—of privacy advocacy—going back 130 years—but also from an antitrust sentiment and an attachment to the values of the free software movement,[12] partly veering toward crypto-anarchy.[13] This long history had also given rise to earlier electronic currency projects such as DigiCash, conceived by the cryptographer considered to be the forefather of the cypherpunk movement, David Chaum; B-money, designed by the cypherpunk developer Wei Dai; and BitGold, the brainchild of the cryptographer and legal scholar Nick Szabo; as well as to technical breakthroughs in distributed computation and distributed consensus cryptosystems that would directly influence Bitcoin.[14] Similarly, if Bitcoin publicized the concept of blockchain, the theorization of this "mathematically sound and computationally practical solution to the time-stamping problem" of digital documents dates back to some seventeen years earlier.[15]

10 Daniel Suarez, *Daemon* (Pasadena: Verdugo Press, 2006).

11 Satoshi Nakamoto, "Bitcoin: A Peer-to-Peer Electronic Cash System," *October* 31, 2008. *Daemon* is not the first prescient novel when it comes to depicting the transformations induced by electronic and global peer-to-peer networks. We have to mention at least Neal Stephenson's *The Diamond Age: Or, a Young Lady's Illustrated Primer* (1995), which already described such a system "designed from the ground up to provide privacy and security so that people could use it to transfer money," and Bruce Sterling's *Heavy Weather* (1994), which mentioned an "electronic, private cash, unbacked by any government, untraceable, completely anonymous, global in reach, lightninglike in speed, ubiquitous, fungible, and usually highly volatile."

12 Essentially, the history of civil software was congruent with that of open-source code until the US Computer Software Copyright Act of 1980 (Pub. L. No. 96–517, § 10, 94 Stat. 3015, 3018) that categorized software as a "literary work," and thus rendered it copyrightable. As early as 1983, GNU, a free operating system, and eCash, an anonymous digital currency, were conceived by the MIT programmer Richard Stallman and the cryptographer David Chaum respectively, initiating the free software movement. "Our code is free for all to use, worldwide. We don't much care if you don't approve of the software we write. We know that software can't be destroyed and that a widely dispersed system can't be shut down." Eric Hughes, "A Cypherpunk's Manifesto," March 9, 1993.

13 See Timothy C. May, "The Crypto Anarchist Manifesto," 1988, available at https://groups.csail.mit.edu/mac/classes/6.805/articles/crypto/cypherpunks/may-crypto-manifesto.html (accessed August 23, 2021); Timothy C. May, "THE CYPHERNOMICON: Cypherpunks FAQ and More, Version 0.666, 1994-09-10"; Timothy C. May, "Crypto Anarchy and Virtual Communities," 1994.

14 Such as the research of Cynthia Dwork, who is notably the co-creator of the proof-of-work algorithm, central to the design of Bitcoin.

15 If the Bitcoin white paper provides a detailed explanation of the first real-world use of a chain of blocks to authenticate transactions in a peer-to-peer network, the first description of the concept is to be found in Stuart Haber and W. Scott Stornetta's article "How To Time-Stamp a Digital Document," *Journal of Cryptology*, No. 3, 1991, 99–111, available at https://link.springer.com/content/pdf/10.1007/BF00196791.pdf (accessed August 23, 2021). The "block chain" was first mentioned by the developer and cryptographer Hal Finney in a response to Nakamoto's paper, on November 8, 2008.

In a nutshell, blockchains—and by that we mean public ones, such as the Bitcoin or the Ethereum blockchains—are cryptographically secure decentralized records of information that do not rely on any trusted third party to guarantee the authenticity of the recorded information. The decentralization of the system enables it to avoid single points of failure, be they technical or political, such as censorship, and therefore "blockchains are tools for the circumvention of systems of control" as the protocol architect and Ethereum researcher Vlad Zamfir would put it.[16]

Despite cryptography being used to form and secure the chain of blocks, that is not what guarantees the trustlessness of the system. Trustlessness is achieved when a majority of participants in the chain agrees on the current state of the chain. Coordination between networked devices is at stake here, and, as we find humans behind those networked devices, it is possible to describe blockchains as a form of cooperation technology. Indeed, what a system requires to operate without the need for a trusted third party, is a way to implement honesty as a Nash equilibrium, that is to say, that honesty is the optimal strategy for every participant.[17] Bitcoin was the first peer-to-peer system to embed incentives in its code for humans to cooperate in a way that is, at times, the best for themselves and the best for the system.[18] Participation, in this case, cannot be merely cosmetic.

Yet, it is a certain idea of human automation that was instrumental in what is probably the most important advance regarding human coordination: Decentralized Autonomous Organizations, or DAOs. The phrase, which has evolved from "decentralized autonomous corporations" mentioned in a publication by the blockchain developer Daniel Larimer,[19] first appeared in this sense in the white paper on the protocol that would soon become the second most important blockchain: Ethereum.[20] This concept was actively being developed in the field in the fall of 2013, and, in an article he published two months before the Ethereum white paper, Vitalik Buterin asked nothing less than "do we really need the people?"[21] Under its provocative guise, this question unveiled what this new kind of organization, automated at its core, was really about, as Buterin elaborated further:

> The industrial revolution allowed us, for the first time, to start replacing human labor with machines on a large scale, and now we have advanced digitized factories and robotic arms that produce complex goods like

16 Vlad Zamfir, "The Potential Impact of Blockchains on Society," Sydney Blockchain Workshops, 2015, available at https://www.youtube.com/watch?v=RzXL_6ZiY8E (accessed August 23, 2021).

17 In game theory—largely used to conceive cryptographic networks that do not need oversight yet produce positive outcomes for the greater good—a Nash equilibrium leads to a stable state of a situation, provided none of the participants finds the incentive to exit that situation. Merging individual with collective rationality is essential to guarantee the validity and thus the security of a blockchain as the system can only be robust if all players, or a majority follow one dominant strategy.

18 For an insightful overview of some of the pitfalls of the Bitcoin protocol regarding this point, see Barnabé Monnot, "Research diaries: Anarchy in Creta," *hackingresear.ch*, July 2019, available at https://hackingresear.ch/diaries/anarchy-creta/ (accessed August 23, 2021).

19 Daniel Larimer, "Overpaying For Security, The Hidden Costs of Bitcoin," *LTB Network*, September 7, 2013, available at https://letstalkbitcoin.com/is-bitcoin-overpaying-for-false-security#.UjtiUt9xyow (accessed August 23, 2021).

20 The term first appeared in a research article by the computer scientist Werner Dilger, but there it referred to a system of intelligent home appliances modeled on the immune system. For the origins of its contemporary meaning, see Vitalik Buterin, "Ethereum whitepaper," November 2013, available at https://ethereum.org/en/whitepaper/ (accessed August 23, 2021).

21 Vitalik Buterin, "Bootstrapping A Decentralized Autonomous Corporation: Part I," *Bitcoin Magazine*, September 19, 2013, available at https://bitcoinmagazine.com/technical/bootstrapping-a-decentralized-autonomous-corporation-part-i-1379644274 (accessed August 23, 2021).

> automobiles all on their own. But this is only automating the bottom; removing the need for rank and file manual laborers, and replacing them with a smaller number of professionals to maintain the robots, while the management of the company remains untouched. The question is, can we approach the problem from the other direction: even if we still need human beings to perform certain specialized tasks, can we remove the management from the equation instead?[22]

And this is what the first decentralized autonomous corporations (DACs) seemed to be aiming at: lines of code becoming autonomous agents, that is to say, able to calculate "a desired action to take," given a certain input within a certain environment, without being stoppable by any human agent thanks to "the kind of distributed computing that we see in Bitcoin: a set of rules that decentrally self-validates its own computation."[23] Those futuristic ideas were enabled by way of smart contracts, automated formalized relationships between parties as conceptualized by Nick Szabo some sixteen years earlier.[24] Thus, in its white paper, Ethereum was first introduced as "A Next-Generation Smart Contract and Decentralized Application Platform," or, as the Ethereum biographer Camila Russo would put it, "Bitcoin wanted to be peer-to-peer money. Ethereum wanted to be peer-to-peer everything."[25]

With governance being the crux of human societies[26]—which "includes human rights, freedom of speech, economic transactions on a worldwide basis,"[27] as Vint Cerf, one of the fathers of the internet, argued—usually implemented by centralized authorities, smart contracts appear to be a liberating technology, as "blockchains, and smart contracts especially, give us the power to alter and align social incentives. All without introducing inevitably corrupt central authorities," summarizes Luke Duncan, now a specialist in DAO infrastructure.[28] But if one of the simplest descriptions of DAOs is making it possible for people to gather to do things they could not do individually—such as organizing, raising funds, managing these funds, aligning toward a common goal—without the need to trust, and, consequently, to know each other, the absolute opposite is also true: DAOs can be used and be useful at the local scale.

Such an intuition fuels CultureStake, an experiment led by the London-based arts organization Furtherfield. One of its founders, Ruth Catlow, relates a sense of dissatisfaction in their practice which consists, in her words, of "funneling artworks that we think are fantastic, from the international digital art scene into a local gallery and benevolently bestow[ing] them on the locality," adding "that was starting to feel just wrong."[29] A feeling I had been sharing for years, which had also led me to explore collaborative and distributed decision-making processes in general and within my own curatorial practice in particular. This feeling that it was wrong, in some way, to impose on people the art they would live with, especially in public space, brought

22 Ibid.

23 Ibid.

24 Nick Szabo, "The Idea of Smart Contracts," 1997, which is an executive summary of the longer essay "Formalizing and Securing Relationships on Public Networks." Available at https://www.fon.hum.uva.nl/rob/Courses/InformationInSpeech/CDROM/Literature/LOTwinterschool2006/szabo.best.vwh.net/idea.html (accessed September 14, 2021).

25 Camila Russo, *The Infinite Machine* (New York: HarperCollins, 2020), XIII.

26 For a very detailed and enlightening history of the word governance, see Alain Deneault, *"Gouvernance," Le management totalitaire* (Montréal: Lux, 2019).

27 J. O'Dell, "Vint Cerf: The Government Is Going Overboard in Internet Copyright Control," *VentureBeat*, November 14, 2011, available at https://venturebeat.com/2011/11/14/vint-cerf/ (accessed August 23, 2021).

28 "Team Interviews: Luke, Research at Aragon One," Aragon One Official Blog, October 26, 2017.

29 Ruth Catlow, in conversation with Ela Kagel, "DAO, DGOV, DIWO, DECAL—a roundup of shared experiences with empowering self-organised collectives through distributed forms of governance and technology," MoneyLab, Berlin, March 26, 2021, available at https://www.youtube.com/watch?v=qIrSWczeT2o (accessed August 23, 2021).

Furtherfield to design an interactive system for their visitors to be given a voice. A system to be formalized as a DAO.

The definitions of DAOs may seem to be manifold, but those differences mainly come down to a question of degree, of intensity to which the core concepts are interpreted and applied. Building a DAO, be it by using a template or coding its rules from absolute scratch, does not merely make a group of people a decentralized autonomous organization. As the complex systems engineer Michael Zargham reminds us, "the technology facilitates decentralization, i.e., makes it easier to have a social system which is decentralized, but decentralization is a property of the social system, it's a political concept, it's not a technical concept."[30] Crucially, decentralized does not mean opening up to everyone without any restriction. Anyone can join permissionless DAOs—Bitcoin, Ethereum, or the DAO to-be CultureStake—but some DAOs—such as Moloch DAOs, as I outline below—are permissioned. Many different levels can be observed here, as the infrastructure on which those structures are running is neither (yet) fully decentralized, nor fully permissionless. The hacktivist and DAOist Sacha Saint-Leger rightly notes that, like decentralization, permissionlessness is not binary, but a spectrum.[31] However, those different levels of decentralization and of permissionlessness do not only result from technological attributes, but also proceed from cultural choices, or, in other words, "while a system might appear technically decentralized, the culture utilizing the system determines the extent to which it is decentralized in practice."[32] It is therefore necessary to point out, together with Zargham, that "the political and the technical concepts of decentralization are related but they are not the same. And it's exactly the same when it comes to the word 'autonomous.'"[33]

Autonomize

Explaining his prescient exploration of the tentacular expansion of automation of society, Suarez writes that "The Daemon posits tasks for humans to achieve, provides incentives (or delivers threats) to achieve them, and then scans multiple public newsfeeds to determine when/if those tasks are completed. In no case does the Daemon actually 'understand' the events it's monitoring; it relies instead on its human network to serve as its eyes and ears—people invested in the survival of the system."[34] The parallel with the early delineation Buterin gives of DAOs is striking: "The ideal of a decentralized autonomous organization is easy to describe: it is an entity that lives on the internet and exists autonomously, but also heavily relies on hiring individuals to perform certain tasks that the automaton itself cannot do."[35] Thus, as tempting as it can be to imagine electronic agents endowed with a will of their own, the autonomy of the automaton is, once again, a question of intensity. Obviously, self-executing code leans toward a certain degree of independence in functioning, but some human input is still

30 Michael Zargham, "Deep Dive 5: Unpacking decentralization and autonomy in DAOs with Michael Zargham," *Square I* podcast, April 22, 2021, available at https://anchor.fm/square1/episodes/Deep-Dive-5-Unpacking-decentralization-and-autonomy-in-DAOs-with-Michael-Zargham-evejuu (accessed August 23, 2021).

31 Sacha Saint-Leger, "like decentralisation, I don't see permissionless as binary, but a spectrum," May 7, 2021, 5.23 pm, tweet, https://twitter.com/oxMiel/status/1390688660505481220 (accessed August 23, 2021).

32 James Duncan, May 4, 2021, 9.14 pm, tweet, https://twitter.com/OKDunc/status/1389659667173806081

33 Zargham, "Deep Dive 5."

34 Rieger, "Understanding the Daemon."

35 Vitalik Buterin, "DAOs, DACs, DAs and More: An Incomplete Terminology Guide," Ethereum Foundation blog, May 6, 2014, available at https://blog.ethereum.org/2014/05/06/daos-dacs-das-and-more-an-incomplete-terminology-guide/ (accessed August 23, 2021).

necessary at both ends of the action of this agent. As it happens, Buterin frames it straightforwardly: "automation at the centre, humans at the edges."[36]

Yet, how may autonomy at the infrastructure level enable autonomy for the people? For Zamfir, there is no real technological autonomy, emphasizing that "protocols are not immutable, they are governed."[37] This is a crucial point that tends to be ignored in the general discourse on blockchains. "One merely escapes to a different set of rules, not one controlled by 'politicians,' but one in the hands of programmers and those in control of computing power," writer and financial hacker Brett Scott observed at a time when Ethereum had not even publicly launched.[38] This issue is not only related to blockchain but permeates the automation sector as a whole. As a matter of fact, AI researchers Mike Annany and Kate Crawford point out that "an algorithmic system is not just code and data but an *assemblage* of human and non-human actors—of institutionally situated code, practices, and norms with the power to create, sustain, and signify relationships among people and data through minimally observable, semiautonomous action."[39] Semiautonomous action appears to be a more accurate phrasing to outline the agency of the smart contracts underpinning DAOs. Indeed, the rules coded in the contracts are as human-made as the rules about the possible changes to those rules, which the author Kei Kreutler stresses when asking "[w]ho is responsible for making the decision on how to make decisions?"[40] Thus, contrary to widespread belief, and despite their automation, the immutability of smart contracts and blockchain protocols is not guaranteed, and, what is more, as Zamfir underlines, "immutability is not a fact, it's more of a crypto legal doctrine."[41]

And even though the father of cybernetics, Norbert Wiener, already warned that "the future offers very little hope for those who expect that our new mechanical slaves will offer us a world in which we may rest from thinking. Help us they may, but at the cost of supreme demands upon our honesty and our intelligence" almost sixty years ago, when it comes to the dominant narrative, this still is the most pressing issue.[42] The autonomy for the people here refers much more to the kind of autonomy of a Temporary Autonomous Zone or TAZ,[43] or a Zone to Defend or ZAD,[44] than to the autonomy of software; it is an autonomy true to both its original moral and political senses of acting for oneself, voluntarily or spontaneously, but also of governing oneself according to one's own rules. And this autonomy is, in

36 Ibid.

37 Vlad Zamfir interviewed on BlockTV on the occasion of EthCC, Paris, March 9, 2020, available at https://www.youtube.com/watch?v=wIvJTVuX3PE (accessed August 23, 2021).

38 Brett Scott, "Visions of a Techno-Leviathan, The Politics of Bitcoin Blockchain," Policy Paper, February 2015, available at https://www.rosalux.de/en/publication/id/6154/visions-of-a-techno-leviathan/ (accessed August 23, 2021).

39 Mike Ananny and Kate Crawford, "Seeing without knowing: Limitations of the transparency ideal and its application to algorithmic accountability," *new media & society*, 2016, p. 11.

40 Kei Kreutler, "The Byzantine Generalization Problem: Subtle Strategy in the Context of Blockchain Governance," *Technosphere*, August 19, 2018, available at https://technosphere-magazine.hkw.de/p/The-Byzantine-Generalization-Problem-Subtle-Strategy-in-the-Context-of-Blockchain-Governance-8UNNcM8VShTpBGWRuob1GP (accessed August 23, 2021).

41 Zamfir interviewed on BlockTV.

42 Norbert Wiener, *God and Golem, Inc.* (Cambridge, MA: MIT Press, 1964).

43 See Hakim Bey, *Temporary Autonomous Zone* (New York: Autonomedia, 1991).

44 A ZAD is a site created through a militant occupation in order to prevent a development plan. The most famous one in France is the occupation of Notre-Dame-des-Landes in protest against plans for a European airport hub unveiled by the French government in 1970. Over fifty years the zone has gradually become a symbol of the contestation of major development projects through non-violent civil disobedience actions.

a way, the exact opposite of the one attributed to software, to code, which has to run according to the rules embedded within itself. This autonomy tends to be defined negatively, proclaimed, as a form of resistance. "DAOs are decentralized organizations autonomous from some existing power structures, as Zargham states, or at least, that is what they aspire to."[45]

The question of these organizations' legal personality has been a subject of public debate since the creation of the first widely public DAO, in 2016.[46] By then, the idea was to enable people to pool capital and, thanks to a token allocation proportional to their investment, have them vote on the uses of this capital. The lack of legal structure turned every token holder into a general partner of the organization and thus made them personally liable. Nowadays, the debate has permeated institutional discourse so much that the State of Wyoming has, as of July 1, 2021, recognized a DAO and its members as a legal entity. If this step makes DAOs simply a new type of limited liability company, it is not only extremely reductive, but above all a subversion of the original borderlessness and even statelessness at the core of DAOs. "By equating DAOs to state-chartered entities, Bill 38 implicitly colonializes the anarchist concept of 'DAOs' to facilitate re-intermediation and rent extraction by [traditional finance] intermediaries such as lawyers, registered agents, and secretaries of state."[47]

If for some, "DAOs are often technology before communities," those that interest us here are precisely the ones that counter this statement.[48] Both orientations coexisted since the advent of the concept, and Griff Green, a chemical engineer turned core member of this first DAO to become publicly known, reminds us that "decentralized autonomous corporations, companies,[49] cooperation,[50] ... The C in DAC could stand for many different ways of organizing, and it could also stand for communities."[51] The aforementioned DAO, which was known as The DAO, was a for-profit organization, a crowdfunded investment fund, but the underlying goal of this unprecedented structure was "to create a universal sharing economy, a universal sharing network, using The DAO as a Schelling point or a governance mechanism." Via a system of smart lockers and possibly drones to deliver the goods to be found in the lockers, "the dream was: let's make it easy for anyone to share anything and be paid for sharing like a rental."[52] This project, led by the start-up slock.it, was fulfilling the ideas of the first uses for smart contracts ventured by Szabo as early as 1997, but in a peer-to-peer fashion.[53]

From planetary systems of coordination to rather simple applications, DAOs are deployed on many different scales that make it possible to define them with different levels of complexity,

45 Zargham, "Deep Dive 5."

46 At the time, DAOs were on everyone's lips, and, early November 2015, during the Devcon1 conference held in London, two DAO projects that were about to deeply influence the field were announced: Maker DAO and The DAO. While the first was building a stablecoin pegged to the US dollar, the second realized the biggest crowdsale in history at that time and raised about US$150 million in just a month, before seeing the funds hacked a few months later, the unfortunate event leading to the first "hard fork" of the Ethereum blockchain and probably the most important dissent in Ethereum's history: is the smart contract's code really immutable or can it be bypassed for its operations to be reversed?

47 Gabriel Shapiro and Sydney Abualy, "Wyoming's Legal DAO-saster," April 10, 2021, *Substack*, available at https://lexnode.substack.com/p/wyomings-legal-dao-saster (accessed August 23, 2021).

48 Grace Rachmany, MoneyLab, Berlin, community call, March 26, 2021. The topic of the technological tools designed for DAOs largely exceeds the scope of this essay but will be explored in the book I am currently writing.

49 Buterin, "DAOs, DACs, DAs and More."

50 BitShares white paper, updated on March 14, 2021, available at https://docs.bitshares.build/docs/get-started/bitshares-whitepaper/ (accessed August 29, 2021).

51 Griff Green, "Deep Dive 10: The Web3 experience with Griff Green," *Square I* podcast, May 28, 2021, available at https://anchor.fm/square1/episodes/Deep-Dive-10-the-Web3-Experience-with-Griff-Green-e110mli (accessed August 29, 2021).

52 Ibid.

53 Szabo, "The Idea of Smart Contracts."

the simplest of them probably being "Internet piggy bank for communities."[54] Why? Because, as Catlow straightforwardly states, "there is no neutral money, the funding you receive means something."[55] And even though there is obviously no clean money, as money is always already circulating through both transparent and opaque economies, and from one to the other, pooling money from a community toward goals chosen by this same community means a lot more freedom for this community than, for instance, applying for public or private funding and risking censorship or, at the very least, control and interference in decision-making. These communities can preexist the DAO as much as they can gather around its goals. Sometimes it happens that these communities emerge from another type of organization, such as a corporation, and that the corporation itself turns into a DAO.[56] At other times, DAOs are the formalization of communities that formed organically. When asked to introduce the MetaCartel DAO, its initiator Peter Pan responded: "I guess it's just a group of people who really like each other and trust each other, it's like a guild."[57]

Organize

"Thinking of the system as an agent throws into relief the degree to which the system *isn't* an agent," the blogger and psychiatrist Scott Alexander wrote in "Meditations On Moloch," a text inspired by Allen Ginsberg's poem "Howl" (1955–56) that heavily influenced the creation of the Moloch DAO, but that is also an important point of reference in the general reflection on how blockchains and especially DAOs can be used to solve human coordination problems.[58] From a scary daemon to an even scarier demon—here an ancient funeral deity who came to be known as the god of coordination failure—the mythology behind decentralized autonomous organizations is one of humans subdued by systems they themselves have created; it is Fritz Lang's *Metropolis* in which Moloch is a god-like machine to which workers are sacrificed that seems to best instantiate the issue.

What is to be done when a system is so overwhelming that only massive coordination to stop abiding by its rules could result in its abolition, but that establishing this very coordination is somewhat impossible? Bypassing the national rules and borders can be a way to not only raise general awareness around the tragedy of the commons, but also to offer solutions both on the global and local levels.[59] In this perspective, one network cannot go without the other, and society may not find the answer to

54 Luis Cuende, "DAO feels quite a challenging term sometimes—I like 'Internet piggy bank for communities.'" March 22, 2021, 6.51 pm, tweet, https://twitter.com/licuende/status/1374056114195726337 (accessed August 29, 2021).

55 Catlow, "DAO, DGOV, DIWO, DECAL."

56 A process that Shapeshift, a decentralized finance company created in 2014, undertook during the summer of 2021, see https://shapeshift.com/shapeshift-decentralize-airdrop (accessed August 29. 2021).

57 See "Humans of Ethereum, episode 9: Peter Pan," September 2019, available at https://www.youtube.com/watch?v=2bnQS9SZjxs (accessed August 29, 2021).

58 Scott Alexander, "Meditations On Moloch," July 30, 2014, *Slate Star Codex*, available at https://slatestarcodex.com/ (accessed August, 2021).

59 The title of a Garrett Hardin's 1968 article, "The Tragedy of the Commons," (*Science*, Vol. 162, Issue 3859, December 13, 1968, 1243–48, DOI: 10.1126/science.162.3859.1243), describes a phenomenon that applies to non-excludable and rivalrous resources such as the oceans or biodiversity: how is it possible to incentivize people to take care of the common goods when being careful will not get them anything more than if they did not? Elinor Ostrom's principles, derived from her studies of collective organization to govern those goods—such as clearly defined limits, explicit rules, effective oversight, gradual sanctions for offenders, conflict resolution mechanisms, broad participation in governance, and relative autonomy from higher authorities—are an essential influence for many DAOists and a ground to build on for the Commons Stack, an organization whose goal is to enable communities to co-own and co-manage shared funds as a commons.

both the free rider problem and the always lurking abuses of power without those global and local networks overlapping.[60] To get there, DAO-to-DAO relations will be essential to think through, and the matryoshka dolls model may be one of those possible relations.

For Ameen Soleimani, who gave himself the title of "summoner" of the Moloch DAO, a minimum viable decentralized autonomous organization relies on two smart contracts: a governance contract and a guild bank.[61] Inspired in part by the weak points of The DAO,[62] and by Alexander's text, Moloch DAO launched early 2019 as a collaborative fund dedicated to the development of the Ethereum ecosystem, and soon became one of the most popular models for DAOs, while other forms of templates were being worked on by entities such as Aragon, Colony, DAOstack, DAOhaus or The Commons Stack.

The funding of public goods and common goods—such as the Ethereum ecosystem, but also open-source software in general, and of course educative initiatives, clean air and water, legal systems or voting models ...—is an important constituent of the DAO ethos, in keeping with the cypherpunk spirit. In the words of the editor of *Week in Ethereum*, Evan Van Ness, Ethereum exists to "change the game of game theory," that is to say, empowering people to coordinate on a planetary scale, and this is what DAOs are specifically about.[63] Moloch DAO overcomes the free rider problem as funding can be allocated to a project if, and only if, other members agree to fund it too. It also enables any Ethereum project bearer to contribute to the improvement of the blockchain technology it needs to function properly without dedicating much funding or their own team to it.

Quadratic funding, pioneered by Gitcoin—the largest crypto platform for the collaborative funding of open-source projects and public goods, which recently evolved into a DAO—aims to compensate for the tragedy of the commons effect. The idea behind this mechanism is "to encourage cooperation across diversity rather than coordination of selfishness for the social good,"[64] according to Glen Weyl, one of the brains behind the concept.[65] In essence, quadratic funding automatically and exponentially matches a pool of subsidies to the contributions of individuals following a quadratic equation, multiplying small contributions more than the bigger ones. Here again, it is not only the economics but also the social properties of the mechanism that matter. Signaling one's interest in the system can quickly make participants sense that their voice is a strong one: "Gitcoin makes you feel you are part of something even though you are playing by yourself. [...] It bolsters the individual action by connecting it to a larger whole" explains its founder, Kevin Owocki.[66]

A few months after the launch of Moloch DAO, a small group of artists decided to adapt its code to create a grant distribution fund, this time aimed not at blockchain developers but artists. While this is not the first DAO with an artistic purpose, it is the one with the most intense activity for the moment.[67] Born in Athens,[68] in a post-recession time, with the ambition to

60 The free rider problem is an economic concept that describes a situation in which people who are not participating in the maintenance of shared resources get to use, or even overuse those anyway. This is particularly frequent with non-excludable and non-rivalrous public goods.

61 The smart contracts at the basis of Moloch DAO were activated in public during the ETHDenver conference on February 14, 2019, see https://www.youtube.com/watch?v=abTRJZcmPwI (accessed August 29, 2021).

62 As detailed in Dino Mark, Vlad Zamfir, and Emin Gün Sirer, "A Call for a Temporary Moratorium on 'The DAO,'" *Hacking Distributed*, May 27, 2016, available at https://hackingdistributed.com/2016/05/27/dao-call-for-moratorium/ (accessed August 29, 2021).

63 Evan Van Ness, "EthCC[4] A Brief Recap," *DoinGud*, July 30, 2021, available at https://www.youtube.com/watch?v=iSRZnUDWoNA (accessed August 29, 2021)

64 Glen Weyl, "RadicalxChange 2.0," RXC Berlin, November 22, 2019, see https://www.youtube.com/watch?v=5Lqn1eVUzf4 (accessed August 29, 2021).

65 See Vitalik Buterin, Zoë Hitzig, and Glen Weyl, "A Flexible Design for Funding Public Goods," *Management Science*, Vol. 65, No. 11, August 2020, 5171–85, DOI: 10.1287/mnsc.2019.3337.

propose an alternative to the bureaucratic and financial hierarchies of the art world,[69] “the Trojan DAO doesn't have employers and employees, it has active participants.”[70] These latter are currently at work on a community-owned biennale: Hackumenta.[71] The ambition for this project is to operate transparently and trustlessly at every level constituting the biennale, be it raising and governing resources, commissioning artworks, renting exhibition spaces, but also to participate in the growing peer-to-peer art market enabled by NFT technology.

For its part, CultureStake aims at connecting communities, artists, and cultural organizations through collective and playful decision-making.[72] Public art audiences have very little say in decisions about what works are funded in their city, even in their neighborhood, and yet it is they who live with them. Institutions, public authorities, and patrons always have control over these decisions, which often results in monolithic programs that give pride of place to the same blockbuster artists. CultureStake emerged from conversations within the Furtherfield community of artists, technologists, and activists, later joined by developers who are also artists and share these concerns. But the enterprise also grew out of a post-Brexit awareness of the failure of systems that look like fair democracy but are anything but. Thus, in order to truly democratize artistic commissioning by offering audiences and artists a way to make decisions together, CultureStake turned to quadratic voting, conceptualized by Weyl, among others, and from which quadratic funding derives.[73] This voting model, which provides the voter with the means to not only express several choices, but also to mark the intensity of these choices by allocating a certain number of votes to the candidates or proposals that they prefer, is more effective than the traditional “one person = one vote” that we are used to in our political democracies, because it favors the ideas supported by a large number of individuals over those supported by smaller but more powerful groups. Here, voting works with a system of credits that can be transformed into votes according to a quadratic equation: to cast one vote, one credit will be needed, but to cast two votes, four credits will be needed, and so on. Ten people voting for the same proposal will express a stronger and more economically balanced result than one person using ten votes at their disposal to support the same proposal, because the ten individuals will have used a total of ten credits, whereas the person casting ten votes on their behalf will have used one hundred credits.

In short, a quadratic vote is not a majority vote, but rather allows the coexistence of different opinions and, as a result,

66 Kevin Owocki, “Slaying Moloch | Ameen Soleimani & Kevin Owocki,” *Bankless*, episode #33, October 5, 2020, available at https://www.youtube.com/watch?v=903tHM4RA9k (accessed August 29, 2021).

67 DAK, which stands for Decentralized Autonomous Kunstverein, the first blockchain-based art center, was established in summer 2018. See https://dak.international/ (accessed August 29, 2021).

68 The Trojan DAO was born on July 23, 2019, commemorating the first hard fork in the history of the Ethereum blockchain following the ill-fated hack of The DAO, in June 2016.

69 “We imagined social sculptures, able to be participated in and exited with equal ease, in the place of the age-old systems. Structures that would more closely resemble living adaptive organisms and collaborative distributed works of art, that cannot be censored and that can operate without middlemen and beyond borders. We began to imagine creating a performance-as-institution, an experimental coordination game for the creation of an art world beyond the artificial scarcities and competitive practices that are holding creativity back.” “The Trojan DAO,” *Medium*, September 16, 2019, available at https://trojandao.medium.com/the-trojan-dao-859b866a15ee (accessed August 29, 2021).

70 See https://www.trojanfoundation.com/ (accessed August 29, 2021).

71 See https://hackumenta.webflow.io/ (accessed August 29, 2021).

72 See https://www.furtherfield.org/culturestake-2/ (accessed August 29, 2021).

73 See, for instance, Eric A. Posner and Glen Weyl, “Voting Squared: Quadratic Voting in Democratic Politics,” *Vanderbilt Law Review*, Vol. 68, No. 2, 2015, University of Chicago Coase-Sandor Institute for Law & Economics, Research Paper No. 657.

thwarts the traditional problem of the tyranny of the majority as well as plutocracy, since the participants with the most credits will not be given the strongest voice. While quadratic voting is already used in politics, other types of voting mechanisms that are also not majority votes are being conceived and implemented in the DAO arena to overcome the illusion of consensus as much as to fight voter apathy.[74] Indeed, even though taking an active role in the decision-making of an organization usually ignites the desire to join a DAO, voting in time on every single decision can be highly demanding, especially since DAOists are usually members of several or even many DAOs simultaneously. Thus, vote delegation has been chosen by Gitcoin DAO. Dandelion Voting, inspired by the Moloch DAO decision processes and made available as a ready-made app by Aragon and as a DAO template by 1Hive, allows members to easily exit the DAO before the passing of a vote if they disagree with the proposal.[75] Conviction Voting, in turn, resulting from Zargham's research and used by DAOs such as The Commons Stack and 1Hive, is based on the aggregation of preferences expressed in a continuous manner, with the strength of the conviction being expressed by its duration.[76] It offers a real-time reflection of opinions within an organization and makes governance more fluid by eliminating the restricted decision-making periods of traditional voting methods.

This research in voting systems is fundamental to advance the field, but also to increase its accessibility. Not only is it necessary to design voting, but the engineering of conflict appears to be essential in such horizontal structures, providing for pluralism and even agonism, and possibly reconciling the political with the technological meaning of decentralization.[77]

Why Wouldn't You?

"The power of a DAO doesn't stem from its token, or even the tech infrastructure it uses, its power arises from the simple fact that a group of people has gained complete autonomy on the internet."[78] If the words of the developer, founder and DAOist Mark Beylin can sound like a tale of anarchist fantasy, it is useful to remember that, as of today, more than 50,000 active DAO participants are deciding on how to deploy more than US$12 Billion to solve the world's most pressing issues. Web 3.0 is unfolding as the new *res publica*, where DAOs are forerunners in terms of the future of global organizations, public and private, putting non-profits as much as corporations back in the hands of those who make them work and work for them. Whereas the technological components of such blockchain-based organizations can be intimidating at first sight, no technical knowledge to set them up is required thanks to the DAOs that are already providing templates to do so—Aragon, Colony, DAOstack, DAO-haus, The Commons Stack or 1Hive to mention just a few. Or, to reference Catlow once more, "the complexity lies less in the difficulty of the technology than in doing any governance in any

74 The Colorado House of Representatives, the Taiwanese government, and the German branch of the European Volt Party have already experimented with quadratic voting in 2019 and 2020.

75 See https://token-engineering-commons.gitbook.io/tec-handbook/ (accessed August 29, 2021).

76 See Michael Zargham, "Sensor Networks and Social Choice," BlockScience research proposal, July 30, 2018, available at https://github.com/BlockScience/conviction/blob/master/social-sensorfusion.pdf (accessed August 29, 2021).

77 Dispute resolution protocols that provide arbitration for the type of subjective conflicts that smart contracts do not address are an integral part of some DAO mechanisms. Kleros Court (https://kleros.gitbook.io/docs/) and Celeste (https://1hive.gitbook.io/celeste/) are pioneering examples of these.

78 Mark Beylin, May 17, 2021, 8.27pm tweet, available at https://twitter.com/MarkBeylin/status/1394358892369522688 (accessed August 29, 2021).

way at all: the difficulties of organizing, coordinating, finding ways to come to common agreements, to negotiate for mutual interest and to understand that sometimes it is simply not possible." She follows on, stating that "all the really strong and interesting projects are those that understand that culture has to come before structure, then build the minimum structure to allow those cultures to thrive."[79] What Matan Field, co-founder and CEO of DAOstack, phrased as "DAOs are operative systems for collective intelligence."[80]

From a collaborative investment vehicle (The DAO), to a way of creating micro-economies (The Commons Stack, 1Hive, Trojan DAO ...), through a mode of financing work (Moloch DAO, metaCartel ...), and the automation of relations to the amplification of communities, DAOs could be seen as a certain undoing of the industrial revolution, and even of the information age, re-empowering people detached from the product of their labor, from their own data, from their communities, and from largely obsolete nation-states. Besides, as Sacha Saint-Leger underlines, "thinking of community as co-designer is perhaps the most effective way for a DAO to prosper and continue innovating over the long-term,"[81] which could lead DAOs to see the future Hakim Bey described for the temporary autonomous zones: "In the end the TAZ is almost self-explanatory. If the phrase became current it would be understood without difficulty ... understood in action."[82]

79 Catlow, "DAO, DGOV, DIWO, DECAL."

80 Matan Field, "The DAO Stack," EthCC Keynote, March 2018, available at https://www.youtube.com/watch?v=799_Ikg1yMs (accessed August 29, 2021).

81 Sacha Saint-Leger, "DAOs and the pitfalls of progressive decentralization," "Gardens," *Substack*, April 15, 2021, available at https://gardens.substack.com/ (accessed August 29, 2021).

82 Bey, *Temporary Autonomous* Zone.

Infrahauntologies:

3

On Invasive Legacies and Futures

AFFORDANCES: DEGREES OF FREEDOM WRESTED FROM PHANTOM NARRATIVES

Nancy Adajania

When we think of the origins of any institution, we tend instinctively to think that it must have a unique point of origin or distinctive *raison d'être*. But, as Jacques Derrida argues effectively, most institutions carry within them the phantom presence of seemingly defunct philosophies and the currents of ongoing debates. To that extent, they are part of an always already present field of motifs, motivations, and aspirations. In this essay, I present the Madhya Pradesh (MP) Tribal Museum in Bhopal, located in Central India, as an example of an infrastructure marked by such a Derridean "hauntology."[1] Its express purpose is not only to preserve and collect "the endangered art forms" of the states of Madhya Pradesh and neighboring Chhattisgarh (which was once a part of MP), but also to "breathe a new life into them."[2] This mandate is especially salient as tribal communities such as the Gond, Pardhan, Bhil, Baiga, Sahariya, and Korku, among others, form 21 percent of the population in MP and nearly 31 percent in Chhattisgarh. Claiming to reject the conventional museum model, the Tribal Museum has fashioned itself as a "collection of liveliness," yet remains haunted by unresolved narratives: the specters of long-running discussions and the demons of socio-economic asymmetry.[3] No amount of appeasement of ancestors and apotropaic chants can reverse this situation.

At the same time, what I have come upon in the interstices, cusps, and thresholds between these haunted and haunting histories is a series of affordances that add a further layer of complexity—as well as ambiguity—to the experience of this museum. An affordance is a capacity latent within an environment, which may be activated by any being that regards that environment, however temporarily, as its habitat. These affordances can be conceptual, visceral, spatial, infrastructural; some may lie unused and unrecognized forever, others may spring into life under the appropriate circumstances. It is these phantom histories and affordances that occupy my attention here. I shall dwell, especially, on two potential spaces that I would designate as the Room for Rebellion and the Room for Jangarh. But first, as the Lonely Planet guides used to put it, a note on getting there and getting away.

1 Jacques Derrida, *Specters of Marx: The State of the Debt, the Work of Mourning and the New International*, translated by Peggy Kamuf (New York: Routledge, 1994).

2 Ashok Mishra, curator of the Tribal Museum, quoted in Shuchita Jha, "Decoding Tribal Museum Motif," *Times of India*, February 24, 2019, available at https://timesofindia.indiatimes.com/city/bhopal/decoding-tribal-museum-motif/articleshow/68136135.cms (accessed June 13, 2021). Jha clarifies that the museum was conceived by the Jan Jati Evam Boli Vikas Academy to keep tribal art forms alive for future generations within these communities: "[The Academy] did thorough research and joined hands with the culture department to turn their dream into a reality in 2011."

3 Ashok Mishra quoted in Smita, "Marked increase in tourists' footfall at India's 1st live tribal museum," *Free Press Journal*, August 9, 2018, available at https://www.freepressjournal.in/bhopal/marked-increase-in-tourists-footfall-at-indias-1st-live-tribal-museum (accessed June 13, 2021).

Arrival

We arrived, along a curved driveway, at the entrance of the Madhya Pradesh Tribal Museum. The façade of the building, which was inaugurated in 2013, is lavishly animated by a grand tableau of images, each a painted cutout—children hiding in trees, women with winnowing pans, grazing animals, and guardian figures with tridents—the entire mural dynamized by the onrush of a long, meandering river. Created by the well-known artist Durgabai Vyam, of Pardhan origin, these cutouts inhabit their own mythopoetic time and are silhouetted by the auspicious *digna* pattern, a corded and crenelated line with which Durgabai's community members decorate the walls and floors of their village homes.[4]

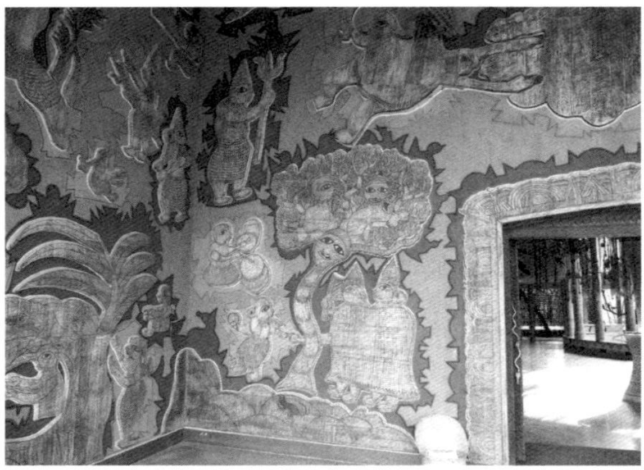

Entrance Tribal Museum Bhopal; all photos by the author

It was fascinating to see how the *digna* pattern had migrated from its original ornamental function in domestic spaces to the Tribal Museum mural. Durgabai and her husband, the artist Subhash Vyam, first experimented with this pattern in their illustrations for a graphic book on the life of the revolutionary leader Babasaheb Ambedkar, who fought against the pernicious caste system with its brutal insistence on untouchability. S. Anand, the publisher of the graphic book, was faced with the challenge of creating a coherent narrative out of the Vyamses' drawings, which happily disregarded the Western convention of using strips of boxed-in panels. After much brainstorming, Subhash came up with the idea of the *digna* pattern as a mode of generating a fluid paneling method that would visually propel the narrative forward.[5] In the Tribal Museum cutouts, the versatile *digna* pattern is used to link and loop various figures and episodes, with the pattern acting variously as separator, bridge, and aureole.

While the wall text provides the origin myth of the Narmada river—considered one of India's holiest water bodies—the credits mention "Durgabai and others" in a tiny font size, disregarding the artist's development or agency in formulating

4 Durgabai corroborated the use of the *digna* pattern in the Tribal Museum mural in a telephone conversation on May 26, 2021. I had met the artist on April 13, 2018, when I visited the Tribal Museum and she had shared with me that most of the myths that she works with were inherited from her grandmother.

5 S. Anand, "A Digna for Bhim," in *Bhimayana: Experiences of Untouchability* (New Delhi: Navayana, 2011), 102. Anand, who co-wrote the text for *Bhimayana*, observed that the Vyamses had complete artistic agency during the project: they "introduce[d] narrative elements, situations and characters not provided for in the storyboard," such that "40 percent of the text and dialogue was generated or re-edited to suit the[ir] drawings."

a language of her own. The parsimonious font size emphasizes the museum's valorization of the community over the individual artistic subjectivity, rendering the latter almost anonymous. For those who do not know of Durgabai's struggle to become an artist, the exhibition didactics turn her into a simple custodian of timeless and presumably changeless folklore.

According to the shared Gond and Pardhan mythology, Rewa Nayak and Nayakin were a nomadic couple who had settled down in a forest near the Amarkantak hill in Madhya Pradesh, the source of the Narmada. When Rewa Nayak was suffering from a terrible skin disease, the water of a stream flowing from a cluster of bamboo and banana trees in the forest healed him. When he and his wife Nayakin went to work, their daughter Johela became friends with a little girl, Narmada, who appeared and disappeared in a cluster of bamboo-banana trees. Johela unfortunately betrayed Narmada on her wedding day by stealthily marrying Narmada's groom. Furious, Narmada flowed away in the opposite direction, and not even the gods could control her as she disappeared into the Gulf of Khambat or Cambay.[6]

I am startled by the positioning of this story of betrayal—an ambiguous sign—which greets us at the entrance. Normally, one might expect that a Tribal Museum would greet viewers with a pictorial rhetoric of cosmic inclusiveness, using archetypal motifs from the web of life. On the other hand, I think how appropriate it is—given the colonial and the postcolonial state's history of visiting systematic oppression and marginalization, false promises and broken treaties on the communities designated as "tribal." Was this narrative an expression of institutional intentionality? In a conversation that I had with Durgabai,[7] I learned that she had proposed several mythic narratives; the Narmada story was chosen from among these by Harchandan Singh Bhatty, who is effectively the exhibition designer and curator of the museum.[8] It is most likely that Bhatty chose this story to emphasize the sacred aspect of the river rather than fold an indirect political critique into his *mise-en-scène*.

Naming and Power

I entered the museum, pondering on the nomenclature used in its title. The English word "tribal" encodes everything, from paternalism to exotic romanticization, to genocidal ambition. While the general understanding is that tribal communities in Indian society lie outside the pale of caste society, the reality is that they have historically been caught up in an uneven process of economic and social transition between forest-dwelling, pastoral, and caste-based agrarian ways of life. The historian Shashank Kela calls this a "dual process of assimilation and separation" of tribal communities from a caste-based agrarian order, which "eventually produced a fluctuating equilibrium marked by conflict and coexistence."[9] With the onset of colonialism, the mobility of the "tribal" communities was severely

6 The wall text notes: "In every marriage ceremony, people belonging to Gond, Baiga tribes living in this region offer their apology to the river Narmada for the betrayal done to her."

7 In conversation with the author, May 26, 2021.

8 In the credits of the film promoting the Tribal Museum, Bhatty is acknowledged as the "Creative Coordinator."

9 Shashank Kela, *A Rogue and Peasant Slave: Adivasi Resistance, 1800–2000* (New Delhi: Navayana, 2012), 45.

curtailed with the diabolical intention of eventually turning them into a reserve army of labor. The colonizers wished to extract revenue from every possible taxable source. By denying the tribal communities access to forest produce, and turning the forests into profit-spinning plantations, they alienated these communities from their habitat and forms of being, utterly subjugating and immiserating them.

If the term “tribal” is a colonial construct, its official Hindi translation, *jan-jaati*, with its associations of a clan-based group, carries a connotation of exotic primitivism, implicitly contrasting it to *jaati*, the caste system that defines mainstream Hindu society. A more legalistic term, *anusuchit jati* (Scheduled Tribes), conveys constitutional safeguards, and, theoretically, positive discrimination as a guarantee for the groups defined as such. On the other hand, the more popular term *adivasi* (“first inhabitant” in Sanskrit) could be proposed as an alternative to *jan-jaati*. This term was first used during the nationalist struggle by the Gandhian social worker A.V. Thakkar, when he was working with the tribes of Chhotanagpur in the 1930s.[10] The Gandhian approach toward the *adivasis* was paternalistic and fiduciary, but according to Bina Sengar, this attitude “would continue till the rise of genuine leadership among the tribals.”[11] This marks an insidious infantilization of the tribal communities, who have produced leaders in every century, some of whom organized the Santhal and Munda uprisings that shook the British colonial regime during the late nineteenth century.

After Independence in 1947, the term *adibasi* (the regional version of the Sanskrit term) found robust articulation in the voice of Jaipal Singh Munda (1903–1970), himself a member of the Munda tribal community from Chotanagpur, and the president of the Adibasi Mahasabha in 1938. During the deliberations of the Constituent Assembly of India in 1946, he reasoned: “Sir, if there is any group of Indian people that has been shabbily treated it is my people. They have been disgracefully treated, neglected for the last 6,000 years.”[12]

The term *adivasi* is also unstable because it does not encompass all of India’s highly heterogeneous tribal communities. In the seven states of northeastern India, for instance, ethnic groups self-identifying as tribes account for an average of 58 percent of the population, ranging between roughly 31 percent in Tripura and nearly 95 percent in Mizoram. In several of these states, these are dominant, articulate majorities that enjoy social privileges and cultural prestige. To them, the term “tribe” signifies the pride of clan heritage and lineage lore. By contrast, the term *adivasi* carries a political valence and is a tool of resistance for Central India’s tribal communities, who are at risk from infrastructure projects and other forms of state intervention that can deprive them of their hereditary occupations, displace them from their traditional lands, and alienate them from their sacred environments.

It should also be understood that, while the term *adivasi* is of strategic importance, it is not necessarily historically accurate.

10 See footnote 30 in Bina Kumari Sengar, “Gandhian Approach to Tribals,” in *Proceedings of the Indian History Congress*, Vol. 62, 2001, 634. According to Sengar, Thakkar had already begun to work with the *adivasis* in 1919–20. A severe famine had affected the regions of Mahikantha, Rewakantha, and Panchmahals of Bombay-Gujarat, dominated by a large population of Bhil *adivasis*. Gandhi sent Thakkar to these areas to alleviate their misery [629]. Available at http://www.jstor.org/stable/44155809 (accessed June 13, 2021).

11 Ibid., 633.

12 Jaipal Singh Munda quoted in Ram Guha, *India after Gandhi: The History of the World’s Largest Democracy* (Delhi: Picador India, 2007), 116.

Many tribal communities have migrated from one part of the subcontinent to another—as their foundation myths often attest—and they have also often slipped between nomadic and settled forms of life, between tribe membership and subscription to an artisanal caste-like group. The bitter truth is that 74 years after independence, the *adivasi* communities, which constitute 8.6 percent of India's population according to the 2011 census, continue to be oppressed and marginalized. Displaced from their lands by big dams, heavy industries, and mining corporations, exiled from the forests by colonial-era forest acts, forced by Hindutva militants to "return" to the Hindu fold—a specious claim of original identity indeed—and caught between Maoist insurgents on the one hand and the Indian State on the other, they have fought back and attempted to resist all forms or authority and exploitation.

Durgabai's mural for the Madhya Pradesh Tribal Museum reveals several forms of betrayal folded into it. The Narmada story reminds us of the people's mass movement in the 1980s, the Narmada Bachao Andolan, in which *adivasis* facing displacement due to the construction of a large-scale dam across the Narmada river and its tributaries in Madhya Pradesh, Gujarat, and Maharashtra, vehemently opposed the project and demanded information and compensation from the government. Even if this welcome mural was never meant to be a provocation, I recognize, in a flash, that it is the first of many affordances that we encounter in this museum.

Phantom Histories

While the Tribal Museum seems to exert its exclusivity as a living museum, it is haunted by another cultural institution of iconic importance, which has had its moments of incandescence in Bhopal: Bharat Bhavan, a multidisciplinary arts center founded in 1982, designed by the legendary architect Charles Correa. At Bharat Bhavan—which stands not far from the Tribal Museum in Bhopal's elite Shyamla Hills district—its visionary director, the artist and cultural activist J. Swaminathan, founded the Roopankar museum. In an unprecedented move, Roopankar showed works by academy-trained metropolitan artists and works by so-called folk and tribal artists in adjacent galleries. By doing so, he pioneered, according to the cultural administrator and poet Ashok Vajpeyi, who was responsible for the establishment of Bharat Bhavan, "a new institutional statement of what is contemporary in Indian art." Bharat Bhavan was intended as a platform, Vajpeyi recalled, where "you could see each art form in the neighborhood of other art forms."[13]

This was a radical redefinition of the contemporary at a time when a strict hierarchy was observed in India between art and craft, urban and rural, Anglophone and vernacular. Vajpeyi explains how the pecking order functioned: "The 'modern' in the National Gallery of Modern Art, Delhi, was perceived exclusively as urban and therefore contemporary; and the works

13 In conversation with the author, October 2015. Bharat Bhavan has instituted the following cultural wings: Roopankar Museum for the visual arts, Rangmandal for theater, Vagarth for poetry, Anhad for music, and Chhavi, the recently opened center for cinema. Its programming is multidisciplinary and multi-lingual, doing away with the hierarchy between classical and folk music and dance, modernist and "folk" art, Anglophone and regional languages. Vajpeyi, who set up the libraries for poetry and music at Bharat Bhavan, recalls: "The theater repertories staged plays in different dialects of Hindi—Samuel Beckett in Chattisgarhi, Brecht in Bundelkhandi. The world poetry festival hosted the Czech poet Miroslav Holub, the British poet Stephen Spender, the Argentinian poet Roberto Juarroz and the Nicaraguan poet Ernesto Cardenal, among others. Peter Brook held a ten-day inaugural workshop in 1982, which was attended by Shambhu Mitra and Habib Tanvir. Bharat Bhavan also established the International Print Biennale in 1989."

of the folk and tribal artists at the Crafts Museum, Delhi, were seen as craft and therefore rural and traditional."[14] Despite this radical departure, something that has disturbed me for a long time is that the works of these two sets of artists were shown in adjacent galleries at Bharat Bhavan, and thus still separate, rather than literally positioned side by side. In my conversation with Vajpeyi, I learned that a heated debate had taken place between Swaminathan and his artist friends regarding the art-historical genealogies and material practices of these art forms of uneven privilege. Eventually, they arrived at the compromise that "both forms should be given a place of equality, but putting them side by side would complicate people's understanding and appreciation of them."[15]

Perhaps they missed an opportunity in doing precisely that—of complicating the distances and adjacencies between the respective art forms. I asked Vajpeyi if, given the chance to restage Bharat Bhavan's inaugural exhibition today, they would do things differently? "Yes," he affirmed, "because there is a greater understanding of this issue today," reiterating that "a pluralistic approach is paramount."[16] It was this pluralistic approach at Bharat Bhavan that nourished the remarkably gifted painter Jangarh Singh Shyam (1962–2001).

A Room for Jangarh?

Once upon a time, a boy was born in a Pardhan family in a village in Patangarh, on a day when government officials had come to conduct a census of his community. The story goes that the officials named him Jangann, deriving this neologism from the Sanskrit *jana-gannana*, the "enumeration of the people." The boy's family recorded it, in their local inflection, as Jangarh. This would not be the only way in which his name and destiny would be linked to those of his people. Growing up, he would travel from Patangarh to Bhopal at the invitation of J. Swaminathan to join him at Bharat Bhavan.[17] Unlike the practitioners of Warli or Mithila art, Jangarh could not call into play existing community traditions of ritual painting that could be used as convenient points of departure. The Pardhan community, to which he belonged, were not traditionally painters—although Jangarh did make clay reliefs on walls—but the hereditary minstrels and balladeers of the Gonds. Through his magnificently expressive oeuvre, Jangarh created a new iconography based on the creatures and gods that haunt Pardhan folklore and myths, as well as his childhood memories of the Narmada river, animals, birds, and trees. His artistic development was also enriched by the ongoing exhibitions of contemporary art, music performances, and multilingual theater repertories and poetry festivals that he could savor at Bharat Bhavan. As Shampa Shah writes, hailing as he did from a community of balladeers, Jangarh took naturally to "listen[ing] to Pandwani and other folk singing traditions with narratives from *Mahabharata*, *Bhartrihari Shatak*, ballads

14 In conversation with the author, October 2015.

15 Ibid.

16 Ibid.

17 See Jyotindra Jain, *Jangarh Singh Shyam, A Conjuror's Archive* (Bangalore and Ahmedabad: MAP & Mapin, 2018), 8.

of local heroes, and [he] also saw plays by stalwarts like B.V. Karanth, Habib Tanvir and others, whose rehearsals he would often attend."[18]

In the process, Jangarh pioneered a new idiom of painting. As his projects expanded in scale, he brought together, trained, and mentored a number of his fellow Pardhans, including relatives like Durgabai and Subhash Vyam—Jangarh's wife Nankusia is Subhash Vyam's sister. The style with which they are associated has been mistakenly called Gond art.[19] However, it would also be an error to try and correct this by renaming it Pardhan art. The claim that this style goes back to time immemorial is, in Terence Ranger's phrase, an "invented tradition."[20] Its only real origin lies in Jangarh's experiments, for which reason the poet Udayan Vajpeyi correctly calls it the *Jangarh kalam*, the Jangarh style. Durgabai Vyam has expanded the *Jangarh kalam* by investing it with her own subjectivity, as have a number of other acolytes and apprentices from Jangarh's circle.

Jangarh, whose name and circumstances may have limited his fate to becoming a government statistic, went on to show in major national and international exhibitions, including the famous but controversial "Magiciens de la Terre" in Paris (1989).[21] But not all the affordances of Bharat Bhavan could save him. The pressure of market forces, his vulnerable position as an *adivasi* artist despite having achieved renown, and his inability to say "No," eventually led him to take his own life. He committed suicide at the age of forty in Japan's Mithila Museum in 2001. What was ostensibly called an artist residency was, as his wife and artist Nankusiya says, "a place where they made him work like a laborer—*mazdoori karvate the*. They did not look after him as hosts would or should have done. They forced him to make, within a few weeks, works that would have taken a few months to complete."[22]

I would strongly propose a Room for Jangarh, who inspired many of the artists showing their work at the Tribal Museum. The gesture would honor his brilliance and act as a cautionary tale to the unscrupulous dealers and ill-informed gallerists. This would also be a dynamic memorial —not a static monument— to an artist whose practice outpaced the canons, conventions and economic asymmetries of his time, but was ultimately overwhelmed by them. Jangarh's journey toward full autonomy and agency was thwarted because there was no institution that could insulate him from the twin dangers of exoticism and exploitation. Paternalism rather than agency continues to be the norm informing the attitude of the state and the art market toward *adivasi* artists. In this context, what further role can the Tribal Museum play? It provides them with a hospitable environment; it gives them a livelihood and a production system. But could it not play a role in advocacy and discourse formation, to ensure that *adivasi* artists are not either treated as purveyors of the exotic or relegated to a vulnerable position in the art economy? There is a profound need for institutional self-criticism and reconfiguration.

18 Shampa Shah, "Jangarh Singh Shyam: The Gond Art Pioneer who created his own idiom, but left the world too soon," April 19, 2021, available at https://abirpothi.com/jangarh-singh-shyam-a-dream-sojourn/ (accessed June 13, 2021).

19 Jyotindra Jain has argued that what is erroneously called Gond art is actually practiced by artists of Pardhan origin. The Pardhans are the bards of the Gond community, and they share religious practices and myths with the Gonds. However, the Gonds see the Pardhans as belonging to a lower social order. The epithet Gond art is a creation of observers and market players who depend on the better-recognized Gond community appellation as a brand, so to speak, to sell Pardhan art. See Jain, *Jangarh Singh Shyam*, 13–15.

20 Eric Hobsbawm and Terence Ranger, *The Invention of Tradition* (Cambridge: Cambridge University Press, 1983).

21 See Lucy Steed et al., *Making Art Global (Part 2): Magiciens de la Terre 1989* (London: Afterall, 2013).

22 In conversation with the author at Nankusiya's home in Professors' Colony, Bharat Bhavan, Bhopal, April 16, 2018.

The Unrelenting Forest

The supremely cluttered foyer of the Tribal Museum gives us a foretaste of the chaos that continues to grow as we pass from one of the institution's six galleries to the next, traversing Cultural Diversity, Tribal Life, Tribal Aesthetic, Tribal Spiritual World, Chhattisgarh Gallery, and arriving at the Raku Gallery, dedicated to *adivasi* children's games. Gigantism and proliferation seem to be the key drivers of the museum's exhibition scenography: a mammoth Gond granary that feels like an unintended ironic gloss on *adivasi* hunger; Bhil votive offerings piled high and multiplying rapidly through the gallery like the ghosts of unfulfilled wishes; a fertility bangle traditionally made by the Bhareva, Jhara, and Ghadwa communities of MP and Chhattisgarh, magnified here to look like a Ferris wheel. Not content with destroying the power of sympathetic magic associated with the bangle, a quasi-naturalistic rural scape has also been imposed upon it. Why should a bangle held in a bride's palm while sowing seeds be turned into a piece of fairground entertainment? The curatorial intention behind the magnification of this bangle symbolising "various aspects of the cycle of life" is explained as follows: "It has been created in a sculpturally magnified form, using iron and bronze, by the region's Bhareva sculptors—Baldev Waghmare, Dashrath Waghmare and others—so that the beauty of its shape and the glory of its conception may be better recognized."[23]

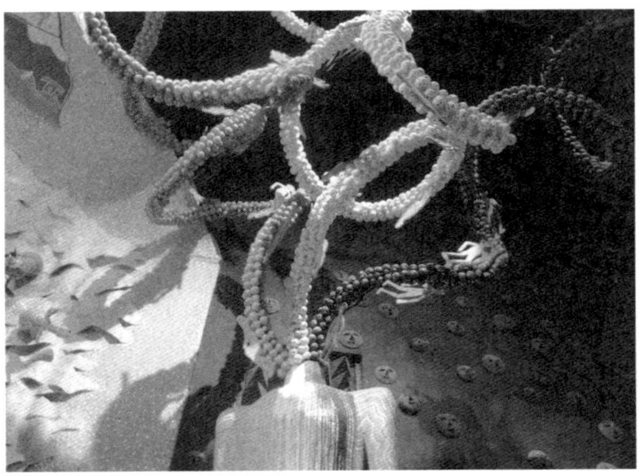

Detail of the installation based on a Bhil myth; the community's ancestors come down to earth to bless people and cattle. Artists: Bhuribai, Anil, Savita, Shanta Bhooriya, Ramesh and Geeta Bariya

By turning a ritual object into a hypertrophic art installation, the museum has reduced it to a kitsch fetish. If indeed it was felt that this object should be made relevant for contemporary times, the *adivasi* artists could have been consulted to reinterpret this object in the age of endangered agricultural practices, climate change, and vampiric capitalism. On the other hand, the installation based on the Bhil myth about the community's ancestors coming down to earth to bless people and cattle is relatively more successful. Tiny ancestral figures travel along fierce

23 Quoted from the online Hindi brochure, available at https://mptribalmuseum.com/brochure.pdf (accessed June 13, 2021). Translation by the author.

bloodstreams gushing out of a gigantic headless sculpture. Based on the artist Bhuribai's painting of the same subject—an imaginative rendering of the myth—this three-dimensional manifestation has a powerful performative dimension. What destroys it are the lurid lights, which imbue the installations in this museum with an unfortunate air of theatricality.

Subject Positions

What is the real subject of the Tribal Museum? What is being museumized here? Is the museum trying to offer a simulacrum of the lived environment or lifeworld of the *adivasi* communities? This is a heroic but doomed project—the forces of modernization and urbanization have destroyed that world while their culture has been embalmed in museums. In its mission statement, "The idea resonates within," which is full of contradictions and windy abstractions, the Tribal Museum presents itself as the "bridge of dialogue between these two streams of life (tribal and modern philosophy of life)." While wishing to initiate such a dialogue, the museum remains trapped in essentialist dogmas: "modern urban life is based on scientific views and tribal life on mythical [*sic*] views."[24] This is a static, ahistorical view. The *adivasi* consciousness can hardly be untouched by the forces of modern life and is not lacking in a scientific understanding of its ecosystem. At the same time, "modern" sensibilities are often marked by unscientific prejudice, superstition, demagoguery, and are also sustained by their own mythology of aspiration and success.

In a desperate attempt to produce a living museum, the exhibition scenography has tried to tweak traditional museum approaches to retrofit its purpose. Consider the following museal and archaeological hauntologies: the *son et lumière* shows at Indian archaeological monuments, which were designed for outdoor evenings, have been adapted to all-day interiors, making for a garish effect. The diorama model has been amplified massively, such that the viewer is made to feel that they themselves are figures in a gigantic diorama. What was meant to generate an immersive effect—with the aim of lessening the distance between the city dweller and the *adivasi* lifeworld—comes across as an oppressive experience, in which the viewer is overwhelmed with material excess. Organic and inorganic elements—straw, plywood, clay, bamboo, iron, dried branches, leaves—compete for space and attention.

The full-scale models of houses belonging to the Gond, Baiga, Sahariya, Korku, and Bhil *adivasi* communities, clustered together and bathed in red and blue lights, add to the sense of clutter. Clearly the curators have not learned the lesson of "less is more" from the *adivasi* building techniques and spare domestic interiors that they display with such elan. The sheer overproduction and waste of material and artistic labor is staggering. In the name of creating a "collection of liveliness" against a sanitized white cube, something new is being produced all the

24 See "The idea resonates within" on the Tribal Museum website, "About the Museum," available at https://mptribalmuseum.com/english/about-us.html (accessed June 13, 2021).

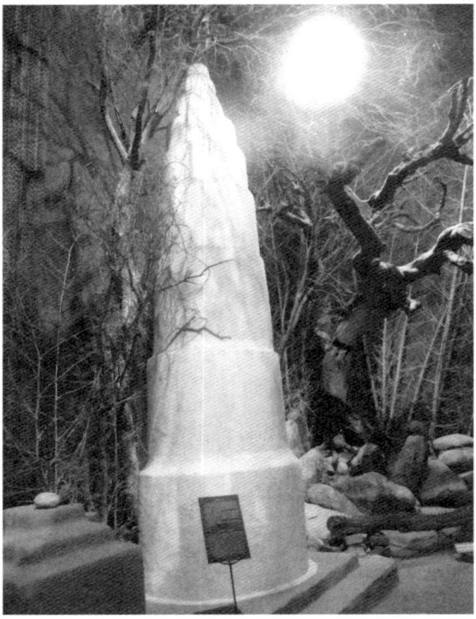

The Pagal Dev Khambh, found in Gond villages, is supposed to cure mental illness. In the Tribal Museum, it is exhibited in lurid blue light and framed by an artificial moon

time. Artists are engaged in stone carving or making furniture for the canteen. We could speculate that, in trying to recreate the magic of *adivasi* animism—in which nothing is inanimate, and everything is alive and has a soul—the museum was allowed to run wild, like an overgrown forest. As if, at some subliminal level, the *adivasi* Other was being imprisoned in a dark and mysterious primitivist fantasy. We walk through this haphazard simulacrum of a forest illuminated by an artificial sun and moon, our sadness increasing with each step.

Art versus Ethnography

Harchandan Singh Bhatty, who is responsible for the exhibition design at the Tribal Museum— and also currently in charge of the Roopankar Museum at Bharat Bhavan—was mentored by J. Swaminathan. In the early 1980s, Swaminathan had assembled teams of young artist-researchers to assist him in building up a collection of *adivasi* art for Bharat Bhavan. He devised an orientation course for them, comprising lectures on anthropology, sociology, and folk art. This course enabled Bhatty and his fellow artist-researchers to develop an eye for collecting art and objects of everyday life for the museum collection, and for identifying unrecognized talent in the villages of Madhya Pradesh.

In asserting the right of artists of so-called tribal background to be seen as individual contemporary artists, Swaminathan sometimes argued that their creativity should be viewed as exuberantly autonomous of an ethnographic account of their lives and circumstances.[25] Of course, he remained fully cognizant of their socio-economic struggles; indeed, his championing of their right to imaginative self-fulfillment was an expression of a pro-*adivasi* politics, as many of his essays attest. “It would indeed ... be convenient, if one were to undertake a study of tribal art, to locate it in communities as closed systems. Such, however, is not the case,” he wrote in the essay “Submerged Archipelago.” “In dealing with tribal art we are dealing with the art of people very much with us and of us, forming a sizeable part of our population, living under the same skies and on the same earth, *though historical time seems to lie like an insurmountable barrier between us*.”[26] A complex thinker, Swaminathan was not the uncritical primitivist he is sometimes made out to be, but more a romantic realist.

However, taking issue with the theoretical consequences of Swaminathan’s strategic move to “sever” tribal art from ethnography at Roopankar Museum in order to establish for it a parity with the art of modernism, the art historian Jyotindra Jain has

25 See J. Swaminathan, “Submerged Archipalego,” *Lalit Kala Contemporary*. No. 40, special issue on J. Swaminathan, edited by Amit Mukhopadhyay, Lalit Kala Akademi, March 1995, 59. He writes: “Ours is not a socio-economic or anthropological study of adivasi communities. Our is an attempt to open our eyes to their art.”

26 Ibid., 57.

written that Swaminathan's project of "emphatic disassociation of the 'art' [aspect] of the tribal works from the 'ethnographic', while prioritising the former" was a "modernist/formalist one."[27] Jain—a former director of the Crafts Museum in Delhi—is right to critique Swaminathan's emphasis on the formalist aspect of tribal art. This strategic move, made in response to the deep-seated social and aesthetic prejudices that tend to fix folk and tribal art as "craft," has not eventually helped to advance the cause of *adivasi* art, which, in comparison with Indian modernism, has its own distinct historical trajectory—one marked by ruptures and experiments rather than by an illusory traditional continuity.

At the Tribal Museum—at a time when there are a number of *adivasi* artists in MP who have received a measure of success in the post-Bharat Bhavan experiment—Bhatty has gone to the other extreme in reversing his mentor's strategy. Ethnographic context dominates the wall texts, while the *adivasi* artists' formal and political choices are not given any consideration. The tribal gallery at the Roopankar Museum in Bharat Bhavan—more of a multipurpose hall than a white cube—has been substituted with the chaotic galleries at the Tribal Museum.

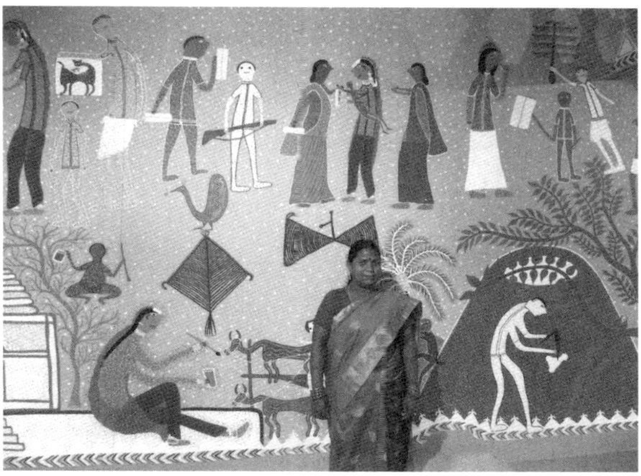

Bhuribai in front of her mural

Bhuribai's seventy-foot autobiographical mural, painted along the long enfilade on the ground level, has escaped the museum's strongly ethnographic bias and composed itself across the museum wall: a long sentence punctuated by a series of intensities, with no full stop in sight. Bhuribai is one of the first women painters from the Bhil community. In the early 1980s, her husband brought her to Bhopal to work as a laborer on the Bharat Bhavan complex, which was then under construction. While she appears in the mural carrying a headload at the construction site, a figure resembling the architect Charles Correa is shown, holding a pair of dividers, in one of the building's domed structures. It is not unusual to see underpaid and overworked woman headloaders on Indian construction sites. What is unprecedented, though, is the miraculous transformation of a laborer into an award-winning artist.

27 See Jain, *Jangarh Singh Shyam*, 16.

Nearly four decades after the event, Bhuribai rehearses the arguments she had with J. Swaminathan on the fateful morning that changed her life. Despite his encouragement, she refused to paint, because she had to earn her livelihood. "Swami-ji asked me how much are you paid for your *mazdoori*, labor. I said six rupees. He said he would pay me ten. I was stubborn. I said no, I only want six, but I will paint." And so Bhuribai began to "play with colors and forms like a child," making organic "village colors"—green from *sagwan*, teak leaves, black from the burn marks on her earthen cooking pot, and red from *sindhoor*. "Nobody told me what to do, I went by my own instinct."[28]

Hybrid Institutions, Necessary Protocols

In the run up to the inauguration of the museum in 2013, 1,500 artists from MP and Chhattisgarh came in batches to work for two years on its "artistic interiors." Bhatty expresses his delight that "[w]hen we asked tribals to help [*sic*] for the construction of the museum, we realized that even masons and home-makers had an artistic inclination ... [and could make] intricate designs on walls and wood."[29] He reasoned that "unlike the plain walls of the city houses and museums that are decorated by an interior decorator ... [he could] let the tribal artists decorate the museum."[30] The museum's curator, Ashok Mishra, emphasizes the role of the artist-decorator in the making of the museum: "Visitors who come here often speak to the artists and hire them to decorate their offices and homes. [Bollywood] actors like Rani Mukherjee and Jackie Shroff who visited the museum were so impressed by it, that they asked the artists to do the interiors for their homes in Mumbai."[31] This instrumentalization of *adivasi* talent and skills, and the channeling of these artists into the function of interior decoration, tends to reinforce the prevailing misunderstanding that such artists—who have individuated themselves through exemplary struggles—are no more than interchangeable bearers of inherited myths and crafts. It also paves the way for a deliberate and disturbing blurring of the boundaries between artwork, installation, and *mise-en-scène*. By rendering these three exhibitionary categories unstable and therefore confused, the curator/exhibition designer is able to exert disproportionate power over what is shown and how it is shown.

From its inception, the museum has propagated, so to speak, a counter-intuitive Magrittean mantra—"This is not a museum"—to emphasize its continuous growth, presenting itself as a hybrid space: a museum that is also a hectic production system. But hybridity has its consequences, and such a stance cannot simply wish away the questions one could legitimately ask. Where does the museum shade into the *karkhana*, a word used both for the painterly ateliers of the Mughal Empire and a humble workshop or factory? Where does the curatorial mandate end and artistic desire begin? Although the institutional rhetoric suggests that the artists are equal partners in the making of the museum, it is the scenography that dominates and

28 Bhuribai quoted in Nancy Adajania, "Village," *Aroop*, Vol. 3, No. 1, January–June 2018, special issue on "Totems and Taboos: What can and cannot be done," edited by Nancy Adajania.

29 This information is mentioned in the credits of the museum's promotional film.

30 Bhatty quoted in Jha, "Decoding Tribal Museum Motif."

31 Ashok Mishra quoted in Jha, "Decoding Tribal Museum Motif."

32 Shilpa Baburaj, "Architect picks holes in Tribal Museum fire-fighting system," *Times of India*, July 30, 2013, available at http://timesofindia.indiatimes.com/articleshow/20890280.cms?utm_source=contentofinterest&utm_medium=text&utm_campaign=cppst (accessed June 13, 2021). The department of culture director Mr. Tiwari rubbished the charges and said that the museum had forty firefighting systems. But Kamath's point was that although "the infrastructure has a fire suppression tank ... there are no pumps and hydrants that run around the building, hence mak[ing] it almost non-existing."

controls the exhibition narrative. The individual artworks—and with them, artistic agency—are subsumed into the overpowering installations that proliferate in a fashion that embraces disorder as an organizing principle.

This blurring of exhibitionary categories creates a series of problems in terms of accession, documentation, and conservation protocols. With the distinction between object and scenography eliminated, how are these installations to be classified in the accession register? In a situation of ceaseless production, where is the line between the changing display, the permanent collection, and the reserve collection? Are the wall murals ephemeral or permanent? If they are ephemeral, can they be re-plastered and re-made annually? What, then, of the authorial signature of the individual artist—who is not interchangeable with other artists? And how will the museum cope with the on-site installations, which—given their heterogeneous materials and improvised techniques—will inevitably pose conservation challenges?

Clearly some of these anxieties had manifested themselves to the architect of the Tribal Museum, the late Revathi Kamath (1955–2020). Shocked by the congested interiors, in which some of the smoke detectors were covered by the display, and apprehensive about the fire suppression system, Kamath had written early on to warn the authorities about the building's vulnerability to a major fire hazard.[32] Kamath's museum design could be read as a series of clusters built around a sequence of three voids that are open to the sky in varying degrees: a funnel-like void for the auditorium, an atrium with a water body at the center, and an amphitheater. The museum, laid out across a sequence of galleries and courtyards, exudes transparency and fluidity. As Madhavi Desai observes, "[t]he galleries are raised above the ground on columns forming a continuous multi-levelled verandah."[33] The buoyancy of the steel trusses and the discreet ornamentation of the castellated girders punctuate, even as they carry forward the continuous spatial flow. The vast double-height gallery spaces reveal Kamath's desire to make the exhibition spaces participatory by enabling "the tribal communities ... to represent themselves and express their own ideas and way of life."[34]

Much of the museum rhetoric regarding a "living heritage" or "living traditions" is presented through a series of affordances embedded in Kamath's built fabric *itself*. These affordances can be activated by artists, curators, and viewers. Among these are spaces of sociality in which artists can gather and converse; occasions of amusement where audiences more used to popular entertainment of the Disneyland variety are not alienated by classical museum displays; double-height galleries that could be turned into multi-level spaces equipped with viewing platforms and observatory perspectives by curators to generate unexpected sightlines and forms of scenography, thresholds of intimacy among which young people can paradoxically craft privacy in public space.[35]

33 See Madhavi Desai, *Women Architects and Modernism in India: Narratives and Contemporary Practices* (Oxford: Routledge, 2017).

34 Ibid.

35 See Ina Ross, "The museum as a dating venue: Couples in the Madhya Pradesh Tribal Museum in Bhopal, India," *Museum and Society*, Vol 16, March 2018, available at https://www.researchgate.net/publication/321357560_The_museum_as_a_dating_venue_Couples_in_the_Madhya_Pradesh_Tribal_Museum_in_Bhopal_India (accessed June 13, 2021). Ross conducted a study at the Tribal Museum to see how dating couples appropriated the museum space and made it their own. She found that it "offered the couples a space of well-ordered freedom within which 'liberation' and 'disciplining' paradoxically go hand in hand." The dating couples could enjoy their freedom as long as they did not transgress the bounds of social propriety.

A Room for Rebellion

While we wrestle with the ethnography-over-art narrative of the Tribal Museum or the phantom narrative of art-over-ethnography as institutionalized by Bharat Bhavan, the story that has gone missing from the representation of *adivasi* art is the ethnography of rebellion. By which I mean the forms of political resistance that *adivasi* communities have developed to combat the colonial and postcolonial state. This is over and against the customary ethnographic study of their social customs, religious rites, or cosmogonic views, which are all abundantly attested to at the Tribal Museum.

Even before the Gandhian reformers descended on the *adivasi* communities in the early 1900s to "civilize" them, they were perfectly capable of producing their own leaders and leading their own uprisings against colonial administrators, local landowners, and the moneylenders who brutally exploited them. I would cite here the Santhal rebellion of 1855–56 led by the Murmu brothers—Sidhu, Kanhu, Chand, and Bhairav—which, importantly, took place before the First Indian War of Independence in 1857, and the Munda rebellion led by the legendary freedom-fighter and leader of a millenarian movement, Birsa Munda, in the late nineteenth century in Jharkhand. And in the post-Independence period, *adivasi* women have played an active role in fighting the repression of the Indian State, whether during the Narmada Bachao Andolan in the 1980s, or during the spirited agitation of the Dongria Kondh in Orissa, which succeeded in ousting the mining giant Vedanta from their sacred Niyamgiri Hills in 2013. In Chhattisgarh, *adivasi* women have survived sexual violence and other brutal human-rights violations because of the intense militarization of the region by the state in a bid to counter Maoist insurgency.

Is there room for rebellion at the Tribal Museum? Would Shantibai's sculpture, paying homage to the trauma of a woman raped by the police in Chhattisgarh, find a place here? During her research into this outrage, Shantibai, who lives in the Dialogue Centre in Chhattisgarh's Kondagaon village, which she has built with her fellow *adivasi* artists and Bombay-based artist Navjot Altaf, found out that "the police laughed at the woman and her parents and told them to go home, else they will rape her again." This columnar wood sculpture's synoptic narrative has many interlocking episodes, but it is the details that are striking. Shantibai has depicted the raped woman's tears as furrows in her cheeks, which could well be considered in the great artistic tradition of the *lachrymae*, or holy tears.[36]

While avoiding the art/ethnography binaries of Swaminathan and Bhatty, I would like to clarify that my proposal for a Room for Rebellion in the Tribal Museum should not be misconstrued as another simplistic dichotomy, one where *adivasi* art is seen to be radicalized only when it comments on political urgencies. As I have shown, *adivasi* art has never

36 See Nancy Adajania, "In the sculptures of these two artists, you can see the burning tragedy of Bastar," *Scroll.in*, December 12, 2016, available at https://scroll.in/magazine/823703/authoring-post-epic-narratives-shantibai-and-rajkumar-address-the-world (accessed June 13, 2021).

been stagnant. It has always responded in its own way to unfolding cultural and political changes. Nor is *adivasi* art that deals with origin myths or cosmogonies a-political. On the contrary, the animistic beliefs of the *adivasis* function, in effect, as a system of checks and balances against the ruination of the Earth unleashed by the forces of the Capitalocene. Compared to their urban fellow denizens of the planet, the *adivasis* are better equipped to grasp the dangers of the Capitalocene era through their myths and folklore, which emphasize the ethics of interspecies coexistence, but also from having historically faced displacement and dispossession. The Room for Rebellion would gesture toward making space for debate and dissensus. It is a modest proposal for a change in curatorial strategy, one which could accommodate and annotate the historical and political agency of the *adivasi* people and their artists without pandering to the facetious dichotomy of ethnography and art.

Affordances

In the print media and in my conversation with some of the artists, their instinctive grasp of the affordances offered by the museum is very palpable. By inhabiting a museum solely devoted to tribal art, they have the freedom to walk in and out of the space without the burden of comparison with other kinds of artists. Within this zone, they are emancipated from the deficits they have to negotiate perennially elsewhere, regardless of how successful they have become. Their work will not be unconditionally legitimized by the art world—like in the case of Anglophone, metropolitan artists—but they do not need such validation in a space that ostensibly belongs to them, and which they have made their own in actuality. When we see the artists sitting in the canteen or standing in front of their works and conversing with curious viewers, we know they have a strong sense of ownership of the museum. The Baiga artist Ladlibai proudly declares: "This is not a *sangrahalay* [museum], but our *ghar* [home]. Things are changing in villages. But here, our children and grandchildren will know what our culture, past and present, means."[37]

One way to look at the Tribal Museum is indeed to see it as the artists' home, a place they have "decorated" with their own hands. But we also know that it is a home whose contents are framed by someone else, whose identity is always already determined—consider the persistent vocabulary of tribal, *jan-jaati*, primitive, innocent, spontaneous—and whose inhabitants are aware that the curator-patron giveth and the curator-patron taketh away. That, while he will create messy interiors to unmake the museum's white cube dogma, he expects you to behave yourself and draw within the boundaries of the designated grid. The artists seem to be adept at playing along—they are able to instinctively tell the difference between an opportunity and an affordance. The former is an official

37 Ladlibai quoted in Gowri Ramnarayan, "The Art of the Adivasi," *The Hindu*, July 13, 2013, available at https://www.thehindu.com/features/magazine/the-art-of-the-adivasi/article4912171.ece (accessed June 13, 2021).

guarantee against precarity, the latter a site of genuine, even if temporary freedom. When the idea of instituting the Tribal Museum was in its initial stages, Bhuribai asked a pertinent question: "Shouldn't a tribal museum be made by the tribals themselves?"[38] Her words ricochet against the museum walls, under an artificial sun.

38 Bhuribai quoted in Ramnarayan, "The Art of the Adivasi."

ABSTRACTION, ABJECTION, AFFECTIVITY: ONTOLOGICAL HORIZONS OF CONTEMPORARY ART

Václav Janoščík

This text is about the economy of ontologies. While there has been a lot of discussion on how the economy as a system, particularly with capitalism and neoliberalism, involves certain metaphysics, there has been little focus on how ontology itself has its own economies. I take the position that we live in a time of demand for new notions of ontology. Environmental doom, a rising disbelief in science, and social discord around inequality but also at identitarian and epistemological levels, all involve problems that the current ontological horizon is unable to resolve. The demand for a renewed ontological concern feeds diverse conspiracy theories, or populist and ultra-conservative sentiments, since the assumption is that they offer simple answers for our hyper-complex problems. I argue that not only philosophy, but also art practices may be able to intervene in this economy of ontologies, without providing direct answers or streamlined ontological systems, but rather offering strategies and forms of coexistence. I also claim that this renewed interest and understanding of ontology is far more appropriate for our current state of affairs.

Speculation, Infrastructures, and Affect Theory

After almost two centuries of corrosion and discredit, we can observe a renewed interest in ontologies in twenty-first-century philosophy. Speculative Realism, with its various strands—ranging from Object-Oriented Ontology and Neo-Rationalism to Speculative Poetics—presents maybe the most ambitious current in contemporary philosophy and the most direct attack on post-Kantian critical (anti-)metaphysics. Yet, despite its main aim—to establish a new post-anthropocentric metaphysics—if falls into diverse folds and niches, or to put it in Jaques Derrida's term, events.[1] Many things have occurred since the founding conference "Speculative Realism" (2007), which gave its name to the new ontological movement, and the publication of Ray Brassier's *Nihil Unbound: Enlightenment and Extinction* (2007), which is still unparalleled in terms of bringing into relief the various strands and perspectives of speculative thinking.[2]

1 Jacques Derrida, "Structure, Sign and Play in the Discourse of the Human Sciences," in *Structuralist Controversy: The Languagese and Criticism and the Sciences of Man*, edited by Richard Macksey and Eugenio Donato (Baltimore: Johns Hopkins University Press, 1970), 247.

2 Ray Brassier, *Nihil Unbound: Enlightenment and Extinction* (London: Palgrave Macmillan, 2007).

We have the devastating critique of Speculative Realism by Pete Wolfendale,[3] attempts to bridge speculative traditions with poststructuralist legacies that are usually extrapolated from it,[4] and spectacular success of speculative thinking in the arts.[5] It may be precisely through its encounter with art that speculative thinking has had a decisive role in not only popularizing speculation, but in loosening its link with academic ontologies, represented mainly by Graham Harman, Quentin Meillassoux, Levi Bryant, and Ian Hamilton Grant. Surely, speculation can be seen as a trend in both art and philosophy, a hashtag used without proper conceptualization, nonetheless it is precisely through its mainstreaming that we can learn more about it, and also how speculative tendencies are already operative in wider society.

Infrastructural, network-oriented or platform thinking can be seen as an even more loosened strand somewhere on the edges of speculative philosophy. In this respect we have some already classical and ongoing approaches, such as Bruno Latour's, who achieved massive popularity with his Actor-Network-Theory (and critique of modernity or laboratory life), or Manuel Castells and his academic blockbuster, the concept of the "network society."[6] More recently, two books have gained immense traction—*Extrastatecraft: The Power of Infrastructure Space* (2014) by Keller Easterling,[7] and Benjamin Bratton's *The Stack: On Software and Sovereignty* (2016)[8]—to which we can also add the concepts of "cosmotechnics" and "cosmopolitics," developed mainly by Yuk Hui.[9] The stark absence of political critique in these sources is somehow counterbalanced by the discourse around acceleration, which ties the critique of capitalism to technological or infrastructural perspectives, with speculative tendencies.[10] Infrastructural thinking can thus be seen as a very broad range of critical approaches, both academic and political, toward the usage of networks and/or AI. What ties these diverse perspectives together is their challenge to the general view on these phenomena in at least two respects. Firstly, in terms of an underestimation of the public, assuming its lack of knowledge or emphasizing its technological conditioning and its political relevance; secondly in respect to tech industry "thinking," with its enduring techno-optimism and the complete corporate hold over new media and technologies. Perhaps, this is the basic encapsulation of platform thinking: it is fueled by efforts to understand and redirect current technological and media vectors.[11]

3 Peter Wolfendale, *Object-Oriented Philosophy: The Noumenon's New Clothes* (Falmouth: Urbanomic, 2014).

4 Armen Avanessian and Suhail Malik (eds.) *Genealogies of Speculation: Materialism and Subjectivity since Structuralism* (London: Bloomsbury, 2016).

5 Suhail Malik, Christoph Cox, Jenny Jaskey (eds.) *Realism Materialism Art* (Berlin: Sternberg Press, 2015). In art itself, the speculative trend has materialized in a trilogy of exhibitions curated by Susanne Pfeffer, including "Speculations on Anonymous Materials" (2014), "Nature After Nature" (2014), and "Inhuman" (2015). See Susanne Pfeffer (ed.) *Speculations on Anonymous Material, Nature After Nature, Inhuman* (Berlin: König Books, 2015).

6 Manuel Castells, *The Rise of the Network Society, The Information Age: Economy, Society and Culture*, Vol. I (Oxford: Blackwell, 1996).

7 Keller Easterling, *Extrastatecraft: The Power of Infrastructure Space* (London: Verso, 2014).

8 Benjamin Bratton, *The Stack: On Software and Sovereignty* (Cambridge, MA: MIT Press, 2016).

9 Yuk Hui, "Cosmotechnics as Cosmopolitics," *e-flux journal*, # 86, November 2017, available at https://www.e-flux.com/journal/86/161887/cosmotechnics-as-cosmopolitics/ (accessed January 19, 2021).

10 Robin Mackay and Armen Avanessian (eds.) *#Accelerate: The Accelerationist Reader* (Falmouth: Urbanomic, 2014); Nick Srnicek, *Platform Capitalism* (London: Polity, 2016).

11 The concept of vector and its articulation by McKenzie Wark is most helpful and instructive in respect to platform thinking. See McKenzie Wark, "A Hacker Manifesto [version 4.0.]," available at http://subsol.c3.hu/subsol_2/contributorso/warktext.html (accessed January 19, 2021).

The third plane in my triangulation of the contemporary ontological demand is maybe less visible, but academically even more proactive, which is the so-called “affective turn.” One genealogy of theorizing affect comes from post-Marxism and the discourse on care. The rather cursory account of affective labor as famously outlined by Antonio Negri and Michael Hardt in their book *Empire* (2000) sparked a whole new area or perspective of research.[12] In their analysis of our current era of “late capitalism,” Hardt and Negri start from the usual assumption of the immaterialization of labor. For them, this means not only the turn to digital economies or a form of customization predicated already in post-Fordism, but they emphasize the affective nature of this labor. It consists of manipulation with affect, ranging from the work of the marketeer—making you buy one product after another—to the context of nursing, care, or reproductive labor. Like in our daily lives filled with social contact and support, in these cases we are preoccupied with creating, attuning toward or manipulating by way of affects. Again, this may seem obvious, but my argument is that this shift in focus is an ontological shift. Nowadays we no longer speak about emotions, products, ecosystems, but rather about bonds, desires, or “the world.” This apparent rhetorical shift has generated an entire affect theory, or an affective turn.[13]

It appears to me that rather than successfully delivering on their explicit promises (new post-anthropocentric metaphysics), Speculative Realism or Object-Oriented Ontology present other agents and shifts in what I term the new *demand for ontologies*, and need to be grasped in connection to other strands of thought—namely infrastructural and affective thinking—that also purport the turn to ontology. This *demand* is generated by the contemporary condition of continually accumulated distrust in the current ideological framework, its institutions—including science and democratic politics—and last, but not least, its very own ontology. This ontology can only be described with great difficulties, since it tries to omit any explicit commitment to an actual ideology or ontology. Probably the most famous and concise definition of this doxa has been put forth by Alain Badiou and his idea of “democratic materialism,” when he argues “[t]here are only bodies and languages.”[14] No truth, real commitment, love, ideology or ontology, nothing except for bodies and languages, desire, and games. I am unable to go deeply into this here, since I want to address the new artistic alternatives of this mainstream anti-metaphysics, but allow me to at least expand briefly on the very masking of its own ontological tenets as the backbone of this everyday ontology. It can very roughly be delineated along the axes of consumerism and identity politics. Let’s tentatively connect these to the idea that (my) freedom precedes the factuality of the world and (my) identity precedes community. In this light we can tackle, otherwise barely imaginable, worlds of conspiracy theories, and the general distrust in shared or institutionalized knowledge production. In this ontology it is entirely permissible to choose your president and ignore

12 Michael Hardt and Antonio Negri, *Empire* (Cambridge, MA: Harvard University Press, 2000), 292–93; and Michael Hardt, “Affective Labor,” *Boundary*, Vol. 2, No. 26, 1999, 89–100.

13 Melissa Gregg and Gregory J. Seigworth (eds.) *The Affect Theory Reader* (Durham: Duke University Press, 2010); Patricia Ticineto Clough and Jean Halley (eds.) *The Affective Turn: Theorizing the Social* (Durham: Duke University Press, 2007).

14 Alain Badiou, *Logics of Worlds* (London: Continuum, 2009), 1.

elections, to choose your version of reality (conspiracy theory) and ignore the intricate process of generating a shared one.

In my view this is the context from which we can actually understand (or even criticize) recent speculative, infrastructural or affect theories. But what interests me here, is how these questions and the recent *ontological demand* are operative in the arts, so that we can outline some fresh strategies for speculation, infrastucturalization, affectualization, or re-ontologization. From the opposite direction, this perspective can shine a different light on the role of contemporary art itself. But first of all let me get to a more lighthearted, decentered, or indirect account of these three theoretical planes.

Mytho-poietics of Contemporary Narration

Lovecraft Country (2020), *Raised by Wolves* (2020), and *I know this much is true* (2020) are some of the recently most discussed TV series that seemingly fit their genre confines. The first presents us with individual and prototypical horror stories tied to the fate of a few African Americans, dealing with monsters and their own anxieties, with mystical roots of their family and the racist society of the 1950s. The second leads us to a seemingly traditional post-apocalyptic future in which mankind seeks a new home on a different planet, fueled by the most traditional sci-fi tension between androids and humans. On the other hand, the mini-series *I know this much is true* takes resort in art cinematography or social realism, involving paranoid schizophrenia, family curses, and recurring traumas. But despite and in conjunction with its overly lighthearted fantasy stylization, *Lovecraft Country* purports a strategy of reframing the white cultural imagination and world-fictioning. An explicit argument with Lovecraft racist poetry, the monsterization of white elites and even its focalization[15]—the representation and construction of African American perspectives—all these aspects of the series show how imagination is operative in creating the world we live in, and its values or identities. In *Raised by Wolves*, on the other hand, the colonization is not just a setting for the plot, but the competing factions and perspectives are directly engaging in projecting their future and society on the platform of a new planet. Their specific visions and beliefs determine not only their actions, but the whole framework that makes it meaningful or convincing. *I know this much is true* cannot but be read as a meticulous procedural analysis of affective labor.

In all their introductory brevity, these television series show how we can put speculative and infrastructural theory into practice. Since speculative philosophy lost its close connection with academic ontologies (Speculative Realism, OOO, or Neo-Rationalism),[16] it can be seen to manifest more in relation to speculative fiction and the operationalization of our imagination.[17] More specifically, infrastructural, network-oriented, or platform thinking are not so much focused on networks, algorithmic, or automated landscapes, but rather open up to

15 Focalization was originally developed by Gérard Genette, and denotes the perspective of the narrator, or even more generally, the locus from which the story is narrated. Gérard Genette, *Narrative Discourse: An Essay in Method* (Ithaca: Cornell University Press, 1972).

16 Levi Bryant, Nick Srnicek, and Graham Harman (eds.) *The Speculative Turn: Continental Materialism and Realism*. (Melboure: re:press, 2011).

17 See, for instance, Andreas Töpfer and Armen Avanessian, *Speculative Drawing* (Berlin: Sternberg Press, 2014).

broader societal possibilities of platforming.[18] So, as speculation need not come with a fully fledged ontology, platforming is not about the sheer description and understanding of platforms, rather it focuses on their repurposing and redirection, and addresses the pressing issue of how we live in and through contemporary media. Thus, these broad strands of thinking are not only academic trends, but I would like to position them in the perspective of some of the underling tensions of today. Fact and fiction, identity and community, local and global, private or public—these constitutive concepts seem to be blurred, or even under siege from populism, conspiracy theories, disinformation, or identity politics. As diverse as these problems are, they all tend to involve fiction or imagination in shaping our shared reality, and the circulation through platforms to gain the traction they need to materializee these imaginaries.

Let me consider one last, most apocalyptic show on air most recently—the attack of Trump supporters on the US Capitol. This groundbreaking unrest revealed not only the toxic affluence of Trump's populism and the divide in US society, but also many interesting ontological assumptions. A seamless transition of power, Trump enablers, and mytho-poetic force of conspiracy theories or alt-right memetics are not only political issues, but they call into question the very existence of ever-vigilant power structures, problems of monstrosity and summoning, the plasticity of a shared reality and its susceptibility to viral economies. While critical voices in philosophy and academia focused on the epistemological and political level—be it institutional, personal, or programmatic—I suggest that there is a far more intimate and indirect engagement with its ontological tenets in art.

Abstraction

The first examples I want to outline are concerned with *abstractive* tendencies in today's art practices. In these approaches, abstraction is of course not to be taken as formal, but as the appropriation of the political abstraction we are witnessing.[19] Hito Steyerl may be the best known artist applying such tactics, using patterns of abstraction to elucidate the algorithmic or biopolitical conditioning of ourselves. Her well-known video *How Not to Be Seen: A Fucking Didactic Educational .MOV File* (2013), for instance, tackles the problem of oppressive transparency of today's media, and the fact that while until recently politics was a fight for representation and visibility, now we often have to fight in order *not* to be seen. In her instructional videos, Steyerl repeatedly appropriates martial arts (in *Liquidity Inc.*, 2013, and *Factory of the Sun*, 2015) or even bondage (*Lovely Andrea*, 2007), not only as a metaphor of survivalist culture and ideology, but also of productivity and self-entrepreneurship. Abstractive logic can even more explicitly be seen in her project *The War According to eBay* (2010), in which she uses Nazi photographs sold on ebay. Erasing the picture and only leaving

18 For an example, see Alfie Bown, *Playstation dreamworld* (Cambridge: Polity, 2017).

19 A problem that is central already for Marx and the entirety of Marxist thought. For a recent approach, see, for instance, Alberto Toscano, "The Open Secret of Real Abstraction," *Rethinking Marxism*, Vol. 20, No. 2, April 2008, 273–87.

the outlines of Nazi insignia, she shows the abstraction of how images are circulated and commodified online. Similarly known is Trevor Paglen's practice, who works with the abstraction of surveillance systems and data extraction. Virtually all his photographs and videos work with the abstracted beauty of the medium obsessively, underneath which we should sense the surveillance drone, military base, or the infrastructure of algorithmic control.

But here I want to focus on a more recent and maybe even more topical usage of abstraction, which goes more directly beyond its critique toward creative or even accelerationist usage of abstractive tendencies. Among many environmentally oriented artists, I want to look specifically at Paul Chaney, who works with algorithmic gardening, survivalist strategies, interspecies politics, and collaborative research. In his *Lizard exit plan* (2014) and *Lizard Exit Plan: Goonhilly Sector* (2019), both of which are based on extensive research, the artist creates a meticulous plan of survival for the population at Cornwall's Lizard Peninsula, cut off from the surrounding world due to an unknown environmental catastrophe. For his *Hypothetical Reterritorialization of Žižkov as an Enclave for 2720 Vegetarians* (2018) he designed software (Fieldmachine) for the computation of a nutritionally balanced diet, based on plants that fit the territory's particular ecosystem, providing comprehensive agricultural planning and redesign of the Žižkov neighborhood in the center of Prague. In the course of his artistic practice, Chaney has engaged with knowledge production, concerns about scale and language, based on the horizon of survival as opposed to our current continuation to fetishize progress, and notions such as GDP. The very mechanisms, economical principles, or measurements that lie at the heart of exploitative tendencies, the colonial perspective of the modern West and the nature/culture divide are here reversed and put forward as if after an apocalypse to which these unrestrained modes of thinking and techniques are leading—as if Chaney is holding up a mirror, or giving us a glimpse from the other side of the cataclysmic doom. But this shows us not just a glittering re-instantiation of ever-present images of discord, chaos, and post-apocalyptic nature. In fact, it is a scientific, comprehensive, and algorithmic perspective of how we can live on, closer to a Russian cosmist perspective than to any pop-cultural apocalyptic aesthetics.[20]

Contours of abstraction are even more visible in *Donetsk Syndrome Diagrammatic* (2016). The central point of this project is a timeline that accurately represents the duration between the Big Bang, the creation of minerals such as iron and coal, and the recent war in Eastern Ukraine. Astronomical, geological, and historical time collide on the walls of the gallery. Here we abstract from our usual perception of time to see the very process of abstraction in the form of a diagram. But abstraction is coupled with extraction in the form of abrupt human intervention in otherwise slow geological time. Yet again, this human history may appear rather as an effect of underlying geological agency,

20 This broad intellectual and cultural cosmist movement spread across Russia at the beginning of the twentieth century, opening up questions of space exploration, human enhancement, or scientific revolution. In contemporary thinking, cosmism was brought up mainly by Anton Vidokle in his film trilogy *Immortality for all* (2014–17).

as was the case in producing this project. Paul Chaney started to develop this project for Izolatsia, an art center in Donetsk, right before the war started, and he was forced to move to Prague where he realized the exhibition for Tranzitdisplay. He has himself been affected by coal and iron that define the history of the area and make it "strategic," where Donetsk was founded by British entrepreneur John Hughes as a mining colony in 1869.

Even in this brief overview, it appears that abstract art can finally be productive again. Almost exactly a century after its avant-garde aligned inception, and after its countless formalist exploitations, abstraction must be thought through the lens of our experience of abstractive tendencies in today's capitalist societies. Of course, the abstractive take on capitalism is by no means new and can already be seen in Marx. But, with the cataclysmic images of identitarian politics and ecological catastrophes today, we need to deal with abstraction more directly. As it is not only an economico-political principle but an engine of our ontology, simultaneously driving us towards a world of "endless opportunities" and inevitable self-exploitation, techno-corporate utopias, and ever-enlarging inequality. What constitutes such abstraction is not form but method.

Abjection

The second example of a form that is highly operative in recent art is the image-object. The approach in such work was assumed to play a dominant role in the New Museum's show "Unmonumental: The Object in the 21st Century" (2007), curated by Richard Flood, Massimiliano Gioni, and Laura Hoptman. However, in the next decade such shows became precarious close to shows about post-internet art, with exhibitions such as "Speculations on Anonymous Materials" (Susanne Pfeffer, 2014) or Berlin Biennale IX (2016), including artists such as Oliver Laric and his mining of the potential of 3D printing (*Versions*, 2009–ongoing), or Marisa Olson, who coined the term post-internet. Iconic and most explicit coverage was given to the image-objects by Artie Vierkant with his eponymous project (2011–ongoing). His collages oscillate between the space of the gallery and online photo documentation, commenting on, and capturing the ever-accelerating spinning of our attention and identities from online to so-called real space. Another backing of the image-objects has been provided by critiques of the anthropocentric perspective on art or the Anthropocene, in, for instance, dOCUMENTA 13 (Carolyn Christov-Bakargiev, 2012), "Inhuman" (Susanne Pfeffer, 2015), "Rare Earths" (Boris Ondreička, Nadim Samman, 2015) or "Stories of Almost Everyone" (Aram Moshayedi, 2018). In its core installation, called "Brain," dOCUMENTA 13 featured many objects generating their own narratives or images. Artefacts such as Bactrian Princesses (2200–1700 BCE), Eva Braun's perfume bottle, or melted pieces of metal from artworks housed in the National Museum in Beirut until it was bombed and burned, all these were meant to produce a non-human community of objects-stories-images. Abjection in all these cases means that we challenge our everyday ontologies. Where images are firmly situated in a spectatorial perspective, objects belong to the world of function, with the former under control of the viewer, the second subjugated to the user. Here objects and images tend to free themselves from pre-established hierarchies, trying to gain their own specific sensitivity, narration, or even agency.

Again I want to turn to the more recent use of image-objects in order to spoil its now bitter post-internet bias. Among the plethora of artists exploring and exploiting this direction, I see at least two variegating vectors. Artists like Berenice Olmedo, Shana Moulton, Anna Uddenburg, or Tenant of Culture work with the abjection of the human body. They tackle its subjection to abstractive mechanisms of normative and oppressive cultures (body and wellness), the global circulation of bodily images and norms. In this respect they continue in a very long and vivid tradition of the abjection of human bodies, usually tied to feminism and authors as diverse as Cindy Sherman and Alina Szapocznikow. But there is a strand of VR engagement too: in her project *Rigged* (2014), Kate Cooper worked with CGI characters to ponder on realism and authenticity and perfection through its "rigged" details such as cellulite, braces, or large pores. Even more comprehensively, Cecile B. Evans confronts our engagement with avatars and artificial subjectivities—in, for instance, *Hyperlinks or It Didn't Happen* (2014) and *What the Heart Wants* (2016). Another engagement with image-objects and human bodies may be traced in textile works that subconsciously bring about the dialectic of visible and invisible, figurative and formless, personal and fabricated, including work by artists such as Anni Haunia, Centre for Style, Nik Timková, and Tenant of Culture.

But I want to get to the second vector of image-object form, which is connected to geological, post-anthropocentric thinking, usually tracing the circulation of materials. In this strand, artists and curators work quasi-archaeologically—examples are Otobong Nkanga and Yuji Agematsu—or even xeno-archaeologically—among whom Boris Ondreička and Nadim Samman, Moon Kyungwon and Jeon Joonho.[21] However, it is Iain Ball that I want to focus on here, due to his obsessively persistent work with his own original speculative ontology. Since 2011 he has been developing his series *Rare Earth Sculptures*, connecting mysticism with hyper-capitalism, speculation and irony, engagement and distraction. One of the earlier and more graspable projects is *(RES) Dysprosium* (2011), related to a uranium mining site in Akbastau, Kazakhstan.[22] The tailings, a byproduct, are transported to another facility where Toshiba is using some rare earth derived from this ore, comprising Dysprosium and Neodymium. Iain Ball devised a stretcher with a vernacular design with which the workers are supposed to transport the tailings. The object is accompanied by text, marketing images, and infographics. The author is clearly not aiming at some real practical

21 Xeno-archaeology can quite simply be understood as the excavation of a past that has not happened (yet), as a deep and material inquiry into what the future, or the other, is.

22 Iain Ball, *(RES) Dysprosium*, 2011, available at http://energypangea.org/dysprosium.html (accessed January 19, 2021).

usage of the device, rather he teases our imagination, making us think about the clash between local and global capital, material and infrastructural exchanges between culture, design, and exploitation. In this respect humans and object somehow fuse into Ball's abjective artwork.

Ball's project *Post.Consumer.Cult* (2010) compresses this tension even more, mapping hyper-capitalist imagery with a touch of anachronistic mysticism, a sense of religious or otherworldly culture.[23] This "transmedia content cloud" consists of a web page or collage, a remix of changing images, videos, other projects, web pages, and collages, and even electronic music tracks.[24] In retrospect, the author claims the project is concerned with the potential collapse of the global system, stating that "*Post.Consumer.Cult* is orientated towards the aesthetics of dissolution. It's a representation of the fallout of liberal progressivism and the onslaught of the post-industrial tech revolution, computational automation, technological acceleration and cybernetic control."[25] But upon closer observation we see images of hyper-consumerism, non-Western engagement with new technologies, and the hacking of human bodies. This appropriation of weird imagery of flexibility, edibility, affectivity, malleability of consumerist culture and the human body again point to a weird abjection, not only in the sense of spoiling the traditional Western subject-object dyad, but also as abduction/abjection of our dreams, media, technologies, and bodies. As if our desires are dreamt not by us, but from the outside.

Affectivity

Apart from the perennial tendency of art to abstract from a specific reality and find general, or even universal points of interests in our world, and apart from the ceaseless processes of abjectification of relations, perspectives, percepts, or thought into an artwork, there is a third similarly integral strand, which is characterized by the urge to affect. Not only to convey some emotional charge, or to induce an (a)effect, but to concentrate forces that can spoil and shatter the distinction between the one who perceives and the one being perceived. Affectivity is not the same as generating feelings, rather it presents a deep engagement with our world and in doing so challenges our everyday ontologies in similar ways as abstraction and abjection. Even Alois Riegl, one of the founders of scientific art history and herald of formalism finds in art primarily a mood, *Stimmung*, which can also be translated as "attunement." This atmosphere presents a "presentiment of order and legitimacy over the chaos, of harmony over the dissonances, of rest over movements."[26] In other words, art affords affects that makes us live in a certain world.

In the twenty-first century, affective qualities of art are often invoked in the wake of (post)conceptualism and its slow decline in the past two decades, reviving aesthetic, sensorial, and material aspects of artworks, elucidating the present as opposed to

23 Iain Ball, *Post. Consumer.Cult*. 2010, available at http://iainball.com/postconsumercult.html (accessed January 19, 2021).

24 Iain Ball, "POST. CONSUMER.CULT 2020: Jurassic Accelerationism, Forced Dinosaurisation & Beehive Communism," *Tzvetnik*, 2020, available at https://tzvetnik.online/article/post-consumer-cult-2020-by-iain-ball (accessed March 15, 2021).

25 Ibid.

26 Alois Riegl, "Mood as the Content of Modern Art," *Grey Room*, No. 80, summer 2020, 28.

27 Michal Novotný, "The Emo-Romantic Turn," *Mousse Magazine*, No. 65, autumn 2018, available at http://moussemagazine.it/emo-romantic-turn-michal-novotny-2018/ (accessed January 19, 2021). On the other hand, for the connection of conceptual art with the romantic, see Jörg Heiser, "Emotional Rescue," *frieze*, No. 71, November–December 2002, available at https://www.frieze.com/article/emotional-rescue (accessed January 19, 2021).

28 For a perspective on film, see Josef Früchtl, *Trust in the World: A Philosophy of Film* (New York: Routledge, 2018). Although this problem is already present in Deleuze's tract on film after World War II, that was trying to re-establish the fractured belief in commonality and the social.

representative function. Sometimes it is tied to sincerity and a revival of a certain romanticism,[27] or "trust in the world."[28] Connecting these two points of departure we see once more how direct address, work with presence and emotional drives has its ontological, "world-building" role. I would like to underline the paradoxical proximity of the discourses on care, ecology, solidarity, communing, or belonging. Art on the one hand immediately situates itself into an almost utopia of tolerance and togetherness, on the other hand it is precisely the art world where the neoliberal practice of self-entrepreneurship, which hinges on performance and self-presentation or project-oriented labor manifests itself.[29] Affectivity in recent art practice thus implies the desire for more direct and accessible forms of building a common presence or even shared worlds, but also shows a robust self-reflexivity in terms of conditions of art production in late capitalism.

Looking for examples under this banner becomes even trickier though. I would like to put forth activities of the hybrid collective BCAA systems, also in respect to their base in the Czech art world and its specific conditions. This context represents neither (former) West nor East. Its relative lack in both public and private institutions created an ecosystem of hundreds of smaller off-spaces, hybrids, micro-institutions, or artist-run spaces. The big presence of art academies makes it even softer in terms of access, sociability, or presence discourse. Speculative and accelerationist thinking have been well received here.[30] BCAA systems comes from the context of not only art, but also club music, DJing, and a wide range of collaborations. For instance, they participated in the multifaceted project *Realistic Utopia Velký Krtíš*. Initiated by Martina Růžičková, it revolves around a small post-industrial town in southern Slovakia, which after the collapse of socialism and the end of coal mining faced neoliberal "transformation" and a political vacuum in thinking about peripheries. Structural unemployment, social isolation, or even indifference are all relatively common in post-socialist peripheries, which themselves call for speculative approaches and practices of rejuvenation or commonality. BCAA systems created a speculative documentary, titled *Azero* (2019), about a fictional crypto-community of digital nomads. The project, con-

29 This is best analyzed in Bojana Kunst, *Artist at Work: Proximity of Art and Capitalism* (London: Zero Books, 2015).

30 Rather than pointing at literature, I mention some artists critically working along speculative, or affective strands of thinking and sensitivity in the broadest sense. These are: in respect of curating, Tina Poliačková and Lumír Nykl, Šimon Kadlčák; collaborative research, BCAA system, APART collective, Extrasensory-Aesthetics Research Working Group, and Kolektiv Bjornsonova; direct engagement with philosophy, Class of Interpretation, Katarína Hládeková; ecology and care, Ekobuňka AVU; painting, Jakub Choma; music, Dan Vlček; corporate culture, Jakub Jansa; film, Milan Mazúr; digital cultures, Martin Kohout; performance, Marie Tučková and Lukáš Hofmann; queer, Jan Durina; graphic design, David Koronczi; but also in more specific terms in relation to the genre of fantasy, Anna Slama and Marek Delong; magic, Nik Timková; commodified object, Romana Drdová; or miniature, David Fesl; or "invisible architecture," Artur Magrot. I would like to particularly mention the series *Untitled (Infrastructures and Beach)* by Hynek Alt. Because his seemingly banal pictures of uncovered pipelines in the streets of Prague not only emphasize the underground and infrastructural level, it shows the abstracted, abjected, affective veins of our societies obsessed with smooth circulation of materials and images. For Situationists it was the beach beneath the street, but it is a beach we fight for through both our imagination and labor. See Hynek Alt, *Untitled (Infrastructure & The Beach)* (Prague: Academy of Performing Arts, 2021).

ceived as a "rhizomatic platform," involved research, workshops, urbanist debates, and community engagement.

Even more speculative and particularly affective flows are evident in BCAAS *No~One is an Island* (2019), which involves a video and a music album featuring many other artists.[31] Nineteen tracks of the compilation are conceived as cards in a symbolic deck. A certain level of mysticism and a fantasy setting are even more present in the video that unravels a story of dissipation and rejuvenation. As such it cannot be but read as an allegory of the current state of affairs:

> There once was a plentiful land—or perhaps, it is yet to be—populated with diverse creatures and organisms, mutually nurturing the common web underneath, inside or above them. But balance is always illusory. Things started to change. As if a slinky shadow was cast upon the hills, moors and valleys of the whole wide world. The winds grew stronger, the plants languished, the droughts dried the rivers into frayed, vanishing blue ribbons. All the tissues, structures and substances shivered. Everyone felt it differently, but yet the same. Something was on the move ....[32]

Here, the genre of escapism and the poetics and aesthetic of fantasy are repurposed for an engagement with the traumatic reality of late capitalism and environmental grief. The work's choral-like sound and rhythm underscore this tension between involvement and disengagement, ritual and future. In BCAAS vast body of work, club music and the collaborative nature of their work, much like the internet, are not just a means of production, but constitute a genuinely affective political ecology and mode of activation.[33] As outlined in my understanding of platform thinking, the point is not so much the simple adoption of digital or collaborative strategies, but rather their repurposing and reimagining through practice. In this way the production of art is always a social production.[34]

Image-Object-Platform Complex

Paul Chaney, Iain Ball, and BCAA systems are well aware of recently developed strands in Speculative Realism, and even more so Left-accelerationism; they and their work operate in an intimate, yet critical proximity to these ontological propositions. Generally, I am deeply skeptical about aligning Left-accelerationism and Object-Oriented Ontology directly with art, and therefore don't talk about, for instance, an accelerationist art. What I tried to show here is that we need to devise concepts that are more pertinent to actual art practice. I believe abstraction, abjection, and affectivity are productive notions in this regard, certainly in relation to traditional axes of art production that have come to the fore in recent years. Together, they even form a complex, a language perhaps, one in which shifts in contemporary art can

31 BCAA system, *No~One is an Island*, 2019, available at https://www.youtube.com/watch?v=9SCEWXBueN4&ab_channel=BCAAsystem (accessed January 19, 2021); and BCAA system, *No~One is an Island*, available at https://bcaasystem.bandcamp.com/album/no-one-is-an-island (accessed January 19, 2021).

32 Ibid.

33 "BCAA is an abbreviation of 'based chain amino acid', which is a supplement mostly used by sports(wo)men to surpass tiredness and raise the energy level. When we started doing music streams, three years ago, our vision was similar—we wanted to share positive feelings and create a refreshing vibe. A lot of our activities have since transformed and changed, but, in a way, we still live this spirit." Martina Poliačková, "BCAA system: Binding Tales in Mutual Care," *Pw-Magazine*, November 8, 2020, available at https://www.pw-magazine.com/2020/bcaa-system-binding-tales-in-mutual-care/?fbclid=IwAR1qyyPJ4eepotlrmoFWc_r7yYAn1jzEeOywbWq_DpI-_IXlSYgQPcQNjEo (accessed January 19, 2021).

34 Or, in Deleuzian-Guattarian terms, desiring production is always social production. See Gilles Deleuze and Félix Guattari, *Anti-Oedipus* (London: Bloomsbury, 2012), 337.

be understood and aligned with the ontological demand that permeates our present situation—a world haunted by environmental doom and rules of ignorance, stripped of its basic political or metaphysical certitudes. From an art, or (post-)medium perspective, abstraction tackles *image* and reinvigorates its abstractive power to draw in an outer world for our understanding; in the opposite direction, abjection controls the ways in which our experience, sensibility, orientation, or stories condense and materialize in an artwork or *object*; affectivity organizes binding and piercing links, *platforms*, through which we not only feel but also share and identify, spoiling the duality of viewer and viewed, art and audience, or even subject and object.[35]

As such, abstraction, abjection, and affectivity present ways in which we can reinvigorate art's perennial preoccupation with existential issues, rather than mere aesthetics, presence, and the representation of our world—and show us ways in which art can push philosophy, rather than the other way around. Therefore, it is AAA instead of OOO—if you like abbreviations and pop-song refrains—where the social and political impact of these concepts becomes clear when we face the abstractive logic of capitalist circulation and our risk society—with its mobility, flexibility, volatility, liquidity[36]—the abjective disposition of ourselves through capitalism of identities or labor market—bullshit jobs, marketing ourselves, self-entrepreneurship[37]—or the affective loops and desperate economy of attention—with its clickbaits, fake news, micro-transactions, looting, dopamine waves.[38] Beyond the usual questions and doubt concerning what art can *do* about these problems, we need an art and a culture conscious about these conditions and experimenting not only with their imaginative or aesthetic aspects, but also their political and ontological ones.

35 As I have recently been preoccupied with electronic sound, let me use a parallel from modular music: abstraction pertains to the sound and the voltage running through the system being generated, filtered, attenuated, or manipulated otherwise; abjection is captured by the various modules used with their functionality and identity within the system; affectivity is the patching, the never-ending rewiring of the system so that it breaks apart from regular instrument-oriented creation of music.

36 Ulrich Beck, *Risk Society: Towards a New Modernity* (London: Sage Publications, 1992); and Elena Esposito, *Future of Futures, The Time of Money in Financing and Society* (Cheltenham: Edward Elgar, 2011).

37 David Graeber, *Bullshit Jobs: A Theory* (New York: Simon & Schuster, 2018).

38 Tim Hwang, *Advertising and the Time Bomb at the Heart of the Internet* (New York: Macmillan, 2020).

CYBERNETIC PASTS, FINANCIAL FUTURES: THE CALCULATION OF THE UNKNOWN

Bahar Noorizadeh

A Cyber-Utopia for All

While the streets of Paris and Prague in the late 1960s were laboring the "new spirit of capitalism," another intergalactic fantasy world was under construction in the southern suburbs of Kiev, USSR.[1] Cybertonia, the autonomous country envisioned by the researchers of the Institute of Cybernetics, administered forged passports, artworks, marriage certificates, a new currency (issued on the researchers' punch card), a map outlining the capital city of Kybergrad, and endless workplace entertainment for these young scientists.[2] This Soviet counterculture was part of a long history of what the media scholar Benjamin Peters calls the making of "the other internet"—decades-long endeavors to network computers for socialist ends.

Around the same time, the American internet gave rise to another sort of imaginary. Their cyberspace was a realm of absolute virtual immersion, of becoming one with the notional space of the machine, and cyberpunk was the indexical analogy for the acid trips of the 1960s.[3] In suburban Kiev, drugs were not part of the psycho-social backdrop, but other technologies of bio-power had marked this region's trajectory. In the late 1940s, a group of electrical engineers moved to the forest of Feofania, under the directorship of academician Sergei Alexeevich Lebedev, to settle in the St. Panteleimon's cathedral complex, an icon of Eastern Orthodox faith, built to a Russian revival design. It was in the adjoining monastery that the first electronic stored-memory computer in Europe, BESM, was engineered.[4]

The forest of Feofania and the historic cathedral was a "complicated intersection of faith, madness, murder, and science," as Peters puts it, and an eccentric site for the invention of the first Soviet computer for more than one reason.[5] After the 1917 revolution, the building was pillaged by the revolutionaries and converted into a mental sanatorium. Later, during the Axis invasion of the USSR, the Nazis executed the inmates and established a field hospital in its place. Seven years later, Lebedev and his team reoccupied the vandalized premises to build the Soviet computer, the communist prototype of modern

1 See Luc Boltanski and Ève Chiapello, *The New Spirit of Capitalism* (London: Verso, 2005 [1999]).

2 See Benjamin Peters, *How Not to Network a Nation* (Cambridge, MA: MIT Press, 2016), 130.

3 In William Gibson's account of cyberspace.

4 The computer's full name was Bol'shaya Electronicheskaya Schetnaya Mashina.

5 Peters, *How Not to Network a Nation*, 128.

prometheanism. Despite Lebedev's technical prowess and extensive experience with the principles of computer engineering, one consequential calculation blunder was made. The colossal mainframe, including 6,000 vacuum tubes, was located on the first floor of the two-story monastery building. Turning up the device raised the room's temperature to such an extent that the workers had to demolish parts of the ceiling to allow for the circulation of air.[6]

By 1952, the monastery lab received frequent visits from top Soviet scientists to take advantage of BESM to solve their sundry military and planning problems—from thermonuclear technology to space flights and stochastic quality control in factories. Despite all this, the Ukrainian Academy of Science failed to recognize the significance of automated computers, allocating a dismal budget to Lebedev's lab for the following decade. In a letter addressed to the Communist Party of Ukraine, Lebedev's former colleagues voiced the graveness of these decisions: "The position that our Republic has taken regarding computer technology is equivalent to a crime against the State."[7]

When Scale Became Imagination

Economic efficiency, as the Russian-American Nobel laureate Wassily Leontief notes, has not always been the hallmark of economic debates since the genesis of political economy.[8] Until the mid-nineteenth century, the followers of Adam Smith, including Marx, had been primarily concerned with economic growth—the rising accumulation of wealth and its redistribution among the owners of labor power. It was the combination of war and revolution, the wreckage of World War I in Europe, and the practicalities of running a worker-owned state with the epic size of Russia, that made *scale* synonymous with imagination. Particularly in the field of economics, a transition to efficiency sciences—management, logistics, planning—was in order as early as the communist revolution took place. Economics at this time advanced into the science of building the most accurate *scale model*—let's call it an algorithm—for the biophysical reality of nation-wide production and distribution.

A source of creative abundance and concomitant anxiety for the early revolutionaries, however, was that this phantasm—of scaled management—had to be summoned from scratch, as there was no historical precedent. Marx, as Leontief writes, "was a prophet of socialism, but he was a student of capitalism."[9] More specifically, Marx was a student of capitalism's initial hundred years. His theory was more a description of private enterprise rather than a command economy. For the Bolsheviks, to replace market mechanisms with socialist planning was to concoct an interpretation of Marx and Engels's teachings that was not included in any chapter of Marxist orthodoxy. It had to be invented in the corridors of GOSPLAN, the newly founded State General Planning Commission, for its seventy years of experimental life.

6 Boris Malinovsky, *Pioneers of Soviet Computing*, translated by Emmanuel Aronie and edited by Anne Fitzpatrick (2007, second edition 2010 [1994]), 12, e-book, available at https://www.sigcis.org/files/SIGCISMC2010_001.pdf (accessed April 25, 2021).

7 Ibid., 15.

8 Wassily Leontief, "Scientific Economic Planning," *Foreign Affairs*, Vol. 38, No. 2, 1960, 261–72.

9 Ibid.

But this was not an easy assignment. The pressures from Stalin's state to bend the economic theories to fit the new agricultural policies and boost the Soviet defense program turned economics into an instrument of rapid industrialization and militarization. This effectively silenced the innovations brought forth by a number of mathematicians, most notably Leonid Kantorovich, who, in his seminal essay in 1939, had outlined the schema for linear programming in a jargon-free advisory format for the economists of his time. Twenty years later, this paper saw the light of day in a book titled *The Use of Mathematics in Economic Research*.[10] Linear programming, originally applied to the problem of optimizing a plywood factory, was essentially the inception of information management and control systems on an industrial scale. In parallel, the demands of military logistics of World War II for the United States—concerned with the allocation of airplanes, food, trucks, and optimizing enemy casualties during combat—brought about a version of linear modeling by American economists.[11]

Besides linear mathematics, the movement toward rationalization of economics in Russia was a cutting rejoinder to the hegemonic reign of Marxian political economy that provided no clear guidance other than ideological soundbites for the Soviet economists. Simply put, organizing the national economy on the basis of socio-hermeneutics of Marx's oeuvre proved futile for the revolutionaries. A similar sentiment toward rationalization was shared in Europe by market socialists—the epigones of neo-classical economics—during the interwar years, with the pressing concerns around the reconstruction of the wrecked continent.

The shared roots of mathematization of economics in both socialist and market-based countries often escapes common accounts. In this historical moment, large-scale planning echoed across the communist and capitalist divide. In Europe, the backlash against economic scientism, however, was not met by the proponents of *Das Kapital*, but by a group of Viennese economists that formed what would later be known as the foundation of neoliberal philosophy. More specifically, and from a historical perspective, the tenets of neoliberal thought originated in opposition, or as a direct reaction to the rising global attraction toward planning of any kind, be it in the Soviet Union, or in the political and intellectual spheres of Vienna at the time. Recounting this moment in the twentieth century's formation of economic thought, and its peculiar alliances and antagonisms, is enlightening for today's horizon of economic justice.

Civilization and Its Markets

The first attack on optimized planning was launched by Ludwig von Mises, the Austrian school economist largely influential for the emergence of neoliberal doctrine. Von Mises was adamant about the impossibility of a socialist system to lead to anything but failure, because rational calculation of a large-scale economy

10 Michael Ellman, *Planning Problems in the USSR* (New York: Cambridge University Press, 1973), 4.

11 Koopman and Kantorovich would share the Nobel prize in Economics (1975) for their contributions to linear programming.

was, rationally speaking, impossible. The amount of information that had to be collected, stored, processed, analyzed, and circulated at every fraction of a second by the centralized planners was simply unachievable. In contrast, the market, with the mysterious sophistication of a black box, did not require any such laborious information technology. This argument, visited time and again as the most fervent economic dispute of the twentieth century, was labeled the Socialist Calculation controversy. The Socialist Calculation debate was "the starting point of the economics of information," a conversation that worked to classify perspectives on the role of knowledge in economics into its primary constitutive camps.[12] But even more consequential for the history of economics, the dispute impelled the opponents of socialism to formulate their core ideas of what the market *is* and what it *does*, as Erwin Dekker remarks, as nothing less than the bedrock of civilization.[13]

It was Friedrich Hayek, Von Mises's protégé, who laid the foundation for the modern philosophy of the market as an articulation of its unchallenged primacy over socialist planning. For Hayek there was something essentially utopian about socialist projects of any kind, which ran counter to the real-world experience of life, with all its irrefutable pain and suffering. The drive to perfect rationalization of the study of society, and the insistence upon applying methods of natural sciences to social phenomena such as the economy, was a grave mistake—an inheritance of war-time planning and socialist fantasies of organization. In *The Road to Serfdom* (1944), Hayek would criticize strategies once designed as transient policies geared toward military defense, to be extended into the civilian and creative domains.[14] The very assumption that social order must arise from a type of organization was at stake here: civilization ultimately was the highest achievement of the *spontaneous order* of a society, not the application of a well-articulated *model* on the reality of human life. Hayek's anti-utopian neoliberal realism, in contrast, had at its core an unreserved mistrust of people. Because the masses were essentially under the illusion that they had a rational choice, the opportunity to oversee the public's ideas was laid bare to intellectuals—those "professional second-hand dealers in ideas"—who would misunderstand and mislead the people.[15] As far as civilization, in its Western, modernist essence, was concerned, such delusions of rationalist primacy were only indications of primitivist and naturalistic detours from the discourse of civilization. To submit to the limits of human rational faculties and their capacities to know and design, was a coda to civilizational progress. For the neoliberal primogenitors, this was a consequential underestimation of "cultural institutions such as the market."[16]

Hayek himself did not hold a consistent position throughout his life: much of what is understood as neoliberal doctrine today is only a snippet of his ever-changing ideas. In regard to the challenge of accounting, Hayek's early work would extend Von Mises's rather reductive opposition to calculation of any

12 Philip Mirowski and Edward Nik-Khah, *The Knowledge We Have Lost in Information* (New York: Oxford University Press, 2017), 60.

13 Ola Innset, *Reinventing Liberalism: The Politics, Philosophy and Economics of Early Neoliberalism (1920-1947)* (Cham: Springer Publishing, 2010), 35.

14 Friedrich Hayek, *The Road to Serfdom* (London: G. Routledge & Sons, 1944), 3.

15 Friedrich Hayek, "The Intellectuals and Socialism," in *The Intellectuals: A Controversial Portrait*, edited by George B. de Huszar (Glencoe: The Free Press, 1960), 371.

16 Erwin Dekker, *The Viennese Students of Civilization* (New York: Cambridge University Press, 2016), Part 1, paragraph 8.

kind in his theorization of price as the sole carrier of information in the market, and therefore society at large. At stake was the perfect apparatus of the market that would make such astronomical calculations not on paper, and not inside a giant mainframe computer, but within (social) practice. The gears of this social calculator were essentially the dispersal of facts among all individuals, plus the liquidity of price itself in capturing the slightest change in its numerical index—importantly without the need to have knowledge of the workings of the entire system. As Hayek put it:

> It is more than a metaphor to describe the price system as a kind of machinery for registering change, or a system of telecommunications which enables individual producers to watch merely the movement of a few pointers, as an engineer might watch the hands of a few dials in order to adjust their activities to changes of which they may never know more than is reflected in the price movement.[17]

That is, the market for early neoliberalism was a computer, and price was not only one of its properties but the measure of change in society at large, the ledger capturing the archive of humanity-as-civilization. In such an atmosphere, it is not difficult to imagine what the arrival of computers meant for the buzz around mathematization of economics in the West, and its strange kinship with planned variants in the East. Oskar Lange, a passionate advocate of market socialism, would respond exuberantly to the Socialist Calculation debate in the 1960s: "So what's the trouble? Let us put the simultaneous equations on an electronic computer and we shall obtain the solution in less than a second."[18] The computing device would show that the market process "with its cumbersome *tatonnements*" was passé, belonging to the mechanical age.[19] Not a mere stand-in, here the electronic computer would achieve a performance unlike the market was ever able to. Computers were more than enough to take on the function of informatic distribution that the market had been shouldering until that point. If this statement held true, a planned socialism could take the lead over capitalist markets.

The Sundry Blueprints for the Communist Network

In the meantime, the new information age was catching up with the mid-century chaos of the Soviet Union. The decades-long shock tactics that Stalin's "Revolution from Above" had bred, supplemented by the mass wreckage of the war, laid waste to the Soviet industries, often falling far behind the central planning system and resulting in shortages and erratic discrepancies. To resolve these irregularities, the state would continuously amplify the administrative apparatus contributing to the proliferation of wide-scale bureaucracy. According to Peters,

17 Friedrich Hayek, *Individualism and Economic Order* (Chicago: Regnery, 1948), 86.

18 Oskar Lange, "The Computer and the Market," in *Socialism, Capitalism and Economic Growth: Essays Presented to Maurice Dobb*, edited by C.H. Feinstein (Cambridge: Cambridge University Press, 1967), 158.

19 Ibid.

"[t]he terror of Stalin's rule was not its rigid centrality but its informal uncertainty."[20] It wasn't the bulletproof institutionalization and airtight regulations that fostered the chaos of the Stalinist USSR, but the absence of any due process and formalized citizenry guidelines.

The indispensable role that the Soviet mafia—the *tolkachi* (or pushers in English)—played during these years is witness to the fallacy of a perfect top-down state. In an industrial system motivated by punishment based on shortage of products—failure to deliver the required amounts of goods—factories were incentivized to hoard rather than to sell, slowing down the entire chain of production. Lubricating the wheels of exchange and pushing factories to sell necessitated the quasi-illicit activity of *tolkachi* as master negotiators running the scene through backdoor deals and personal favor trading. The informal favor economy was not a by-product of a sluggish centralized industry, but the very means through which the industry functioned, as Francis Spufford writes. "The money was there, the price of a transaction had to be paid, but the object was to find non-money reasons for the transaction to take place."[21]

In such an environment, the economy at the time of Stalin's demise "resembled an exhausted beast."[22] As part of the de-Stalinization of the USSR, Nikita Khrushchev aimed to decentralize authority over the industry. Fifteen percent of the national workforce in 1954, as statistics go, comprised administrative and managerial personnel. Administrative reforms, Khrushchev hoped, would distribute and accelerate planning processes and curtail the exorbitant red tapes of the Soviet post-war economy. The reforms, however, did not work exactly as planned—the year of Khrushchev's forced resignation from office saw the lowest GNP growth, of -1.1 per cent, until the fall of the Soviet Union.[23] This new spirit of reform, be that as it may, left a significant mark on the science of governance: applied mathematics at this time was revived out of its repudiated corner and put to work at the new Academy Council on Cybernetics, and mathematical planning accordingly was rebranded as economic cybernetics.[24]

After Lebedev's initial victories of mainframe computer developments and Kantorovich's conceptual framing of economic mathematics, the foremost proposal to network a set of computers came directly from the military: Anatolii Kitov, who had published the first book on digital computers in the Soviet Union and was heading the computation center at the Ministry of Defense, mailed his book to Khrushchev. Along the writings came a message advancing structural improvement in the methods of management by transitioning from manual administration to automated systems relying on the electronic computer machines.[26] In the letter he described the automation of planning as "a revolutionary leap in the development of our country that would ensure a complete victory of socialism over capitalism."[27]

Although the Soviet leadership took the call for employment of new technologies seriously, they did not implement

20 Peters, *How Not to Network a Nation*, 75.

21 Francis Spufford, *Red Plenty* (London: Faber & Faber, 2010), Chapter 4, part 3, paragraph 1.

22 Richard Judy, "Information, Control, and Soviet Economic Management," in *Mathematics and Computers in Soviet Economic Planning*, edited by J. Hardt et al. (New Haven: Yale University Press, 1967), 642, quoted in Slava Gerovitch, "InterNyet: why the Soviet Union did not build a nationwide computer network," *History and Technology*, Vol. 24, No. 4, 2008, 336.

23 Peters, *How Not to Network a Nation*, 64.

24 Gerovitch, "InterNyet," 337.

25 Ibid., 339.

26 Anatolii Kitov, "Chelovek, kotoryi vynes kibernetiku iz sekretnoi biblioteki," *Komp'iuterra*, No. 43, November 18, 1996, 45, quoted in Gerovitch, "InternYet," 339.

27 Malinovsky, *Pioneers of Soviet Computing*, 49.

Kitov's most revolutionary plan, which involved a countrywide automated network for the management of the economy. To reduce the cost of this exorbitant program, Kitov suggested a dual network for both civilian and military uses. Those in the Ministry of Defense committee rejected the idea, partly for fear of bearing responsibility for the civilian sector, and partly worries about their personal loss of power.[27] Infuriated when Kitov took his complaint to the communist party, the committee removed him from his position at the Ministry of Defense and he was eventually dismissed from the party.

The most crucial takeaway from these early cybernetic dreams is the incommensurability of technological and political systems. These proposals turned a blind eye to the reality of informal practices and nepotistic dynamics of life in the USSR, similar to how liberal media theorists have over-emphasized the non-hierarchical functions of technology in democratic systems: "Centralizing computer networks and centralized socialist states have as little to do with one another as the digital does with democracy."[28] This lesson would resonate with the ideals of early cybernetic theorists, such as Norbert Wiener's vision of power as external to the cybernetic feedback loop. Khrushchev's reforms would demonstrate this misunderstanding in the nature of power: authority could not automatically be dispersed within decentralized models, rather power was embedded within the protocols and managerial apparatus that overlooked the system.

The Soviet Internet That Never Was

Taken by its congruence with an organized command state, Khruschev himself was in favor of the cybernetization of not only the economy, but of society altogether. This vision was closer to Kitov's original plans of central control than the liberal ideals of seamless communication and systemic freedom. This later vision of a decentralized network, often attributed to Wiener's idea of feedback and communication between various parts of a democratic society, was being developed in-house in the USSR, but never saw the light of day. The unfulfilled Soviet internet in the service of the economy was called OGAS, conceived and survived during the 1960s under the leadership of Viktor Glushkov, the new director of the Institute of Cybernetics at Kiev's Feofania campus.[29] Two years before Khrushchev's government came to an abrupt end, Glushkov extended Kitov's national network blueprint with a tendentious upgrade: elimination of paper money and its substitution with digital payments. Glushkov's network schema, although hierarchical, was in essence decentralized and geared toward the workers: the perfect synergy between streamlined management and peak surveillance.[30] Contrary to the previous proposals, Glushkov set out to work not only with mathematicians but also economists.[31] This included the director of the Central Mathematical Institute Nikolai Fedorenko, with whom he published a proposal for a unified planning system.

28 Peters, *How Not to Network a Nation*, 104.

29 OGAS was short for The All-State Automated System for the Gathering and Processing of Information for the Accounting, Planning, and Governance of the National Economy, USSR.

30 Peters, *How Not to Network a Nation*, 113.

31 Gerovitch, "InterNyet," 341.

Glushkov put forward his updated plan for an electronic socialism, the OGAS network, in 1962. Together with his team in Kiev, he envisioned the national economy as a complex cybernetic system incorporating innumerable, yet interconnected control loops. The key was to optimize a planned economy based on a three-tiered structure that included thousands of local computation centers that would compile "primary information," tens of mid-scale computation centers in larger cities, and one top-level center concurrently overseeing the entire network and aiding the government.[32] If successfully implemented, this mechanism would eventually replace regional managers with computers that extracted, analyzed, and circulated economic data in a single nationwide network. The popular press began to call computers *machines of communism*. At the peak of the technology race with the US, cybernetic economics drew the outline of a communist internet in the service of socialist planning. The communist authority eventually gave the nod for the first cybernetic reform of the economy via OGAS in 1963.

Glushkov had predicted that if economic data processing remained operated manually, the entire adult population of the Soviet Union would be employed in managing its own bureaucracy by 1980. Unlike ARPANET, the American project that would support the internet, OGAS wasn't merely interested in facilitating communication among scientists, but its higher ambitions were to digitize all matters of bureaucracy and convert government documents to electronic records, enable remote access to all workers, and allow decentralized command over those documents. OGAS envisioned the economy as one domain within the larger science of governance, challenged relentlessly by the scientific-technical revolution. It took the factory unit as a model for the entire national economy, setting it apart from other contemporary networks: the network was "an expression of the nervous system of a factory, writ large across a nation [...] a sort of simultaneously metaphorical and mechanical collectivization of the industrial household (or what Hannah Arendt calls the oikos)."[33]

Despite initial victories, OGAS was never realized. In its place, hundreds of local computer centers had been built by the end of the 1970s, but they were never connected. Glushkov and his team faced endless opposition from various groups: the military support that the project was originally reliant on had no interest in the civilian promises of a networked architecture. Competition between the ministries who wanted sole ownership of OGAS obstructed any productive collaboration between state agencies. There was a major backlash from the bureaucratic body, which suspected an automated management would drive them to unemployment. Emerging liberal economists in the Soviet Union also feared that a networked management would further embed the ineffective central planning, which they were striving to correct by introducing market incentives.[34]

More importantly, by the 1970s the Soviet economy was anything but a well-ordered hierarchy: decades of mismanage-

32 Ibid., 342.
33 Peters, *How Not to Network a Nation*, 109.
34 Ibid.

ment had driven the system to be heavily reliant on interpersonal bonds and incestuous cliques. The *tolkachi* were also active during these times, and actual negotiations happened in long corridors, train stations, and suburban summer houses, rather than in the ministries' conference rooms. Glushkov's unbiased computers lacked popular support, because they threatened the existence of these well-entrenched and corrupt friendship networks. Frustrated by the incongruity of the political system to the abstract image of a unitary communist nation, Glushkov hinted at the limits of Soviet techno-utopianism short of a political program in an interview:

> If we put truthful information about the capabilities of every workplace and every production area in the machine, the machine will combine them and get enhanced opportunities of enterprises, branches, republics, and the country as a whole. That is, on the basis of truthful information, we can really get an amplification of human intelligence with the help of machines. It's what can't be done without machines. But, if we put a deliberate lie in the machine, it will amplify this lie and spit out a lie that will be impossible to sort out.[35]

The Specter Haunting Amazon

Though cybernetic dreams could not save the Soviet Union from collapse, a faction on the Left today is hopeful about the valences of big data, marking the concluding passage of the long century of the Socialist Calculation debate.[36] Capitalism at its current stage, according to those holding these views, works on the clock not due to the affordances of the market and the price system, but because it plans.[37] From our contemporary perspective, the means of information infrastructures and the massive increase in computer processing speed renders Von Mises's forewarnings obsolete: if the early-day mainframes were promissory of a socialist match for the market, the current supercomputers used in climate modeling and meteorological facilities alone can easily handle the required large-scale planning and analysis of the global economy without a hitch.[38]

This remarkable efficiency today is incarnated in retail mega-platforms such as Amazon and Alibaba. The revolution in barcode scanning and the introduction of Amazon's "Chaotic Storage"[39] and "Anticipatory shipping"—the knowledge of what the customer wants before they even want it—culminates in the extraction and mining of future demands, by way of engineering an archetype subject. Not only do platforms embody the bygone socialist imaginary of scale, but the building blocks of socialism, Kantorovich's linear modeling, are coded into their DNA. Needless to say, this massive potential runs parallel to corporate mainstays of anti-union practices, intensive workplace surveillance, record-high unsafe working conditions, and monopolizing tendencies and increasing market shares,

35 Victor Glushkov, *Pioneer of Soviet Computing*, no date, available at https://www.youtube.com/watch?v=lMS1hBhV2-4 (accessed April 24, 2021).

36 Nick Dyer-Witheford, "Red Plenty Platforms," *Culture Machine*, Vol. 14, 2013, available at https://culturemachine.net/wp-content/uploads/2019/05/511-1153-1-PB.pdf (accessed April 21, 2021); Benjamin Bratton, *The Stack: On Software and Sovereignty* (Cambridge, MA: MIT Press, 2016); Thomas Ramge and Viktor Mayer-Schönberger, *Reinventing Capitalism in the Age of Big Data* (New York: Basic Books, 2018).

37 Leigh Phillips and Michal Rozworski, *The People's Republic of Walmart* (London: Verso, 2019).

38 Dyer-Witheford, "Red Plenty Platforms," 8.

39 "At Amazon, employees armed with barcode scanners take incoming products and place them in unoccupied shelf positions, regardless of what other products are around them. Since each product and shelf have unique barcodes, the staff is able to record where each product was placed, so when the time to ship out comes another employee just reads off the computer's picking list." From "Why Chaotic Storage is Perhaps the Best Inventory," no date, available at https://www.systemid.com/learn/why-chaotic-storage-is-perhaps-the-best (accessed April 25, 2021).

all exacerbated in the course of the global pandemic and its aftermath.[40] What is more, the image of an Amazon-like entity governing the planet is equally disturbing to any non-centralist and participatory communist tradition. One adequate response, however, is Glushkov's original OGAS, or the decentralized Chilean cybernetic schemes developed by Stafford Beer, stirring a democratic imagination of feedback structures. Rather than adjusting user behavior according to institutional norms, Beer's design of cybernetic freedom modifies the institutional protocol to be inclusive of singularities and systemic anomalies.[41] Despite all the deficiencies of platform capitalism, its compatibility with the project of cybernetic revolutionaries are much more evident to be simply overlooked. "A fortiori, Amazon offers techniques of production and distribution that are just waiting to be seized and repurposed."[42]

It is crucial here to change the terms of the debate. Efficiency—the hallmark of cybernetic philosophy—was never the epitome of the neoliberal theory of the market. The efficiency discourse maintains a non-dynamic view of information, presuming information to be entirely constrained to commodified data in the age of platforms. This is a distorted account of the process of opinion formation that precedes market exchange: the background negotiations, reputation inspections, and the informal substrata that underpin the expression that is the price index. Opinion formation, in other words, is the processual practice that precedes price numbers, and where market competition commences. Competition, in its original neoliberal formulation, was not limited to the discovery of lower prices and higher profits, but was also competition for reputation, or the discovery of non-price knowledge by way of familiarity with the *people* that supply commodities, in the absence of knowledge regarding the commodities or services themselves: "The function of competition is here precisely to teach us who will serve us well: which grocer or travel agency, which department store or hotel, which doctor or solicitor, we can expect to provide the most satisfactory solution for whatever particular personal problem we may have to face."[43] This process is enabled by, and entirely dependent on capitalist institutions: advertising, press, and the process of market discovery via competition. As journalist and writer Evgeny Morozov states, "[t]he price system worked so efficiently only because capitalism did the rest."[44]

The Roots of Anticipatory Capitalism

The seeds of this epistemic rift were envisaged in Hayek's seminal early essay "The Use of Knowledge in Society" (1945).[45] He argued that a single mind could never contain the sum of data for the whole society "in concentrated or integrated form," and this information could exist "solely as the dispersed bits of incomplete and frequently contradictory knowledge which all the separate individuals possess."[46] These theoretical meditations implied, first and foremost, that economics was no longer

40 Lisa Fickenscher, "Workers at Amazon's Staten Island warehouse hold rally over high injury rates," *New York Post*, November 25, 2019, available at https://nypost.com/2019/11/25/workers-at-amazons-staten-island-warehouse-to-hold-rally-over-high-injury-rates/ (accessed April 25, 2021).

41 Stafford Beer, *Designing Freedom* (Toronto: House of Anansi Press, 1993 [1974]).

42 Phillips and Rozworski, *The People's Republic of Walmart*, Chapter 4, paragraph 2.

43 Hayek, *Individualism and Economic Order*, 97.

44 Evgeny Morozov, "Digital Socialism?," *New Left Review*, Nos. 116–17, 33–67.

45 Hayek, *Individualism and Economic Order*.

46 Ibid., 77.

concerned with the allocation of resources—the world of matter—but the allocation of knowledge—the world of information. The early Hayek maintained that the knowledge prerequisite to any scaled planning, could not be *given in advance*, as such an *a priori* status assumes localization in one body, and that it would necessarily be time-dependent, resting on the exchange of information between distinct individuals.[47] The socialist planners' cardinal oversight was not their fallacious faith in computation with a view to economic optimization—the calculation debate—but an epistemological chimera that deluded them in thinking that it was possible to get the better of the market by simply removing its chronological index, i.e., what transpires during exchange itself.

The question of time at the center of economic information was augmented in Hayek's later work until it reached its occult status: it was not knowledge, but the absence of knowledge—the ontological impossibility of accessing this knowledge *in advance*—that underpins economic activity. The Hayekian knowledge/non-knowledge dichotomy, then, making a transition from the realm of epistemology to ontology, was no more concerned with economic psychology as was previously theorized in the work of his antecedents, but came closer to Freud's theory of the unconscious as anterior to conscious phenomena. Despite this theoretical resonance, there was no acknowledgment or serious consideration of the psychoanalytic discourse in Hayek's later work. Psychoanalysis was indeed entirely absent from "The Sensory Order," Hayek's venture into the foundations of psychology in which he realized it was up to an outsider to diagnose a great neglect of "the nature of mental phenomena," as a result of what he described to be psychology's entirely empirical methodology, and, even more, "an excessive contempt for 'speculation' [...] which is another word for thinking."[48] This was in line with his critique of social sciences as they insisted on the realm of objective facts rather than the speculative activity of the mind. He reproached the—then rising—neoclassical economists for their negligence of the speculative foundation of the market, forgoing it for their delusions of perfect optimization and efficiency.

The economists who took this challenge to heart emerged primarily out of the Cowles commission based at the University of Chicago. Cowles's economists, led by two avid econometrics advocates, Oskar Lange and Tjalling Koopmans, strongly opposed Hayek's cognitive theories, and for the same reason were committed to overrule his metaphysics of the market with more enhanced information pragmatism. It was in Chicago that the neoclassical science of economy—popular at the time in the US—was married to the neoliberalism of Hayek and his ilk through a subtle appendage: the introduction of advanced probability theory and Bayesian statistics through the emerging field of game theory.[49] In short, that the shadow of the future surfaced into economics as a numerical factor has directly to do with the chaotic feud with the Hayekian market-unconscious.

47 "The common idea now seems to be that all such knowledge should as a matter of course be readily at the command of everybody, and the reproach of irrationality leveled against the existing economic order is frequently based on the fact that it is not so available. This view disregards the fact that the method by which such knowledge can be made as widely available as possible is precisely the problem to which we have to find an answer." Hayek, *Individualism and Economic Order*, 81.

48 Friedrich Hayek, *The Sensory Order* (Chicago: University of Chicago Press, 1952/1976), Preface, paragraph 4.

49 Prior to the twentieth century, according to Mirowski and Nik-Khah, economics was past-oriented. Values were registered as ramifications of what happened *historically*.

This unholy alliance between American econometrics—itself an uncanny twin of Soviet cybernetics—with early-day neoliberal philosophy resulted in the contemporary monster called "neoliberalism," a mishmash of idealist battles over information with no base in today's lived "reality" whatsoever.

For decades to come, the neoclassical engineers of the market—i.e., economists—would continue to sweep up Nobel Prizes in the field. Since the 1980s there has been a resurgence of physicists, again, in economics' practice as their own discipline has faced shrinkage post the Cold War, and they have entered banks and hedge funds as designers of statistical algorithms and complex predictive models. As economic philosophers Philip Mirowski and Edward Nik-khah emphasize, the discourse of economics since the eighteenth century has been taking its validation from the natural sciences.[50] The Black-Scholes equation, for instance—the principal pricing formula for financial options—is primarily modeled after a heat equation.[51] One would think that the recurrence of financial crises must have rendered these forecasting models subject to constant mutation and change, yet this is hardly the case. Half a century after the publication of the Black and Scholes article, the formula still holds the status of holy writ in finance according to the business tycoon Warren Buffet.[52]

The War on Speculation

The seldom narrated story of twentieth-century economics helps us situate and track the predictive stochastics of finance capital today. That Hayekian speculation morphed into future *engineering* in finance and beyond is nothing normal or natural. It is the root of three major ramifications for those who pursue alternative economic imaginaries on a par with the current byzantine crises of global capitalism. First, to return to the present, the most tech-reverent faction on the Left have presented case after case of hyper-functional *planned capitalism* served by digital platforms—a socialism within reach—primed for capture and control. Celebratory accounts of the ready-made planning apparatus are often accompanied by a disregard for—or an outright critique of—speculation, particularly post-2008.[53] In a way, by dramatizing the current computational affordances of big-data platforms, these arguments revive the Socialist Calculation battle—in its original state pre-World War II—at the cost of overlooking the knowledge problem for centralized authority that, as I have shown here, has spawned *anticipatory capitalism*.

In *Capital and Time* (2018) Martijn Konings problematizes the regressive nature of these heterodox economic wars on speculation. Their appeal to foundationalism is particularly absurd when one considers how every other domain of the humanities and social sciences in the past half century has undergone an anti-essentialist epistemic crisis.[54] In reverting to an essentialist notion of value, critiques of speculation not only miss the autopoietic essence of money—its *a priori* status as a container for

50 Mirowski and Nik-Khah, *The Knowledge We Have Lost in Information*, p. 45.

51 Vipul K. Singh, "Options Pricing Formula: Confluence of Financial Economics, Mathematics and Computational Science," *Asia-Pacific Journal of Management Research and Innovation*, Vol. 10, No. 1, 2014, 49.

52 Warren Buffet, "Berkshire's Corporate Performance vs. the S&P 500," 2008, 20, available at https://www.berkshirehathaway.com/letters/2008ltr.pdf (accessed April 25, 2021).

53 The many vindications of the Keynesian macroeconomics apply here. Misconstruing neoliberalism as an "anti-regulatory" machine, rather than a re-regulatory framework that integrates previous binaries between states and markets, and *laissez-faire* economics and central banks, these accounts revive regulation in the abstract without much valence in relation to how the state-market nexus works today.

54 Martijn Konings, *Capital and Time* (Stanford: Stanford University Press, 2018), Introduction, paragraph 6.

"fictional expectations"—but also rid economics from imagining itself otherwise.[55] Producing unorthodox knowledge, so vital to contemporary struggles, demands imagination. Similarly, exclusive appeals to "regulation" itself, as Mirowski asserts, is a major symptom of such bankruptcy of the economic enterprise.[56]

Secondly, and as a collateral to the above, the Left's essentializing tendencies do not leave room for a distinction between the subjective variant of this epistemic problem and its ontological derivative. The critique of knowledge-qua-information solely concerns itself with the speed of information transfer between social units. It seeks to recalibrate predictive stochastics and preemptive information employed within high-frequency finance toward a *better* model of efficiency, corresponding merely to the subjective epistemic phenomena. But while finance purports to bring future uncertainty under its managerial control, real-world crises interiorize, and therefore sublimate the material ramifications of a yet untamed uncertainty. These are essentially two different registers of uncertainty—a subjective one derived from finance's indebtedness to neoliberalism, and one that categorically cannot be steered, controlled, or governed, and only comes into view at times of *crises*.

Crisis is not an ephemeral error exposing the epistemic problem at large, but it reveals the fundamental rift between the ontology and the epistemology of uncertainty. The former is captured verbatim in Donald Rumsfeld's infamous territory of the "unknown unknowns," or in what Nassim Nicholas Taleb calls the "Black Swan" phenomenon.[57] That is, certain "outlier events" with "massive impact" exist, for which finance can only "concoct explanations for its occurrence after the fact, making it explainable and predictable."[58] It is the reverse-engineering of predictability—*ex post*—that shifts probability's tip of the arrow from the future to the past. Although Taleb's observation is based on what he sees as the epistemic constraints of philosophical and empirical approaches to probability, he remains negligent of the particular epistemic angle that his version of the "Black Swan" presumes. In his theory of the Blank Swan, Elie Ayache adjusts Taleb's epistemic angle: "The Black Swan is a *change of context* and that it is only relative to a given context that we can make causal predictions at all."[59] Briefly put, massive financial crises of the past decades shake the grounds of our forecasting models to reveal that they only apply as long as the context they arise from remains identical.

Lastly, as it concerns a politics of subjectivity, the philosopher Michel Feher shows that what we are left with today is not the entrepreneurial Vitruvian man of early neoliberal aspiration, motivated by profit and revenue, but "the credit-seeking asset manager" aiming at maximizing their creditworthiness and capital value.[60] The financialized subject—enacting an exaggerated species of Hayekian reputation—is spurred on by amplified future gains rather than humble, though guaranteed present income. Being deemed creditworthy, as Feher writes, "can translate into loans, venture capital investments, buzz,

55 Jens Beckert, *Imagined Futures* (Cambridge, MA: Harvard University Press, 2016), 9.

56 Philip Mirowski, *Never Let a Good Crisis Go to Waste* (London: Verso, 2013), Chapter 5, paragraph 3.

57 Donald Rumsfeld, "Rumsfeld/Knowns," *CNN*, 2002, available at https://www.youtube.com/watch?v=REWeBzGuzCc (accessed April 24, 2021).

58 Nassim Nicholas Taleb, *The Black Swan* (New York: Random House, 2007), xviii.

59 Elie Ayache, "Elie Ayache, Author of the Black Swan," *Wilmott Magazine*, July 2007, 47.

60 Michel Feher, *Rated Agency* (New York: Zone Books, 2018), 225.

material support, confidence, and other forms of empathy."[61] In the age of *appreciation*, platform capitalism is far more than an infrastructural substitute for reallocation of goods and services, i.e., the market: alongside financial markets, financialized states, and investee citizens, platforms today are the paramount locations for measuring attractiveness of their users through rating.

Futures of Platform Capitalism

This may indicate that current platforms are enabling speculative infrastructures in their own right, primed for public requisition. The historical battle of socialist planning against neoliberalism, engendering the reign of numerical forecasting and the calculation of the future, however, tells another story. The future-oriented activity currently employed within platforms' marketing strategies is considerably more normalized and regressive than their techno-utopian accounts portray: it is a playground for absolute (decentralized) contingency, holding the prospect of distributed ownership.

Political theorist Nick Srnicek goes so far as saying that far from gesturing at a prosperous era of capital dynamism, the transition toward lean platforms in the aftermath of the 2008 crisis signals that capitalism is on the decline. The giant tech platforms were built on the back of decades of massive public financing, tax cuts, and long periods of unprofitability.[62] Even today, Amazon's delivery system is losing money on every order, but rapid and cheap delivery is the primary incentive for users of the platform to cross-subsidize other sectors. According to any capitalist common sense, however, this business model is not sustainable. The shift toward investment in building data centers, and providing cloud computing power issues from Silicon Valley's educated projection of its own survival. The accelerated growth of the digital sector in the past decade confirms alas that this projection is already here.

The celebratory discussions of big data take it as a marker of the exponential growth of capital and the creation of new possibilities to incentivize underdeveloped peripheries into its dynamism.[63] In these accounts, platforms' fiber-optic speed of communication is to facilitate intra-capitalist competition that, in principle, would translate into diversification and decentralization of enterprises. As Srnicek notes, the shift from the industries of goods to services in the past few decades is a major contributor to this oversight, where it has led some to believe that the era of ownership has come to an end.[64] In reality, network effects do indeed have a propensity for concentration of power and further consolidation of capital—and thus ownership—in their (data) centers.[65] Big tech, likewise, reveals

61 Ibid., 224.

62 Nick Srnicek, "Cloud Platforms," in *Platform Capitalism* (Cambridge: Polity, 2017). Srnicek describes this phenomenon as follows: "The monetary policies set by the US central bank in the aftermath of the Dot-com boom in the 1990s laid down the infrastructure for the forthcoming platformization. This trend continued into what followed the 2008 crisis, where the governments undertook massive amounts of public debt to rescue the private sector through colossal bailouts and emergency tax cuts. Most importantly governments dropped interest rates to record lows—a 10 fold decrease in the US and the UK between 2007 and 2008. The low interest rate conditions that carried on since the crash cultivated the emergence of the new tech industry. This was primarily implemented through the shift towards *quantitative easing*, an unorthodox monetary policy in which the central bank quickly increases the money supply through purchasing long-term securities and stimulating spending. Contrary to the traditional monetary policy—affecting short-term interest rates—quantitative easing lowers the long-term interest rates of assets. Under such conditions, those investors and VC funds that seek higher returns would gravitate towards more risky assets, namely, the 'unprofitable and unproven' tech companies. This, joined with the surge in tax evasion and cash hoarding, has driven the tech sector, left with a whopping amount of money, to invest in ever riskier ventures with the promise of a better yield."

63 Viktor Mayer-Schönberger, *Das Digital* (Berlin: Econ Verlag, 2017); Ramge and Mayer-Schönberger, *Reinventing Capitalism in the Age of Big Data*.

a similar tendency toward monopoly formation. This inclination toward centralization can be explained in terms of the recursive mode of valuation that takes place via platforms, that is, maximizing the value of users' contents, and, by the same token, appreciating their own value. As "temporary higher order aggregations," as design theorist Benjamin Bratton writes, platforms *are* what they *do*.[66] It is not only that they slow down competition, but that they change the coordinates of competition, away from a sole dependence on the difference between costs and prices, and toward a new field of data extraction and analysis.[67]

To further Feher's argument, Amazon not only heralds the monopolization of digital infrastructures, more and more indispensable from our livelihoods, but also of reputational infrastructures, as it continuously strives to top the chart of service providers worldwide. Platforms flatten the diversity of social organization into one based on the principle of competition, though construed via a complex algorithmic architecture. Marrying the essential constituents of the market—reputation and information—platforms bring together the logic of finance with the logic of data, consolidating their own formidable share in the twenty-first-century economy. By all accounts, the path forward has to involve the construction of public rating agencies and collectivized platforms with truly distributed ownership, governed by the people.

Speculative Socialism: What's after Imagination?

In his keynote at the annual conference of Digital Capitalism at the Friedrich Ebert foundation, a short while before the onset of the global pandemic, Morozov offered an unorthodox definition of neoliberalism. He stated that "neoliberalism is about preventing any form of non-market coordination from scaling up."[68] Coordination, to wit, can take place inside households, schools, local trust funds, and food banks, in ways that are not conditioned upon the market and the price system, but the instance in which any such social experiment poses a danger to capital accumulation—the moment these experiments aspire to *scale up*, as Morozov warns—they are quelled by neoliberalism. In this understanding, any attack on neoliberalism is necessarily a schema that relies on scaled organization.

As I claimed earlier, with the projects of socialist universalism in the twentieth century *scale* became a surrogate for *imagination*. As the battle over scale appeared more despondent, an era of imaginative malady prevailed. The much bemoaned lack of imagination could itself effectively be reframed as a symptom of the psychic dimension of planetarity. The pressing question for the Left, to extend Morozov's ideas, is not only how to imagine the new scale, but how to do so not forgoing the requirement of temporal property prior to planning of any kind. How to reckon with speculation, in lieu of imagination, of scalable and universal justice?

64 Srnicek, *Platform Capitalism*, Chapter 2, conclusion, paragraph 3.

65 See, for instance, Manuel Castells, *The Rise of the Network Society* (Hoboken: Wiley-Blackwell, 1996); and Saskia Sassen, *The Global City* (Princeton: Princeton University Press, 1991).

66 Bratton, *The Stack*, Chapter 3, section 9, paragraph 1.

67 Srnicek, *Platform Capitalism*, Chapter 3, section 1, paragraph 3.

68 Evgeny Morozov, "Competition and Cooperation in Digital Capitalism," talk Friedrich Ebert Stiftung, 2019, available at: https://www.youtube.com/watch?v=FKOKjDQ662A (accessed April 25, 2021).

Feher and Morozov put forth two parallel possibilities: as far as a subject position is concerned, Feher stresses the necessity of active participation in the rating economy of platforms to instantiate the mode of activism commensurate with our financialized age. The systemic analogue to Feher's rating subject is drawn by Morozov in his discussion of platforms as "feedback infrastructures." Digitized rating, operational in platforms like Uber and Amazon, implements a paradigm shift in the previous contractual system, traditionally formalizing prices and the rights of the sellers and buyers. Reputational feedback—as a diversion or upgrade to traditional law—allows price-setting activity to take place outside the formalizing mechanisms of either governmental regulations or worker union petitions, making it a function of opinion-formation that happens through the platforms' algorithmic frameworks. In this sense, reputational feedback enables speculative participation and distributed risk management, countering heterodox proclivity of law-based social coordination and risk aversion. As Morozov states, platformization is not solely about the replacement of prices with information—the cybernetic dream of a streamlined economy conjured in mega-platforms today—but shifts the grounds of socio-political practice as it exchanges law for the atomized consumer-based solutions based on competition and reputation—the logic of the market.[69] In short, for a socialist future on a par with the latest stage of capitalism, the ownership of "feedback data" cannot be the only ground for politics, but the "feedback infrastructures"—platforms as the marketplace of reputation and rating—are equally important sites for future political battles. For the Left, this project may look like "the ownership and operation of the means of producing feedback data."[70] This speculation-compatible future socialism would seek non-market applications of feedback infrastructures on the basis of solidarity instead of competition.

The cybertonians in southern Kiev would have never imagined the current technologies of computation. If anything, this daunting vision of the codified rating future, whether in its state-centralized modality or its privatized techno-positivist analog, signals the need to shift the terms of the Socialist Calculation debate toward a discussion of the reputation infrastructures. Sweeping all domains of social coordination and political traction, as Cambridge Analytica's complicity in the triumphant isolationist and neocolonial political campaigns around the world has magnified, digital reputation needs to be reassessed today with far greater attention. This is a conversation directed not merely at the sphere of technological innovation—as the prevailing sentiment has it—but also at the sphere of policy, empowering experimentation around solidarity-based frameworks that are extendible from the city unit to the nation-state, and ultimately planetary governance. Although our imagination may fall short of picturing it at this dystopian present, one pivotal infrastructural piece underlying our future commons is a scalable and speculative platform for all.

69 Morozov, "Digital Socialism?," 50.

70 Ibid., 52.

HOW TO BREAK FREE FROM THE GHOSTS OF THE FUTURE?

Cassandra Collective (Laura Cugusi, Chiara Di Leone, and Anastasiia Noga)

"World-building" is the single most important task in writing; it is the infrastructure of the narrative and if done unconvincingly, it can make it all crumble. Every successful screenwriter's advice on "how to build a world" of speculative fiction will point out the canonical five elements: character, want and need, plot, structure and conflict, but most importantly, the imperative "never start with a blank page."

World-building is sometimes looked at with disdain in design theory circles as an activity appropriate for art or speculative fiction, but entirely divorced from the rough realities of hard science or, say, engineering. In Cassandra's vocabulary, however, world-building is not limited by these interpretations and simply relates to all phenomena responsible for actualizing the future. Whether material or intangible, these processes bring the world into being. The real implications of the word "building" often fly over one's head, but as all matters of construction, it should be a reminder that world-building is necessarily structural.

"Radical imagination" is an often-abused label in design practices, intuitively connoting bold, groundbreaking creative ideas that "challenge" the familiar. However, these premises barely hold when working with future scenarios in the field of institutional climate governance, where some of the variables that compose the methodological framework refer to hard facts of science, mixed with qualitatively different, historically specific descriptions of transient and volatile human experiences.

World-building and radical imagination are not binaries, only subtle fluctuations within the same process, sometimes engulfing one another, sometimes going their separate ways. Radical imagination may lead to a staged rupture in the trajectory of movement, but not necessarily to the world being built. It can also set someone free so that new structures can appear in the now empty space of the present.

In the past fifty years, scenario planning techniques have been proliferating:

either simulating different versions of the same dystopia

or painting a frictionless fantasy defined by the absence of its opposite.

Not only is the future haunted by the specter of ossified forecasting techniques, but the practices of futuring themselves are haunted by binary models.

> *Time becomes human to the extent that it is articulated through a narrative mode, and narrative attains its full meaning when it becomes a condition of temporal existence.*
>
> *We are following therefore the destiny of a prefigured time that becomes a refigured time through the mediation of a configured time.*
>
> —Paul Ricoeur[1]

> *toxicity can occur in the opposite direction: by preserving what is internal to its self-referential modes of thought.*
>
> —Patricia Reed[2]

Scenario Planning: Defining the Problem Space

Scenario planning (SP) is a world-building technique, a literary genre, and a strategic analysis tool. It consists of writing quasi-fictional episodes—scenarios—about the future, as if the writer and the reader were already living in that specific future. Today, scenario planning is the most popular long-term strategic analysis method across the world. Born as a military technique aiming to rationalize the anxieties and endless stalemates of the Cold Wars, it was an instant hit in the planning and forecasting fields. SP started a field in its own right: of

1 Paul Ricoeur, *Time and narrative. Volume 1* (Chicago: University of Chicago Press, 1983), 3.

2 Patricia Reed, The Toxicity of Continuity," *Pages*, March 18, 2021, Version # 1, available at https://pagesmagazine.net/en/articles/the-toxicity-of-continuity (accessed August 31, 2021).

futurology, growing in popularity in the following decades, also and especially outside of the military.

In the 1970s, Pierre Whack, head of the French branch of Royal Dutch Shell and a former magazine editor with a bent for Eastern philosophy and mysticism, made SP rise to prominence after writing convincing scenarios about the future of the company. Some of them—especially their "energy crisis" scenarios—ended up being prophetic, resulting in steep advantages over Shell's competitors. They also served as positive advertisements for business intelligence and other applications of the old military forecasting techniques.

After Shell's successes, SP became pervasive in the corporate and bureaucratic world. It has been used without fail by governments, coastal guards, universities, charities, business schools, hospitals, management consulting firms, museums, cities, design schools, and climate panels in order to anticipate and manage unknown events—always located beyond the horizon of the known present. The field counts endless consultants, gurus, specialized science-fiction writers, service design firms and various fortune tellers, who distinguish themselves from tarot readers only because of their meagre intellectual honesty.

SP's language and constructs of time—through the development of worst-/best-case scenarios, pathways, variables, probability space, known unknowns—inform geopolitical shifts, including the management of energy sources, the financial crisis, tax reforms, and even artworks. It is no stretch to say that today SP is used in all organizations, one way or another. Despite its ubiquity, its specific conceits of time remain as widespread as they are unscrutinized and unquestioned. Scenario planning has become infrastructural, albeit not in a bricks-and-mortar sense, but in the sense of knowledge infrastructure as defined by Paul N. Edwards in his seminal book on climate sciences, *A Vast Machine* (2010).

In Edwards's words, knowledge infrastructures are "robust networks of people, artifacts, and institutions that generate, share, and maintain specific knowledge about the human and natural worlds."[3] Similar to physical infrastructures, they may appear elusive for "they are composed of many interacting, yet largely independent groups and institutions, each with its own imperatives, values, resources, revenue streams and temporal orientations."[4]

Like many things infrastructural, SP is invisible, ghostly, even. But how did it mature to the point of seamlessly pervading the fabric of knowledge infrastructures of the Future? How did we come to a point where all forms of institutional and organizational long-term thinking are caged into this paradigm?

It is hard and perhaps impossible to offer a clean, linear trajectory for the birth of SP. The canonical story names the RAND Corporation military strategist Herman Kahn as its father. Khan was a founder of the Hudson Institute and one of the preeminent futurists of the latter part of the twentieth century. He came to public notice with the publication of *On*

3 Paul N. Edwards, *A Vast Machine: Computer Models, Climate Data, and the Politics of Global Warming* (Cambridge, MA: MIT Press, 2010), 17.

4 Paul N. Edwards, "Knowledge infrastructures for the Anthropocene," *The Anthropocene Review*, Vol. 4, No. 1, 2017, 36.

Thermonuclear War (1960), in which he accomplished a goal for which he is remembered and was, at least partially, resented: holding up a mirror for the public to the American fears of a nuclear war by narrativizing its possible unfolding. Through his applications of statistical simulations—especially the Monte Carlo methods, borrowed from physics—he modeled various "scenarios" for nuclear military strikes and their, until then, unimaginable consequences.

But Kahn was better known for his performative and provocative communication style rather than his accurate calculations. According to his most important scholar, Sharon Gamiri-Tabrizi, model design was artisanal and subjective.[5] The process of setting up an efficient Monte Carlo problem depended on the intuition of the human analyst and model operator rather than on their ability to evaluate the formulae given. Khan certainly tried to maintain the "sleight-of-hand" impression of the process instead of backing up the methodology behind it. He routinely hired Hollywood screenwriters to craft convincing scenarios based on mathematical models and simulations that, if we look at them now, appear closer to cinematic props than the result of rigorous scientific research.

In *The Future of the World* (2018), Jenny Andersson contextualizes SP within the wider history of Futurism and shifts the focus toward computational advances and mathematical calculations underpinning science-fiction writing, which received less attention than Kahn's theatrical Hollywood-style writing of scenarios and preaching, but which were arguably infinitely more structural and influential to the field.[6] The key futurist at RAND, Andersson argues, was not the flamboyant Kahn, but the much more discreet mathematician Olaf Helmer, who developed the so-called Delphi Oracle—a compilation of experts' predictions, according to which we should have alien farming by now.

In his "World Futures" (2016) paper, John R. Williams emphasizes the "Orientalist" influences at the root of the paradigm shift in futurology that happened in the 1950s and 1960s, namely the transition from predicting the future to outlining *all* possible futures.[7] This new form of projecting forward—a mode he refers to as World Futures—posited the capitalizable, systematic immediacy of multiple, plausible worlds, all of which had to be understood as equally potential and nonexclusive. The influences that made this shift possible came from the East, Williams argues, or rather, the mental images of Eastern philosophies that Californian strategists, including Kahn, had in mind; a particular kind of futurity—of a plurality of worlds existing at the same time—in endless fractals and branching paths of possibilities.

All these accounts bring forth important aspects of the birth and rise and institutionalization of SP within the most powerful and influential organizations. Orientalism and Monte Carlo methods, technics and mysticism, simulations and science fiction have all contributed to the maturing of SP to the infrastructural and invisible levels at which it is applied today. But understanding the history of this technique is only useful to

5 Sharon Ghamari-Tabrizi, *The Worlds of Herman Kahn: The Intuitive Science of Thermonuclear War* (Cambridge, MA: Harvard University Press, 2005), 128.

6 See Jenny Andersson, *The Future of the World: Futurology, Futurists, and the Struggle for the Post-Cold War Imagination* (Oxford: Oxford University Press, 2018).

7 See R. John Williams, "World Futures," *Critical Inquiry*, Vol. 42, No. 3, spring 2016, 473–546.

us in order to explain how SP has infiltrated a very particular pocket of institutional thinking: the imagining, planning, (mis-) management, and dead-ends of climate-change policy making.

Ossified Infrastructure and Scenario Planning

Diagnostics of the future have become central to the way we talk about climate change. Almost all discourse is concerned with catastrophic consequences unless we act now, and implement some drastic policy measures that never seem to question the economics and premises of the systems they operate within. Instead, climate-change agreements and policies often seem to merely circumvent, if not continue to accommodate, the economic and social systems in place.

We feel a sense of hopelessness and stasis, inertia, and often real rage, yet we are unable to point the finger at where the bottlenecks to actual change really are. Some say they are located at the level of inept older generations—"those in power"—incompetent and "not wanting to listen to the scientists," as Greta Thunberg, rightly, points out in her emotionally charged speeches. Others point the finger at the difficulties of asking countries of the Global South to reduce their emission, just when they are starting to be able to provide a better quality of life to their citizens—international coordination is arguably always a zero-sum game.

The reasons for inaction and stasis when it comes to climate change are many. They are interconnected and incredibly complex, but a fundamental (and overlooked) root cause for the systemic inaction at governmental and supranational levels is the use of scenario planning techniques and their impact (or lack thereof) when it comes to preventing tragic, planetary events.

SP, as applied to climate-change policymaking, has generated a particular kind of self-perpetuating disaster through its reliance on a specific knowledge infrastructure, which depoliticizes language, incentivizes a politics of stasis, and reaffirms old and unhelpful economic models.

The Intergovernmental Panel for Climate Change (IPCC), for instance, produces reports about how socio-economic factors are likely to influence future emissions. In the panel's own words about its first report of this kind, "[i]n 1992 the IPCC released emission scenarios to be used for driving global circulation models to develop climate change scenarios. The so-called IS92 scenarios were pathbreaking. They were the first global scenarios to provide estimates for the full suite of greenhouse gases."[8] In reality, these IS92 scenarios were a far cry from pathbreaking; they assume that socio-economic paths are based on "business as usual" analysis and do not consider the potential effects of different climate policies.

This sense of acceptance of the status quo and relinquishment of the potential for change is further testified by the reports' writing style. In IPCC reports, the language is appropriately corporate and diplomatically bland. Glaciers don't melt, they

8 See Nebojsa Nakicenovic and Rob Swart (eds.) *Emissions Scenarios* (Cambridge: Cambridge University Press, 2000).

"continue their widespread retreat," as the example from 2000 states. They write their own questions and answer them too: "This Report reinforces our understanding that the main driving forces of future greenhouse gas trajectories will continue to be demographic change, social and economic development, and the rate and direction of technological change."[9] Among the hundreds of different scenarios and pathways produced by the IPCC over decades, no signs of fundamental changes in economic and finance models, extraction strategies, and taxation regimes are to be found—not in writing, and certainly not in practice.

The ways in which SP makes sense of the future, models it, sketches its possible unfolding is a very particular one: it fosters passivity, fear and stasis, while also creating a veneer of multiplicity—a false sense of choices, possibilities, agencies, and the familiar relief that comes with making grandiose-sounding plans that do not need to be implemented. Of all the paradoxes to emerge in the last few decades, none is as consequential—and, alas, as tragically overlooked—as the Paradox of the Future(s). Why is it that the more we accept the idea of futures, in the plural, the more resigned we are to the inevitability of a singular future—that of climate collapse?

Beyond the Paradoxes

The rigidity of outdated methods of scenario planning contrasts with emerging attempts at speculation in design and architecture, which have been appropriating artistic license to push the boundaries of the possible in creative and conceptual practices. Speculative design leverages the luxury of being afforded exceptional freedom to outline a vision that starts with an evocative abstract sketch and eventually manifests in three-dimensional form in physical, or increasingly in virtual space. In other words, this radical imagination that promises total freedom without consequences as traditionally afforded to architects and designers clashes with the rigidity of the material conditions as the logical limits of the possible. As a result, most recently, practice is becoming almost exclusively speculative without even aspiring at infrastructural solidity and functionality—see the proliferation of SP workshops.

In a variety of discursive practices in architecture, design, politics, and visual culture, the borders of the possible are interpreted through distinct subjectivities and modalities of perception aligned to cultural specificities. They are articulated through narratives encompassing these disciplines and their own particular knowledge infrastructures, framing their scope of action. They are haunted by bottomless archives of models, simulations, databases, reports, projections, and exponentially accumulating data. These, in turn, generate the demand for larger and hungrier data servers collecting invaluable information, the vast majority of which is destined to decay or remain perpetually unread. Contemporary monsters are to be found in the uncertainties hiding among this abundance of data—like

9 Ibid., 5.

those needed to produce IPCC reports—rather than beyond the borders of the existing map.

Knowledge infrastructures that emerge when the rigorous study of a phenomenon combines data with imagination still hold a degree of potential for the field of institutionalized climate futurology—the potential that doesn't seem to be explored yet, judging by the pervasiveness and rigidity of SP. Simulation and data visualization as aesthetic practices can offer unexpected insights in the framing of the problem space, like the experimental scientific research in VR that shows significant progress in the analysis of biological processes and diseases.[10] Rather than replicate natural phenomena or aspire at reaching verisimilitude, augmented vision techniques provide additional angles and vantage points for the observation of a problem.

That said, aesthetic practices are often culturally positioned as if they are uniquely suited for dealing with imagination and experimental methodologies only. This assumption often implicitly goes hand in hand with a distrust in science as the domain of rigid, inherited modes of thinking and inquiry. In these assumptions, science cannot be associated with profound epistemological reconsiderations and is only useful as source material for artists and designers to take as ground zero and radically reimagine. The productive kind of speculation is relegated to the field of artistic production. Even if science is not explicitly attacked as a form of unproductive speculation, its omission from these discussions is still unhelpful. That is not to mention the cases in which scientific inquiry becomes tainted by its value for corporate R&D departments, the culture of Silicon Valley innovation and, therefore, capital. Needless to say, science has always been as fit for radical imagination and re-imagination, as well as philosophical paradigm shifts, as the art and design world. When this is written down it is painfully obvious, and yet in the popular imagination artistic practices are heroically responsible for imagining radical possibilities of the future, while science can barely keep up with making sense of the present.

It was the field of quantum physics that opened up an epistemological question, complicating the notion of the binary—like the (false) one of art and science. In quantum physics experiments, the spectrum of high and low energy is equally important, but it is not possible to collect more data for low energy, so the relevant information needs to be gathered in another way. There is no evidence of the existence of dark matter, but there is a ghostly presence, a trace for which we haven't found a way of defining yet, and which could dismantle the tools with which we see the world, the future, and how we plan for it. Success in this field of research means finding a new flaw in our ways of understanding. As Carlo Rovelli illustrates "Science is not clean, especially on the boundary between what we know and we don't know [...] the idea of certainty is one of the most devastating and useless ideas ever produced in the history of culture."[11] Similarly, as Tamara Vázquez Schröder, physics

10 Theia, a virtual reality cancer lab, is an example of the application of VR that made such discoveries possible. These tools were developed in the field of artistic expression, such as the gaming and entertainment industries, yet they are increasingly applied in industrial design, medicine, health care, and education. See https://www.biorxiv.org/content/10.1101/2021.06.28.448342v1 (accessed September 2, 2021).

11 Carlo Rovelli, interview in *Tank Magazine*, issue 86, February 11, 2021, available at https://tankmagazine.com/issue-86/talk/carlo-rovelli (accessed September 2, 2021).

researcher working on the ATLAS experiment for the LHC (Large Hadron Collider), points out, it is more the experiment rather than the theory that guides us through the next step in terms of the exploration of physics. She underlines that

> [t]he history of physics, in particular particle physics, proves that it has always been necessary to take a fresh look, to climb a tree and scan the horizon, to live in the treetops like Italo Calvino's Baron in the Trees, in order to discover the fundamental structure of a reality that is much more universal that the one that surrounds us here and now.[12]

The standard scientific model itself is entering a crisis, as discoveries in quantum physics and mathematics are highlighting that the model based on observation and evidence is limited by default. Blind spots in maps and data sets require maximum creativity and intuition—unlike the hygienic separation of these two areas seems to suggest. In absence of instructions on where to look, technology can assist in translating concepts and meaning that are beyond or between the senses. Art practices reveal modes of looking beyond and between and which can be systematized and applied as rigorous research methodologies.

It is almost as if the Paradox of the Future(s), as it has become manifest in the field of institutional climate strategy, stems exactly from the fact that SP has over time managed to embrace the worst of both worlds. In order to justify its own legitimacy, it has often served arbitrary and randomized choices under the veneer of scientific methodology. Because the results of SP are produced in a seemingly structured manner—like scenarios that are based on methodically combining a limited set of variables chosen to perpetuate the status quo in the first place—it is rational enough to be fit for strategy development and policymaking.

On the other hand, SP's embrace of subjective creativity—albeit only in its limited interpretation—allowed it to fit very well into the established mode of neoliberal knowledge production. Scenario planning as a narrative technique doesn't always revolve around first-person narration—in fact, as a rule it doesn't, it relies on the much more "neutral" eagle-eye perspective of the third person singular. But it is impossible to think of its history without the centering of a protagonist and a subjectivity inherently tied to personhood, since this has been key to SP's institutionalization.

As the short article "A Primer on Futures Studies, Foresight and the Use of Scenarios" states,

> Scenarios are a valuable part of foresight work ... and need to be seen within the context of an on-going, long-term, "closed-loop" organisational foresight process. With this understanding of their place in foresight work, they are a useful tool for generating *shared*

12 Tamara Vázquez Schröder, "The Elementary Bestiary," CCCBLAB, May 15, 2013, available at https://lab.cccb.org/en/the-elementary-bestiary/ (accessed September 2, 2021).

forward views, helping to align strategic action across an organisation *on its journey into the future*.[13]

What this suggests is that sometimes scenarios are turned into narratives, often without specific individuals in mind—such as the members or employees of an organization that is using SP to develop a strategy—but with an institution as a presumed individual. The institution assumes the characteristics of personhood—a collating of heroes within one hero's journey.

In other SP workshops, participants are explicitly asked to use their first-person perspective when imagining all possible futures. If the goal is to test the validity of a concept, for example a new technology, participants are asked to speculate how their individual life would be changed if that technology were widespread. At other times, creativity extends to the realm of actual aesthetics, for example by questions such as "tell us what you see and feel in that imagined future: textures, sounds, images, things, etc." Scenarios are then abstracted from these exercises to map a strategic pathway for an institution—which are mostly infrastructural, dispersed entities. For these entities, a path forward would practically mean a sequence of decision-making protocols and resulting decisions made by a very small group of executives. What scenarios contribute to the process, is the anthropomorphization of these entities within the narrative as elements that have autonomous agency to walk those routes, when, in fact, this is never the case.

The culmination of this logic lies in the fact that the subjectivization of these infrastructural entities is allegedly undertaken in order to explore radically different possibilities of their future. However, in SP, radical speculation rarely overcomes the logic of individualized creativity, subjective expression, and individual choice. The seemingly "structural" and "systemic" approach in method and world-building exercises gives credibility to the idea of radical imagination—which cannot overcome the limits of privileged personhood.

The combination of the worst of two worlds is what allows SP to be institutionalized into a formal practice. Its roots in systems thinking turn it into a suitable technology for "rationalized" governance and bureaucracy, while narrativized imagination is what allows it to be non-committal. Presenting corporations—like strategy scenario planning workshops do—or societies—like the IPCC reports do—as unified entities with agency absolves the decision-makers responsible for bringing the world into being from that very responsibility.

These flickering versions of unrealized futures haunt our present in the company of two other great spectral presences: the ghostly knowledge infrastructure that produced them itself, and the shadowy agencies that shape the world as they see fit but are hard to pinpoint. As a result, scenario planning has evolved into a machine aptly fit to produce ghosts, and ghosts only—the possible versions of the future that will remain imagined and never constructed.

13 Joseph Voros, "A Primer on Futures Studies, Foresight and the Use of Scenarios," *Prospect: The Foresight Bulletin*, No. 6, December 2001. Emphasis added by authors.

Coda: COP26, Glasgow, Scotland, UK, November 2021

We walk along a recently built corridor. We are in Glasgow, but we could be anywhere.

The hashtags #climateactionnow printed on a polyester wall, the non-place of the conference/art fair makeshift architecture with Old World ventriloquists stomping over it: the junglecore sans-serif logo with the usual images of polar bears and melting glaciers. Lady Gaga gives a speech this year, last time it was Enrique Iglesias's turn.

The first workshop is inspired by The Future board game, a wargame designed to teach US defense professionals how different strategies could affect key planning factors at the intersection of force development, force management, force posture, and force employment. Everyone is in a good mood. We win. We take pictures for the press. It does not matter.

After the session, we move to the main conference hall for the plenary session, a swarm of prime ministers coming to congratulate us on our game victory, like a shoal of small, aged fish. We shake hands, Greta is there too.

I don't want to be here, none of us does. The sadness of seeing how things really are at the top, how brittle and superficial "those in power," is a weight that's too much to bear. I would prefer to believe the worst of conspiracy theories in which the master puppeteers who rule the world do that out of principle, even an evil and destructive one—here is all a vanity, a choreography, a vacuous performance.

Scenes oscillate between the makeshift and the ossified: the prefabricated architecture of international climate summits, where testimonials of electoral consensus unironically pontificate about resilience and sustainability.

Everyone eats their vegetarian sham lunch, the air is soporific. I take out my notebook and write:

> *In IPCC meetings the starkest contrast between different temporalities is staged: the modes of futurity of the non-place corporate aesthetics of repeatable and formulaic interiors, populated by the archaic ideologies of national sovereignty. In this setting, ghosts of both past and future show up to the party. The ones from the past wear suits and champion flags, shake hands and mentally rehearse their speeches. The ones from the future hide more gracefully in the big, pompous plans—and there are many more of them.*

ARCHITECTURE IS OBSOLETE: FINANCIALIZATION NOSTALGIA AND REAL ESTATE POWER

Adham Selim

New Cairo is evidenced fiction: it is not real (yet), but its traces in the future are already visible.[1] Keller Easterling describes the combined effect of unfolding relationships in complex infrastructural systems as a *disposition*—something that often escapes detection or explanation.[2] New Cairo is such a disposition, an effect taking place between a present that cannot be fully described yet, and a future whose impact can already be imagined. It is an oasis, a locus for an exceptional enterprise of city-making, one that is nevertheless often copied elsewhere. Its illusory exceptionality is also part of how it works. The redundant diction of exceptionality that seemed hitherto to counterweigh the city's iconographic deficit, actually turns out to complement a swinging back and forth between its controversially unique market offering and financializable modularity of assets—a continuous coupling and decoupling of architectural simulacrum and "finance-power."[3]

New Cairo is, in fact, not new; its long pedigree stretches from the Renaissance bank states of Italy all the way down to Dubai and Shenzhen. What is relatively new, however, is its outsized capacity to render the city as an investment strategy, where real estate is the sole manifestation of power at both physical and systemic levels. It celebrates the gradual re-emergence of the "city" in globalized design, distribution, and absorption of a variety of forms of finance capital after the global financial crisis.[4] It is the world capital of what Samuel Stein calls the "real estate state," a political formation in which real estate capital has inordinate influence over urban form and power.[5] In that sense, it is stale, empty, and haunted by a pervasive

1 "New Cairo" must not be confused with the "New Administrative Capital" of Egypt currently under construction. In fact, the latter is never referred to as New Cairo. Rather the term refers to a compounded phenomenon at the intersection of the latest iteration of the new cities scheme in Egypt and the increasing financialization of housing in the Global South over the last decade. Since 1976, and in close conjunction with the liberalization of its economy, Egypt has built 27 new cities, a number that according to Egypt's New Urban Communities Authority (NUCA) should have reached a total of 44 by 2017 if it were not for the political turmoil following 2011. The seemingly never-ending supply of new cities, alongside massive infrastructure projects over the last few decades turned construction, real estate, and mortgage into Egypt's favorite businesses, absorbing about half of Egypt's labor power and about one third of its total spending. In relative terms, Egypt's construction market comes only slightly second after the UAEs, silently posing as both a template and testing ground for what post-Dubai urbanism could be. This construction surge coincides locally with a regulatory framework that not only grants state-owned holding companies a monopoly over half of the settled land in the country, but also extreme speculative powers over asset pricing. On a global scale it also echoes the rising importance of housing-generated financial instruments in extending the terrain of finance capital into highly unregulated markets of the Global South. See Saskia Sassen, "Expanding the Terrain for Global Capital: When Local Housing Becomes an Electronic Instrument," in *Subprime Cities: The Political Economy of Mortgage Markets*, edited by Manuel Aalbers (Oxford: Wiley-Blackwell, 2012), 74–96; and Amr Adly, *Cleft Capitalism: The Social Origins of Failed Market Making in Egypt* (Stanford: Stanford University Press, 2020), 152–76.

2 Keller Easterling, *Extrastatecraft: The Power of Infrastructure Space* (Brooklyn: Verso, 2014), 112.

lack of urgency. However, like a Ballardian fiction, New Cairo's dullness is what keeps things interesting. It is mostly conceived by middle management as a systemic recipe for urbanism on Excel, and it develops as an agnostic side effect of a complex array of financial interventions and construction management ploys. Contrary to the belief that such a brand of cities stands for absolute hegemony over the production of urban form born out of a single vision, authority here convenes liberty to act upon exception: a material "metaverse" that gives a wide range of players—military despots, Arab royals, Chinese construction tycoons, Russian oligarchs, overseas venture capitalists, among others—endless trials and errors for sourcing, moving, and transforming matter and capital.

Topology

New Cairo is designed, if also by accident, in episodic patches connected with super highways that sharply distance development from the surrounding otherness—from the chaos that is everything else. Frictionless mobility is ensured by a network of riot-proof tunnels and flyovers straddling different security zones. By infringement on scale, it is vast, yet so sparse that next to it previous urban substance is sometimes naturalized as landscapes of exposed red brick and concrete shrouded in traffic smog. Unlike other cities, where a duality of center-periphery intensities modulates where, when, and how space is capitalized and recapitalized—a process otherwise known as gentrification—New Cairo's network topology suggests more connectivity without center or periphery. It shows metropolitan activity continuously migrating toward a ring road, where maximum exchange takes place. It makes way for a thinning historical core in the middle, something that, on a real estate metric, renders a non-financializable blob begging to be broken up and scattered.

New Cairo only gets bigger, and when the maximum holding capacity of its ring road is reached, the ring widens in diameter and another ring road is added. New, longer flyovers and wider tunnels generate low pressure zones that absorb more slums. As a result, New Cairo constantly foams its countryside outward, inseminating its periphery with enclaves mimicking former downtowns. Asset value is maximized by blowing the density of former centers into spongy real estate matter of minimum weight per unit volume, to a point at which the oversized periphery-turned-center becomes weightless. New Cairo's tragedy is caught in loops of revivalism that affirm the center by actively eradicating it.

Real Estate Power

To understand how New Cairo works, we have to consider real estate first. Real estate is slow, it takes a relatively long time to materialize. However, its capitalization is instant, and sometimes even happens irrespective of whether the underlying

3 An extended discussion of the term "finance-power" can be found in Suhail Malik, "The Ontology of Finance: Price, Power, and the Arkhéderivative," in *Collapse, Volume VIII*, "Casino Real," edited by Robin Mackay (Falmouth: Urbanomic, 2014), 637.

4 Jeroen Klink, *Metropolis, Money and Markets: Brazilian Urban Financialization in Time of Reemerging Global Finance* (London: Routledge, 2020), 55.

5 An extended definition of the "real estate state" is found in Samuel Stein, *Capital City: Gentrification and the Real Estate State* (London: Verso, 2019), 5–45.

asset—the actual property—exists.[6] It builds on the promissory discrepancy of an asset value in the future in an attempt to make profits against its value in the present. While not impossible to imagine, such discrepancy between "real" and future prices is a nuisance to economists. From a neoclassical perspective, this discrepancy, particularly in extreme market swings, cannot be rationally measured or explained—unless maybe in units of speculators' greed or fear. This is perhaps why it is commonly rendered as an aberration. On the Marxian side, this aberration is often explained by real estate's relationship to the production of value. Simply put, real estate profit hails from a non-produced asset that has no fundamental price: land, and as such real estate is considered a "fictitious" commodity that is expected to defy any rational pricing system.[7] Much like finance capital, real estate thus follows what Michel Aglietta describes as a logic of momentum. It moves, by its very nature, in erratic cycles of booms and busts.[8]

Upon closer examination, however, the discrepancy between capitalization and real assets appears to be the norm rather than the aberration. Based on his reading of Jonathan Nitzan and Shimshom Bichler's seminal work *Capital as Power* (2009), Suhail Malik explains:

> contrary to how Marxian and Neoclassical doctrines determine prices to be set by inter-firm rivalry given exogenous conditions (such as supply-demand, labor and capital costs, consumption, etc.), such that the supposed priority of the latter casts finance capital as parasitical, supplementary, or "fictitious," according to the power theory of price, financially-set prices are the *primary* elements for the dynamic organization of capital-power.[9]

Nitzan and Bichler note that major market players often begin with a long-term target rate of profit, and henceforth calculate the markup price backward. Furthermore, they add that "the markup [is] not simply a vague social convention, but a measure of power."[10] According to them "the primary line of causality runs not from [real] production to [fictitious] distribution, but from [fictitious] distribution to [real] production."[11] In other words, the hierarchy of reality and fiction observed above, is in fact reversed, the "fictitious" future price is the source rather than a derivative of the "real" present price and power.

This is particularly reinforced by the very nature of real estate markets. What constitutes the distinction in our case is the relatively long duration a construction takes to materialize. Combined with inelastic supply on the one hand—slow responsiveness of the construction industry to increases in asset prices—and positively elastic demand on the other—rising asset prices induced by an air of profitability driving an accelerating demand—the material slowness of real estate establishes an interesting condition for political power.

6 David Harvey, *Rebel Cities: From the Right to the City to the Urban Revolution* (London: Verso, 2019), 45–49.

7 Recent studies criticize this as a false generalization, originating from a feudal agricultural order in which productive (peasants and artisans) and unproductive activities (nobility and merchants) were fairly clear-cut. See Jonathan Nitzan and Shimshom Bichler, *Capital as Power: A Study of Order and Creorder* (London: Routledge, 2009), 112–15.

8 Michel Aglietta, *Money: 5,000 Years of Debt and Power* (London: Verso, 2020), 3.

9 Malik, "The Ontology of Finance," 655–56.

10 Nitzan and Bichler, *Capital as Power*, 242.

11 Ibid., 221.

Whereas real estate supply is virtually independent of momentary price increases over the course of a given contractual term, demand builds up on the bouts of these increases, meaning that price-setting mechanisms in real estate are tied only on one end—demand—which is in this case subsumed by supply. Ownership of real estate is therefore not ownership of its production inasmuch as it is of price-setting agency as political power. New Cairo is not only the source of the "underlying"—commodities whose value is the base for derivative assets traded on the market—rather, and more importantly, a structural condition of power.

Real Estate Time

The only bound to real estate power is the finitude of city's buildable topology and the technological capability to stack this topology vertically in the form of floor plates. Growth is not just the *modus operandi* of New Cairo, rather it is its *raison d'être*. This continuous growth implies that at some point in the future users of the city will never be able to reckon with a possible past. Amnesia is the only possible form of ideology here—it forges into being a subject whose field of experience is real estate time.[12]

Real estate time is New Cairo's internal time. In the same way that its artificial microclimate is divided into zones, time in New Cairo is divided into different time zones based on the complexity of where stocks from each zone are traded. Each zone runs to its own tempo, always premediating an affectivity of anticipation at crossings. Real estate time is inseparable from real estate power; if anything, it is the cause for, rather than the effect of New Cairo's design of real estate power.[13] Instead of organizing the city as a techno-capitalist system so that it creates new perception of time, New Cairo constantly rearranges time, giving rise to emergent forms of capital-power.

Real estate time subordinates the present and the past in favor of the future. As a result, buildings become dumping sites for fainting memories, an archive of digitally stretched, scaled, and skewed slices of places and times. Buildings in New Cairo are designed as if they were part of an algorithmic collage, nurtured by the continuous browsing and editing of countless CAD blocks, stored and rated on the cloud in order of their market performance.

In New Cairo, architecture is obsolete and the city is absolved of the guilt of apathy. Floors, walls, roofs, stairs, doors, windows, how people dine, go shopping or socialize, are all re-enactments of performances whose facticity is not entirely certain. Nostalgia here is not about affinity to more historical forms, but sentimentality for the future. In this reproductive time warp, everything becomes an imitation of itself. Yet the true horror does not lie in the gap incurred in consuming the future as present, rather it resides in the inexorable authority over futurity epitomized by the very prefix "New." Jumping back to *Capital as Power*, Nitzan and Bichler describe this authority

12 The concept of real estate time derives from Armen Avanessian and Suhail Malik's Speculative Time Complex. See Armen Avanessian and Suhail Malik, "The Time-Complex. Postcontemporary," *Fear of Content*, Berlin Biennale 9, 2016, http://bb9.berlinbiennale.de/the-time-complex-postcontemporary/ (accessed April 24, 2021).

13 Although repeated references to "real estate time" in this text draw heavily on Malik and Avanessian's Speculative Time Complex, this particular modeling of a techno-social system in reciprocal relationship with a specific conception of time is indebted to Bernard Stiegler's extensive work on the subject: "specificity of modern technics resides, in essential part, in the speed of its evolution, which has led us to the conjugation of the question of technics with the question of time [...] having come full circle in our investigation of technical evolution, that is, of technics in time, the possibility will arise that technics, far from being merely in time, properly constitutes time." Bernard Stiegler, *Technics and Time, 1: The Fault of Epimetheus* (Stanford: Stanford University Press, 1998), 21–27.

in terms of capital-power as "creorder"—a paradoxical dynamic *creation* of a static *order*. "The form of the process is the quantitative redistribution of ownership, its content the qualitative transformation of power relations. The transformative feature is crucial because it means novelty."[14] This novelty is predicated on nothing but power: "Power means the ability to impose order, and imposition presupposes resistance [...] And since to overcome resistance is to create a new order, the very presence of power spells a built-in pressure for change."[15]

Sabotage

Rather than the canonical image of a class struggle between those who own capital and those who do not, Nitzan and Bichler's formulation of strife for power creorder runs along the lines of intra-capitalist rivalry. They suggest a model in which those accumulating capital are locked in a death race of *differential accumulation*—not to maximize profits, but to "beat the average." Yet, exerting a new order against the *average* invites an additional operator: *sabotage*. According to Nitzan and Bichler, sabotage has a double aim: first, it raises one's own earnings, while second, cutting the rest who make up the benchmark.[16]

New Cairo propagates sabotage on two scales—systemic and infrastructural. On the systemic scale, composing a hypothetical average portfolio to gauge asset returns requires elaborate parameters and metrics to price the trade-off between risks and returns. In other words, in order to beat the average, one has to define it first. The absence of sufficiently deep and consolidated capital markets, as is the case with New Cairo—and with cities in the Global South more generally—renders the *average* untenable. This is usually mitigated by sovereign interventions such as favorable regulatory frameworks, subsidies, and tax incentives to attract investment. While their overall effect is market enabling, these interventions in fact absorb risk and propagate it as systemic sabotage.[17] New Cairo is both instrument and medium for the continuous propagation of sabotage through maintaining an active involvement in the false valuation of risk. Often concealing existing patterns of market vulnerability, especially in times of crises, involves channeling systemic sabotage to the municipal level in the form of austerity. If anything, said market enabling interventions feed off public funding roll-backs, tax increases, and massive privatization of infrastructure, among others.

Like a voracious alien life-form, New Cairo's physical infrastructure forms an endless network of ventures developed out of precarious dependence on centralized resource extraction and distribution. It does not necessarily imply enabling those who live in the city, inasmuch as disabling others who do not. Like all capital-power systems, capital here is rather necessarily counterproductive. But infrastructural sabotage is not limited to this. In her influential book *Extrastatecraft: The Power of Infrastructure Space* (2014), Keller Easterling examines the effects of

14 Nitzan and Bichler, *Capital as Power*, 325.

15 Ibid., 305.

16 Ibid., 315

17 For example: "rescue operations that emerged after the global financial meltdown have, by and large, transformed the subprime crisis into a widely disseminated regime of fiscal crisis, accompanied by calls for fiscal austerity and state roll-back. This subsequent rescaling of crises and austerity has increasingly targeted cities." See Klink, *Metropolis, Money and Markets*, 57–62.

large-scale spatial organizations and infrastructure projects, as both site and instrument for producing political power. According to Easterling, infrastructures create

> the need for an administrative authority comparable to that of the state, and they continue to require direction from new constellations of international, intergovernmental, and nongovernmental players. As a site of multiple, overlapping, or nested forms of sovereignty, where domestic and transnational jurisdictions collide, infrastructure space becomes a medium of what might be called extrastatecraft—a portmanteau describing the often undisclosed activities outside of, in addition to, and sometimes even in partnership with statecraft.[18]

If New Cairo's infrastructure is a logical, spatial, and jurisdictional exception, its infrastructural sabotage must then circumscribe state sovereignty itself.

Risk Society

At user level, the city's design focuses on the statistical optimization of risk. As spatialized power, New Cairo relays the societal through continuous statistical dividualization. It continuously extracts and parses large amounts of data to build information models of everything—every user, asset, property, etc. Since risk is the measurable probability of an occurrence, these models need not be accurate, but they always need to be measurable and comprehensive. The continuous calibration of society forges and maintains a society of transitory anonymity akin to the populations of highways, parking lots, and airport terminals that thrives on the rapid turnover of acquaintances. This gives rise to a new social type: cool, impervious to psychological pressure and with minimal needs for privacy. As Randy Martin observes:

> Risk awareness engenders a kind of complacency [...] Routinization of risk makes a particular historical and economic arrangement appear to be natural [... It] makes common sense out of what was hitherto nonsensical. Which matters appear dangerous and which should be ignored have been part of consensus arrangements in society.[19]

To beat the average, however, is to win over the economy, suggests a caution with norms, distrust in conventional wisdom, and an aversion of common sense. When you play against the game itself, no one but yourself is responsible for a safety net. This is the reason why risk can also be a register of extreme pleasure, transcendence, and self-actualization. For the new social breed, compulsive skepticism and embrace of fatality go hand in hand. When you play at life, euphoria and paranoia tend to be one and the same thing. New Cairo removes the

18 Easterling, *Extrastatecraft*, 1.
19 Randy Martin, *Financialization of Daily Life* (Philadelphia: Temple University Press, 2002), 104–07.

need to repress or caution risk takers. It often leaves them free to explore whatever deviant impulses they may entertain. It is precisely in these areas that the most interesting social effects of New Cairo take place. Secured by the distance as though they are in the wilderness, users of New Cairo embody the final and total assimilation of finance power order as *nature*.

RESTAGING INFRASTRUCTURAL IMAGES THAT MAKE THE WORLD: RECONFIGURING SCALE

Tom Clark

Mnemiopsis leidyi or "comb jellies" are walnut-shaped ctenophores; they are similar to jellyfish, but stingless, moving by pulsing cilia along their length. They have also secured "a slot on the International Union for Conservation of Nature (IUCN) list of 100 World's Worst" invaders.[1] Scientists' best guess is that they arrived on ships traveling west into the Black Sea at the beginning of the 1980s—released when the contents of the cargo ships' ballast tanks they'd been traveling in was emptied at port.[2] Comb jellies are native to the coastal waters of the North and South American continents. They cause relatively little harm in these native environments, being preyed on by several species of fish.[3] But in a dynamic familiar to many of the impacts of standardized and global infrastructure systems, the introduction of this quickly reproducing and adaptable species in many regions around the Mediterranean set off massive ecosystem shifts.[4] The effect of the arrival of *M. leidyi* is two-fold. Able to capitalize on other environmental changes occurring after its introduction—such as excessive nutrient levels allowing the sea to support more biomass (or "eutrophication"[5]), warm summers and mild winter temperatures,[6] as well as consuming the zooplankton many fish rely upon for food as well as the eggs of plankton-feeding fish such as anchovies (which themselves had become the top predator after previous fish species depletions in the 1960s)—the comb jellies exert a profound and irreversible "influence on the functioning of marine ecosystems." In the Black Sea, this precipitated a "major [fish] stock collapse" from the end of the 1990s, with ecosystems only very slowly and only partially recovering since.

This is just one account of the consequences of Anthropocene infrastructural imaginaries, their instituting and unfold-

1 Bell Galil, Nurit Kress, and Tamara Shiganova, "First Record of Mnemiopsis Leidyi A. Agassiz, 1865 (Ctenophora; Lobata; Mnemiidae) off the Mediterranean Coast of Israel," *Aquatic Invasions*, Vol. 4, No. 2, January 2009, 357, DOI:10.3391/ai.2009.4.2.8.

2 See Tamara A. Shiganova et al., "Population development of the invader ctenophore Mnemiopsis leidyi in the Black Sea and other seas of the Mediterranean basin," *Marine Biology*, Vol. 139, No. 3, 2001, 431–45, DOI:10.1007/s002270100554.

3 Bettina Fach, Baris Salihoglu, and Temel Oğuz, "Alien species can cause severe disturbance," 2021, available at https://feralatlas.supdigital.org/poster/the-invasion-of-alien-species-can-cause-severe-disturbance-and-regime-shifts-to-ecosystems (accessed September 13, 2021); H. Mianzan, N. Marí, B. Prenski, and F. Sanchez, "Fish predation on neritic ctenophores from the Argentine continental shelf: a neglected food resource," *Fisheries Research*, Vol. 27, Nos. 1–3, 1996, 69–79, https://doi.org/10.1016/0165-7836(95)00459-9.

4 The vectors of invasion are quite complex, with transportation between the Black Sea and the Mediterranean Sea—a body of water that is particularly susceptible to ship-transported bio-invasions: with one fifth of the alien species recorded in the Mediterranean having been introduced by vessels. See Galil, Kress and Shiganova, "First Record," 358.

5 "Eutrophication" makes the system vulnerable to exploitation by species able to dominate through additional feeding. See Fach, Salihoglu, and Oğuz, "Alien Species."

6 Shiganova et al., "Population development of the invader," 431.

ing in various locations told in and by *Feral Atlas: The More-Than-Human Anthropocene*.[7] A punctuation point in a five-year research and curatorial exploration of how "ecologies have been radically transformed by imperial and industrial infrastructure projects," *Feral Atlas* is an online platform and conceptual model of the Anthropocene. Not a story of infrastructural success, but of a 500-year period of "ecological-transformation projects of long-distance conquest, governance, and investment for the accumulation of wealth," the platform explores how the human-made infrastructures of the Anthropocene "have unleashed a set of catastrophic *feral effects* that endanger life at a planetary scale." It comprises seventy-nine case studies in which these "feral effects" are located on one of four scenes of human and more-than-human entanglement represented in the platform's maps.

The platform describes the assemblages that engender the feral effects it explores through the coming together of three key dynamics. The first of these is a series of consequential infrastructure projects or imaginaries that the Anthropocene has instituted or *detonated*, which carry the labels "Empire," "Invasion," "Capital," and "Acceleration." These imaginaries are made manifest through a second axis of so-called "tippers"—repeatable modes of state-change mediated by world-forming infrastructures such as "GRID"(s) of standardization and "ecological simplification,"[8] how "CROWDS" pack together population or object density to "further political, economic, or scientific programs,"[9] or the "SMOOTH"(ing) and "SPEEDING" up of temporal and spatial rhythms. The third axis is defined by the qualities of these feral effects as they emerge from the ruins, edges, unintended consequences of planetary infrastructure projects, and local ecologies or social relations that infrastructural tippers enact. Such labels as "Accelerated by Climate Change," "Thrives with the Plantation Conditions," or in the case of the comb jellies, "Industrial Stowaways," offer a final axis used to conceptualize the more-than-human Anthropocene summarized as "feral qualities."

Each of these axes serves to conceptualize specific layers of Anthropocene effect in a model of infrastructural mediation and construction, and acts as one of multiple, non-hierarchical entry points through which these case studies are organized and accessed on the platform. Firstly, through the interaction of these axes, infrastructure acts as much to produce uncertainty as it does as a locus for world-making. Shipping, in the example I started this essay with, "TAKE"(s) products from one place to another place, but also carries other cargo which is deposited or extracted by it—such as "INVASIVE" species being moved by accident, rendering an ecosystem degraded. Secondly, they are brought together as means of navigating its platform and conceptual frame; a platform user can follow, compare, and explore feral entities according to the category of detonation, tipper, or feral quality, or vice versa. The intersection of these axes enables a description of the complexity of the

7 Anna L. Tsing, Jennifer Deger, Alder Keleman Saxena, and Feifei Zhou, *Feral Atlas*, 2021, available at http://feralatlas.org/ (accessed September 19, 2021).

8 See https://feralatlas.supdigital.org/index?text=isc-grid&ttype=essay&cd=true (accessed September 19, 2021).

9 See https://feralatlas.supdigital.org/index?text=isc-crowd&ttype=essay&cd=true (accessed September 19, 2021).

Anthropocene from the point of view of the non-uniform ways in which the planetary practices of Invasion, Empire, Capital, and Acceleration are disrupted by the feral practices of "other species, as well as nonliving things, [that] make it possible to be human" and that are more or less attuned to the assemblages that the Anthropocene has gathered.[10]

And while "feral effects" can kill both humans and non-humans, the argument is that without feral effects humans would all be dead: "If human landscape transformation was as effective as modernist dreamers claim in replacing earlier ecologies, we might have no more forests or fisheries. [But] forests grow back, fish escape and reproduce."[11] As such, *Feral Atlas* argues that to understand the extension of infrastructure as a means of knowing and making the planetary, it is key to look to the more-than-human ecological patches of planned and unplanned infrastructural effects to understand how this world is held together—from suburbs to plantations to plastic ocean gyres.[12] In doing so, *Feral Atlas* offers a potentially transformative image and effect of infrastructural collaboration—especially amid evermore images of the planetary scope of such unplanned effects.

*

On August 9, 2021, ahead of COP26, a major international conference to limit climate warming held in Glasgow, Scotland, the Intergovernmental Panel on Climate Change (IPCC) Working Group 1 released another kind of ecological image in its Physical Sciences Basis report (part of the Sixth Assessment Report). The IPCC report states that the link between human-induced CO_2 emissions—spiking since the industrial revolution at levels unseen in two million years (measured in 2019)[13]—is "unequivocal," with climate change already affecting every region of the planet.[14]

Two weeks earlier, the River Lea, a tributary to the Thames running through London's East End, burst its banks after heavy rain and flooded the former Olympic Park, a Docklands Light Railway station and part of the Hackney Wick area. A video posted on Twitter, which has been viewed millions of times, documented the scene as flood water charged through the ticket gates and lower levels of the Pudding Mill DLR station.[15] Behind the raw, singular, emotive ability of these images to consolidate the realities of climate change lay an unseen history of official acceptance of how the city would suffer the known consequences

10 See https://feralatlas.supdigital.org/index?text=introduction-to-feral-atlas&ttype=essay&cd=true (accessed September 19, 2021).

11 Ibid.

12 Ibid.

13 V. Masson-Delmotte, P. Zhai, A. Pirani, S.L. Connors, C. Péan, S. Berger, N. Caud et al. (eds.) "IPCC, 2021: Summary for Policymakers" (SPM), in *Climate Change 2021: The Physical Science Basis. Contribution of Working Group I to the Sixth Assessment Report of the Intergovernmental Panel on Climate Change*, (Cambridge: Cambridge University Press, 2021), 9.

14 Ibid. Models include Equilibrium Climate Sensitivity (ECS) (Technical Summary, 45), which models change over centennial timescales; Transient Climate Response (TCR), which models change over 5–10 year periods (Technical Summary, 46); Transient Climate Response to Emissions (TCRE).

15 The DLR, or Docklands Light Railway, is part of the London transport system. The video, available at https://twitter.com/Robday/status/1419339808372142083 (accessed September 17, 2021) was one of many of extreme rainfall in 2021, which also included one of a NYC subway station after tropical storm Ida (September 3, 2021), and earlier that month from Zhengzhou, where flood water from the Yellow River caused scores of deaths, including 14 people on the underground. See https://news.sky.com/story/flooding-kills-more-than-300-in-china-including-14-trapped-in-subway-12372343 (accessed, September 16, 2021).

of entirely predictable flooding in these areas.[16] In this context—alongside many others—and synthesizing an unprecedented level and scope of observational data,[17] and further updates to models used to predict climate trends, the IPCC report offers a "reality check" and a guiding narrative in five emissions scenarios ranging from the catastrophic to the potential of managing current levels, into which images such as those in the London Underground can fit.[18]

At one level, and in contrast to the weight of evidence, the IPCC report's authors hope to catalyze a picture of the required scope and scale of collective action to mitigate the planetary effects of climate change.[19] At another, the goal of the report is more straightforward: to provide the technical basis for agreeing the Nationally Determined Contributions (NDCs) to the remaining net-zero-carbon budget. This framework defines the distribution of substantial emissions reductions that signatories of the 2015 Paris Agreement will have to commit to in order to stay within the range of a 1.5°C temperature rise, balancing this with continued economic activity, and the "international development agenda," through Sustainable Development Goals supported by the UN Addis Ababa Action Agenda.[20]

Feral Atlas, the IPCC report, and the visualizations and representations of the effects and models it discusses each dramatize different ways to approach how to image and how to act in regard climate: whether to scale up a common response or address the creation of a planetary problem by scaling activities down. If images of flooding, forest fires, and droughts can only visualize climate effects, adding to a real-time modeling of changes already happening, and targets are precisely organized to be nested into existing infrastructural-economic conditions, each of these examples poses a stark question: How to act in relation to the planetary demands of Anthropogenic climate change?

With its targets and impactful graphs, scatter plots, and regional heat maps showing ranges of temperature changes, desertification, sea level rise, and CO_2 sequestration, the IPCC report not only prompts the question of how to make the infrastructural changes necessary to change the direction of travel, but also how to register and model them: physically in terms of emissions mitigation, and politically in terms of public will. Similarly, by exploring the both "wonderful and terrible feral effects" of the last 500 years of human-made infrastructures, *Feral Atlas* suggests that the models of infrastructural expansion that undergirded the Anthropocene, are either unsustainable or undesirable. It reads feral effects as both signs of unsustainability and of other modes of sustaining a system. Where climate change is both caused by and cause of a precipitous loss of ecological diversity, the planetary offers a site and conceptual frame for the changes necessary to mitigate its worst effects.[21] These two approaches can be used to compare different kinds of speculative effect in relation to the infrastructural images and collaborations mediating the planetary.

16 As architect/editor Christine Murray made clear in a seventeen-tweet thread, various degrees of infrastructural mitigation indicated how differing interests were represented in the architectural relation to the flood plain. The shopping center was built with raised areas because "everything was going to flood" and over 2,500 homes were built with floodable ground floors, despite the risk of residents being trapped, because the housing shortage outweighed an as yet unrealized risk of flooding. See https://twitter.com/tcmurray/status/1419542653105025024 (accessed September 16, 2021).

17 Masson-Delmotte et al, "IPCC, 2021: Summary for Policymakers," 5.

18 IPCC, "Climate change, widespread, rapid and intensifying," available at https://www.ipcc.ch/2021/08/09/ar6-wg1-20210809-pr/ (accessed November 1, 2021).

19 Chair of the IPCC, "CHAIR'S VISION PAPER," in *AR6 Scoping Meeting Addis Ababa, Ethiopia, 1–5 May 2017* (Geneva: Intergovernmental Panel on Climate Change, 2017), 4.

20 Ibid., 2–4, and 28.

One way to consider the speculative potential of the differences between these models, is to explore their implications as responses to the question of scale through what Bogna Konior describes as a particular kind of planetary-scale contemporary image simulation—analyzing these against the infrastructural collaborations necessary to stage them.[22]

Real-Time Images

Composed from multiple, often contested data models, whose effect is indexed to the various experiences and capacities of the infrastructures that make them possible, climate models offer images that cannot be seen in their entirety—be it spatially or temporally. Rather than an experiential fact, they are instead paradigmatic of what Konior describes as a contemporary form of real time, embedded images, composed and realized where "flows of data are carves into climate risk visualizations, [where] satellite monitoring produces pictures for both machine and human eyes [...] and apps on our phones visualize for us the invisible pollution that permeates our bodies." This is a mode of image-making through which, "our planet has become a giant [composite] camera [...] with which we produce simulations, predictions, and visualizations."[23] They may be understood as climate models of what Wendy Chun calls "hypo-real tools"—tools for making hypotheses on an unfolding reality.[24]

The impact of this kind of image is to enmesh more deeply what is being represented with how it is being represented. Whereas what Geert Lovink has described as the "image as evidence" can be viewed as referring to a "somewhat nostalgic idea of a reality that precedes its representation,"[25] these are images that do not simply represent an object, but should be understood as being "part of an operation," as Harun Farocki suggests.[26] Continuously and dynamically indexed to how it is infrastructurally situated and compos(it)ed, the contemporary image Konior describes is "no longer simply a moving still" whose representational claim is to be contested. Instead, it constitutes "a running hypothesis that keeps re-actualizing and updating itself."[27] Our contemporary surround of images does not represent a universal, or even global, albeit diverse, whole, but rather exists as multiple, parallel hypothetical presents.

So, while the scale and complexity of these simulated images generates forms of representation that consolidate a story of infrastructural conditions gone awry and exist at a scale that puts demands for action at individual, state, and collective level in tension with the planetary infrastructural conditions they speak to and from, we could, Konior suggests, also look to a fictive dimension in climate modeling as a different mode of engagement. Constantly contested and reconfigured, as well as reverse-engineered against data from previously observed trends, climate models simulate entire earths in which to spool out the potential future of climate dynamics according to certain given environmental parameters. As a running simulation,

21 The term "planetary" refers to Gayatri Spivak's introduction of the word in 1997, where she used it to advocate forms of life that in their non-abstract relation to a context such as "the globe" were distinct from the imaginaries of globalization. It offers an embedded account of the multiple scales of thinking and cognition of being a part of the planet. See Gayatri Spivak, "Imperative to Re-imagine the Planet," in *An Aesthetic Education in the Era of Globalization* (Cambridge, MA: Harvard University Press, 2013), 335–35.

22 Bogna Konior, "Modelling Realism: Digital Media, Climate Simulations and Climate Fictions," *Paradoxa*, Vol. 31, 2019–20, 55–75.

23 Ibid., 56.

24 Wendy Chun, "On Hypo-Real Models or Global Climate Change: A Challenge for the Humanities," *Critical Inquiry*, Vol. 41, No. 3, 2015, 678.

25 Geert Lovink quoted in Konior, "Modelling Realism," 56.

26 Harun Farocki, "Phantom Images" (2004), in *Picture Industry: A Provisional History of the Technical Image, 1844–2018*, edited by Walead Beshty (Zurich: JRP|Ringier, 2018), 660.

27 Konior, "Modelling Realism," 56.

the efficacy of climate models also rests, following Konior, on a form of *fiction*: a "prognostication [...] in the form of complex simulations of the planet used to predict [climate change's] environmental consequences," grounded by what can be sensed and how this is constructed into a model in the present.[28] Climate futures are inherently uncertain, however, seeing this openness as a condition of the compositional and propositional nature of contemporary image models, prompts for Konior the possibility of the fictive dimension of climate as a kind of hypothetical, propositional realism. This highlights "the place of the digital in our epistemolog[ies]" and avoids restricting an object such as the future to its knowns while still aiming at "a knowledge of reality."[29] This composite image opens the future out to "fictionalizing," to making possible objects that do not yet exist, including the infrastructure that might make livable futures knowable, possible, and scalable.[30]

To stage a claim on a different future, the simulations in the construction of climate models can for Konior be brought into contact with the fictive dimension established most explicitly in so-called "climate fiction," in which various scientifically modeled futures are expanded into social, political, cultural, and aesthetic narratives. By connecting such infrastructurally mediated climate modeling, the speculative capacity of fiction to simulate reality from multiple forms of data offers a link in the flow of information composed by multiple real-time simulations that expand possibility in the infrastructural worlds and collaborations that have both made and now shape the planetary. Climate fiction may therefore be how the implications of climate modeling are made *more* real. But another perspective could be raised here. One impact of this mode of image-making hinges on the ability of these images to be known, and what such real-time images make knowable about the world, as itself a situated model. In the case of climate modeling, relevant layers, resolutions, or facets—such as rainfall distribution—cannot be understood without taking into account the simulations to which they contribute and that they support: the connection between human-induced CO_2 emissions and climate change. Likewise, where climate models exist in systemic collaboration with the targets their predictions are used to set, climate fictions are also tied to the infrastructural layers they are built on.

For instance, while images of climate effects on infrastructure—such as videos of flooded railway stations—offer a pause in the unfolding of an infrastructural assemblage, a single image or video is not enough to reflect and shape the complexity and depth of meaning bound up in the infrastructure concerned. Instead, it must become part of the infrastructural composite or simulation Konior describes to take effect, but the infrastructure that mediates this simulation can also determine what that effect is. In the case of a video posted on Twitter timelines, such an image is either overwhelmed by the flow of all other content and information it adds to, or it demands that an individual user must keep up with, rather than act on, the running simulation

28 Ibid., 57.
29 Ibid., 69–70.
30 Ibid., 70.

of the reality the timeline helps form—reacting through likes, reposts, comments, and so on. The infrastructural protocols and practices that hold a world in transition together, as composite images or models, are in some cases more likely to detach the image from the scales it refers to, situating it according to the act of an individual. This generates what Chun refers to elsewhere as a sense of crisis driven by an inability to ever attain enough information in real-time media.[31]

The fictional openness to the future proposed by Konior is a hypothetical future, whose claim to realism is modeled as well as enabled according to its index to the operational infrastructures in the present. While allowing different kinds of fiction to be scaled up to meet the climate crisis, this conversely suggests that without a means of differentiating the effect of these images within systemic models of climate future, the greater the claim to realism, the greater the need there is to rely on the systemic assemblages through which they may become possible. While infrastructure can serve as a venue for speculative formations, or "social prognostications," could these fictions change the conditions from which they emerge and in which they are relevant? How would these fictions make a difference in the mediation of planetary scales that make part of their reality—anthropogenic climate change—possible, but in which the status quo can persist—in images and videos that add to, but do not change, the timeline of events—and be further nested into emission reduction frameworks? This is not just about difference for difference's sake. When IPPC findings are bound to targets that can maintain current infrastructural conditions—dialling down CO_2 output while also continuing to scale up growth—an important question is how to scale down while also reflecting the planetary scale and distribution of the problem. If *Feral Atlas* can already offer one lesson, it is that the assemblages in which such fictive infrastructural realities are nested must remain adaptable.

Feral Atlas: Scalability and Non-Scalability

To read infrastructure as the outcome of a particular assemblage model is also to trace how, why, and from where we enter, know, and interact with that infrastructure. Infrastructure is not an *a priori* object, but constructed through what Geoffrey Bowker calls "infrastructural work," a series of organizational techniques that enable higher-order outcomes.[32] Another way to image the planetary would be to see infrastructural collaborations and how they mediate their internal and external context as dynamics in more unstable and uncertain assemblages.

As points of convergence in assemblages constructed by Anthropocene infrastructure, feral entities in *Feral Atlas*—and the intersection of the three axes of Anthropocene imaginaries, infrastructural tippers, and feral qualities of those entities in this context—invoke different interpretations of how infrastructure might be brought together to mediate alternative

31 Wendy Chun, "'Crisis, Crisis, Crisis', or Sovereignty after Networks," *Theory, Culture and Society*, Vol. 26, No. 6, December 2011.

32 Ashley Carse, "Nature as Infrastructure: Making and Managing the Panama Canal Watershed," *Social Studies of Science*, Vol. 42, No. 4, 2012, 539–63.

models of possible scale in these assemblages. *Feral Atlas* poses a definition of infrastructure as a kind of mediating interface or practice in different interpretations of the assemblages, gathering of parts, dynamics, and changes of state already enacted in the Anthropocene.

One reading of *Feral Atlas* that could offer an answer to how to scale down, is that by disrupting the scalability of Anthropocene infrastructural plans and realized forms, feral entities enact the transformative possibilities of what Anna Tsing has developed with the concept of "non-scalability."[33] As expression of infrastructural imaginary and the collaborations that make them, qualities such as scale are not just technical achievements, but are used to mediate the world as a consequence of the logic of infrastructural organization at stake. In contrast to the feral, Tsing contends that the scalability of infrastructure seeks to expel what is seen to be redundant and different so that a system of production can be scaled and expanded without having to change basic parts.

Basing her analysis of scalability in the establishment of the Portuguese colonial sugar cane experiments, scalability began as an infrastructural accident of the plantation. Organized according to the grids of irrigation canals that made growing sugar cane possible in non-native sites such as Madeira, plantations also meant that cultivation of cane could be standardized, making it easier as well as "necessary" to manage all other areas of the environment, labor, and resources. By banishing the "meaningful [ecological] diversity" that might "disturb the design of the system,"[34] and by cleansing the transformative social relations of its labor that might "change things"[35]—through the social and cultural displacement of enslavement and the Atlantic Middle Passage—the plantation became a model for expansion that nested regionally distributed, but standardized plantations into an expansive colonial logic and infrastructure of trade. Like this, scalability projects provide an infrastructurally extractivist, imperialist, and expansionist logic for growth, which means that supporting resources, dynamics, and contexts—labor, soil ecologies, regulations, etc.—are what must change, be displaced, or eradicated.

As Tsing argues, global supply chain capitalism built on colonial economic infrastructure expands and entangles the plantation logic into myriad locations. One effect of scalable infrastructure is to enforce a slow violence to keep those worlds repeating: the exclusion, extraction, displacement of relations that may organize its parts differently. However, this continued expansion without change, of exclusion of the transformative dynamics that sustain the adaptability of a system, also creates uncontrollable edges and breakdowns. Whether in the collapse of markets due to lack of demand, like in the case of timber forests, the expenses of sustaining degraded soil, or in the organizing of labor against control, when a system or ecosystem can no longer be supported without change, the accidental or exploitative introduction of new relations by a feral entity or

33 Anna L. Tsing, "On Nonscalability: The Living World Is Not Amenable to Precision-Nested Scales," *Common Knowledge*, Vol. 18, No. 3, 2012, 505–24.
34 Ibid., 513.
35 Ibid., 507.

uncontrolled actor—a vine that swamps former cotton plantations (kudzu)[36]; a virus that moves by air transport, later keeping populations in lockdown (sars-cov-2)—means the flow of an infrastructural assemblage can be drastically changed. In the unfolding of scalability also resides a consequence in its opposite: non-scalability.

Drawing on the matsutake mushroom blooms and harvests that emerged in the wasteland of abandoned industrial forestry in the Pacific Northwest of the USA, Tsing establishes non-scalability as the tracing and production of relations that are highly situated and localized—mushrooms that can only grow around certain trees—and are disruptive to scalability; they cannot be cultivated, although they can be made addressable as they are loaded into the belly of aircrafts in global trade. Non-scalability is for Tsing both before and the epiphenomenon of scalability. Neither good nor bad, it is simply the absence of scalability. But since "relationships are a potential vector for transformation,"[37] non-scalability therefore is a measure and staging of the capacity for diversity of relations and transformation in the system. By tracing the relationships that cohere around the ruins of scalable effects, Tsing argues that the possibility of non-scalability—transformation in relation—can be found.

The implication to be explored here is how each axis in *Feral Atlas* describes where a model of infrastructural collaboration mediates the assemblage according to models of scale that exclude diversity, but also operates as a locus of relational diversity established as feral interventions produce the conditions of alternative interpretations of that locale. If the effects *Feral Atlas* discusses are feral "because they emerge within human-sponsored projects, but are not in human control,"[39] non-scalability introduces the possibility of intentionally creating feral effect in the infrastructures of the present. Can these models of non-scalability be used to mobilize a different kind of image and effect to that of real time simulations? Can it mobilize a more generative relationship to the scalable infrastructural operations that enable them?

A Non-Scalable Platform

Feral Atlas describes the unintended consequences of the intersection of Anthropocene imaginaries and infrastructural design in a kind of assemblage whose dynamics are shaped by exploitation or interpretation of these conditions by various feral entities. Seeing these dynamics as embodiments of different models and interpretation of scalability and non-scalability, feral processes also mediate the practices that hold together, pattern, and make knowable the intentional and unintentional worlds generated by the Anthropocene at present. They enact images of scalability and non-scalability. This is manifest as a tension between non-scalable and scalable dynamics—beginning on the conceptual axes it is built around, between the promises of infrastructure and feral effects, between shipping

36 See https://feralatlas.supdigital.org/poster/kudzu-pueraria-montana-history-physiology-and-ecology-combine-to-make-a-major-ecosystem-threat (accessed September 16, 2021).

37 Tsing, "On Nonscalability," 507.

38 Ibid., 515.

39 See https://feralatlas.supdigital.org/index?text=introduction-to-feral-atlas&ttype=essay&cd=true (accessed September 16, 2021).

as logistical achievement and invasion propagated as its edge. This tensioning is used to invert infrastructural intention and imaginaries—seamless interoperability, invisibility to outcome, exclusion of indeterminacy and the political. How this might be staged as a speculative infrastructural image is reflected in the platform itself.

The research collection at the core of *Feral Atlas* is built around Contentful, a content management system that allows the creation and storage of information (and associated metadata) and pulls it into a variety of platforms, devices, and uses through an application programming interface (API).[40] As a so-called headless database tool, Contentful is not tied to a front-end webpage that displays content according to predetermined rules, such as how a tweet or Facebook post always looks familiar. This means that the relationship between entities in the database—such as which tippers and detonators are relevant to the emergence of a feral entity, or how a number of entities emerge through a similar mediation of state-change like "INVASION"—can be designed more thoroughly, as can how this content is displayed and therefore used according to these relationships.

Where the organization of entities is defined by the convergence of axes used by researchers on the one hand, and by users exploring the platform on the other, the parameters of entities are both descriptively non-scalar, and prompt non-scalar narratives in their reading. Access of information is driven not by scalability of carefully hierarchized categorization—such as Wikipedia, and traditional encyclopedias—but the comparatively erratic scaling of navigation by relations and parameters set by each user to visualize and manifest patterns in its database. This allows a horizontal view of each layer of importance, but by connecting these layers in a platform that must be navigated through clicks, hyperlinks, scrolls, and location—as well as reading, watching, and listening—one must reconstruct the feral entanglements of these assemblages through decision trees of how to approach each case study, which mimics the chaotic but conditional unfurling of the feral effects.

However, opening up the constraints of one infrastructural layer—web platforms which host relatively traditional content forms—creates a relationship to a different kind of infrastructural layer, and thus impacts the claims of *Feral Atlas* accordingly. The platform of *Feral Atlas* is itself built using React, an open-source application builder developed by Facebook for the design of interactive user interfaces.[41] React is a code library established and maintained by Facebook.[42] Contentful is hosted by Amazon web servers (AWS), and delivers its managed content using Content Delivery Networks (CDNS),[43] including Fastly, to distribute copies of the source information to users held on CDN servers around the world, and closer to the user.[44] As a result, the architecture supporting *Feral Atlas* is both technically scalable, efficiently pushing content out to multiple users and platforms, tesselating with a powerful and dominant infrastructure,[45] and conceptually non-scalable.

40 Email correspondence with designer, April 2021.

41 Ibid.

42 See https://opensource.fb.com/projects/react (accessed September 16, 2021).

43 A CDN serves content copied and cached on distributed and localized servers where and when it is needed rather than all users downloading from a single hosting server. Though making things faster and therefore scalable, with many content- and user-heavy services using CNDS, this reliance and complexification can make such infrastructure more precarious, as happened when Fastly suffered an hour-long outage in 2021, causing a large portion of the web to go down. See https://www.cloudflare.com/en-gb/learning/cdn/what-is-a-cdn/ (accessed September 16, 2021); and https://constellix.com/news/fastly-global-outage-2021 (accessed September 16, 2021).

44 See https://www.contentful.com/legal/faq/ and https://www.contentful.com/security/ (accessed September 16, 2021). This interface is, however, key to the construction of an inter-layer infrastructure stack, whose meaningfulness is derived from its entanglement and integration with its context.

Reflecting the claim that the Anthropocene must be understood through local ecological patches, this construction creates a tension between platform user and its content—as well as between the non-linear parallel routes possible to be explored between multiple axes and entities, and the multiple intersections caused by the Anthropocene from which these case studies and frameworks emerge. However, the confusion created by the platform—and enabled by its underlying architecture—about what aspect is most important, about what direction of cause and effect is relevant, not only reflects the epistemic role of digital media in the understanding of the planetary as Konior would argue. It also means that these effects must be pieced together and re-assembled through the relationships, dynamics, mediators that cohere in each case as conceptual, critical devices in the use of the platform. More specifically, these feral narratives or flows can be thought of as what N. Katheryn Hayles would refer to as choices or interpretations cohering in a "cognitive assemblage."[46] In this case, a cognitive assemblage established between each individual user, the platform infrastructures, and those of whatever feral effect it refers to.

For Hayles, the spread of computational media into virtually all complex technical systems, as well as the increasing integration of human and non-human actors in complex societies, ecologies, and technologies has vastly expanded the sphere of cognition and meaning. This has opened up interaction between "[biological,] human and technical" conscious and non-conscious cognitive actors or "cognizors," systems, and processes to produce multiple kinds of "cognitive assemblage."[47] Accordingly, the cognitive assemblage describes how, despite profound differences, functionally similar biological and technical cognitive processes can become enmeshed by actors able to sense and interpret information shared in these systems to produce and mediate distributed and relational meaning made in the dynamic arrangement of information flows and cognitive interactions.[48]

Focusing on the mediation, recognition, and interpretation of "information within contexts that connect it with meaning" and where the meaning of information is "given by the processes that interpret it," the effect of meaning made in the cognitive assemblage can be boiled down to the capacity to make a choice about the flow of information within a system. This focuses on the complex interrelations in the flows "of information through a system and the choices and decision that create, modify and interpret that flow."[49] Outcomes vary from low-level choices or responses to changes in contextual information, and consequentially very simple cognitions—for example, where plants release chemicals to warn others of predators, or to lure back pollinators—as well as higher cognitions and interpretations. These include the interaction between a trading algorithm and human regulator, and between technical autonomous systems—such as self-driving cars or traffic controls, regulatory and legal frameworks, and actors not in its control such as pedestrians.[50]

45 Indeed, Facebook intersects the Anthropocene not only trough the energy it uses for its vast data centers, but also in how it is rewriting subjectivity in relation to its communication and economic infrastructure, whether demanding that legal identity is transparent to profile identities. See https://en.wikipedia.org/wiki/Facebook_real-name_policy_controversy (accessed November 1, 2021), or in the construction of what Shoshana Zuboff calls "surveillance capitalism."

46 N. Katherine Hayles, *Unthought: The Power of the Cognitive Nonconscious* (Chicago: University of Chicago Press, 2017).

47 Ibid., 1–3.

48 Ibid., 11.

49 Ibid., 116.

50 Ibid., 20, 13.

A decision is based on the interpretation of information in a variety of cognitive processes; choice does not imply free will here, but is the result of a dynamic that unfolds in the conditions of the assemblage mediating it, and by comparing incoming information against known and simulated models.[51] The qualities of this meaning are therefore not based on what they represent, but on the kinds of systemic effect they (are able to) have on the assemblage as a whole and established as a flow of evolving relationships; as a systemic concept of meaning, the *specific* points and connections in cognitive assemblages where information flows are initiated, modified, or transformed by what Bruno Latour called mediators.[52] These determine "the kinds and scope of decisions possible within milieus and the meanings that emerge within them,"[53] at the point in which they hold together a cognitive process. The idea of cognitive assemblage therefore offers an intersection at which patterns of information, affect, and signals moving through infrastructural collaborations and given meaning by this context—the context "in which its activity makes a difference"—can be described, simulated, and tested.[54]

Cognitive Assemblages, Feral Interpretations, and Non-Scalable Models

In this context, *Feral Atlas* describes in feral effect examples not only non-scalable relations, but what can be read as relational modes of interpretation and choice that express non-scalable patterns and effects in the information flows, distributions, and models described by the infrastructurally mediated worlds of the Anthropocene. By mediating feral effects through both non-scalable and scalable infrastructures, the platform itself offers a speculative mediator that temporarily joins together feral entities and users in scalable infrastructural conditions and local relations in speculative interpretations that could transform the kind of infrastructural collaboration possible. Returning to my opening example, for instance, *Feral Atlas* underlines that when comb jellies enter a new location, industrial shipping composes a cognitive assemblage between them and Black Sea ecologies. These industrial stowaways interpret the changing flow of resources defined first by this infrastructurally mediated assemblage—created by shipping, taking invasive species from one location to another—and then by their ability to sense, model, and generate new systemic relations between the ecological, infrastructural, and climactic factors in the interpretation of this assemblage.

The introduction of non-scalability into the cognitive assemblage opens up a distinct ethical/aesthetic framework in the analysis, making, and instituting of infrastructural images such as those staged by *Feral Atlas*, in which the question is not only which actors are given agency in this frame.[55] An additional question is what interpretations are possible given the various conditions and mediators of the systems, and dependent on perspective, also putting into question the particular mediating

51 Ibid., 22, 23, 26

52 Bruno Latour, "Morality and Technology: The End of Means," in *Theory, Culture and Society*, Vol. 19, Nos. 5–6, 2002, 247–260.

53 Hayles, *Unthought*, 117.

54 Ibid., 26.

55 Ibid., 116.

arrangement in each, and whether alternative actors have agency in this flow. Reading the novel situation in which they landed as both viable and devoid of predators, the comb jellies could become top mediators in the assemblage detonated or set into play by the Anthropocene imaginary of invasion, taking it from an ecologically balanced assemblage to one less adapted—but this is not immutable. The changing dynamics of an assemblage can mean that a once non-scalable feral entity can become too powerful a mediator; a non-scalable, feral interpretation can also be scaled up to, again, limit the possibility of further change. In the ecology of the Black Sea, the comb jelly came to dominate the conditions, until a new predator entered.[56] The continued production of diversity of mediation is then key to an infrastructural collaboration being transformative or not.

Like this, the cognitive assemblage offers a different mode of imagining and staging change. Scale is not an achievement of *Feral Atlas* but is put in tension by feral effects and by the platform: as an interpretive non-scalable effect or by acting to mediate a non-scalable flow of information. While there is agency in making an interpretive choice in using the platform, by assembling what can be described as a cognitive assemblage, it is more evidently conditional and constrained by how these feral effects and feral user journeys are mediated. The platform uses this inversion of scale to show how tensioning an assemblage—making new relations that cannot be contained by the existing system—can create tipping points in that system, whether in how the cognitive entity interprets it (comb jellies, for instance), in the ability of mediators to shape systemic effects (ballast tanks carrying and releasing invasive species), or it the arrangement between the platform itself, its content, the delivery of this content, and its users.

By staging such tensions between the extensive scale of access and complex content delivery using dominant infrastructures, and the complexifying relations of non-scalable axes and user journeys through the infrastructural conditions and organizing frameworks of its platform, *Feral Atlas* enacts a different kind of hypothetical realism that understands the epistemological role of digital images but isn't determined by this. Although only speculative, built into the platform is a tension that allows it to link between multiple contexts—both scalable and not—by extensive software infrastructures and the errant mediations and user journeys it enacts. The platform is not mediating a response to an apparently real-time image but entangling the user in the uncertain dynamics of feral response to scalable infrastructures and imaginaries extended too far. In this sense, *Feral Atlas* also offers a speculative frame that stages a different relationship to the uncertainty of environmental futures, in which the infrastructural collaborations from which they emerge is unstable, but relationally generative. It shifts from expanding what is thought possible, like in fictioning, to an image that enacts different kinds of non-scalable effect in the flow of information of which it is a part.

56 In the case of *M. leidyi*, fish stocks recovered, temperatures changed and "the ctenophore *Beroe ovata*[41]—also accidentally introduced—started preying on *Mnemiopsis*, so that extreme outbreaks were not observed again." Fach, Salihoglu, and Oğuz, "Alien species can cause severe disturbance."

The starting point of this exploration was the question how infrastructure is known and makes worlds known by holding together traces of effect, layers of sensing, and relations between things. The expansion of infrastructural collaborations discussed here—through platform, integrated data-driven, mobile locative technologies—shows how infrastructural work is performed and maintained in real time; not only as a condition of infrastructural access and operation, but of particular modes of meaning formation too. The real effect of the hypothetical nature of composite images, such as climate models, manifests the performative dimensions of infrastructure—what Gilbert Simondon calls the circular causality of infrastructure.[57] In this sense, infrastructure is (a set of) cognitive relations and flows that create the object on which it has an effect, such as a user, a climate model, or a feral entity. It is constructed in advance to make what it can make known known. The real-time image described by Konior, and those models that emerge in the relationship between feral entities and the assemblages that contextualize them, can then be seen as the patterns, thresholds, feedback loops, and transformations mediating possible choices in the flows of information assembled by infrastructure around certain climatic conditions, or feral qualities. Perhaps a simple concluding question, then: By seeing that unfolding as a mode of infrastructural practice staged into both the not-yet of speculative modeling and into specific infrastructural collaborations in which its speculative propositions come and have effect, can infrastructural models of scale learn from the feral, to be relational and adaptive rather than extractive?

This article was written as an extension of / in parallel to PhD research for "Reality Constructions: Changing What Infrastructure Means" (working title), 2022, Goldsmiths, University of London. The research was supported by a CHASE PhD Studentship, funded by the Arts and Humanities Research Council (AHRC), UK.

57 Gilbert Simondon, *On the Mode of Existence of Technical Objects*, translated by Ninian Melamphy (London: University of Western Ontario, 1980), 62.

END MATTER

Nancy Adajania is a Bombay-based cultural theorist and curator. She has curated a number of research-based exhibitions, including the Nelly Sethna retrospective "The Unpaved, Crusty, Earthy Road," Chatterjee & Lal with Cymroza Art Gallery, Bombay (2021); "Zigzag Afterlives: Film Experiments from the 1960s and 1970s in India," Camden Art Centre, London (2020); the Sudhir Patwardhan retrospective "Walking Through Soul City," NGMA, Bombay, with The Guild art gallery (2019); and "Counter-Canon, Counter-Culture: Alternative Histories of Indian Art," Serendipity Arts Festival, Goa (2019). Adajania has proposed several new theoretical models through her extensive writings on subaltern art, media art, public art, transcultural art, and biennial culture of the Global South. She conceptualized and led the online curatorial workshop "Once Upon a Cultural Famine: A Curatorial Thought Experiment" for the Kochi Biennale Foundation (2021). She was the juror for the video/film/new media fellowship cycle of the Akademie Schloss Solitude (2015–17).

Sabeth Buchmann is an art historian and critic who lives and works in Berlin and Vienna. She is Professor of History of Modern and Postmodern Art at the Academy of Fine Arts, Vienna. Together with Helmut Draxler, Clemens Krümmel, and Susanne Leeb she co-edits PoLyPen, a series on art criticism and political theory, published by b_books, Berlin. Recent publications include *Putting Rehearsals to the Test: Practices of Rehearsal in Fine Arts, Film. Theater, Theory, and Politics* (edited with Ilse Lafer and Constanze Ruhm, 2016); *Textile Theorien der Moderne. Alois Riegl in der Kunstkritik* (edited with Rike Frank, 2015); *Hélio Oiticica, Neville D'Almeida and others: Block-Experiments in Cosmococa* (with Max Jorge Hinderer Cruz, 2013); *Film Avantgarde Biopolitik* (edited with Helmut Draxler and Stephan Geene, 2009); *Denken gegen das Denken. Produktion—Technologie—Subjektivität bei Sol LeWitt, Yvonne Rainer und Hélio Oiticica* (2007); and *Art After Conceptual Art* (edited with Alexander Alberrro, 2006).

Cassandra Collective are Laura Cugusi, Chiara Di Leone, and Anastasiia Noga. Laura is an artist, writer, and researcher living in Berlin; Chiara is a writer and design researcher living in London; Anastasiia is a writer living in Moscow. Together they form the research collective Cassandra through which they investigate institutional practices in the field of ecosystem governance. They explore how climate change is not only constructed through discourse and rhetoric but produced through protocols of action, gestures, rituals, and choreographies that corporate and state institutions perform. Most recently, Cassandra's research has focused on complex temporalities, the blurring of the boundaries between physical and digital spaces (between speculation and reality), and possible strategies for shaping a future that is already here by acknowledging the recursive power of sensing technologies in ensuring the habitability of Earth.

Tom Clark is a curator and writer. He has worked on curatorial and publishing projects internationally and also teaches. He is currently an AHRC/CHASE-Funded PhD Candidate at Goldsmiths, University of London. His research explores infrastructural figures, politics, and imaginaries as they relate to critical practices in the institutions of art.

Diakron are David Hilmer Rex and Aslak Aamot Helm. David is an artist based in Copenhagen, Denmark, and co-founder of Diakron, a studio for transdisciplinary research and practice. He is currently a PhD candidate at The Royal Danish Academy of Fine Arts and Aarhus University. His research, titled "Artistic Practice and Systems Change," proposes a framework for a mission-oriented sector of art, based on foundational principles of diversification and specialization of the sector of art, as guided by articulate missions. Aslak works on building alliances, experiments and organizations across art, science, technology, and industry. He is the co-founder of Diakron, as well as Primer, a platform for artistic and organizational development housed in the global water- and biotechnology company Aquaporin. Aslak is currently a postdoctoral researcher with Medical Museion, Diakron, and Serpentine Galleries. His project, titled "Re-energizing art institutions at the intersection of art, science and technology," aims to study and further para-organizational missions and strategies across a diverse selection of transdisciplinary arts organizations and practices.

Bassam El Baroni is assistant professor in curating at the School of Arts, Design and Architecture, Aalto University, Finland. Formerly, he lectured at the Dutch Art Institute, ArtEZ University of the Arts, Arnhem (2013–19) and was artistic director of the now folded non-profit art space ACAF—Alexandria Contemporary Arts Forum in Alexandria (2005–12). His current research engages with financialization in relation to artistic practices, artists' engagement with infrastructural futures and histories, and new forms of artist-led activism. Recent curatorial projects include: "Infrahauntologies" at the Edith-Russ-Haus for Media Art, Oldenburg, and La Box ENSA, Bourges (2021–22). Previous curatorial projects include: "What Hope Looks like after Hope (On Constructive Alienation)," at HOME WORKS 7, Beirut (2015); "Agitationism," the 36th Eva International—Ireland's Biennial, Limerick (2014); the Lofoten International Art Festival (co-curator with Anne Szefer Karlsen and Eva González-Sancho, 2013); and Manifesta 8, Murcia (co-curator, 2010). He is the author of various essays on artists, art, and curating, and co-editor, together with Ida Soulard and Abinadi Meza, of *Manual for a Future Desert* (Mousse Publishing, 2021). He holds a PhD in Curatorial Knowledge, Department of Visual Cultures, Goldsmiths, University of London.

João Enxuto and Erica Love work on projects about the technopolitics of work, institutions, and economies connected to contemporary art. Enxuto received an MFA in Photography from RISD and Love holds BAs from Brown University in Economics and Visual Arts and an MFA from UCLA. Together they were fellows at the Whitney Museum Independent Study Program and were awarded a New York Foundation for the Arts Artist Fellowship and a Creative Capital Andy Warhol Foundation Arts Writers Grant. They have given talks and exhibited work at the Centre Pompidou, Whitney Museum of Art, New Museum, Walker Art Center, Louisiana Museum in Denmark, Anthology Film Archives, Carriage Trade, ArtCenter/South Florida, Tamayo Museum in Mexico City, and other venues worldwide. Enxuto and Love's writing has been published by Verso, *Mousse Magazine*, *Art in America*, *Walker Artist Op-Eds*, *Wired Magazine*, *X-TRA Contemporary Art Quarterly*, and elsewhere. They currently teach at the Cooper Union, New York University, City College New York, The New Centre for Research and Practice, and Maumaus in Lisbon.

Václav Janoščík is pedagogue, theorist, and curator currently teaching at the Academy of Fine Arts in Prague (AVU) and Academy of Arts, Architecture and Design in Prague (UMPRUM). He has edited several volumes on problems of contemporary thinking, ranging from new materialism, speculative realism, acceleration, future, and media theory, including *Speculative Ruinology* (2020), *Back to the Future* (2019 [CZ]), *Mind in Terrain* (2018 [CZ]), *Reinventing Horizons* (2016), and *Object* (2015 [CZ]). His solo-authored books are *Nonsleeping* (2018 [CZ], which gives a highly personal account of social acceleration or abstraction), and *Straining the Contemporary, Detective Search for Shared World* (2020 [CZ], which tries to reinterpret and weaponize pop culture). He curates extensively, and is specifically interested in expanding art into gaming, technology, or experimental and collaborative practices. He focuses on political ecology, philosophy of technics and media, democratization of contemporary art or thinking, and gaming.

Bogna Konior is an Assistant Professor at the Interactive Media Arts department and a Research Fellow at AI & Culture Research Centre at NYU Shanghai. She investigates how humanist conceptions of species, causality, and agency are dislocated across global technological networks and environmental crises, and how digital culture fuels and registers this process. She was previously a Lecturer in New Media and Digital Culture at the University of Amsterdam, and a Research Fellow at the International Research Institute for Cultural Techniques and Media Philosophy at the Bauhaus-Universität Weimar. Her recent work can be found at www.bognamk.com.

Aude Launay is an independent researcher, writer and curator, with philosophical training. For the past five years, her focus has been on distributed decision-making and democratic processes prototyped with blockchains. She is currently writing a book on decentralized autonomous organizations (DAOs), aiming to bring a theoretical perspective to the concept by putting it in the context of the history of ideas and political philosophy.

Ilan Manouach is a conceptual comics artist, AI entrepreneur, and strategy consultant for Onassis Publications. He is currently doing a PhD at Aalto University on comics epistemology, exploring the effects of frontier technologies, synthetic media, fintech, and globalized logistics on the comics industry. He is mostly known for Shapereader, a system for tactile storytelling initially designed for people with visual disabilities. He is the founder of Applied Memetic, an organization that researches the political repercussions of synthetic media in graphic narratives, as well as director of Futures of Comics, an international research program that examines the ongoing historic mutations of the comics industry in the midst of increasingly financialized, globalized, and technological affordances. With Kenneth Goldsmith, he co-curated *Shadow Libraries*, a festival that probed the conceptual consistency and the ethics of digital preservation and distribution in web libraries, through the lens of its users and makers. He is also the curator for the collections of Conceptual Comics for Ubuweb and Monoskop.

Bahar Noorizadeh is a filmmaker, writer, and platform designer. She works on the reformulation of hegemonic time narratives as they collapse in the face of speculation: philosophical, financial, legal, futural, etc. Noorizadeh is the founder of Weird Economies, an online art platform that traces economic imaginaries extraordinary to financial arrangements of our time. Her work has appeared at the German Pavilion, Venice Architecture Biennial 2021, Tate Modern Artists' Cinema Program, Transmediale Festival, DIS Art platform, Berlinale Forum Expanded, and Geneva Biennale of Moving Images, among other contexts. She is pursuing her work as a PhD candidate in Art at Goldsmiths, University of London, where she holds a SSHRC Doctoral Fellowship.

Matthew Poole is a curator and writer living in Los Angeles. He is a Professor of Art History & Theory at California State University, San Bernardino. His practice involves producing exhibitions, publishing artists' projects, writing on topics related to the relations of production and distribution of art, and teaching. Prior to moving to California in 2012, Poole was a faculty member in the Department of Art History & Philosophy at the University of Essex, UK, where he ran the postgraduate curatorial programs. Some of his work can be seen online at www.kynastonmcshine.org.uk.

Ghalya Saadawi is Senior Lecturer at Goldsmiths, University of London. She works and teaches across the domains of critical theory, art and the broader economy, Lebanese art, critical human rights with an interest in witnessing and testimony, among others. She holds a PhD in sociology from Goldsmiths, where her doctoral dissertation underscored the art practices and theoretical considerations that informed a rethinking of witnessing, representation, and state-economic ideology at the declared end of the Lebanese civil wars. She was adjunct lecturer at the American University, the Alba, and the USJ in Beirut, offering courses in Lebanese contemporary art, and twentieth- and twenty-first-century art, with an emphasis on social art history and Marxist and post-Marxist approaches (2011–19). In 2015–17 she was Resident Professor of the Ashkal Alwan Home Workspace Program, an art study program in Beirut, where she organized a year around art, finance, and the future. Saadawi has been a theory tutor at the Dutch Art Institute since 2018. She has written for a number of art publications, artist monographs, and academic journals, and has most recently been working on an auto-theory manuscript on hypochondria, and a forthcoming essay-fiction titled "Capital as a State of Mind." Saadawi is affiliated with *Makhzin* magazine and the Beirut Institute for Critical Research and Analysis (BICAR).

Adham Selim is a transdisciplinary architect and managing editor of the Archilogue, a crowd-sourced electronic shelf for translating and publishing critical design literature in Arabic. His current research project "Digital Arabs," supported by the Andrew W. Melon Grant for Research on Arab Humanities and Arts, is an inaugural attempt at understanding the "digital South," which is to locate the origin of digital thinking and tooling in alternative academic geographies and temporalities not necessarily synonymous with the Global North or advanced capitalism. Selim was a former panelist at the Digital Earth Symposium 2019 and a finalist co-curator for the National Pavilion of the United Arab Emirates in the Venice Architecture Biennale 2020.

Nishant Shah is the Director of Research and Outreach at ArtEZ University of the Arts. He is an endowed Professor in Aesthetics and Cultures of Technology at Radboud University and University of Twente, the Netherlands, and a faculty associate at the Berkman-Klein Centre for Internet & Society, Harvard University, Cambridge, MA. He works on questions of digital infrastructures, collectives, and identities at the intersections of feminism, humanities, and critical technology studies. He is currently working on AI values and future of platforms in Asia. His recent book *Really Fake* (University of Minnesota Press, 2021) is available via open access through Meson Press.

Vermeir & Heiremans live and work in Brussels. Through their work, the artist duo investigates the complex relationship between art, architecture, and the economy in today's highly globalized world. Having designated their own house an artwork, the artists use this "house as artwork" concept as a framing device that questions the role the arts play within the ever-growing entanglement of finance, urban development, and governance. Their practice employs financial tools, historical references, technology, and cinematic language to reflect on social codes as well as on the production of value in today's artistic and non-artistic realms. Vermeir & Heiremans have presented work at Musée de la Ville d'eaux, Spa (2021), Edith-Russ-Haus, Oldenburg (2021), Museum of Modern Art, Aalborg (2020), Carico Massimo, Livorno (2019), Pump House Gallery, London (2018), The Atlantic Project, Plymouth (2018), Glassyard Gallery, Budapest (2018), Bucharest Biennale 7 (2016), Transmediale, Berlin (2016), Dojima River Biennale, Osaka (2015), Triennale Brugge (2015), Rotwand Gallery, Zurich (2014), Riga Art Space (2013), Extra City, Antwerp (2012), Argos, Brussels (2012), Manifesta 9, Limburg (2012), 7th Shenzhen Sculpture Biennial (2012), Viennale, Vienna (2011), Nam June Paik Art Center, Yongin (2010), Arnolfini, Bristol (2009), and the 10th and 13th Istanbul Biennials (2007 & 2013).

Marina Vishmidt is a writer and editor. She teaches at Goldsmiths, University of London. Her work has appeared in *South Atlantic Quarterly*, *Artforum*, *Afterall*, *Journal of Cultural Economy*, *e-flux journal*, *Australian Feminist Studies*, and *Radical Philosophy*, among other platforms, as well as a number of edited volumes. She is currently editing a reader on speculation for the Documents of Contemporary Art series (Whitechapel/MIT 2022). She is the co-author of *Reproducing Autonomy* (with Kerstin Stakemeier, Mute, 2016), and the author of *Speculation as a Mode of Production: Forms of Value Subjectivity in Art and Capital* (Brill 2018 / Haymarket 2019). She is one of the organizers of the Centre for Philosophy and Critical Thought at Goldsmiths, a member of the Marxism in Culture collective, and is on the board of the New Perspectives on the Critical Theory of Society series (Bloomsbury Academic).

Tirdad Zolghadr is a curator and writer, and currently artistic director of the Sommerakademie Paul Klee. Curatorial work includes biennial settings as well as long-term research-driven efforts, most recently as associate curator at KW Institute for Contemporary Art, 2016–20. Teaching engagements have included the Dutch Art Institute and the Center for Curatorial Studies, Bard College. Writing includes *Traction: An Applied and Polemical Attempt to Locate Contemporary Art* (Sternberg Press, 2016). Zolghadr is currently grappling with his third novel, titled *HEADBANGER*.

Natalia Zuluaga is a curator and editor based in Miami. Since 2014, she has been the co-director of [NAME] Publications, a non-profit press with an emphasis on histories and practices often marginalized in dominant art and design histories. She previously served as the Artistic Director at Oolite Arts (formerly ArtCenter/South Florida), Miami. Recent exhibitions and projects include "Migrant Archives" (with Gean Moreno), initiating research, programs, and publications around cultural archives that stem from displaced communities; "Novo Pan Klub," a three-week summer intensive in collaboration with Materia Abierta in Mexico City; "SupraCitizenship": "Future of Demonstration," Vienna; and for ArtCenter/South Florida, "A.S.T.: Intertidal; The Recalibrated Institution" (co-organized with Victoria Ivanova and Armen Avanessian); 'Parallax Drift: The Program for Applied Artistic Research"; and "An Image" (co-curated with Domingo Castillo). She is currently a guest editor for the online journal *Shift Space*. Zuluaga has been a Visiting Lecturer at the Pacific Northwest College of Art (Portland, Oregon) and Florida International University (Miami). She has lectured at various institutions, including The New Museum (New York), the Kadist Foundation (Paris), the Pérez Art Museum Miami, and Es Baluard (Palma, Spain). She received an MA from the Center for Curatorial Studies, Bard College, in 2015.

I would like to thank all of the contributors to this publication, many of whom developed their essays during the pandemic and in a surrounding air of uneasiness that has only heightened the questions and issues this book responds to. I want to express my gratitude to the Edith-Russ-Haus for Media Art, in particular Edit Molnár and Marcel Schwierin, who were pivotal in making this publication happen. Thanks also go to my colleagues and fellow workers at the School of Art, Design and Architecture, Aalto University, for their support during the development and production of this volume. Particular thanks go to Professor Kevin Tavin, who deserves much credit for his backing of the project, and my colleagues at the Visual Cultures, Curating and Contemporary Art (ViCCA) major, who have all been encouraging and accommodating during some difficult times in 2021. I would like to extend my sincere thanks to Gerrie van Noord, whose management of the publication process has been seamless, but also for being a caring individual whose support was invaluable for this book. I would also like to thank An Endless Supply for their work in making this book look so striking and their generosity with their time. Thanks to my friends and network in Helsinki with whom I have had many great conversations about this publication, in particular Paul O'Neill and Constantinos Miltiadis. My love and thanks go to my family, my partner Mona Marzouk and our son Zinedine, for their continuing support. I dedicate this publication to my parents, my late father Dr. Mohamed El Baroni (1944–2021) and my mother Sawsan Abou Gereeda.

Between the Material and the Possible
Infrastructural Re-examination and Speculation in Art

Published by Sternberg Press, London, and
Edith-Russ-Haus for Media Art, Oldenburg

Editor
Bassam El Baroni, Helsinki

Managing Editor
Gerrie van Noord, London

Design
An Endless Supply, Birmingham

Printing and binding
Graphius, Ghent

Typefaces
Neue Haas Unica, Arnhem, ABC Gravity

Paper
Munken Print White 15, 115gsm
Symbol Freelife Tela Fine 250gsm

ISBN 978-3-95679-600-5

Distributed by The MIT Press, Art Data, and Les presses du réel

Sternberg Press
71–75 Shelton Street
London WC2H 9JQ
sternberg-press.com

Edith-Russ-Haus
Katharinenstraße 23
D-26121 Oldenburg
edith-russ-haus.de